ISLAM, CHRISTIANITY AND THE MYSTIC JOURNEY

Other books by Ian Richard Netton

Across the Mediterranean Frontiers (ed. with D. A. Agius)

Allāh Transcendent: Studies in the Structure and Semiotics of Islamic Philosophy, Theology and Cosmology

The Arab Diaspora: Voices of an Anguished Scream (ed. with Z. S. Salhi)

Arabia and the Gulf: From Traditional Society to Modern States (ed.)

Encyclopaedia of Islamic Civilization and Religion (ed.)

Al-Fārābī and his School

Golden Roads: Migration, Pilgrimage and Travel in Mediaeval and Modern Islam (ed.)

Islam, Christianity and Tradition: A Comparative Exploration

Islamic and Middle Eastern Geographers and Travellers (4 vols) (ed.)

Islamic Philosophy and Theology (4 vols) (ed.)

Middle East Materials in United Kingdom and Irish Libraries: A Directory (ed.)

Middle East Sources (ed.)

Muslim Neoplatonists: An Introduction to the Thought of the Brethren of Purity (Ikhwān al-Ṣafā')

A Popular Dictionary of Islam

Seek Knowledge: Thought and Travel in the House of Islam

Studies in Honour of Clifford Edmond Bosworth, volume 1: Hunter of the East: Arabic and Semitic Studies (ed.)

Ṣūfī Ritual: The Parallel Universe

Text and Trauma: An East–West Primer

ISLAM, CHRISTIANITY AND THE MYSTIC JOURNEY

A COMPARATIVE EXPLORATION

◆ ◆ ◆

IAN RICHARD NETTON

EDINBURGH UNIVERSITY PRESS

Edinburgh University Press Ltd
22 George Square, Edinburgh
www.euppublishing.com

Typeset in Goudy by
Koinonia, Manchester, and
printed and bound in Great Britain by
CPI Antony Rowe, Chippenham and Eastbourne

A CIP Record for this book is available from the British Library

ISBN 978 0 7486 4082 9 (hardback)
ISBN 978 0 7486 4081 2 (paperback)

CONTENTS

PREFACE AND ACKNOWLEDGEMENTS

There is a journey which every believer in most faith traditions must make – and that journey leads to the Divine. For some, this is articulated as *the Way of the Mystic*. The present volume attempts to survey and analyse, in a comparative fashion, the roadmap for that mystic journey as espoused by two major religions, Islam and Christianity. Its signposts progress from the *quinque viae of perfection* – an indicative but by no means exclusivist mode of analysis – through the *caves and clouds of unknowing* and on to the *mountain caverns of revelation and knowledge* whereby the thirsty traveller may attempt to slake a thirst for the Divine. And every mystic traveller has a library of roadmaps whereby that attempt may be facilitated and eased. As we read the roadmaps, we note, *en passant*, as Fran and Geoff Doel remind us, that green is 'a colour of enchantment'.[1] It was also the favourite colour of the Prophet Muḥammad himself. It is thus fitting that this colour will feature in diverse places as an occasional adjunct in our mapping of the mystic journey.

Kenneth Cragg was kind enough to describe my earlier *Islam, Christianity and Tradition: A Comparative Exploration*[2] as a 'masterly study of faith-identity';[3] and it was a particular pleasure to find that book shortlisted for the 2007 British–Kuwait Friendship Society Prize for Middle Eastern Studies, a prize awarded for the best scholarly book on the Middle East published in Britain each year. The present companion volume is intended as the second part of a comparative-religion trilogy whose final volume will be entitled *Islam, Christianity and the Realms of the Miraculous: A Comparative Exploration*.

Like the first *Tradition* volume, the present volume is not a textbook. Fully aware of the dangers of essentialism, it presents a series of analytical case studies of mystics and mystical writings and seeks to discover an inner dynamic, coherence and relationship *between these selected authors and their writings*. The usual diacritics have been deployed, with the exception of the words Sufism, sufi and Allah.

I must acknowledge huge debts of gratitude: to my colleagues and friends at Edinburgh University Press, especially Eddie Clark, James Dale and Nicola Ramsey;

to Ivor Normand, who remains the best copy-editor in the world; and finally, and most importantly, to my wife Sue, who has tolerated, with wry patience, abundant affection and practical care and help, the manifold idiosyncrasies of her author-husband completing *yet* another book!

Ian Richard Netton
Sharjah Professor of Islamic Studies
University of Exeter
August 2010

Notes

1. Fran Doel and Geoff Doel, *The Green Man in Britain* (Stroud: Tempus/Charleston, SC: Arcadia, 2001), p. 31.
2. Edinburgh: Edinburgh University Press, 2006.
3. *The Muslim World Book Review*, 27:4 (Summer 2007), p. 15.

ABBREVIATIONS

EI^2	*Encyclopaedia of Islam*, 2nd edn
EIS	*Shorter Encyclopaedia of Islam*
EQ	*Encyclopaedia of the Qur'ān*
ME	Middle English
Q.	*Qur'ān*

For Deborah, Alex and Thea, with much love

CHAPTER

1

EXPLORING THE MYSTICAL IMAGINATION: PERFECTION AND ITS *QUINQUE VIAE*

1.1 *The Sacred Way*

In one of her sublime mystical poems, Annemarie Schimmel evokes the quiet of the night and envisages the 'purple wing' of the archangel which covers 'the eyes' of her heart. Only God remains.[1] In the depth of feeling conveyed by the poem and the aura of transcendence which illuminates it, these verses bear comparison with the famous *Noche Oscura* poem of the Spanish mystic, Juan de la Cruz, to which we will have occasion to refer in considerable detail later in this text.

And perhaps it is only in poetry that the essence of Sufism, Islamic mysticism, may truly be captured and evoked. Professor Schimmel's magisterial volume *Mystical Dimensions of Islam*, however, also captures in a rare, lucid and profound manner her almost boundless *knowledge* of Sufism, drawing on her skills in diverse relevant languages.[2] But, like the great Persian mystical poet, Jalāl al-Dīn Rūmī (AD 1207–73), before her,[3] Schimmel expresses the *essence* of Sufism best in her poetry. The verse cited above captures one of the most commonplace, and yet deepest, of all sufi themes, the yearning of the terrestrial-bound soul for communion, intimacy and ultimate union (whatever that might mean!) with the Divine 'Object' and focus of sufi love, God Himself.

Yet these perennial themes of yearning and love are but two in what is an 'ocean of themes'. As the Qur'ān puts it in another context:

> And if all the trees
> On earth were pens
> And the Ocean (were ink)
> With seven oceans behind it
> To add to its (supply),
> Yet would not the Words
> Of God be exhausted
> (In the writing) ...[4]

Such *topoi* of yearning and mystical love occur over and over again in the diverse mystical and ascetical literatures of both Islam and Christianity. And their essential adumbration, *in terms of neat definition*, has been perceived as unproblematic by some and almost impossible by others.

The Concise Oxford Dictionary does not seem to have any problem: a mystic is 'one who seeks by contemplation and self-surrender to obtain union with or absorption into the Deity, or who believes in spiritual apprehension of truths beyond the understanding'.[5] A quick trawl of key words and themes in this succinct definition would include 'contemplation', 'self-surrender', 'union' and a Gnostic-type knowledge.

By contrast, Annemarie Schimmel, while noting that 'mysticism can be defined as love of the Absolute'[6] and that 'in its widest sense it may be defined as the consciousness of the One Reality – be it called Wisdom, Light, Love or Nothing',[7] clearly believes that, ultimately, such definitions are jejune. Right at the beginning of *Mystical Dimensions*, she warns that 'to write about Sufism, or Islamic mysticism, is an almost impossible task. At the first step, a wide mountain range appears before the eye – and the longer the seeker pursues the path, the more difficult it seems to reach any goal at all'.[8]

As in the story of the blind men and the elephant, narrated by Rūmī, where the particular localised touching of the animal by each man fails to interpret and identify the whole beast,[9] or as when mere words became like straw for the formerly prolific Thomas Aquinas (c. AD 1225–74) after his famous vision in December 1273,[10] it is clear that, for Professor Schimmel, Sufism is ultimately to be *experienced* rather than merely defined, or described, in writing; for the Divine Goal is hidden.

When Schimmel doffs her purely academic hat and dons that of the mystic poets with whom she has so much in common, she acknowledges that the only true love is for 'the First Friend' (= God) and His real glory is hidden behind numerous veils, a standard Islamic mystical *leitmotiv*.[11]

Mystery, then, is at the heart of the mystical. Semantically, Schimmel holds that the two words are underpinned by the same Greek root, meaning 'to close the eyes'.[12] A standard *Greek–English Lexicon* translates *mustikós* as 'mystic, connected with the mysteries' and *mústēs* as 'one initiated',[13] while *Cassell's New Latin–English/English–Latin Dictionary* translates *mysticus-a-um* as 'relating to the mysterious, secret, mystic' (and deriving from the Greek *mustikós*); the noun *mystēs* is rendered as 'a priest at the mysteries' and derived directly from the Greek *mustēs*.[14] The intriguing semantic subtext here is that we have not just *mystery* but *The Mysteries*!

Margaret Smith believed that mysticism was 'historically connected with the mystery-cults of the Greeks'.[15] Such mystery cults were well known from antiquity – but, as R. A. S. Seaford notes, 'the secrets of the Mysteries were fully known only to those who had been initiated into them. We have to help us no ancient text which expounds these secrets'.[16] This reference by Seaford is to the fresco in the 'Villa of the Mysteries' near Pompeii which portrays the Dionysiac Mysteries.[17] St Paul's reference in 1 Corinthians 13:12 to the idea that 'at present, we are looking at a confused reflection in a mirror'[18] – a line famously translated in the King James Version as 'For now we see through a glass darkly'[19] – may well be a literary reference to these Mysteries.[20]

Indeed, John S. Kselman and Ronald D. Witherup note that W. Bousset (AD 1865–1920) went so far as to claim that 'Paul or his successors transformed primitive Christianity into a mystery cult'. They continue: 'Many of the early Christian groups in the Hellenistic world had been mystery fellowships, which now simply worshipped a new god, Jesus, as *Kyrios*, a title commonly given to the god-hero in the cult and ritual of the mysteries'.[21] However, other scholars have 're-emphasised' another paradigm, namely 'the uniqueness of the claims of Pauline Christianity ... against the background of Judaic Messianism'.[22]

Certainly, 'the variety of mystery cults makes them exceptionally difficult to summarize both briefly and accurately'.[23] Richard L. Gordon stresses the 'limp' nature of the category 'mysteries' and holds that 'it is clear that they cannot be considered independent movements, let alone religions'.[24] 'After [U.] Bianchi and others', he identifies a triple typology of '"mystery" proper', '"mystic" cult' and '"mysteriosophic" cult'.[25] There is clearly scope for confusion, then, in the use of the word 'mysteries', whether one is dealing with Eleusinian, Dionysiac, Orphic or other 'mysteries' and mystery cults.[26] Whatever the differences, similarities and ideal[27] typologies inherent in any examination of 'the mysteries', it is clear, at least, that all partook in 'an air of mystery' in its simplest sense. In this sense, there may be some foundation to Margaret Smith's assertion that there *was* a historical connection between mysticism and 'the mystery-cults of the Greeks'.[28]

It is *not* suggested here, however, that Islamic mysticism, *taṣawwuf*, is a direct product of the cults associated with Orpheus, Dionysos or that part of Athens known as Eleusis, whose fame, Kevin Clinton insists, 'was due primarily to the annual festival of the Mysteries'.[29] For Margaret Smith, 'the mystic was one who had been initiated into the secret knowledge of Divine things'.[30] And the cultic follower of 'the Mysteries' in antiquity, the Gnostic of early Christianity[31] and the Islamic sufi all breathe the air of 'Divine mystery', whether or not a formal induction, initiation or *bayʿa* (oath of allegiance to a sufi shaykh or master) is undertaken.

Rituals which were originally outside that sphere of 'Divine mystery' could develop. Thus Ninian Smart notes:

> It is possible for a ritual which was originally magical or at least on the edge of it to be adapted later for some spiritual purposes – for instance, the Eleusinian rituals, originally designed to promote agricultural fertility (but in so far as they embodied belief in gods they belong to the devic theory of causation, which is not strictly mantric), but which emerge in Graeco-Roman culture as a mystery religion of deep existential purport to the initiates.[32]

Moving on from the intertextual spheres of 'mystery', 'mysteries', 'mysticism' and the sacred, it is interesting that many of the secondary sources which deal with, or survey, Islamic mysticism take a syncretic approach and stress the essential harmony of the Islamic and Christian mystical traditions. Reynold A. Nicholson, for example, stresses that 'if Judaism, Christianity and Islam have no little in common in spite of their deep dogmatic differences, the spiritual element of that common element can best be appreciated in Jewish, Christian and Islamic mysticism ...'[33]

A. J. Arberry concurs with this syncretic approach: 'The Way of man's approach [and the capital "W" for "Way" is significant in the context of this volume] or return to God is in essence the same, in Christian and in non-Christian teaching. It has three stages: an ethical stage, then one of knowledge and love, leading to the mystical union of the soul with God.'[34] The key words in this quotation from Arberry's classic work *Sufism*, which have a massive intertextual resonance for this work, are 'love', 'knowledge' and 'union' and also, significantly, 'Way'. Elsewhere, Arberry emphasises that 'it has become a platitude to observe that mysticism is essentially one and the same, whatever may be the religion professed by the individual mystic: a constant and unvarying phenomenon of the universal yearning of the human spirit for personal communion with God'.[35] Here, the two significant key words are 'yearning' and 'communion'.

However, there are obvious dangers in too indulgent an irenicism in the sphere of mysticism. The danger of essentialism is always present to the student or scholar in this field, and we shall explore this in more depth later in this book. 'Similarity' must not be confused with that which is 'identical'. With Geoffrey Parrinder, we might proclaim that 'nowhere are religions closer than in mysticism';[36] but all mysticisms are not identical, and real Islamic mysticism (*taṣawwuf*) is rooted in Islam and the Holy Qur'ān and these only. It is not a part of a vague world 'religion' called 'mysticism', even if, with Margaret Smith, some may choose to hold that 'to the mystic, Ultimate Reality, true Being, is One'.[37]

We have examined the intertextual sphere of 'mystery' and the syncretic and irenical approach favoured by scholars. We have identified certain key favourite motifs which have surfaced in quotation from the writings of the latter on the Islamic mystical tradition. It remains, in this first section, to identify and underline some of the key definitions of modern scholarship which will serve as *foundations* for what follows and illuminate other parts of our text. As with 'the mysteries' which we surveyed earlier, precise definitions of *taṣawwuf*, which we will translate as Islamic mysticism, can be somewhat slippery and variable.

Alexander D. Knysh defines Islamic mysticism as 'an ascetic-mystical trend in Islam characterized by a distinct life-style, values, ritual practices, doctrines and institutions'.[38] Here, we may identify two new key words: ritual and asceticism. In Julian Baldick's view, 'Sufism is a mystical tradition which, when compared to Christian and European institutions, could be put somewhere between monasticism and Freemasonry. It has many of the characteristics of monasticism, but does not usually preach celibacy.'[39] Elsewhere, he reminds us of the traditional definition: 'The English word *Sufism* is used to designate a set of practices, an ideal, and one of the Islamic religious sciences. It is employed to translate the term *tasawwuf*, which means literally "wearing wool" (wool, *suf*, being the dress of eastern Christian and Muslim world renouncers) ...'[40]

Seyyed Hossein Nasr holds that 'to follow Sufism is to die gradually to oneself and to become one-Self, to be born anew and to become aware of what one has always been from eternity (*azal*) without one's having realised it until the necessary transformation has come about. It means to glide out of one's own mould like a snake peeling off its skin.'[41]

In view of the stress in this volume of mine on such words as *journey*, *way* and *path*, Professor Nasr's later words have a particular significance: 'It [Sufism] is the path within Islam that leads from the particular to the Universal, from multiplicity to Unity, from form to the supra-formal Essence'.[42] What Nasr emphasises here, then, in a nutshell, is that Sufism is *the* preferred way or path to Allah, within the framework of the Islamic tradition. There is also a fundamental emphasis on *tawḥīd* in this definition, that is, on the declaration of the sublime Oneness of God, the first of the Five Pillars (*arkān*) of the Islamic faith.

Carl Ernst defines Sufism as 'a mystical tradition that is Qur'anic and Muhammadan'[43] and also emphasises the concept of path: 'Sufism is a path of mystical life, which begins with the souls's conversion, or turning, towards God. The end of this path is human perfection in union with God.'[44] Here, then, is another fundamental key word which will be pursued and elaborated upon in what follows: perfection. Nicholson reminds us of the elemental keynotes which will lead to the establishment of human perfection and union with the One Real Unique Perfection Himself: 'Light, Knowledge and Love'. He deliberately capitalises each of these key motifs in Sufism.[45] They will be recurring *leitmotivs* in our text as well.

Finally, in this brief introductory survey of themes and definitions, we note that Annemarie Schimmel reminds us of 'the importance of Neoplatonic influences upon the development of Sufism'.[46] This is a *topos* to which we will also return at a later stage in this book. For 'yearning' and 'love' are key *topoi* in both Sufism and Neoplatonism.

What we have surveyed thus far is a plethora of varying themes and definitions associated with *taṣawwuf*, Sufism, Islamic mysticism. And what becomes clear from these, and many others which have not been cited, is that there is a multiplicity of themes and a multiplicity of definitions and that perhaps no single theme nor definition does full justice to the reality and richness of Sufism.

With Julian Baldick, therefore, it seems useful to eschew further

> dictionary-style definition, and concentrate instead on isolating specific elements which the label 'mysticism' covers. *Secrecy* is certainly one, indicated by the word's root meaning, from which we also have the idea of *mystery*. The sense of a higher, privileged *knowledge* is another element, connected to the idea of intimate communion or experience [*dhawq*, literally 'taste'] which, perhaps by its very nature … cannot be disclosed. Other elements which must be included are the *means* indicated to obtain this experience, and the thinking that surrounds both the means and the final goal.[47]

In this quotation, Baldick alludes to a theme already adumbrated above, as well as some of the other classic themes of Sufism like knowledge, experience (I suggest there is a reference here to *dhawq*), communion or union with the Deity and, significant for our purposes, the *means* to that union, whereby he must mean *The Way*. These themes will imbue the five ways or, to borrow Aquinas' term, *quinque viae*, of perfection which we will now use to explore the dimensions of the mystical tradition, both in Islam and Christianity. The Five Ways which we have chosen are by no means meant to be regarded as the *only* ways in which our material can be evaluated and sieved; they are indicative and illustrative, rather than exclusive.

This first section, then, deals with *the Sacred Way of Perfection*. At its heart is the Prophet of Islam, Muḥammad (c. AD 570–632). In a seminal article, Alexander D. Knysh draws attention to the mystical visions and experiences of the Prophet as articulated in the Qur'ān and stresses how such experiences could form a bedrock for mystically inclined believers who wished to follow the *sunna* (example) of the Prophet.[48] Knysh refers to the relevant verses in the Qur'ān by number (Q.17:1 and Q.53:1–18) in his article but does not quote them in full. It is worth citing the first here:

> Glory to (God)
> Who did take His Servant
> For a Journey by night
> From the Sacred Mosque
> To the Farthest Mosque
> [*al-Masjid al-Aqṣā*]
> Whose precincts We did
> Bless, – in order that We
> Might show him some
> Of Our Signs: for He
> Is the One Who heareth
> And seeth (all things).[49]

The reference here, of course, is to the famous Night Journey (*isrā'*) of the Prophet on the winged beast Burāq from Mecca to Jerusalem, in the company of the angel Jibrīl, and the consequent Ascension into Paradise (*mi'rāj*).

> By Muslim theologians the question has been discussed, whether the *isrā'* happened while Muḥammad was asleep or awake and whether it was his spirit or his body which journeyed. The orthodox opinion is that the journey was performed by Muḥammad with his body and awake[50]... [However] Mystics and philosophers often favour an allegorical interpretation.[51]

The whole narrative of the *isrā'* and the *mi'rāj*, incorporating as it does conversations between the Prophet Muḥammad and Allah Himself,[52] and articulating a 'perfect' physical and spiritual *way* or path to Paradise, is a glowing testimony to the human perfection which Muḥammad is believed to have attained; it is little wonder that this narrative is one beloved by the sufi tradition.

The second 'mystical' set of Qur'ānic verses, to which Knysh refers, is Q.53:1–18. In these verses, 'Muhammad's truthfulness', as W. M. Watt puts it, is 'supported by two visions'.[53] Does the Prophet actually encounter God at one moment of revelation 'as seems to be suggested by Q.53:1–18'?[54] There is some vagueness on the matter here.[55]

Certainly, it is clear from al-Bukhārī that Muḥammad *does* speak with God Himself during the *mi'rāj* as, at the instigation of Mūsā, he bargains with the Deity for a reduction in the initially prescribed number of prayer times, reducing this from a heavy fifty per day to a more manageable five.[56] It is abundantly clear for the Muslim that, for Muḥammad to have been admitted as a living mortal to the sublime presence of God Himself, and to have been allowed both to speak and to *bargain* with the Deity, bespeaks not just the infinite mercy, graciousness and generosity of Allah, but also a level of perfection attained by Muḥammad himself far beyond that achieved by other mortals.

What is also clear is that this whole passage (Q.53:1–18) is suffused with mysteries, mystical words and phraseology, a vocabulary in other words which accrues to the aura of perfection surrounding the classical view of the Prophet:

> He was taught by one
> Mighty in Power.[57]

The reference, of course, is to the revelation of the Qur'ān via the angel Jibrīl.

> For indeed he saw him [Jibrīl]
> At a second descent,
> Near the Lote-tree [*sidrat al-muntahā*][58]
> Beyond which none may pass:
> Near it is the Garden
> Of Abode.
> Behold, the Lote-tree
> Was shrouded
> (In mystery unspeakable).[59]

Yusuf Ali interprets the first two lines as a reference to the *miʿrāj* and notes that the first occasion when the Prophet actually saw Jibrīl was during the first revelation (see Q.96:1–4). Yusuf Ali continues: 'The [later] Mi'raj appearance [of Jibril] was near the Lote-tree in the highest heaven, above which (figuratively) is the Throne of God'.[60]

Watt interprets slightly differently: 'The lote tree ... the Garden ... probably places in the region of Mecca, but commentators have often taken them to be celestial'.[61] The latter is certainly the case with the great ḥadīth-collector al-Bukhārī (AD 810–70),[62] who describes the lote tree in both mystical and grandiloquent terms: its blossoms or fruits resemble the earthenware bottles or pitchers of Hajar [near Medina] and its leaves are like elephant ears![63]

Thus far, we have associated 'mysticism' and 'mystery' with the Prophet, drawing our evidence from the Qur'ān, in an endeavour to demonstrate the charism of 'perfection' by which he was, and is, regarded. The actual 'perfecting' of the Prophet, *per se*, however, does have a formal record both in the revelation and the tradition literature, as well as the *Sīra*:

> Have We not
> Expanded thee thy breast? –
> And removed from Thee
> Thy burden
> The which did gall
> Thy back? –
> And raised high the esteem
> (In which) thou (art held)?[64]

Yusuf Ali comments: 'The holy Prophet's human nature had been purified, expanded and elevated, so that he became a Mercy to all creation'.[65] Watt, however, is more physical in his exegesis and notes that 'some commentators took [these verses] as a reference to the "opening" of Muhammad's breast when a child by angels in order to remove the blood clot of sin'.[66]

The whole event is elaborated upon in the infancy narrative section of the *Sīra* by the early Medinan biographer of Muḥammad called Ibn Isḥāq (c. AD 704–c. 767). Here we are told how his wet-nurse, Ḥalīma,[67] was informed that two white-robed men had seized the child Muḥammad, thrown him down on the ground and torn open his stomach. Ḥalīma ran to the boy and, to her intense relief, found that no harm had come to him but his visage was changed. Muḥammad related to his nurse exactly what had happened and later provided a fuller account. Apparently the two white-robed men had carried a golden plate containing snow and, when they had opened his chest, they had taken out his heart and, after removing a lump of black blood, they had washed the stomach and heart of the Prophet with snow to purify those organs.[68]

The infancy narrative from the *Sīra* is paralleled, in slightly different circumstances, when the Prophet has become a fully grown man. In the ḥadīth literature, as recorded by al-Bukhārī, we are told that the angel Jibrīl opens the roof of the Prophet Muḥammad's house in Mecca and proceeds to open the Prophet's chest and wash it with water from the Spring of Zamzam (*fa-faraja sadrī, thumma ghasalahu bi-mā zamzam*). After this, the angel brings a basin (*ṭast*) made of gold filled with wisdom and faith (*ḥikma wa īmān*). These are poured into Muḥammad's chest. Thus purified, fortified and perfected, the angel takes the Prophet's hand and the *mi'rāj* begins.[69]

W. Madelung reminds us that the word *'iṣma*, meaning, theologically, 'immunity from error and sin'[70] or, broadly, 'infallibility', is un-Qur'ānic and is also absent from the classical ḥadīth literature.[71] Nonetheless, he concludes: 'Particular views on *'iṣma* were developed in Ṣufī circles in connection with their doctrine of mystical sainthood. Some Ṣufīs from al-Djunayd (d. 298/910) to Ibn al-'Arabī (d. 638/1240) have attributed virtually complete impeccability, far beyond the common Sunnī doctrine, to Muḥammad as the ideal Ṣufī saint.'[72]

Paul E. Walker stresses that the issue of *'iṣma* of a particular prophet is a God-given charism and the doctrine had a particularly pragmatic role in safeguarding the idea that the prophets who brought revelations always told the truth.[73]

However, Madelung's earlier quotation, with its references to the mystic Ibn al-'Arabī (AD 1165–1240) and the Prophet Muḥammad 'as the ideal Ṣufī saint'[74] connects neatly and intertextually with the sufi ideal of *al-Insān al-Kāmil*, The Perfect Man. And this is how sufi mystics down the ages have regarded Muḥammad. Citing Q.33:21, which in Yusuf Ali's translation reads: 'Ye have indeed in the Apostle of God a beautiful pattern (of conduct)',[75] Claude Addas emphasises that such mystics hold Muḥammad to be the supreme spiritual exemplar who is both the model, indeed fullness, of saintliness, and the Perfect Man 'on the cosmic scale'.[76]

One of the best-known exponents of the doctrine of *al-Insān al-Kāmil* was the sufi 'Abd al-Karīm Quṭb al-Dīn b. Ibrāhīm al-Jīlī (AD 1365–c. 1428). A notable ancestor of his was the mystic 'Abd al-Qādir al-Jīlānī (AD 1077/8–1166), eponym of the Qādiriyya *ṭarīqa* (sufi Order). Intellectually, however, al-Jīlī is a disciple of Ibn al-ʿArabī.[77] Of al-Jīlī's many books, the most famous, and most relevant for our purposes, is his *al-Insān al-Kāmil fī maʿrifat al-Awākhir waʾl-Awāʾil (The Perfect Man Via Knowledge of the Last and First Things)*. Although there have been many 'Perfect Men', the focus here is on Muḥammad the Prophet as the supreme exemplar.[78]

Nicholson notes: 'Jílí holds that in every age the Perfect Men are an outward manifestation of the essence of Mohammed, which has the power of assuming whatever form it will ... In the 60th chapter of the *Insánu 'l-kámil* he depicts Mohammed as the absolutely perfect man, the first-created of God and the archetype of all other created beings'.[79] For Nicholson, this is 'an Islamic Logos doctrine', though he surely goes too far when he says that 'it brings Mohammed in some respects very near to the Christ of the Fourth Gospel and the Pauline Epistles'.[80] In the next breath, and admitting as much, Nicholson observes that 'the Mohammedan Logos tends to identify itself with the active principle of revelation in the Divine essence',[81] but there is no question of co-equality or co-eternity with the Godhead, however much Muḥammad is cherished as Perfect Man and Perfect Image of God by Jīlī and other sufi mystics.[82] Jīlī stresses many times that 'while at supreme moments a man may lose himself in God, he can never be identified with God absolutely'.[83]

Cornell elaborates:

> Al-Jīlī cites the following hadith: 'The Qur'an was sent down to me in a single sentence (*unzila ʿalayya al-Qurʾānu jumlatan wāḥidatan*)'. For al-Jīlī, this tradition meant that Muḥammad, as the final historical manifestation of *al-insān al-kāmil* in the form of a prophet, was infused with the Qur'ān in a single instant and became the embodiment of revelation itself. As such, he epitomizes God's desire to maintain His creation ...'[84]

While R. Arnaldez emphasises that the whole concept of *al-Insān al-Kāmil* is not directly Qur'ānic,[85] he also points to how the medieval mystics like Ibn al-ʿArabī had no problems in *developing* the doctrine from the verses of the sacred text.[86] A good example lies in the latter's *Fuṣūṣ al-Ḥikam (Bezels of Wisdom)*;[87] the text is replete with Qur'ānic references, and, in the last chapter, entitled 'The Wisdom of Singularity in the Word of Muhammad', Ibn al-ʿArabī observes of the Prophet: 'He is the most perfect creation of this humankind, for which reason the whole affair (of creation) begins and ends with him'.[88] This is his conclusion from all that he has found in the sacred text of the Qur'ān.

With this necessary charism of Perfection, the Prophet Muḥammad stands, in a very Islamic and mystical sense, between the heavens and the earth:

1. He is the vessel through which Jibrīl channels the revelation of the Qur'ān from Allah:

> He was taught by one
> Mighty in Power,
> Endued with Wisdom:
> For he appeared
> (In stately form)

While he was in
The highest part
Of the horizon:
Then he approached
And came closer,
And was at a distance
Of but two bow-lengths
Or (even) nearer;
So did (God) convey
The inspiration to His Servant
(Conveyed) what He (meant)
To convey. [89]

2. During the *isrā'* and the *mi'rāj*, he encounters Jibrīl and the beast al-Burāq, rising from the terrestrial Mecca, via Jerusalem, to the highest heavens and conversing with the great prophets of the past who have preceded him to Paradise like Adam, Idrīs, Yūsuf, Yaḥyā, Hārūn, Mūsā, 'Īsa and Ibrāhīm.[90]
3. Finally, as we have seen, Muḥammad speaks with Allah Himself, bargaining, at the instigation of Mūsā, over the number of times the prayer ritual (*ṣalāt*) should be undertaken each day.[91]

And these are not the only celestial figures with whom Muḥammad has contact in his life. It is significant to note for this particular book that Fritz Meier draws attention to the fact that 'an initiation of Khaḍir by the Prophet during the latter's lifetime is referred to in Muḥammad b. 'Alī al-Sanūsī: *Al-Manhal al-rāwī 'l-rā'iq…*'[92] A. J. Wensinck, in the *Encyclopaedia of Islam*, notes that Ibn Ḥajar al-'Asqalānī (AD 1372–1449) 'describes a meeting between al-Khaḍir and Muḥammad in various versions' in his famous biographical *Dictionary* entitled *al-Iṣāba fī Tamyīz al-Ṣaḥāba*.[93] Now, *al-Khaḍir* means literally 'the Green Man' and has another Arabic form also, which is *al-Khiḍr* ('the Green').[94] Furthermore, it is well known that green was the favourite colour of the Prophet Muḥammad himself, and so we shall allude to this link between prophethood and colour at various times throughout this book.[95]

The following case study, drawn from the great Islamic mystic Ibn al-'Arabī (AD 1165–1240), provides a graphic and succinct illustration and encapsulation of what has gone before in our discussion of *The Sacred Way of Perfection*. Many of these key themes with regard to the Prophet Muḥammad as *The Perfect Man* are brought together in a mystical work attributed to Ibn al-'Arabī entitled *Shajarat al-Kawn (The Tree of Being)*.[96] A translator, or 'interpreter' of this work as he prefers to designate himself, Shaykh Tosun Bayrak al-Jerrahi al-Halveti, suggests that *The Tree of Being* suffices as an exoteric title only and draws attention to the translation by Sayyid Sharif al-Jurjani of *Shajara* 'as Perfect Man and *Kawn* as the Expression of Existence'.[97]

Thus, for this shaykh, 'this book is the description of a perfect human being, Allah's best creation, the Prophet Muhammad, Allah's peace and blessings upon him, written by someone who loved him. Therefore we also chose as a title An Ode to the Perfect Man: The Prophet Muhammad'.[98]

The work opens with a quotation from the Holy Qur'ān:

> Seest thou not how
> God sets forth a parable? –
> A goodly Word [*kalimat*]
> Like a goodly tree,
> Whose root is firmly fixed,
> And its branches (reach)
> To the heavens.[99]

The verses which immediately follow are worth citing here because of the very vivid contrast between the 'goodly tree' (= Muḥammad) and the evil tree, which could be said to represent the wilful sinner:

> [The goodly tree] brings forth its fruit
> At all times, by the leave
> Of its Lord.
> So God sets forth parables
> For men, in order that
> They may receive admonition.
> And the parable
> Of an evil Word [*kalima*]
> Is that of an evil tree:
> It is torn up by the root
> From the surface of the earth.
> It has no stability.[100]

In both the initial Qur'ānic quotation cited by Ibn al-ʿArabī, and the verses which succeed it in the Qur'ān, there is reference to 'Words', the one 'good' and the other 'bad'. While this is not the *Logos* doctrine of St John[101] in Islamic garb, and 'the Word' here in the Qur'ān is never made incarnate, it is strikingly clothed in an arboreal simile, giving it an intertextual depth beyond the purely literal.

The whole of Ibn al-ʿArabī's text is replete with praise of the Prophet Muḥammad in one form or another. He relates how God, after purifying 'the quintessence' of the seal of the Tree of Being, 'created the light of our Prophet Muhammad' and that this light was the origin of all else that came to be.[102] Allah's beloved last Prophet Muḥammad was created from the Divine imperative *Kun*.[103] The revelation of the Qur'ān confirmed the presence of Muḥammad on earth and precipitated a joyful efflorescence from the Tree of Being.[104] Elsewhere, Ibn al-ʿArabī compares the light of Muḥammad to life-sustaining water: the former 'gives life to every heart', and the mystic emphasises that Muḥammad's existence 'is Allah's mercy upon the universe'.[105]

He lauds the sublime beauty of the Prophet's human form and states that God endows him with the ability to be known in the celestial spheres.[106] Daringly – provocatively? – Ibn al-ʿArabī, with an excess of devotion, goes so far as to say that God has infused into Muḥammad – according to al-Halveti's translation – 'some of His own divinity and lordship'.[107] This is a very powerful theological statement which must have caused many who read it to wonder how it accorded with the fundamental Islamic doctrine of *tawḥīd*.

Ibn al-ʿArabī's text also portrays Muḥammad coaching the faithful in the correct responses to those questions with which they will be interrogated on the Last Day when Allah comes as the supreme judge.[108] But perhaps one of the most interesting sections of the text is that which describes the famous *isrā'* (Night Journey) and *miʿrāj* (Ascension into Paradise), which are elaborated in a truly mystical vein.[109]

Miʿrāj is now the name given to 'a second mystical beast' which conveys the Prophet 'above the world's atmosphere'.[110] Jibrīl carries Muḥammad to the Lote Tree in the Seventh Heaven, Muḥammad pierces 70,000 veils of light and finally arrives at the Throne of Allah. The Throne, anthropomorphised, speaks to the Prophet, non-verbally, deploying 'the soundless language of love'.[111] Finally, he comes face to face with God and communicates with the Creator Himself.[112] Ibn al-ʿArabī concludes with the Qur'ānic words:

> So did (God) convey
> The inspiration to His Servant –
> (Conveyed) what He (meant)
> To convey.[113]

Shaykh Tosun Bayrak al-Jerrahi al-Halveti, the translator and interpreter of Ibn al-ʿArabī's mystic text, considers that the *isrā'* or Night Journey of the Prophet Muḥammad was the greatest of the miracles wrought by the Prophet.[114]

Ibn al-ʿArabī's *Shajarat al-Kawn* may be characterised in many ways: certainly, its language is high-flown, devotional, mystical, filled with awe and yet loving and worshipful as well. It breathes the air of the sacred, and it is an almost unparalleled hymn to the perfection, virtues and life of the Prophet Muḥammad. In a nutshell, it is an excellent illustration and case study of *the Sacred Way of Perfection*.

1.2 The Secular Way

The themes of this particular *Way* contrast vividly and starkly with those adumbrated above. The subliminal theme of perfection is still present, but it now has a secular articulation in such *topoi* as courtly love, knighthood, and those qualities which make up the perfect hero, knight or gentleman. They will be explored with reference to a diversity of medieval authors such as Geoffrey Chaucer, Chrétien de Troyes, Guillaume de Lorris and Jean de Meun, and Sir Thomas Malory. Here we encounter *the Perfect Knight* and *the Ideal Woman*, a secular parallelism to the *Perfect Man/Perfect Deity* theme delineated above.

The Secular Way of Perfection is a medieval palimpsest of ideals. It will be articulated here round the twin themes of *courtly love* and *chivalry*. Neither was monolithic; both were often intertwined in a complex meld of actuality, romance and ideal. In an attempt to illustrate this *Way*, we shall examine briefly the origins, definitions and qualities of each of these *topoi*, bearing in mind at all times the multivalent nature of each.

Beverly Kennedy, for example, identifies three types of knight in Sir Thomas Malory's famous *Le Morte d'Arthur*. The author was born around AD 1415–17 and died in AD 1471. His work was completed in AD 1469 or 1470:[115] there was 'the Heroic knight, who has only the basic feudal virtues to recommend him; the True knight who combines feudal and religious virtues (and in some cases courtly virtues as well); and the Worshipful knight, who combines feudal and courtly virtues'.[116] Beverly Kennedy sees the supreme embodiment of each type of knight in the Arthurian Gawain, Lancelot and Tristram: Gawain is the Heroic, Lancelot the True, and Tristram is the Worshipful knight.[117] All are knights, Kennedy stresses, united under the general heading of knighthood, but their natures are by no means monolithic: each has an individual ethos and individual comprehension of the meaning of how one should be a 'good' knight.[118]

Courtly love

The *origins* of courtly love and, indeed, of the term itself have been disputed. Marlé Hammond cites Theodor Frings' view 'that the origins of European courtly love lay in a primordial female lament'.[119] Roger Boase tells us that the actual term *amour courtois* first appeared in an 1883 article on 'Lancelot du Lac' written by the French medievalist Gaston Paris.[120] Boase is at pains to stress, however, right at the beginning of his volume, that the poets of the Middle Ages whose theme was love 'wrote within a literary tradition, inspired by a particular ideal of "true love" which motivated their conduct'[121] and that Gaston Paris was by no means the first to write a study of 'courtly love'; there were, indeed, Renaissance antecedents.[122]

C. S. Lewis, in his famous classic work *The Allegory of Love*,[123] dogmatically held that we have all heard of courtly love and we all know that its origins lie in Languedoc 'at the end of the eleventh century'.[124] But Bernard O'Donaghue is not so sure![125] Boase stresses a possible Arab source,[126] while O'Donaghue points to the popularity and spread of literature dealing with the Arthurian traditions during the twelfth century.[127]

Precise *definitions* of courtly love are no less diverse. Boase holds that 'the meaning of the term has never been satisfactorily defined'[128] and that it is a term which may be characterised as 'inherently ambiguous'.[129] That is certainly true if the designation of love as 'hostile peace' in the medieval *Romance of the Rose* is anything to go by![130] Boase's useful conclusion is worth citing in full: 'Courtly love was ... a comprehensive cultural phenomenon: a literary movement, an ideology, an ethical system, a style of life, and an expression of the play element in culture ...'[131] So, what were its *qualities*?

Lewis prefers to stress the 'specialized' nature of the love involved and, again some may think over-dogmatically, to proclaim that it has four key characteristics; he capitalises each one in his text: 'Humility, Courtesy, Adultery, and the Religion of Love.[132] And, while we may readily accept 'humility', 'courtesy' and 'the religion of love' as possible and admissible aspects of our *Secular Way of Perfection*, the focus on adultery – whatever its prevalence and description in medieval literature – is somewhat disquieting for any paradigm of perfection and has no place within it. This stress on adultery as a component of courtly love is, indeed, questioned by O'Donaghue[133] and others as well.

Maurice Hussey, for example, emphasises that 'C. S. Lewis was wrong to give the impression that all courtly love stories are adulterous, since [Chaucer's] *The Franklin's Tale* has for its opening premise a lover whose end is a marriage of rare distinction'.[134] O'Donaghue, usefully, identifies two main traditions of courtly love poetry, the one deriving from Ovid and the other which he characterises as 'the religion of love, perhaps verging on blasphemy in theory ... *but in practice often metamorphosing into love of God*'.[135] This last statement is of particular significance for any comparison between our sacred and secular *Ways*. O'Donaghue goes on to say that many of the troubadours ended up by embracing the religious life: 'A *virtuous love affair ought to be a figure of the love of man for God*'.[136]

Certainly, love was idealised and its literature was appreciated by people as unlikely as the youthful Teresa of Ávila (AD 1515–82) and Ignatius of Loyola (AD 1491–1556),[137] the first a major reformer with Juan de la Cruz/John of the Cross (AD 1542–91) of the Carmelite Order, and the second the founder of the Jesuits.

Not only was courtly love considered to be an *ideal*, but it was also an *enchantment*.[138] We see this vividly in the thirteenth century in *The Romance of the Rose* (*Le Roman de la Rose*), a dual-authored medieval French poem: Guillaume de Lorris (died c. AD 1237) was the author of the first part in about AD 1230,[139] while its continuation was undertaken by Jean de Meun writing in about AD 1275.[140] The latter died in AD 1305.[141]

In the poem, the narrator dreams allegorically of seeking to pluck a rose in a walled garden named Pleasure (Deduit). He encounters the God of Love as well as such figures named Reason and Jealousy.[142] 'The implicit sexual metaphor of the lover's quest is developed to a final conclusion in the continuation of the poem, added many years later by Jean de Meun, where the dreamer finally succeeds in entering the inner sanctum of the rose before awakening at daybreak.'[143]

C. S. Lewis famously described *The Romance of the Rose* as 'a germinal book' and 'a parent, begetting offspring at once like and unlike itself'.[144] Perhaps part of the *enchantment* lies in the somewhat frustrating fact that, in the poem, we barely perceive the heroine as an actual person, since the description overwhelmingly focuses on her desirability as a rosebud.[145] And perhaps the rest of the *enchantment*, at least for the reader if not the narrator, lies in the two-sided nature of the allegory: it could be interpreted, literally, blatantly, as the narrator's attempt to achieve full union with the Beloved by sexual intercourse; and/or with O'Donaghue, we might view the poem as an essay in 'love-service' and as a 'social drama', imbued with the *topoi* of courtly love, whose goal is love's total conquest of the lover.[146]

The themes of *enchantment* and yearning for the Beloved are developed in many of the great troubadour songs of the Middle Ages, such as that by Gaucelm Faidit, a troubadour of the twelfth century, who wrote a beautiful song entitled *Lo Rossinholet salvatge* (I have heard the wild nightingale), whose first stanza runs as follows:

> I have heard the wild nightingale
> rejoicing with love
> in its own language.
> And it makes me die of envy
> for I can neither see nor gaze upon

the one whom I desire,
nor has wanted to hear me this year,
but because of the sweet singing
of the nightingale and his mate,
my spirits are encouraged a little
and thus do I comfort my heart
by singing
something I didn't expect to do this year.[147]

Courtly love also involved *adoration*, that is, adoration of the Beloved Woman; there is a development of what might be characterised as 'The Cult of the Adored Woman'. Veneration, akin to that which might have been paid by the pious medieval worshipper to the Virgin Mary, or one of the female saints, is paid instead to the sublime human object of Love and Awe. Women are almost objectified as they are placed on mental pedestals. Discussing Chrétien de Troyes' twelfth-century *Lancelot, Le Chevalier à la Charrette* (*Lancelot, The Knight of the Cart*),[148] C. S. Lewis draws our attention to the way in which Lancelot's resignation and meekness mimic feelings implicit in religion. It is true, he adds, that Lancelot's love is sensual, indeed carnal, but the work shows him adopting a virtually 'worshipful' attitude to Guinevere before whose bed he actually kneels down, adoring the woman with whom he is entranced and infatuated.[149] Here, it is not just a case of 'worship' or 'longing' from afar but actual consummation preceded and followed by the rituals of 'adoration': it is the 'cult of the adored woman' made flesh or lustful.

Before Lancelot has intercourse with Guinevere,

He approached the queen's bed,
Bowing in adoration
Before the holiest relic
He knew ...[150]

On leaving her bedroom,

He bowed and crossed himself,
As if acknowledging
An altar ...[151]

We have examined the theme of courtly love respectively as an *ideal*, as an *enchantment* and as *cultic adoration*. Fourthly and finally, we note how it might be considered to be an actual *illness*! Boase observes how 'mystics were also believed to be prone to melancholy on account of their great yearning to be united with God'.[152] Such a statement would harmonise well with our *Sacred Way of Perfection* adumbrated earlier in this chapter. But it is the parallel, secular version which concerns us here.

The notion that love might be a sickness was not an uncommon one; it was recognised in the Islamic East as well as the Christian West. The medieval Islamic historian al-Masʿūdī (c. AD 896–c. 956), for example, in his famous belletrist history known to us as *Murūj al-Dhahab* (*The Fields of Gold*), portrays a *majlis* or seminar at which the nature of love is discussed in pathological terms. The Arabic word used is *'ishq* which is the equivalent of the Greek *éros* or 'passionate love'.

Boase reminds us of the origins of the 'love as sickness' theory in 'the Graeco-Arabic theory of love-melancholy or *amor hereos*'. He notes that 'the term *'ishq*, as used by Avicenna [Ibn Sīnā, AD 979–1037], referred to a mental disorder, caused by excessive meditation on the image of a woman who is sexually unattainable'.[153] In *The Romance of the Rose*, love is characterised, in a typically paradoxical fashion, as 'reasonable madness', 'healthful sickness' and 'an infirm strength'.[154]

In al-Mas'ūdī's Chronicle to which we have just alluded, we find the following, offered Platonic-*Symposium*[155] style, as a contribution to the grand debate on passionate love, *'ishq*, which involves a diversity of attempts at its true definition. The second speaker at the *majlis* affirms the disorderly nature of the desperate lover's thoughts and the way that his whole mind becomes unbalanced; nothing seems pure to him any more, and all is fickle. He is beset by misfortune. Indeed, 'love is a draught from death's cup'.[156] Later in the debate, the medieval theory of the four humours is woven into the fabric of the speaker's definition:

> As [love's] strength grows, the lover becomes more agitated, more irritable. He is absorbed in his thoughts, his vague aspirations, his sorrows. He draws breath with difficulty, is permanently wrapped in his reveries and loses his appetite. His intelligence withers, his brain dries up and his life becomes exhausted, for, through the ceaseless action of desire, the blood becomes heated and converted into black bile. This increases and invades the seat of thought. Fever develops and then the yellow bile becomes inflamed, turbid, decays and ends by mixing with the atrabilious humour, of which it becomes an integral part, increasing its strength. Now one of the properties of this atrabilious humour is to act on the thoughts. When thought weakens, the gastric juices mix and decompose, hence sluggishness, dwindling of the intellectual powers, desire for the impossible and at last, madness. Then the lover either commits suicide or dies of grief and despair.[157]

Here we see the Arab author invoke a whole spectrum of physical disorders moving from the spectre of madness suggested by *The Romance of the Rose*[158] to death itself. What is interesting about the whole of the passage just quoted is how it fits neatly with a general medieval theme which held that passionate love was an actual sickness. Of course, the Arabic passage deploys rhetorical hyperbole, as do the medieval romances like *The Romance of the Rose*; but this is always used to powerful effect to emphasise a fundamental point. However, while love as *ideal*, *enchantment* and *cultic adoration* might justifiably contribute to the establishment of our *Secular Way of Perfection*, this fourth aspect, love as *sickness*, must necessarily be excluded.

Chivalry

We move now to the second major *topos* to be considered under the heading of *the Secular Way of Perfection*: chivalry. Together with the theme of courtly love, the arena of chivalry has much to contribute to any evaluation of this secular *Way*.

There are also several features which bear comparison with the *Sacred Way* in terms of quests for perfection and Perfect Models.

Examining the *origins* of chivalry, Boase situates and confirms its beginnings in a twelfth-century romantic revival whose heroes were Charlemagne and the Arthurian Knights of Round Table fame.[159] He cites Johan Huizinga (AD 1872–1945) as having identified a heroic and a bucolic theme. The former presented 'an ideal hero' as a model for emulation; and this idea became the foundation of medieval chivalry.[160] And, while numerous scholars viewed chivalry as a practice and ideal which derived from the Middle East, either by returning Crusaders or the variegated multi-ethnic channel of the Iberian Peninsula,[161] this is rejected by Boase, who regards it as an institution which emerged in the twelfth century 'distinct from feudalism' as the gulf grew between the knights and their association with the land, and there was an influx of 'new' nobility.[162]

Thus a knightly caste arose, whose minds were filled with the heroic legends and myths of the past, deriving from Arthurian and other sources. And, whatever the real truth about the actual origins of chivalry in Europe in the early Middle Ages, it is clear that this became an ideal and an upper-class *modus vivendi* in the West, and in the East as well, as we shall see.

Definitions of 'chivalry' as a term are many. In *The Concise Oxford Dictionary of Current Usage*, we find the following succinct definitions: 'Medieval knightly system with its religious, moral, and social code ... ideal knight's characteristics, Courage and courtesy ...'[163] And it is on these characteristics or qualities that we shall now concentrate, for it is these with which the *Perfect Knight* was endowed, *in toto* or in part, and which contribute, with the *topos* of courtly love, to our establishment and illustration of a medieval *Secular Way of Perfection*. We should stress here, right at the beginning, that our paradigm thus constituted was – and is – by no means the only possible one. There are many others, but ours is established by way of being a stark *secular* contrast to the *Sacred Way* which we illustrated and analysed above.

C. S. Lewis draws a parallelism between earthly knighthood and angelic knighthood, an antithesis which resonates well with our own *sacred/secular* paradigms.[164] And indeed, there are many stark parallels to be drawn from the whole corpus of medieval literature: one thinks, for example, of virtuous knights (e.g. Gawain) contrasting with sinful, adulterous knights (e.g. Lancelot).[165] Helen Cooper shows that, in the oath sworn by the Knights of the Round Table and the emphasis on fidelity in love, Sir Thomas Malory presents 'an ideal of secular Christian chivalry'; but, in addition to the need for being physically able and faithful to one's spouse, there is a substratum of the sacred in that religious observances are deemed to be necessary as well.[166] Furthermore, just as the *good knight* or the *perfect knight* reveres and respects his God, so the ordinary people, those perhaps working on the land for whom knighthood would be an impossible dream by virtue of feudalism and class or even those who write poems, respect and revere knighthood.[167]

So, what were the qualities that led to such respect and reverence for knighthood and the institutions and ideals of medieval chivalry? Kennedy stresses that there was no single code of knighthood to which every knight might subscribe. Surveying the culture of fifteenth-century England in which Malory was steeped, he identifies three very different styles of knighthood in competition with each other and each possessed of its own ethical code.[168] These were articulated and incarnated in the three types of knight which we quoted Kennedy as identifying earlier: the Heroic, the True and the Worshipful.[169] Agreeing with Kennedy, Helen Cooper stresses that Malory's *good knights* are deployed in such archetypes as 'Lancelot, Gareth and Tristram'.[170] However, Lancelot, as we have already seen, is not always on the side of the angels, at least as far as chastity is concerned! Cooper notes Malory's limited vocabulary for his two types of knight, the good and the bad: 'Noble, worshipful, good against shameful, false, traitorous, ... recreant or recrayed'.[171]

The medieval literature in which the knights, both good and bad, are shown displaying these diverse qualities is vast. We shall examine just two examples here: Roland (the nephew of Charlemagne (AD 742–814), and Chaucer's knight.

In the old French poem known as the *Chanson de Roland* (*The Song of Roland*),[172] whose theme is the Battle of Roncevaux in AD 778, Roland is portrayed as the very paragon of the heroic knight.[173] With a small group of soldiers, he is defeated by the Gascon and Muslim armies and killed with his fellow warriors, being far too proud at first to summon help from his uncle Charlemagne. His ultimate call for help comes far too late to be of any use.[174]

Roland's knighthood embraces the virtue of sublime courage[175] but is flawed by an overweening pride: 'Count Roland was a noble warrior' (*Li quens Rollant fut noble guerrer*)[176] but when he is begged by Oliver to sound his horn to summon help, he refuses:

> *Respunt Rollant: 'Jo fereie que fols'.*
>
> Roland replies: 'I would be behaving like a fool'.[177]

Finally he sounds it, and it is heard by Charles (Charlemagne) and his army, but it is all too late:

> *Li quens Rollant ad la buche sanglante,*
> *De sun cervel rumput en est li temples*
> *L'olifan sunet a dulor e a peine,*
> *Karles l'oït e ses Franceis l'entendent.*
>
> Count Roland's mouth is bleeding,
> The temple of his brain has burst.
> He sounds the Oliphant in agony and in pain.
> Charles heard it, and his Frenchmen too.[178]

It is left to the reader or listener to decide whether the charisms of knighthood have been diluted or enhanced by Roland's stubborn and foolish pride!

Gerard J. Brault lauds Turoldus' (c. AD 1100) *Song of Roland* as 'the greatest French epic' and grants it a most prominent place in the Western literary canon.[179] Aware that the poem was written about three centuries after the actual Battle of Roncevaux in AD 778,[180] Brault draws our attention to Pope Urban II's famous instigation of the First Crusade in his speech at Clermont in AD 1095 and the subsequent fall of Jerusalem to the Christian crusaders in AD 1099. For him, the *Song of*

Roland is a contemporary mirror of the wars between the Muslims and the Christian crusading armies.[181]

Thus medieval chivalry, crusade, Islam and Christianity intertwine seamlessly, and intertextually, in this 'greatest French epic'. Because of his sinful pride, Roland is a flawed knight and hero (rather like Lancelot before him, but for different reasons), but he achieves redemption in the eyes of some scholars through repentance and ultimately death.[182] And Turoldus conforms his poem to an epic tradition of knightly valour and renown, using archetypical themes where 'the myth-making process itself also militates against realism'.[183]

Finally, we note, with Brault, that the sacrifice and death of Roland constitute an *imitatio Christi*.[184] The clear lesson is that the truly chivalrous knight must be Christ-like, must be *obediens usque ad mortem*: to be obedient to the essence of chivalry is to be obedient to the demands of Christ Himself. In Roland, then, there is a near-merging of our *Secular* and *Sacred Ways of Perfection*, diluted only by his sin of pride but redeemed by a valiant death.

Geoffrey Chaucer (c. AD 1343–1400) began his famous *Canterbury Tales*[185] in about 1387/8.[186] Up to the point when he began the composition of the *Tales*, C. S. Lewis insists that he may be considered primarily as an exponent of the courtly love genre.[187] But, while the *Tales* may diverge from what Lewis has perceived thus far as a literary pattern in Chaucer's life, they nonetheless present us with much information about what it meant to be a *good knight* – and herein *does* lie an affinity with aspects of the courtly love tradition. Here, there *is* a parallelism with Malory's own concerns about *good knighthood*.[188]

Chaucer's knight in *The Canterbury Tales* is acclaimed not just as *good* but *perfect* or *complete*:

> *He was a verray, parfit gentil knight.*[189]
> ... he was indeed
> The very pattern of a noble knight.[190]

The Riverside Chaucer, in its footnotes to Chaucer's *General Prologue* to the *Tales*, translates *verray* as 'true', *parfit* as 'perfect' (complete) and *gentil* as 'noble'.[191] Here, then, we can already glean at least two notable knightly qualities from our Chaucerian knight: *nobility*, and *perfection*, perhaps in the sense of being completely rounded in all the requisite virtues.

From the rest of the description, we learn that our knight is fond of his chosen military profession: '*He loved chivalrie*';[192] he cherishes '*trouthe and honour, fredom and curteisie*'.[193] He has fought with great courage in diverse parts of the world,[194] but despite his fame he is wise and eschews a foul tongue.[195] He rides good horses but does not dress to impress, for he has just returned from one set of travels and is now on pilgrimage to Canterbury.[196]

In short, Chaucer presents to us a very paragon of knighthood[197] with all the virtues we might expect from any good medieval Christian knight, whether within or without the courtly love tradition. In the light of this, the lack of resemblance between *The Knight's Tale* and other French and English romances of the Middle Ages is interesting and, perhaps, surprising.[198]

The tale which the knight tells is adapted from the *Teseida* of Boccaccio but transformed into 'a uniquely philosophical romance' by Chaucer and given a happy ending with the marriage of Palamoun and Emelye.[199] There is, then, the usual romantic happy ending, as J. A. Burrow notes; but he also stresses that *The Knight's Tale* is a much more serious piece by contrast with the equally happy endings in *The Wife of Bath's Tale* and *The Franklin's Tale*, and this is manifested in the seeming fragility of the conclusion 'shadowed by thoughts of suffering and death'.[200]

Helen Cooper draws our attention to the similarities between the structure of Chaucer's *Knight's Tale* and that of *Sir Gawain and the Green Knight*.[201] And, while the motif of *greenness* in no way imbues Chaucer's poem, this is perhaps a useful point at which to introduce the concept as we move in our discussions to *the Mystic Way of Perfection*.

Sir Gawain's exploits were clearly well known in medieval literature: there are, for example, overt and covert references to him in *The Romance of the Rose*.[202] And, in *Sir Gawain and the Green Knight*, the colour *green* assumes a quasi-mystical dimension, being interwoven into the very fabric of this heroic tale of medieval knighthood. As Gerald Morgan puts it: 'In the poet's description of the Green Knight as a whole … the greenness is on any view the most outstanding of all the details'.[203] It can stand as a symbol for so much, not least the mystical goodness and perfection with which the *Perfect Knight* should be imbued.

What we also have here, no less, although played down by Morgan,[204] is the establishment of a link covering the colour green, medieval knighthood, their union in the Green Knight, and the Green Man of popular myth. Morgan quotes the following passage from J. Speirs:

> The Green Knight, whose head is chopped off at his own request and who is as miraculously or magically alive as ever, bears an unmistakable relation to the Green Man –the Jack in the Green or the Wild Man of the village festivals of England and Europe. He *is* in fact no other than a recrudescence in poetry of the Green Man.[205]

And there is more: as we shall see, 'the poem locates the foundation of a knightly brotherhood of a green girdle in an erotic text'.[206] In the main, Sir Gawain passes the test, and thus the poem reflects a *way of love* which is slightly different from those adumbrated in our *Sacred and Secular Ways of Perfection*. It is a story of respect for the bonds of married love, with the gift of the green silk girdle becoming a symbol of chastity and fidelity: Sir Gawain's chaste refusal to be seduced by his temptress contrasts vividly with Sir Lancelot's willing adultery with the equally compliant Queen Guinevere; in a nutshell, it is *Virtuous Knight* versus *Sinful Knight*!

1.3 *The Mystic Way*

1.3.1 Sir Gawain, the Green Knight and al-Khaḍir

What have the Middle English poem *Sir Gawain and the Green Knight* and the eighteenth *sūra* (chapter) of the Arabic Qur'ān got in common? At first sight, it would seem that the answer must be a succinct 'very little'! *Sir Gawain* is a masterly romance which Brian Stone has characterised as follows: 'At the very time when Chaucer was flourishing, poets of the west and north-west of England were producing a number of fine long poems in alliterative verse, of which *Sir Gawain and the Green Knight* is the pearl'.[207] The eighteenth chapter of the Qur'ān is entitled *The Chapter of the Cave*. It contains, *inter alia*, a story analogous to that of the Seven Sleepers of Ephesus, an account of a series of mystical encounters between Moses and a mysterious, gnostic-type figure variously identified as al-Khiḍr or al-Khaḍir, and possible references to the Alexander romance.[208]

Yet, closer examination shows that a number of themes are held in common. *The Encyclopaedia of Islam* tells us that 'Al-Khaḍir is properly an epithet ('the green man') ... [and has a] secondary form Khiḍr (approximately 'the green'), which in many places has displaced the primary form'.[209] In *Sir Gawain*, the knight is

> A fellow fiercely grim,
> And all a glittering green
> ...
> The steed that he spurred on was similar in hue
> To the sight
> Green and huge of grain
> ...
> Yes, garbed all in green was the gallant rider.[210]

Both al-Khaḍir and the knight, then, are *Green Men*, mystically and mysteriously so, and both are physically 'green' in their garb.[211]

Scholars have differed over the etymology of the name al-Khaḍir, borne by that strange mystical being who encounters Moses (Mūsā) in the Qur'ānic *Chapter of the Cave*. In one explanation, 'he sat on a white skin and it became green', the skin being the Earth itself.[212] In another, 'al-Khaḍir is told at the spring of life: 'Thou art Chadhir [*sic*] and where thy feet touch it, the earth will become green'.[213] In *Sir Gawain*, the Green Knight is an 'implicitly supernatural ... person'; he is 'more like the jovial demon of old popular tradition, and also, it seems to me, resembles the kind of devil who tempts within the system and on behalf of God, like Satan in the Book of Job ...'[214] Here he contrasts quite vividly with the more sublime, less physical and more mystical figure of al-Khaḍir. Nonetheless, it is clear that both figures, regardless of their moral worth, share a fundamental and mysterious *green* quality.

There is another basic feature which both the Green Knight and al-Khaḍir hold in common. They both belong to a genre which might be characterised simply as 'questing and testing'. And both behave in what seems, *prima facie*, to be an antinomian fashion.

Al-Khaḍir encounters Moses – Mūsā in the Arabic – while the latter is already on a quest and has reached 'the junction of the two seas' which he has sought. Al-Khaḍir is endowed with special, Divinely infused knowledge, and this is clearly recognised by Moses, who begs to be allowed to follow this gnostic-type figure. Al-Khaḍir challenges Moses, saying that he will not be able to have patience with him. Moses begs to differ, and so al-Khaḍir permits him to follow, on condition that he does not question what al-Khaḍir does.

Three tests follow, and, on each occasion, Moses is unable to maintain the requisite silence and patience, and he cries out peevishly. In other words, Moses fails each of the three tests as al-Khaḍir successively scuttles a boat, kills a young man and repairs a crumbling wall. God's ways are clearly not man's ways, as al-Khaḍir explains to Moses: the boat was sunk to prevent it from falling into the hands of a rapacious and piratical king; the young man would have vexed his God-fearing parents by falling into unbelief; the wall had to be rebuilt lest its crumbling state revealed a buried treasure which two orphans were due to inherit.[215] The two themes here are theodicy and the testing of Everyman, the latter epitomised in the confused figure of Moses.

In *Sir Gawain*, 'the Green Knight ... clearly has some of the pagan attributes of stock figures from primitive folklore'.[216] And *green* is a constant *leitmotiv*: not only is our eponymous Knight a 'green knight', but also there is a 'green silken girdle'[217] and a 'Green Chapel'[218] in the story.

Everything begins with the unexpected arrival at King Arthur's court at New Year of

> An awesome fellow
> Who in height outstripped all earthly men ...
> Men gaped at the hue of him
> Ingrained in garb and mien
> A fellow fiercely grim,
> *And all a glittering green.*[219]

This terrifying apparition of a Green Knight starts the 'testing' by issuing a challenge to the effect that any of those present may strike him with his axe, provided that he is allowed to return the blow in a year's time. King Arthur's nephew, Sir Gawain, beheads the Green Knight, but this does not prevent the miraculously still-live figure from picking up his head and bidding Sir Gawain to abide by the terms of the oath he has sworn. In a year's time, he is to

> Go to the Green Chapel without gainsaying to get
> Such a stroke as you have struck ...[220]

'Questing' follows this first test as Sir Gawain, after an interval of ten months, rides forth to seek his potential nemesis at the Green Chapel. Further tests follow. He is entertained over the Christmas period at a castle where, Joseph-like, he is tempted by the wife of the Lord of the castle [221]. The story fits an ancient paradigm of the attempted seduction of a virtuous man and is to be found both in the Judaeo-Christian Book of Genesis[222] and the Islamic Qur'ān.[223] In the *Sir Gawain* narrative, the Lady of the Castle finally abandons her attempts at seduction but bestows on Sir Gawain a protective girdle. He rides forth to the Green Chapel, which has rightly been identified as being 'at the heart of Sir Gawain and the Green Knight',[224] and not just structurally, for it is a powerful semiotic indicator of righteousness, the sacred and, indeed, chastity in marriage itself, given that it would have been a place where wedding vows must at one time, or even recently, have been pronounced.

Sir Gawain then encounters the Green Knight, who gives him two 'feinted blows'[225] but just cuts his neck slightly with a third. To his amazement, he discovers that the Green Knight is really the Lord of the castle! The slight cut on the neck is the punishment for failing to tell the Lord earlier about the present of the girdle. Sir Gawain returns to the court of King Arthur and is received with general rejoicing and comforted by the king and the court. All the knights of the Brotherhood agree that, henceforth, they will wear a bright green band in honour of Sir Gawain.[226]

The distinguished poet and translator of *Sir Gawain*, Simon Armitage, believes that the success of the poems lies in the succession of 'vivid contrasts' which it presents: there is the deployment of standard and colloquial forms of speech; the utterly transparent goodness of Sir Gawain stands in vivid contrast with the blood-thirsty menace of the Green Knight; the *mores* of courtly love contrast powerfully with the explicit and blatant sexuality of the Lady of the castle. For Armitage, 'these contrasts stretch the imaginative universe of the poem and make it three-dimensional'.[227] He sees, in addition, that aspects of Sir Gawain's predicament have a contemporary relevance, especially with regard to man's relationship to nature.[228]

It is true that the story has a wide applicability and an almost infinite capacity for adaptation; the intertextual domain in which such stories as the Arabic al-Khaḍir and Moses on the one hand, and the English *Sir Gawain* on the other, participate is vast. Iris Murdoch, for example, would later devise a version of the story in a modern setting in her novel *The Green Knight*.[229] Semiotic clues infuse her text: Murdoch's hero has a 'green umbrella';[230] he enters a room with a 'green shaded lamp';[231] he has a 'dark green tweed jacket'.[232] And he speaks of 'restitution' and 'justice'.[233] Murdoch's novel, too, embraces the perennial theme of 'questing and testing'.

The common motif and theme in all this, of course, is *greenness*, a colour imbued with, or characterised by, an often mystical or quasi-mystical significance. At the very least, it is the colour of *mystery*. For this reason, we will now move briefly from our consideration of what it means to be green in such knightly and mystical tales as those of al-Khaḍir, Sir Gawain and the hero of Iris Murdoch's novel to a broader consideration of *greenness* and the mysterious, often mystical, figure in English and other folklore of *The Green Man*.[234]

Some associations with this colour are easier to explain than others. Simon Armitage draws attention to the world of nature which we find described in *Sir Gawain*.[235] It is, perhaps, hardly surprising that contemporary political parties which concern themselves primarily with the environment should characterise themselves to the voting populace as 'Green Parties'. The national flag of Pakistan is predominantly green[236] because it was the favourite colour of the Prophet Muḥammad.[237]

Other examples abound: there is a plethora of pubs in the United Kingdom which bear the name *The Green Man*; [238] the ship of the famous Ming-dynasty Chinese admiral Zheng He (travelled AD 1405–33) was called *The Green Eyebrow*:[239] it was 'a renowned Song dynasty junk, named for the menacing glare painted on her bow'.[240] On the Greek island of Skyros, during the pre-Lenten Goat Dance, the genitals of a certain statue are painted green.[241] Here we note the association of a pagan 'liturgy' with the colour green. But we might also note the religious use of the colour green in the older Roman Catholic liturgy, where green vestments had a *non*-festal significance as opposed, for example, to the use of white vestments on major feast days.[242]

Green was also the sacred colour of the ancient Egyptian goddess Hathor, a colour reflected in the early part of the Nile inundation. For Hathor was 'the mistress of the stream who makes the river rise'.[243] And green eye shadow was a symbol of the protection of the goddess.[244]

Now, it is not the intention of this book to explore the mystery or the mysticism behind each of these diverse examples. They are presented here as examples of the variegated nature of the 'green intertext'. What we will explore in greater detail is the association of the colour *green* with knighthood, and its function via the *Sir Gawain* poem as a possible source or inspiration for, or reflection of, the Order of the Garter, founded by King Edward III in about AD 1347–49,[245] together with its *essential* nature in the story of al-Khaḍir[246] and the whole Islamic tradition thereafter. For *green* is the primary colour of *the Mystic Way of Perfection*, whose signposts we adumbrate in this chapter. As we have seen, there is a profusion of intertextual links between our key *topoi* of courtly love, knighthood, chivalry, mystery and greenness which in turn mirror, and thus connect to, *the Sacred Way of Perfection.*

1.3.2 The Green Man in Legend, Myth and Literature

Green Men

M. A. Hall has drawn attention to the fact that the term *Green Man* is a portmanteau term with a whole variety of meanings and types and also liable to many misconceptions.[247] Was this figure a mere 'personification of springtime' or 'a leaf-hidden horror?'[248] Hall points to an essay by Brian Stone, for whom green represents 'everliving and eternal truth'.[249] This type of green symbolism would resonate powerfully with an Islamic audience, where the colour is associated both with the sage al-Khaḍir and the Prophet Muḥammad himself, but perhaps less with a Christian, where the many corbel carvings and bosses of Green Men in churches yield a whole variety of symbolisms and interpretations. Hall notes that such 'foliate head[s]' have decorated churches from the fifth century AD, if not before. They could portray devils, souls in Hell, and poor sinners. They might have a resurrectional significance, reflect man's sinful state and even reflect the brevity of his earthly sojourn, since all that is green must eventually wither and die after its first flourishing.[250]

Despite a possible reference to ultimate resurrection, then, what we have here in Hall's summary of the diverse symbolisms of the *Green Man* is an association of *greenness* with demons, evil, lust, sin and the utter brevity of life – associations which are the very opposite of the symbolism of green as representing 'eternal truth'. For Brian Stone, indeed, in his essay appended to his translation of *Sir Gawain and the Green Knight*, entitled 'The Common Enemy of Man', the Green Knight is precisely that, and, moreover, 'like the jovial demon of old popular tradition, and … the kind of devil who tempts within the system and on behalf of God, like Satan in the Book of Job'.[251]

But there *are* other, more neutral, indeed chivalric, connotations of green as well, forming a kind of half-way house between the sacredness of 'eternal truth' and the purely demonic. We learn, for example, that May festivities associated with the Duc de Berry involved cloth whose colour was *vert gai*, which was called *livré de mai*, and ladies clad in green, riding horses whose bridles were decorated with green.[252] In more sacred mode, the Annunciation scene, in the Master of Mary of Burgundy's *Book of Hours for Engelbert of Nassau* (AD 1451–1504), portrays the angel Gabriel with green-bordered wings whose colour matches the green drapes of the room within which the Virgin Mary receives the angel.[253]

Secular or sacred, angelic or demonic? The colour *green* was clearly multivalent in its usages and symbolisms in the Middle and Later Middle Ages. Thus far, we have encountered green seers (al-Khaḍir), green knights, and angels with wings tipped with green. We have some knowledge of their origins, contexts and roles. But what were the *origins* of *green men*?

Kathleen Basford, after noting how often they appear in medieval church architecture, on roof bosses, tombs and misericords *inter alia*,[254] finds their origins in first century AD Roman art.[255] From the fourth or fifth centuries AD, despite such pagan origins, the Green Man motif became a feature of ecclesiastical architectural symbolism.[256] But, Janus-like, the Green Man had a dual aspect.[257] Basford, stressing the more sinister side, points out that the Green Men, whose carved heads are to be found, for example, in profusion in Devon churches, especially Exeter Cathedral, had a range of meanings moving from the demonic to lost souls.[258] Elsewhere, however, Green Men figures were associated with 'the blessing of the fields',[259] an altogether more benign aspect. But overall, the iconography of the Green Man is a gloomy one.

This is how Kathleen Basford puts it:

> The Green Man's place in the scheme of things may perhaps be better understood from the imagery of the joyous Incarnation group in Exeter Cathedral. The Virgin treads on the Green man as she might tread on the head of the old serpent, the tempter himself, lurking in the Tree of Life. The leaves rise up out of the wide open mouth as from the abyss … [The Green Man here] represents the darkness of unredeemed nature as opposed to the shimmering light of Christian revelation.[260]

All this belies John Satchell's view that the majority of Green Men figures are to be perceived as 'benign, vigorous, cheerful and even noble',[261] though he is aware of some carvings in Cumbria where the Green Man is presented as a totally evil being, as well as a malevolent-looking example in Carlisle Cathedral's treasury and a demonic Green Man on a corbel in Preston Patrick parish church near Kendal.[262] Satchell's conclusion is that, if we seek the origins of the Green Man in the fertility rites and symbols of paganism and then find it later Christianised as a resurrection symbol,[263] then the examples cited above bear witness to a strong pagan milieu whose symbols a nascent Christianity was unwilling to tolerate or absorb into its own regional iconography except as motifs of unregenerate evil.[264]

Throughout his book on the *Green Man*, William Anderson waxes lyrical about the Green Man in a very positive fashion, which again contrasts with some of the demonic images which we have already surveyed: for him, the Green Man is a symbol of 'irrepressible life';[265] it represents 'the union of humanity and the vegetable world'.[266] There is a vision of the Green Man as one who is the custodian and discloser of mystery.[267] The Green Man is a symbol of God's eternal creative power which is disclosed in human time and space.[268]

Anderson himself sees the *origins* of the Green Man as being well before the first century AD, and he is thus at variance with Kathleen Basford. For him, the origins of this figure lie with the Neolithic matriarchal religion of the Europe of antiquity.[269] Down the ages, this has resulted in a being with a variable triple aspect: a head whose form derives from one or more leaves, *or* a human head spewing vegetation which may become types of facial hair, *or* a head which is actually 'the fruit or flower of vegetation'.[270]

In sum, when we survey the divergent views of various scholars, it is clearly impossible to say anything which is absolutely definite about the origins of the Green Man.[271] He may certainly be regarded, as Clive Hicks regards him, as an 'archetype'[272] and a generic term embracing a diversity of architectural images,[273] folk customs and world mythologies.[274] In the Islamic tradition, al-Khaḍir functions as a similar kind of archetype with the important difference, however, that there is no demonic aspect to this Islamic sage.

As we have seen, the Green Man is endowed with positive and negative aspects ranging from the purely evil to the virtually angelic. He has associations with harvests and fertility as well as the decaying of life. It is unlikely that we shall ever know for certain the real antique origins of the myth of the Green Man; these are probably lost in a prehistoric, pre-literate age. What we can do is make intertextual (inter-architectural?) connections and show how the myth was both adopted and adapted down the ages, retaining always its mysterious and mystic aspect of *green* but charging that colour, according to the prevailing context, myth or architecture – or lesson to be stressed – with a benign or sinister power and demeanour.[275]

Christianised, 'the Green Man was a symbol of Divine immanence';[276] demonised, he was a symbol of a pagan past, evil, decay and death itself.[277]

Shakespeare

It is well known[278] that, in Shakespeare's *The Merry Wives of Windsor*, reference is made to 'the ghostly hunter of Windsor Forest, Herne the Hunter'.[279] It has been suggested that the story of Herne and Windsor Forest originates with Shakespeare himself.[280] However, given the antiquity of the Green Man legends, the tale of Herne could also have an earlier provenance. For behind the story of Herne, and, indeed, the Green Men myths generally, lies the brooding figure of the nature god of the Celts whose name was Cernnunos. Dr Wendy Macphee comments:

> The legend of Herne the Hunter, a forester who, guilty of wrong-doing, was said to have hanged himself from an oak in Windsor Forest and subsequently haunted it, follows the universal myth of THE WILD HUNT wherein a devil-like creature followed by savage hounds mysteriously appears in a terrifying hunt. It is said that the fairies the Windsor citizens will dress up as represent the SOULS OF THE DEAD.[281]

Certainly, the whole play has Italian antecedents in the *commedia erudita genre*,[282] and, in the light of what we have observed about *Sir Gawain*, the possible connection – or, at the very least, intertext – between *The Merry Wives of Windsor* and some entertainment celebrating or remembering the Order of the Garter is intriguing.[283] It is true, as one scholar puts it, that 'this is Falstaff's play'.[284] But it could also be characterised as 'Herne's play', given the trick played on Sir John Falstaff in Act V.[285] The 'Merry Wives' of the title prepare as follows: Mistress Page relates the ancient tale of Herne, whom she identifies as a former keeper of Windsor Forest. She tells how, through the winter season, at midnight, Herne is to be seen walking 'round about an oak, with great ragg'd horns; and there he blasts the tree, and takes the cattle, and makes milch-kine yield blood and shakes a chain in a most hideous and dreadful manner'. The wives plot to bring Falstaff to the oak in Windsor Park 'disguis'd, like Herne, with huge horns on his head'. Their children, and others of the same size, will dress up 'like urchins, ouphes, and fairies, green and white, with rounds of waxen tapers on their heads and rattles in their hands … let them all encircle him about, and fairy-like, to prick the unclean knight; and ask him why, that hour of fairy revel, in their so sacred paths he dares to tread in shape profane'. Mistress Ford makes their purpose clear: 'And till he tell the truth, let the supposed fairies prick him sound, and burn him with their tapers'. Mistress Page relishes the forthcoming denouement: 'The truth being known, we'll all present ourselves; dis-horn the spirit and mock him home to Windsor'.[286]

Here, it is abundantly clear that this Herne, this Windsor Forest Green Man[287] whom Falstaff will impersonate, is considered fundamentally to be a figure of evil and fright who will blast trees, cause cattle to give blood rather than milk, and shake chains in the stereotypical fashion imputed to ghosts everywhere in every age. The urchins and ouphes (oafs) of whom Mistress Page speaks are goblins and the children of elves,[288] so the whole scene is to be clad in a ghostly, terrifying garb. Interestingly, in her speech, the fairies are characterised as *green* and white, and the ring they will sing in is *green* – but even more germane for our discussion is the emphasis on 'truth' in the quotations above from Shakespeare's play.

Mistress Page tells us that 'the superstitious idle-headed eld' (= 'ignorant people of earlier ages')[289] have handed down the story of Herne 'for a truth'. We may recall, earlier, in analysing the various dimensions of the Green Man, that, when not viewed in a malevolent aspect, he could be considered as an embodiment or incarnation of (an) eternal truth. Here, however, in Shakespeare's play, it is a false Herne who embodies a false truth. *Inter alia*, the green fairies, as Mistress Ford suggests, will try to force a disclosure of the truth, even though the 'fairies' are themselves but human children and no more real spirits than the false Herne/Falstaff himself.

Finally, it is the purity of the disguised 'fairies' which contrasts with the lasciviousness of 'the unclean knight', who, according to at least one reading of the code of chivalry, is about to betray that code for a night of lust and adultery with a married woman. The Falstaff whom Shakespeare presents to us for our inspection, and ultimate mockery, has none of the noble chivalric qualities even of that other famous knightly adulterer, Sir Lancelot, in the Arthurian epics.

The trick works, the charade is played out, and Falstaff enters in the guise of Herne the Hunter.[290] The intended seduction is then interrupted as planned by diverse 'fairies' (= the children), 'the Fairy Queen' (= Mistress Quickly), a 'satyr' (= Sir Hugh Evans) and a 'hobgoblin' (= Pistol). Falstaff is, at first, terrified and then, when the trick is disclosed, humiliated. Herne, supposedly in Windsor Forest a figure of fear, has become here a figure of fun.[291] The Green Man has been defused and deflated.

Falstaff observes: 'I do begin to perceive that I am made an ass' and listens, dejected, as his 'knightly' character is torn to pieces by the virtuous wives.[292] It becomes apparent that it is they, rather than the knight, who possess some of the real traditional virtues of chivalry like chastity, fidelity and prudence. Sir John's own personal preferred way of life, as Lord of Mis-rule rendered as a proverb,[293] is shown up for all its unchivalrous emptiness and folly: 'When night-dogs run, all sorts of deer [> dear!] are chased'.[294] Sir John Falstaff, a knight of the realm, 'becomes' for a brief period the Green Man in the guise of Herne the Hunter. Here, 'Herne' may be said to represent the less salubrious side of Sir John. He does not resist or fight his 'inner-Green Man': the result is possible chaos but actual humiliation. Sir Gawain, in stark contrast, fights the Green Knight, and his innate virtue wins through with only a minor penalty but with his knightly honour firmly intact.

Ainsworth

Shakespeare was by no means the only author to make much play with the figure of Herne the Hunter in Windsor Forest. The nearly forgotten but prolific Victorian novelist, William Harrison Ainsworth (1805–82),[295] did much the same, in fictional rather than dramatic form, in one of the better-known of his many novels, *Windsor Castle* (1843).[296] It is conventional these days to note the existence of Ainsworth but rarely to go so far as to engage in a 'sustained study'.[297] His work has been dismissed as 'Gothic' and 'formulaic', 'linked by a common thread of Gothic scenery and melodramatic characterisation'.[298] Be that as it may, Ainsworth's fiction, as Stephen Carver has shown, is worthy of a renewed critical debate.[299] However, it is not our purpose here to engage in that debate but rather to appreciate how this Victorian author himself engaged in his fiction with the perennial Green Man, whom he, like Shakespeare, knew as Herne the Hunter. The work may have been despised in its own day as 'a picture-book, and full of very pretty pictures',[300] but it was clearly appreciated by a welcoming public, who bought it in large quantities.[301] And, perhaps not astonishingly, *Windsor Castle* remained in print until the end of the 1960s.[302] This must all have been due in no small part to the fascination exerted by the figure of Herne the Hunter on a nineteenth-century Victorian public eager for such 'Gothic' supernatural fantasies.[303]

The first five books of *Windsor Castle* are set in AD 1529, while the last, Book Six, covers the year 1536. Book One is entitled 'Anne Boleyn', while Book Six is called 'Jane Seymour'. Such nomenclature clearly indicates the meat of the novel, which concerns Henry VIII's attempted divorce from Catherine of Aragon (spelled Arragon by Ainsworth) and his relationship with Anne Boleyn. In the background there hovers, however, as an almost constant presence, the figure of Herne the Hunter, the Green Man of both Shakespeare's drama and Ainsworth's novel. Carver stresses the 'supernatural dimension' with which Ainsworth endows his novel by the addition of this figure, whom Carver characterises as 'an elemental deity who haunts Windsor Forest with a motley band of followers, often helping mortal characters in wicked designs, in order to gain their souls'. He continues: 'Herne kidnaps Mabel [Mabel Lyndwood] and Wyat [Sir Thomas Wyat], and the mortals fall in love while imprisoned, but Mabel is drowned during an escape attempt'.[304]

Carver holds that Herne 'is the most interesting character in the narrative',[305] although he emphasises that Ainsworth's account of the origins of the legend of Herne the Hunter is a complete fabrication, as many Ainsworth scholars have recognised.[306] With Wendy Macphee, Stephen Carver finds the ultimate origins of Herne the Hunter in the Celtic god Cernunnous [Cernnunos or Carnan], who was associated with hunting and whose own antecedents may go back to the Hindu Animals God, Pashupati.[307] And, in the dark recesses of mythological origins, comparisons may be drawn, as Carver points out, with several of the other gods of antiquity, including Pan, Tammuz and Dionysus.[308]

Of such associations, perhaps that with Tammuz is one of the most relevant and interesting. For Tammuz was 'the name by which Dumuzi [a Sumerian god] is known in Babylonian mythology. The consort of Ishtar [a Babylonian goddess], Tammuz is the god of *grain and vegetation*, spending part of each year in the underworld.'[309] Carver holds that 'it is Herne that compels one to keep reading [*Windsor Castle*]'[310] and, from a structural point of view, the whole novel is framed by the legend of Herne, which stands to the story like a pair of bookends.

In the first few pages of chapter 1 of Book One ('Anne Boleyn'), the youthful Earl of Surrey encounters Herne during a solitary walk in Windsor Park, which Ainsworth calls 'the Herne Park'. He has previously been warned by Captain Bouchier: 'Only let me caution you against going near Herne's Oak.[311] It is said that the demon hunter walks at nightfall, and scares, if he does not injure, all those who cross his path.'[312] But the earl does not appear over-mindful of the warning: he plunges into a thorn-filled dell:

> Suddenly, however, he was startled by a blue phosphoric light streaming through the bushes on the left, and, looking up, he beheld at the foot of an enormous oak, whose giant roots protruded like twisted snakes from the bank, a wild spectral-looking object, possessing some slight resemblance to humanity, and habited, so far as it could be determined, in the skins of deer, strangely disposed about its gaunt and tawny-coloured limbs. On its head was seen a sort of helmet, formed of the skull of a stag, from which branched a large pair of antlers; from his left arm hung a heavy and rusty-looking chain, in the links of which burnt the phosphoric fire before mentioned; while on its right wrist was perched a large horned owl, with feathers erected, and red staring eyes.[313]

The earl crosses himself; the figure vanishes with a clanking of chains, 'laughter, then a fearful wail'.[314] The earl then leaves the dell and encounters a forest-keeper below 'a large, lightning-scathed, and solitary oak' – the actual one associated with the Herne legend, and apparently distinct from the huge oak in the dell below which Herne actually appears.[315] The Earl of Surrey tells the keeper: 'I have seen Herne the Hunter himself, or the fiend in his likeness', and he describes to the keeper what he has seen.[316] The keeper replies: 'Ay, ay, you have seen the demon hunter, no doubt'.[317]

Thus, right at the beginning of his tale, in chapter 1 of the first Book, Ainsworth introduces us to his primary anti-hero. And Herne's own words constitute the closing bookend in the last passage of the last Book of the novel. A gun booms to signal the execution moment of Anne Boleyn:

> 'There spoke the death-knell of Anne Boleyn!' cried Herne, pointing to the Round Tower. 'The bloody deed is done, and thou art free to wed once more. Away to Wolff Hall, and bring thy new consort to Windsor Castle!'[318]

Does Ainsworth intend by these words, put into the mouth of Herne, that, as Carver suggests, 'with the death of Anne Boleyn, Henry has surrendered his soul to marry Jane Seymour'?[319] Are we to view Herne the Hunter, the Green Man of Ainsworth's Windsor Forest, as the corrupted *alter ego* of Henry, a 'knight' who loved chivalry and jousts[320] but for whom the lure – political and physical – of an Anne Boleyn has proved as compelling and corrupting as the desire of Sir Lancelot for Guinevere?

However we choose to interpret Herne, and, indeed, Henry VIII, in Ainsworth's fiction, there is no concealing the fact that the demonic hunter is omnipresent throughout the novel, framing the whole fiction, as we have seen, between the Earl of Surrey's first terrifying encounter and the final comment by Herne at the death of Anne Boleyn.

Later, Herne is seen by an, at first, doubting Duke of Richmond[321] and followed by him in the company of Surrey.[322] Sir Thomas Wyat, in love with Anne Boleyn, makes a Faustian pact with Herne in order that he might win her from a besotted Henry VIII:

> 'I would give my soul to win her back from my kingly rival', cried Wyat.
> 'I accept your offer', rejoined the spirit. 'Anne Boleyn shall be yours. Your hand upon the compact.'[323]

Later still, Wyat goes hunting with Herne,[324] and the latter appears to the king himself on the terrace. There is a furious exchange of words, and Herne prophesies an awful death for Henry VIII:

> But now mark me, Henry of England, thou fierce and bloody king! – thou shalt be drunken with the blood of thy wives; and thy end shall be a fearful one. Thou shalt linger out a living death – a mass of breathing corruption shalt thou become – and when dead, the very hounds with which thou huntedst me shall lick thy blood.[325]

And Herne continues to involve himself in the affairs of the human protagonists in the story, going so far as to declare his love for Mabel Lyndwood, who is dragged into a great cave to meet Herne.[326] Here, then, we find the cave as a *locus* of fear, passion and the unknown. Wyat is ultimately abandoned by Herne;[327] Mabel is eventually dragged, dead, from the lake.[328] And Herne appears once more to the king:

> 'Thou here, demon!' cried the King. 'What wouldst thou?' 'You are on the eve of committing a crime' replied Herne; 'I told you that at such times I would always appear to you.' 'To administer justice is not to commit crime', rejoined the King. 'Anne Boleyn deserves her fate.'[329]

And here Herne becomes the discerner of souls and consciences. His final riposte follows:

> 'I know your motives better; I know you have no proof of her guilt, and that in your heart you believe her innocent. But you destroy her because you would wed Jane Seymour.'[330]

It is a strange, mournful insight which the demon hunter articulates in Ainsworth's fiction: here, Janus-like, Herne, the Green Man, reveals another aspect. He has already forecast the king's gruesome death, but now he is almost benign – or, at least, righteous – in the insight which he betrays into the king's very soul. Though Herne is the very incarnation of evil itself, perhaps even the *alter ego* of Ainsworth's conniving Henry, he here exhibits qualities perhaps more akin to those of an Old Testament prophet than the sinister Green Men of antique myth.

On the last page of the novel, disguised as a 'tall archer', Herne proposes a toast to 'the headsman of Calais' who will execute Anne Boleyn the next day, and then he evades Henry's clutches for a final time. The following day, at the moment when a gun signals the execution, 'a wild figure, mounted on a coal-black steed, dashed towards Henry', crying, as we have seen: 'There spoke the death-knell of Anne Boleyn!'[331]

Herne, and Henry, the corrupt 'King-Knight', are the anti-heroes of *Windsor Castle*, and readers will have no difficulty in perceiving the Green Man of Windsor Forest as an incarnation of Henry's evil dreams, ambitions and actions, Henry's *other self*. If, however, we are to look for a *hero* in this fiction, then it is perhaps not too much of an exaggeration to suggest that this is an order of chivalry, rather than an actual person, the very *Order of the Garter* itself. This is a theme to which we shall return after a few pages.

1.3.3 Elijah and al-Khaḍir

The prophets in the Old Testament are Yahweh's own heroic 'knights'; they have their own codes, not so much of medieval chivalry, but, rather, of prototypical 'warning' and struggle. And they fight, for example, distinctive enemies. Thus Elijah, as we shall see, 'does battle' with the priests of Baal.[332] This major Old Testament prophet is of particular interest for our text, since he has frequently been identified with, or, at the very least, associated with, the Qur'ānic al-Khaḍir/al-Khiḍr. So, who was Elijah?

Simply, he was a prophet, chosen and guided by Yahweh,[333] who fulfils his 'knightly'/prophetic role by obeying the Divine command[334] and, Gawain-like, entering upon a process of struggle and testing. In the course of this hectic life he becomes a 'prototype of the hero-archetype', as Aharon Wiener dramatically characterises him,[335] an *alter*-Moses,[336] a lasting symbol of righteousness,[337] and the channel through which 'Yahweh demonstrates his lordship, his boundary-bursting power'.[338]

The story of the prophet Elijah is recorded primarily in the Old Testament's two Books of Kings.[339] The name Elijah itself is interpreted from the Hebrew to mean 'My God is Yahweh'[340] or 'Yahweh is God'.[341] In some Old Testament translations, Elijah is also known in English as Elias,[342] a clear derivative from the Greek *Elias*, which also gives us the Qur'ānic Arabic Ilyās.[343] Aharon Wiener notes that Old Testament scholars accept Elijah as a real historical figure who flourished about 920–850 BC[344] and Philip Satterthwaite and Gordon McConville confirm that his prophetic activity took place during the reigns of the two kings of Israel, Ahab (*reg.* 874–853 BC) and Ahaziah (*reg.* 853–852 BC).[345] These two authors draw attention to the extraordinary wickedness of Ahab with his marriage to the Phoenician Princess Jezebel and his introduction of the worship of the Phoenician god Baal into the region.[346] Indeed, Wiener perceives the real enemy of Elijah to be this Jezebel rather than King Ahab.[347] With Bronner, we may note that the mission of Elijah is precipitated by the deeds of Jezebel.[348] And, if we may very loosely compare the exploits and stories of the later Sir Gawain with those of Elijah, then it is certainly true that the Jezebel of the Old Testament is a far worse character than the wife of the Green Knight. And, in another literary context, the adultery of Queen Guinevere with Sir Lancelot pales into insignificance by comparison.

In 1 Kings, Elijah bursts upon the scene, 'unintroduced',[349] proclaiming before King Ahab: 'By the life of Yahweh, God of Israel, whom I serve, there will be neither dew nor rain these coming years unless I give the word'.[350] From that moment on, Elijah's life assumes an aspect of chaotic struggle.[351] He withdraws to the 'torrent of Cherith',[352] and, *inter alia*, endures a drought,[353] restores to life the dead son of a widow who has been looking after him,[354] vanquishes, and has slaughtered, the 450 prophets of Baal on Mount Carmel[355] and, yet, is threatened by the inexorable Jezebel from whom he flees.[356]

Life has become a veritable rollercoaster; and Elijah is tempted to give up what must seem an insupportable struggle and series of testing battles. (One might compare here the varying trials of Sir Gawain, the triple testing of Moses by the Qur'ānic al-Khaḍir, and the tests set by the Green Man of Knowledge,[357] together with the responses of the protagonists.)

Elijah wishes he were dead, and tells Yahweh: 'I have had enough. Take my life; I am no better than my ancestors.'[358] But he is consoled and fed by an angel; thus fortified, he makes the long trek to Mount Horeb.[359] Here he has a mystical encounter with Yahweh,[360] followed later by a more human encounter with King Ahab, who now repents.[361] Elijah's earthly life concludes by his being caught up to Heaven in a fiery chariot in front of his disciple, Elisha, who picks up Elijah's cloak.[362] He has burst upon the scene in a fairly dramatic fashion with his unannounced proclamation to King Ahab in 1 Kings 17:1; he leaves this earth in an even more dramatic fashion.

Overall, the two Books of Kings present Elijah as a charismatic figure of huge importance for the Judaic history of the prophets of Yahweh, and this is certainly true regardless of whether or not the Elijah of tradition is an accurate mirror of the Elijah of history.[363]

This outline of the life, work and significance of Elijah is presented here because of the traditional identification of the Judaic Elijah with the Islamic Qur'ānic al-Khaḍir by some scholars, and the stress laid by others on, at least, a strong association between the two, while considering them as separate figures.[364] And if al-Khaḍir, the Green Man in Islam,[365] is to be identified or, at least, associated with Elijah, then that makes Elijah, ineluctably, a 'Green Man' too! Aharon Wiener's comment is significant here:

> [Elijah] wanders from place to place, appearing suddenly 'here and now' when a divine call commands him or when he believes of his own accord that he must represent God and act on his behalf. *He appears as 'a hairy man and girt with a girdle of leather' (2 Kings 1:8), resembling a nomadic shepherd or an archaic figure of the time when the Israelites were wandering in the wilderness.*[366]

Let us return now to the relationship between this Biblical prophet of prophets, Elijah, and the Qur'ānic al-Khaḍir (al-Khiḍr). Arabic sources identify the unnamed figure in the Qur'ān, characterised as 'one/Of Our servants/On whom We had bestowed/Mercy from Ourselves/And whom We had taught/Knowledge from Our own/Presence',[367] as al-Khaḍir.[368] And it is not just the case, as Titus Burckhardt observes, that 'for Islamic esotericism, this person plays the same role as Elijah in Judaic esotericism'.[369] That is, indeed, true, but many commentators, both Arab and non-Arab, have gone further than that and stated that Elijah and al-Khaḍir are one and the same person.

Thus the article on Elijah in *the Encyclopaedia of the Qur'ān* notes that 'other reports and traditions claimed that Elijah and al-Khiḍr [al-Khaḍir] were the same person'.[370] W. M. Watt, commenting on *Sūrat al-Kahf* (*The Sūra of the Cave*), has few doubts: '*One of Our servants*: usually identified with a legendary prophetic figure al-Khiḍr (also identified with Elias [= Elijah]'.[371] Another modern commentator, J. Spencer Trimingham, noted that al-Khaḍir was 'generally identified with Ilyās (Elias [= Elijah])',[372] while Aharon Wiener affirms that 'Sura 18 [*The Sura of the Cave*] includes a legend in which there appears a favoured wise servant of God who is not called Elijah in the text but is identified with him in the whole Islamic tradition'.[373] He goes on: 'Islamic literature unequivocally shows that the identification of al-Khadir with Elijah – they are at times called twin brothers – is derived in the first instance from the Koranic story of Moses' encounter with the pious servant of Allah'.[374]

The *Encyclopaedia of Islam* draws attention to three possible sources for the story of Mūsā (Moses) and al-Khaḍir in *Sūrat al-Kahf*: the Gilgamesh epic, the Alexander Romance[375] and, most interestingly for us here, the influential[376] Judaic story of the journey undertaken by Rabbi Joshua ben Levi with Elijah: Joshua 'goes on a journey with Elijah under conditions laid down by Elijah, like those ... of the servant of God in the Ḳur'ān. Like the latter, Elijah does a number of apparently outrageous things, which affects Joshua as it did Mūsā.'[377]

Aharon Wiener, in the same vein, notes the story in the Jewish Aggada according to which Elijah allows Rabbi Joshua to be his companion on a journey, on condition that he refrains from questioning Elijah.[378] The rabbi is then exposed to some examples of seemingly gratuitous and evil cruelty.[379] Rabbi Joshua is forced to speak and is deserted by Elijah, who, however, explains before he goes the meanings of what the rabbi has witnessed. It is made clear that God's ways are not man's ways.[380]

However, this very close identification of the story of Mūsā and al-Khaḍir in the Qur'ān with the Jewish story of Rabbi Joshua and Elijah has been disputed. Brannon M. Wheeler, for example, holds that, if we carefully examine the sources used by Wensinck and other scholars, we find no support for the idea that the story recounted in the Qur'ān (Q.18:60–82) is ultimately beholden to a Christian or Judaic source.[381] Furthermore, he does not believe that the way in which al-Khaḍir and Elijah are frequently merged is a consequence of mere confusion 'but rather that the character of al-Khiḍr was developed to appropriate the characteristics associated with Elijah in Biblical and rabbinic stories'.[382]

Such remarks, whether one agrees with them or not, remind us that there is a parallel tradition among commentators that al-Khaḍir and Elijah (Arabic Ilyās) are actually separate people but often very closely related. Wiener is clearly aware of this when he notes that al-Khaḍir and Elijah have sometimes been designated twins.[383] Schimmel, too, shared this view when she ranked – separately – four prophets who had been assumed into Heaven while still alive: Idrīs (sometimes himself, confusingly, identified with al-Khaḍir), al-Khaḍir, Ilyās (= Elijah) and Jesus.[384]

Eszter Spät reminds us that the Kurdistani Yezidis always refer to Xidir (= al-Khaḍir/al-Khiḍr) in the same breath but make a clear differentiation between the two as separate 'holy beings'.[385] And the medieval Arab historian 'Imād al-Dīn Ismā'īl Ibn Kathīr (c. AD 1300–73) and the story-teller Muḥammad ibn 'Abdallāh al-Kisā'ī (c. twelfth century AD) similarly inclined to the belief that these were two separate persons.[386]

Elijah has been identified with other figures as well, most notably Idrīs[387] and Dhū 'l-Kifl[388] while al-Khaḍir has also been identified with St George.[389] However, such further identifications will not concern us here. What is worth noting is the way in which the Moroccan traveller Ibn Baṭṭūṭa (AD 1304–68/9 or 1377), in his famous *Riḥla* (*Travelogue*) makes several interesting references to al-Khaḍir. For example, he cites a piece of poetry by the Hispano-Arab writer Nūr al-Dīn Abū 'l-Ḥasan 'Alī b. Mūsā b. Sa'īd al-'Ansī al-'Ammārī al-Gharnāṭī (c. AD 1214–86),[390] where the poet notes the presence of al-Khaḍir on the edge of every meadow.[391] Ibn Baṭṭūṭa's translator, H. A. R. Gibb, reminds us that 'the allusion here is to the tradition "Wheresoever al-Khaḍir stands or prays the earth becomes green"'.[392] Ibn Baṭṭūṭa would certainly have been familiar with such popular traditions. Elsewhere, our traveller notes that on 'the mountain of Sarandīb' (*Jabal Sarandīb*: Adam's Peak in Sri Lanka) there was a cave called 'the Cave of Khiḍr' (*Maghāra al-Khaḍir*), and Ibn Baṭṭūṭa follows the pilgrim custom of staying in the cave for three days.[393]

From an intertextual perspective, and from the frequent identification of al-Khaḍir and Elijah/Elias (= Ilyās), the motif of the cave is significant and powerful. However, it is noteworthy that Ibn Baṭṭūṭa himself does not make an identification of the two figures, preferring in various parts of his *Riḥla* to speak of al-Khaḍir and Ilyās (Elijah, Elias) as separate individuals.[394] His translator and commentator, H. A. R. Gibb, however, has no such hesitations and notes that the two (al-Khaḍir and Ilyās) are frequently regarded as the same person.[395] This is an identification shared by Tim Mackintosh-Smith, who conflates al-Khaḍir, Elijah *and* St George![396] And Harry Schnitker, on a more popular level, agrees: 'To Muslims, St George is El Khuddar [*sic*] or The Green One, and he has all the same syncretic elements found with the Christian St George'.[397]

Ultimately, whether or not Elijah and al-Khaḍir are to be identified as one and the same being, or just as two individuals with very close mystical links, is unimportant. What is significant is that they are linked by the triple attributes of *immortality*, *esoteric knowledge* and, perhaps most intriguingly for this section, *fertility production*.[398] The associations with rain, water and the Water of Life are particularly striking.[399] Both are clearly 'Green Men' and represent terrestrial new life as well as a new life which has an eschatological dimension by reason of their continued, indeed immortal, existence in Paradise, albeit with visits to, and circumambulations of, this mortal earth. Spät describes the 'holiday of Xidir Ilyas' as a 'feast, with ... strong undertones of a fertility cult' which is 'clearly of an agricultural character'.[400]

We referred earlier to the *Alexander Romance*; and it is worth noting in passing how the mythological Alexander has almost ineluctably infiltrated the other stories of Elijah and al-Khaḍir. For example, Elijah and al-Khaḍir act as guides for Alexander in his quest for the Water of Life;[401] Alexander sees al-Khaḍir bathing, and thereby becoming immortal, in the Water of Life;[402] he travels with al-Khaḍir in the Land of Darkness;[403] finally, in an episode which has a profound intertextual resonance with the legends of St George, he fights a dragon in a land identified as Ethiopia.[404]

In conclusion, our discussion and analysis of Elijah and al-Khaḍir, 'Green Men' of the Bible and Qur'ān respectively, yield the following intertextual sequence: Judaism and Christianity revere the sublime figure of the Old Testament prophet of prophets, Elijah. Elijah reappears in Islam either in the guise of, or beside, the mysterious Gnostic figure al-Khaḍir/al-Khiḍr. Both al-Khaḍir and Elijah are endowed with immortality and gnostic knowledge as well as a particular interest in fertility. They are associated with questing and, indeed, the testing of lesser beings, although the Biblical Elijah is more the victim of Yahweh's 'testing' than the perpetrator.

Both Elijah and al-Khaḍir are associated with caves, the first in 1 Kings 19:9–18 and the second by virtue of his story being framed in the Qur'ānic *Sūra of the Cave*. Elijah's name is eternally linked to a mountain of struggle and testing, Mount Carmel. And it is from that mountain that the Christian Order of friars to be known as Carmelites would later take its name,[405] in the Middle Ages, incorporating within its framework a profound reverence for Elijah[406] as well as another figure, equally revered in Islam and Christianity, Mary or Maryam.[407] In the words of John Welch O.Carm.:

> The Marian tradition is united with the Elijan tradition in Book Six of the *Institution*.[408] When Elijah sends his servant to look out to sea, the servant reports seeing a small cloud. To the prostrate Elijah, God revealed four mysteries in this vision of the little cloud: 1) the future birth of a girl born

without sin; 2) the time of her birth; 3) that she would be the first woman to take the vow of virginity (after Elijah, who was the first man to vow virginity); 4) that the Son of God would be born of this virgin. The Carmelites, now Christians, understood that these mysteries were fulfilled in Mary.[409]

1.4 *The Way of English Chivalry*

1.4.1 The Order of the Garter

King Edward III officially became king in AD 1327 on the deposition of his father, Edward II (*reg.* AD 1308–27), but he only assumed actual power in 1330, freeing himself finally from the guardianship of Queen Isabella, his mother, and that of her lover, Roger Mortimer, whom he had executed.[410] Edward's reign was to last until his death in 1377 – an incredibly lengthy period of rule, or so it would seem. Yet that reign, with the events which charged it, was so full that one commentator, Christopher Lee, was moved to observe that 'every so often there's a time in history when much happens in a relatively short space of time. The long and vigorous reign of Edward III, and several years after it, was one such time.'[411]

Lee goes on to enumerate, *inter alia*, the beginning of the Hundred Years War, the Battle of Crécy in AD 1346, the Black Death and the foundation of the Order of the Garter.[412] It is a dramatic, diverse and hectic list. The horrors of the Black Death, which arrived in England in 1348, and after which Simon Schama in volume 1 of his *History of Britain* names an entire chapter, entitling it 'King Death',[413] contrast vividly, for example, with the ceremonies and rituals with which England's premier order of knighthood, the Order of the Garter, was inaugurated.[414] Its founder was King Edward III, Britain's 'new Arthur'.[415]

Its historical backcloth, however, was the Black Death. And even St George, now England's patron rather than St Edward the Confessor, seemed powerless in the face of the catastrophe which overtook England in 1348.[416] Windsor might be 'a new Camelot',[417] but the Black Death was no respecter of chivalry. Yet, amid the horrors of the age, the ideals of glory and honour won in warfare and military feats continued to flourish. At the Battle of Crécy in Normandy, for example, in 1346, the English army spectacularly wiped out a larger French army supported by Flemish, German and Genoese soldiers, using their longbows to excellent and deadly effect.[418] The French suffered appalling casualties.[419]

Honour, chivalry and the rituals of chivalry mattered.[420] Thus Hugh E. L. Collins writes: 'Founded in 1348 in the aftermath of Edward III's remarkable victory at Crécy, the order of the Garter was conceived by its founder as a celebration of the deeds of arms of English knighthood'.[421] But, while it is true that twenty-two of the foundational knights of the Order were actually present at the Battle of Crécy,[422] it is no longer suggested that the foundation of the Order of the Garter was as a direct commemoration of this battle.[423] Begent and Chesshyre suggest that the Order's foundation stems from a merging of several factors which included the popularity of tournaments and the proliferation of European orders of chivalry and knighthood, together with the military Orders like the Knights Templar, the Knights Hospitallers and the Teutonic Knights, as well as the abiding impact of the Arthurian saga.[424]

All these very real factors are infused by what we might term the 'Foundation Myth' of the Order, which suggests a reason why King Edward chose to have a garter as the prime insignia of his new Order. According to this, the king attends a ball, which might have been in Calais, and sees that one of the ladies has dropped a garter. Ever the gallant knight, he springs to the rescue and, wishing to spare her any embarrassment, attaches the garter to his own leg with the famous words which afterwards became the motto of the Order: '*Honi soit qui mal y pense*'.[425] But the conclusion by Begent and Chesshyre is that 'the stories associating the foundation of the Order of the Garter with the female sex appear to be incapable of verification …'[426]

Keen stresses that Edward modelled his Order on the chivalric codes of the Arthurian legends,[427] but Begent and Chesshyre, while concurring, detect, by contrast, a religious overtone.[428] Be that as it may, it is clear that the Knights of the Round Table of the legendary King Arthur and the Knights of the Garter founded by Edward III shared many traditional chivalric qualities such as courage, honour, courtesy and loyalty.[429] One was required to be '*un gentil home de sang, et chevalier sans reprouche*'.[430] However, it is salutary to note, with Scott L. Waugh, that there were inherent contradictions in the system, with real warfare contrasting with chivalric ideal, courtesy with ubiquitous pillage. He reminds us of the sack of Limoges and consequent massacres after that city had betrayed him and sided with the French enemy.[431]

We note, finally, in passing, the adoption by King Edward of St George and the Virgin Mary as patrons of the Order.[432] The Chapel of St George in Windsor Castle was refurbished and became the focal point for Garter ceremonial, with a dedication to the Virgin Mary, St George and St Edward the Confessor,[433] thus giving the Order of the Garter a 'triple patronage'.[434] In Shakespeare's *Richard III*, King Richard swears 'by my George, my Garter and my crown';[435] and Shakespeare's editor, Anthony Hammond, notes that 'the Order of the Garter was augmented by the pendant image of St George in Tudor times'.[436] St George, as we have already seen, has also been identified with al-Khaḍir, while Mary (Arabic Maryam) is a significant figure in both Christianity and Islam, as both the Gospel of Luke and *Sūrat Maryam* attest.

Simon Schama clearly views Edward III as a heroic, Arthurian figure. Of his funeral in AD 1377, he writes: 'His body, carried on a bier by twenty-four knights dressed in black and walking to a slow march, was *the last great Arthurian show* of the Plantagenets'.[437]

1.4.2 *Sir Gawain*, *The Merry Wives of Windsor* and *Windsor Castle*

It is possible to view the poem *Sir Gawain*, the play *The Merry Wives of Windsor* and the novel *Windsor Castle* as a Garter poem, a Garter play and a Garter novel. Not all scholars will agree with the application of such an epithet for all three works, but this concluding section of *the Way of English Chivalry* will set out briefly the evidence which is adduced for such designations. Certainly, and intriguingly, however, each of the poem, the play and the novel may be characterised as 'green' by virtue of the presence of the Green Knight in the poem, and the Green Man of Windsor, Herne the Hunter, in the play and the novel. Is it, then, too great an intertextual link to suggest that behind both of these figures lurks the sublime figure of al-Khaḍir/Elijah, identified, as we have seen earlier, with the patron saint of England and the Garter Order itself, St George?

Clive Hicks notes: 'St George was a Christian figure from Palestine also known to Islam, where he is associated with Khidr, the Green One, the supposed identity of an unnamed character in the Koran. Khidr is the Moslem saint of fertility, whose green credentials associate him also with the Green Man.'[438] Begent and Chesshyre draw attention to the confused hagiography of St George, dissociate him from Cappodocia and identify him as one who might have suffered martyrdom in the region of Lydda sometime before the reign of the Christian Emperor Constantine (*reg.* AD 306–37).[439] They suggest that the stories of St George and the dragon are of late twelfth-century origin.[440]

Bowden and Attwater comment: 'St George was a martyr who suffered at Lydda in Palestine, perhaps during the persecution under Diocletian [*reg.* AD 284–305]. That is all that can be confidently affirmed about him; but in later ages it was said that he was a soldier, a favourite of Diocletian, who advanced him to the rank of tribune'.[441] However, George falls from grace and is beheaded after rebuking the Roman emperor for his persecution of the Christians.[442] Bowden and Attwater confess that they are unsure how St George came to be selected as England's patron, and surmise that returning crusaders may have had some responsibility.[443] If the latter were to prove correct, it would provide an interesting and neat physical and intertextual link between a Middle Eastern George and the English protector and patron.

We noted earlier Begent and Chesshyre's suggestion that 'the Garter, although clearly chivalric in concept, had strong, not Arthurian, but religious overtones'.[444] I suggest that the dichotomy is a false one: by virtue of its founder's reputation as the 'New Arthur',[445] the Garter had *both* Arthurian *and* religious overtones. Regardless of *how* St George came to be adopted as patron of the Order and, indeed, of England[446] itself and of other countries, that soldier, saint and martyr embodied all the chivalric and religious virtues, earlier incarnated in the legend-clad figures of al-Khaḍir and Elijah themselves as well as the virtuous Sir Gawain. All four figures of St George, Sir Gawain, al-Khaḍir and Elijah participate in a common intertextual pool of merit, virtue, questing and testing.

Sir Gawain and the Green Knight has, as its dramatic – and mysterious – colophon, the phrase which constitutes the motto of the Order of the Garter: *Hony Soyt qui Mal Pence* (= *Honi soit qui mal y pense*).[447] Was this a later scribal addition, as has been suggested?[448] Stone, in his Notes on the poem, agonises whether the poem was actually written 'for the institution of the Garter' and makes much play with both dates and colour: he notes that Edward III founded the Order around AD 1347 and that the distinctive symbolic garter of the Order was dark blue, rather than green, thus ruling out any affinity between the bright green baldric mentioned in the concluding lines of the poem[449] and the Garter robes.[450] The early statutes insisted that the mantles should be blue, although in later years it is clear that these garments were tinged with various shades of purple or were even purple rather than blue.[451] Begent and Chesshyre do stress that there is some doubt about the nature of the materials and colour of the Garter robes in the early days, but suggest that blue is still likely to have been the colour of choice. They cite as evidence that

> a number made of blue silk ... were provided as decorations and appear in the accounts of John Cook, Clerk of the wardrobe, dated between September 1347 and January 1349, '*ad faciendum xii garteria de blu de auro et serico qualibet habent dictamen "Hony soyt q'mal y pense"*.'[452]

Attempts, then, to associate the *Sir Gawain* poem with the motto of the Garter, *Honi soit qui mal y pense*, might be given some credence, *provided* that the same motto at the end of the poem is not a later addition. Attempts to associate the poem with the Order of the Garter on the basis of colour seem, *prima facie*, doomed to failure. For the dominant colour in the medieval poem, as we have seen, is green; the dominant colour in the Garter robes is blue.

Yet none of this appears to be a problem for Francis Ingledew, whose book *Sir Gawain and the Green Knight and the Order of the Garter*[453] has been described as both 'daring and provocative'.[454] Ingledew deliberately 'pursue[s] a reading of the poem as a reading of history whose point of departure is the founding of this order [of the Garter]'.[455] Central to this reading is a suspected rape by Edward III of the Countess of Salisbury.[456]

Ingledew concentrates more on the shared quality of garter and the poem's girdle (= baldric) 'as intimate and easily sexualised items of female apparel'[457] rather than their respective colours of blue and green. Both are worn to 'solidify ... fraternity'.[458] Ingledew suggests: 'Though Gawain himself is proved chaste, *SGGK's* [*Sir Gawain and the Green Knight's*] green girdle may trade in the blue garter's claim of fidelity for an imputation to Edward of infidelity'.[459] Is the *Sir Gawain* poem, in which a chaste knight resists an attempted seduction by a noble lady, meant to mirror in an opposite fashion, and indeed castigate, the attempted rape of a countess by a king of England?[460]

Ingledew points out[461] that, at one point in the poem, Sir Gawain wears 'a turquoise tunic extending to the ground';[462] and Brian Stone succinctly comments: 'Gawain wears the colour of faithfulness, blue, to perpetrate his one deception!'[463] Here, then, we can detect some kind of affinity between the two colours, perhaps with green representing temptation (albeit withstood by Sir Gawain) and blue representing fidelity both to one's marriage vows and to one's fellow knights. Ingledew's conclusion is that 'Gawain appears to become a Garter knight on the day he receives the girdle as at once a putative love token ... and the sign of Gawain's definitive victory over this lady's attempts to seduce him'.[464]

In a sympathetic review of Francis Ingledew's book, Carolyne Larrington in *The Times Literary Supplement* sees considerable significance in the fact 'that Gawain wears a blue furred robe like those of the Garter knights on the evening he resolves to withhold the girdle'. For her, this detail means that the present reader and, indeed, future scholars will not be able to ignore Ingledew's reading of the poem 'as a critique of the Order and all it stands for',[465] regardless of whether they find his arguments convincing.[466]

The debate about content and the relationship of *Sir Gawain* to the foundation of the Order of the Garter also reflects a scholarly debate about the actual dating of the poem.[467] We find a similar debate imbuing the discussions of Shakespeare's *Merry Wives of Windsor*.

Giorgio Melchiori has identified multiple Falstaffs.[468] We will concentrate here on the figure we find in *The Merry Wives of Windsor*. Melchiori holds that this is a 'small-town' comedy but one with a very special claim to historical fame: for Windsor is the historic seat of the Order of the Garter. It is for this reason that *Merry Wives* deserves to be called a 'Garter play' rather than for its being an epitome of chivalric Garter values, which it is not.[469] Melchiori notes that there has been a general – though by no means universal – consensus that the play was first performed on St George's Day, 23 April 1597, during a Garter celebration at Windsor when George Carey (Baron Hunsdon), one of Shakespeare's patrons, was invested as a Knight of the Garter by Queen Elizabeth I.[470] Certainly, by virtue of Mistress Quickly's speech in Act V, Scene V, *The Merry Wives of Windsor* may be considered a 'Garter' play.[471] But Melchiori, after examining the internal evidence, suggests that it was a new version of an older play from 1597, cobbled together in about 1600.[472] If, however, the former ever existed – actual written evidence is lacking – then it would have been rather shorter than the *Merry Wives* and much more akin to a masque.[473]

Nonetheless, in at least one sense, the actual dating of *The Merry Wives of Windsor* is unimportant. It is a 'Garter play' for the reason adumbrated above, namely that one of its heroes is Windsor itself; it has an anti-hero whose values are at odds with those espoused by the Order of the Garter; embedded within it is the very significant 'Garter speech' of Mistress Quickly;[474] and Falstaff, an unworthy knight, provides a dark contrast to the faithful women of Windsor, 'knights' or 'dames' in their own right as champions of fidelity and chastity.

Finally, by virtue of the references to the legendary Herne the Hunter, the play may also be characterised by the epithet 'green', with green here a potent symbol of lust and desired infidelity. Contrasting with this is 'green' as a symbol of both purity and fertility in Mistress Quickly's famous 'Garter speech', which also embraces a reference to Herne the Hunter:

> And nightly, meadow fairies, look you sing,
> Like to the Garter compass, in a ring.
> Th'expressure that it bears, green let it be,
> More fertile-fresh than all the field to see;
> And *Honi soit qui mal y pense* write
> In em'rald tufts, flowers purple, blue and white,
> Like sapphire, pearl and rich embroidery,
> Buckled below fair knighthood's bending knee:
> Fairies use flowers for their charactery.
> Away, disperse. But till 'tis one o'clock,
> Our dance of custom round about the oak
> Of Herne the hunter let us not forget.[475]

William Harrison Ainsworth's *Windsor Castle* is truly a 'Garter novel' and a 'green novel' in the senses whereby we have considered the poem *Sir Gawain* and the play *The Merry Wives of Windsor*. As with the latter play, Windsor itself (or, rather, the Castle) is the hero; as with the latter play, and even more so, Herne the Hunter is an important figure. Just a cursory reading reveals that the whole novel is replete with references to the Order of the Garter and Garter ceremonial.

In Book One, chapter 1, we encounter the Chapel of the Order, St George's Chapel, in the speech of Captain Bouchier:

> the king's highness, being at Hampton Court with the two cardinals ... proposes to hold the grand feast of the most noble order of the Garter, at this his castle of Windsor, on St George's Day – that is to say, the day after tomorrow – and that it is therefore his majesty's sovereign pleasure that the Chapel of St George, in the said castle, be set forth and adorned with its richest furniture; that the high altar be hung with arras representing the patron saint of the order on horse-back ...[476]

Later, we hear mention of the Garter Tower in the castle[477] – and, in the following chapter, as if by secular contrast, there is a reference to 'a snug little hostel, situated immediately beneath the Curfew Tower', which also rejoices in the name of the Garter.[478] Chapter 3 of Book One then describes in detail the Garter procession to Windsor Castle: we encounter, *inter alia*, the officers and knights of the Order, the Mayor of Windsor, the Black Rod, the Chancellor of the Order, and the Bishop of Winchester, who has the honour to be 'the prelate of the Order',

> wearing his mitre, and habited in a robe of crimson velvet lined with white taffeta, faced with blue, and embroidered on the right shoulder with a scutcheon of Saint George, encompassed with the Garter, and adorned with cordons of blue silk mingled with gold.[479]

King Henry VIII, too, is similarly attired with the Garter: 'About his neck was a baldric of balas rubies, and over his robe he wore the collar of the Order of the Garter'.[480] It is purple passages such as these which led some critics to a particularly severe view of the novel *Windsor Castle*:

> The present popularity of Mr Ainsworth could not have risen out of its own materials. His so-called historical romance of 'Windsor Castle' is not to be regarded as a work of literature open to serious criticism. It is a picture book, and full of very pretty pictures. Also full of catalogues of numberless suits of clothes. Such a passion, indeed, has he for describing clothes, that he frequently gives us two suits with a single body, one being concealed under the other ... As to plot or story it does not pretend to any.[481]

It is clear that we should not pretend that *Windsor Castle* is great literature, even though we may regard the criticism which we have just cited as somewhat harsh and unsympathetic to the 'Gothic' genre in which *Windsor Castle* is undoubtedly written. We should not rank it with the *Sir Gawain* poem, nor with Shakespeare's *Merry Wives*. Yet, for all that, it is still worthy of being remembered as a 'Garter' work which follows in the same 'Garter tradition' as both poem and play.

Chapter 4 of Book One of the novel portrays Henry holding a chapter of the Garter Order, mixing ceremonial with politics by announcing beforehand, in the presence of Cardinal Wolsey and the papal legate, Cardinal Campeggio, his intention to divorce his queen, Catherine of Aragon, and electing Anne Boleyn's father, Sir Thomas Boleyn, as a Knight of the Garter.[482]

Then the king, magnificently arrayed in crimson, garters bearing the Order's motto *Honi soit qui mal y pense*, and 'a mantle of blue velvet with a magnificent train, lined with white damask, and having on the left shoulder a large garter',[483] proceeds to St George's Chapel, where the newly elected knight, Sir Thomas Boleyn, now Viscount Rochford, is invested with the Order of the Garter.[484]

As we have seen, this most ancient of Orders represents the highest peak of chivalry in England. Yet here we are shown by Ainsworth a corrupt king using the Order as a kind of bribe with which to ingratiate himself with the father of his chosen mistress and second wife. There is a kind of 'Lancelot' syndrome abroad here, where the true ideals of chivalry, adumbrated already in several places in this book, are not espoused: the king's passion for a male heir, his fear of a repetition of the Civil Wars of the previous century, and his pure lust for Anne all take precedence over any nobler chivalric considerations.

Ainsworth, attentive and sensitive to the religious scruples articulated by Henry,[485] genuinely or falsely, in the matter of his marriage to Catherine, portrays the king at mass[486] and, the following day, celebrating the feast of St George, the patron of the Garter, at matins in St George's Chapel.[487] Ainsworth might enjoy, more than most Victorian novelists, a grandiloquent turn of phrase, but he does skilfully interweave the religious and the political with the chivalric in his 'Garter' narrative. And this designation of ours of *Windsor Castle* as a 'Garter novel' is reinforced by the author in Book Three, chapter 2, in which the institution of the Order by Edward III is described.[488]

Interestingly, Ainsworth is sufficiently aware of the controversies surrounding the foundation of the Order to write: 'The origin of this illustrious Order has been much disputed'.[489] He *is* prepared, despite this statement, to attach some credence to 'the popular legend', which he articulates as follows:

> Joan, Countess of Salisbury, a beautiful dame, of whom Edward was enamoured, while dancing at a high festival, accidentally slipped her garter, of blue embroidered velvet. It was picked up by her royal partner, who, noticing the significant looks of his courtiers on the occasion, used the words to them, which afterwards became the motto of the Order – '*Honi soit qui mal y pense*'.[490]

And Ainsworth stresses that, regardless of other additional decorations, the *essential* colour of the robes of the Garter was – and is – *blue*.[491]

We have seen earlier how the king's growing attachment to Anne Boleyn takes place in Ainsworth's fiction against the backdrop of Garter ceremonial. The same is the case with Jane Seymour: chapter 1 of Book Six, entitled 'Of Henry's Attachment to Jane Seymour', begins:

> On the anniversary of Saint George, 1536, and exactly seven years from the opening of this chronicle, Henry assembled the knights-companions within Windsor Castle to hold the grand feast of the most noble Order of the Garter.[492]

And it is 'on the day after the solemnization of the Grand Feast of the Order of the Garter' that Anne Boleyn receives 'proof of Henry's passion for Jane Seymour'.[493]

The two wives, Anne Boleyn and Jane Seymour, are thus framed in Ainsworth's fiction by two celebrations of Garter ceremonial. The Garter represents nobility and chivalry; it is, however, the backdrop to devious politics and adultery. Behind all – perhaps incarnating the worst aspects of Henry's character – lurks the fearsome figure of Ainsworth's Green Man, Herne the Hunter. Here we have a Green Man with no benevolent side, nor with the wisdom of an Islamic al-Khaḍir. This Green Man is pure evil, one who exults as, on the last page of the novel, Anne Boleyn is executed.[494] If the rather slighter identification were to be pressed, then the 'good' Green Man of the novel is St George himself, in whose chapel, at various times in the novel, King Henry VIII and his Knights of the Garter gather, resplendent, as Ainsworth insists on showing us, in their splendid robes.

But should we go so far as to regard at least one of their number, the king himself, as a 'whitened sepulchre'?[495] And, for Ainsworth, does England's finest Order of chivalry frame not chastity and fidelity but lust and adultery? The wild, deerskin-clad figure of the Green Man of Windsor Forest, the demon Herne the Hunter, is a clear semiotic indicator of evil in the novel *Windsor Castle*. Does the wearer of the blue of the Garter, for Ainsworth, in at least one royal case, also come to represent the same? The Garter in its essence and chivalric ideals signals a *Way of Perfection*; but in Ainsworth's *Windsor Castle* it frames a *Way to Perdition.*

1.5 *The Way of Sufi Chivalry*

In Hans Wehr's *Dictionary*, a variety of definitions are given for the Arabic word *futuwwa*. *Inter alia*, these include 'adolescence', 'youth', 'bully' and 'racketeer'.[496] Of most relevance to us, however, are the following definitions:

- 'the totality of the noble, chivalrous qualities of a man'
- 'noble manliness'
- 'magnanimity'
- 'generosity'
- 'nobleheartedness'
- 'chivalry'
- 'designation of Islamic brotherhoods of the Middle Ages, governed by chivalrous precepts'.[497]

Very loosely, then, this word, which encapsulates and repeats so much of the Western paradigm, may be translated as 'chivalry' for our purposes in this section.

The *Encyclopaedia of Islam*, in a lengthy article, stresses the original etymology of the word: it signified 'that which is regarded as characteristic of the *fatā*, pl. *fityān*, literally "young man"',[498] and was a term which came into being in about the eighth century AD.[499] Much later, the scholar J. V. Hammer-Purgstall held that the *futuwwa* was 'a form of chivalry', while others stressed the links with Sufism.[500] For his part, the author of the first section of the seminal article in the *Encyclopaedia*, Claude Cahen, draws attention to the fact that, while Arabic in the *Jāhilī* and early historical period of Islam eschewed the actual term *futuwwa*, it did use the singular noun *fatā* to denote 'a man still young and vigorous, valiant in warfare, *noble and chivalrous*'.[501]

Soon afterwards, however, he shows that the plural *fityān* appears, denoting either sufi-style but non-ascetical fraternities or communards on the one hand, or vagrants (*ʿayyārūn*) on the other, as well as '*mafiosi*' in positions of power.[502] Cahen stresses: 'The texts, however, make it clear beyond question that many of the *fityān* ... called themselves or were called *ʿayyārūn* or some equivalent name, while many of the *ʿayyārūn* on the other hand called themselves *fityān* or followers of the *futuwwa*'.[503] It is abundantly clear from all this, then, insofar as any real clarity may be gleaned about the obscure origins of *futuwwa*, that there is at least one sense in which *futuwwa* denoted the very opposite of chivalric ideals and the whole concept of chivalry!

Regardless, however, of the diverse alleged origins and senses of this term, and regardless, too, of the links which Cahen perceives with aspects of *ʿaṣabiyya* or group solidarity,[504] it is clear that the term *futuwwa* did become linked with both the establishment of various guilds *and* Sufism with its heterodox movements and Orders.[505]

The connection with Sufism is powerfully confirmed by Annemarie Schimmel:

> Essentially, the idea of *futuwwa* goes back to early Sufism. The *fatā* is 'the young man', 'the brave youth', generous and faithful. The Koran had called the Seven Sleepers *fityān* (plural of *fatā*; Sūra 18:10). Ḥallāj used the term for those who excel by their absolute faithfulness and loyalty to treaties, including, particularly, Iblis and Pharaoh, who remained faithful to their claims ... The term *jawānmard*, the Persian translation of *fatā*, is used in the hagiographies of many Sufis ...[506]

Other scholars have other emphases. While noting that *futuwwa* (which he translates as 'youngmanliness' rather than 'chivalry') was 'often compared to European chivalry, and was combined with Sufism', Julian Baldick stresses the Iranian origins of the institution[507] and sees the whole concept prefigured in pre-Islamic Zoroastrian literature.[508]

Alexander Knysh is closer to Schimmel in stressing the links with Sufism. 'The doctrine of chivalry (*futuwwa*)', he says, became 'a hallmark of many Sufi associations in the subsequent epochs';[509] elsewhere, he 'loosely' defines 'the ideals of *futuwwa* ... as spiritual chivalry and altruism'.[510] He emphasises that the great sufi Shihāb al-Dīn Abū Ḥafs ʿUmar al-Suhrawardī (AD 1145–1234) was at pains in his writings to show that there was a very real relationship between *futuwwa* morality and sufi ascetical and spiritual practice.[511]

1.5.1 Al-Sulamī and his *Kitāb al-Futuwwa*

It is proposed to examine here not the work of al-Suhrawardī but that of an earlier sufi scholar. Abū ʿAbd al-Raḥmān al-Sulamī (AD 936–1021) is credited with having written one of the earliest – if not *the* earliest[512] – works on *futuwwa* in Islamic literature. *Kitāb al-Futuwwa* has been translated into English under the title *The Book of Sufi Chivalry: Lessons to a Son of the Moment.*[513]

Al-Sulamī, born in Nīshāpūr, is an important figure in medieval Sufism, and his prolific works were much mined by sufi writers who came after him.[514] His education connected him with the Baghdad sufi school.[515] Knysh notes his fondness for ḥadīth and the way in which he travelled through Iraq and Khurāsān, in a classic *riḥla fī ṭalab al-ʿilm* (travel in search of knowledge), in order to study under famous scholars of ḥadīth.[516] He inherited wealth from his teacher, and a house and library in Nīshāpūr which were transformed into a sufi dwelling.[517] Here he spent the last forty years of his life, with, Knysh tells us, the occasional visit to Baghdad.[518]

Al-Sulamī's *Kitāb al-Futuwwa* is clearly not one of his major works. Indeed, Baldick characterises the author himself as 'unoriginal and uninspiring',[519] as well as 'tedious'.[520] He was unimpressed by al-Sulamī's *Kitāb al-Futuwwa*, which, he says, 'contains nothing but a succession of banalities about the ethical implications of sacrificing oneself for others'.[521]

Others have been less harsh in their evaluation: referring to one of the central foci of the book, 'heroic generosity', al-Halveti, the translator of this volume into English, lauds the way in which al-Sulamī gives us some 'extraordinary examples' of what is clearly considered to be a wonderful trait.[522] In effect, it is a book of *adab* (*belles-lettres*, ideal sufi manners).[523]

Whatever the literary qualities of the work – and even if it is platitudinous – the *Kitāb al-Futuwwa* is worthy of brief investigation as a focus for comparison with codes and works of medieval European chivalry and the medieval Western mystical tradition, as well as being a useful exemplar of a medieval sufi code. For in it merge the chivalrous, the mystical, the ethical, the religious and the ritual.

After the usual *basmala*, which sounds a note of man's dependence on Allah, we are introduced to many of the prophets of Islam who have preceded the last of the prophets, Muḥammad; these are said to have embraced *futuwwa*, in a line beginning with Adam and including Ibrāhīm (Abraham), Mūsā (Moses) and the *Aṣḥab al-Kahf* (Companions of the Cave),[524] to whom our text will later have occasion to refer in some detail. All these are exemplars *par excellence* for the would-be *fatā* who wishes to embrace the codes and paths of *futuwwa*. This early history culminates, logically enough, in a brief panegyric to Muḥammad, and we are informed that the early Rightly-Guided Caliphs (*al-Rāshidūn*), Abū Bakr, ʿUmar and ʿAlī b. Abī Ṭālib, became 'guardians' of *futuwwa*.[525]

There are several significant definitions of *futuwwa* in al-Sulamī's *Kitāb*: its true meaning, for example, is the abandonment of evil and the striving after perfect devotion and action.[526] Here we have no proto-Protestant justification by faith alone but a code which stresses both faith and works. This is very much within the ethical framework and general ethos of mainstream Islam. As al-Nawawī quotes:

'Let him who believes in Allah and the Last Day either speak good or keep silent, and let him who believes in Allah and the Last Day be generous to his neighbour, and let him who believes in Allah and the Last Day be generous to his guest'.[527]

We shall have occasion, in a short while, to show how hospitality to guests is considered to be an important element of *futuwwa*. Other elements include the need for loyalty towards other people and being considerate of their needs.[528] It is of the essence of *futuwwa* that one spends little time in argument.[529] Al-Sulamī sums up the many definitions of *futuwwa* by stating that its highest type is when one occupies one's mind with Allah and nothing else.[530] Such an aspiration, of course, is hardly unique to *futuwwa* but is characteristic of the sufi quest in all its many forms. Reynold A. Nicholson, for example, relates a sufi story which coheres powerfully with the above definitions by al-Sulamī.

He tells us that one day the sufi

> Sahl ibn ʿAbdallah bade one of his disciples endeavour to say 'Allah! Allah!' the whole day without intermission. When he had acquired the habit of doing so, Sahl instructed him to repeat the same words during the night, until they came forth from his lips even while he was asleep. 'Now,' said he, 'be silent and occupy yourself with recollecting them.' At last the disciple's whole being was absorbed by thought of Allah. One day a log fell on his head, and the words 'Allah, Allah' were seen written in the blood that trickled from the wound.[531]

Annemarie Schimmel tells us that the author of this story, Sahl al-Tustarī (died AD 896), was again one who stressed faith and works and who, in trying to live the ascetical life, 'tried to combine *tawakkul* [trust in God] and work; for, as he thought, it would be an offense to the Prophetic tradition to avoid or condemn work as a means of gaining one's livelihood, but an offense against the faith to neglect "trust in God"'.[532] In al-Sulamī's *Kitāb al-Futuwwa*, we also find an emphasis on *dhikr* (remembrance of God), and our author proclaims that its effects are *riḍā* (contentment, acceptance, satisfaction) and *khushūʿ* (submissiveness, humility).[533] Here, too, we find devotional and intertextual links with Western spiritual traditions such as the Christian usage of the litany and mantra, the latter espoused and taught in the twentieth century by the Benedictine monk John Main (died 1982).[534]

Al-Sulamī's text identifies different types of *futuwwa*; for example, there is that which regulates one's conduct with regard to God Himself, another suitable for the Prophet, and others with regard to one's companions, brotherhood, shaykh and even the recording angels whose task it is to sit on one's shoulders and record each person's good and bad deeds during this earthly life.[535] Fundamentally, however, the text shows us that the good *fatā*, the good practitioner of *futuwwa*, should mould his character and attributes according to three different foci, concentrating on himself, his dealings with others and his attitude to Allah. The ideal *futuwwa* comprises a striving to achieve *perfection* in three main areas:

- *The self*: The good *fatā* is noble in character,[536] ascetical in lifestyle[537] yet joyful of heart.[538] He will keep his word[539] and love truth.[540] Humility[541] will be his watchword, together with a desire for solitude.[542] The ego is to be renounced: following it will only lead one into darkness, whereas following one's intelligence will lead the true *fatā* to the light of Allah and His realms.[543]
- *Relationships with others*: It is in this area, perhaps, that we find the greatest congruence with some of the essential factors in Western medieval concepts of chivalry as well as in the Western mystical tradition. Cruelty should be responded to with kindness;[544] and love, kindness and gentleness[545] should permeate all the *fatā*'s dealings with others. There must be no discrimination in the way that help i.[546] The would-be *fatā* has a duty of hospitality, and the Prophet is quoted ass offered deploring that society which does not receive guests and the person who does not make guests welcome.[547] In addition, good manners are of the essence of *futuwwa*.[548] At the heart of real *futuwwa* are love and compassion.[549] The modality of this is illustrated by a charming tale recounted by al-Sulamī which, interestingly in view of our previous references, invokes the name of al-Khaḍir, defined in a footnote by the translator of *Kitāb al-Futuwwa*, Shaykh Tosun Bayrak al-Jerrahi al-Halveti, as 'a guiding spirit existing at all times who appears in human form to help those worthy to be guided'.[550] Al-Sulamī tells the reader about a query that is put to a sufi on the subject of love and compassion for one's brothers. He replies that he was once visited in his house by al-Khaḍir, who sang to him, and, in consequence, he found himself wishing that he could listen to him with his whole being (rather than just a pair of human ears). This is the model one should follow, being so taken up with one's brethren's concerns that one identifies totally with them, body and soul.[551]
- *Relationship with Allah*: The true *fatā* must clearly avoid that which Allah has prohibited in the way of sin,[552] and pray without hoping for cosy mystical feelings.[553] Only Allah is worthy of trust,[554] but the sufi master must be obeyed, and preferred by the disciple or novice, since the master will *facilitate the journey*![555] And the journey on the sufi path can be a hard one. Al-Sulamī tells us that one of the most important objects of *futuwwa* is to come to learn about Allah and suffer travail and hardship out of love for him.[556]

In sum, then, the *Kitāb al-Futuwwa*, despite its often seemingly platitudinous nature, constitutes a guidebook for the sufi seeker, formulated in lucid albeit repetitious terms. It portrays what the *fatā* must do to win eternal life and, in so doing, provides a stimulating counterpoint and parallel to the delineation of those virtues which are present both in Western secular medieval chivalry and the Western medieval mystical tradition. In the West, our evidence thus far suggests that the knight was usually apart from the mystic and orientated himself towards secular pursuits, though the two might participate in a common pool of qualities and virtues. In the East, on the evidence of al-Sulamī and using the term *futuwwa* generally and loosely, God's 'knights', the *fityān*, who battled both the *nafs* (ego) and the lures of the terrestrial world, combined a 'military' or militant opposition to the latter with a yearning for the sacred.

Western or Eastern, however, secular or sacred, a common motif which linked all was frequently that of love, either of an unattainable courtly lady or of God Himself.

1.5.2 Ibn Baṭṭūṭa's Encounter with the *Fityān*

In his seminal article on the *futuwwa* in the *Encyclopaedia of Islam*, Claude Cahen draws attention to the encounter between the great Maghribī traveller Ibn Baṭṭūṭa (AD 1304–68/9 or 1377)[557] and the Anatolian *fityān*. Cahen characterises the *fityān* as being

> young adults living in small communities, coming from varied social, ethnic (and, to start with, religious?) circles ... associating together to lead in common the most comfortable possible life in an atmosphere of solidarity, mutual devotion and comradeship (with joint ownership of goods) ... The setting was more extensive than that of a single town, in the sense that a fraternity existed between the *fityān* of each town and others elsewhere by whom they were received when travelling, like the old 'companions' in Europe.[558]

Cahen suggests that they may have worn a special garb, and it was thus that Ibn Baṭṭūṭa found them when he travelled into Anatolia.[559]

Cahen does not elaborate on Ibn Baṭṭūṭa's encounter, so it is worth going to the traveller's own text, his famous *Riḥla* (Travelogue), to see exactly what he has to say. For it is clear that the *fityān* in his account share many of the virtues lauded in al-Sulamī's *Kitāb al-Futuwwa*, especially with regard to hospitality and solicitude for guests.

It is in the city of Anṭaliya[560] that Ibn Baṭṭūṭa encounters 'the Young Akhīs', as H. A. R. Gibb translates the Arabic *al-Akhiyya al-Fityān*.[561] Gibb identifies this city 'at the head of the Gulf of Adalya [as] the ancient Attaleia'[562] and observes that the city walls had been built by the Romans.[563] He notes Ibn Baṭṭūṭa's occasional usage of the words *fatā* and *akhī* as virtually synonymous despite the fact that, semantically, *akhī* was actually a higher grade in the *futuwwa* hierarchy.[564]

Ibn Baṭṭūṭa is generous in his praise of the *akhiyya al-fityān*: for him, they are without parallel in their care of strangers, whose every need they satisfy.[565] He is obviously aware of the differences between the two terms *fatā* and *akhī*, for he gives a formal definition of what he means by the latter word: 'An *Akhī*, in their idiom, is a man whom the assembled members of his trade, together with others of the young unmarried men and those who have adopted the celibate life, choose to be their leader. That is [what is called] *al-futuwwa* also (*wa tilka hiya al-futuwwa ayḍan*).'[566]

The *Akhī*, then, is clearly a designation for one of the *fityān* in a position of leadership and authority, as Ibn Baṭṭūṭa himself stresses in another place: 'The members are called *fityān*, and their leader, as we have said, is the *Akhī*'.[567] The latter is characterised as a kind of head of a commune: he is responsible for building a *zāwiya* (a sufi house, but translated by Gibb as 'hospice'),[568] which he furnishes. It is then the task of the *fityān* to fund and provision this *zāwiya* with what they have earned at work. Thus all is ready to give the highest levels of hospitality, board and lodging to the itinerant traveller (*musāfir*);[569] as we have seen, their treatment of such travellers evokes the highest praise from Ibn Baṭṭūṭa.[570] The latter has a direct experience of the hospitality of the *zāwiya* in Anṭaliya, for he is invited to dine with the *fityān* in a splendidly appointed building by a shabbily dressed man who proves to be one of the shaykhs of the *Akhīs*: Ibn Baṭṭūṭa is treated to a magnificent feast which is followed by dancing and singing. His admiration, he tells us, knows no bounds as he basks in the generosity of his hosts and their chivalric demeanour.[571]

Insofar as they may be separated, Ibn Baṭṭūṭa encounters the secular rather than the 'sacred' side of *futuwwa* in a 'secular' banquet. But the element common to both the secular and the sacred in *futuwwa* – generosity, self-abnegation, sublime hospitality, carelessness of outward appearance – shine through in Ibn Baṭṭūṭa's account. And this emphasis on hospitality and courtesy towards strangers has a profound resonance with many of the classical elements which we have surveyed in European chivalry.

It is interesting to note here that one of the tasks of the *Akhīs* listed by Ibn Baṭṭūṭa is the killing of evildoers and their associates deployed by those in authority to maintain control.[572] We may compare this with the medieval European knight and his courtly code of rectitude and pristine morals.

Futuwwa, or 'spiritual chivalry' as it has been translated,[573] was, indeed, an interesting mix of the secular and the sacred. We have demonstrated earlier its association with the higher aspects of Sufism. And there were other, more secular aspects which will not be covered in detail here. It is clear, for example, that *futuwwa* was associated with the post-medieval Turkish guilds, producing guild documents known as *Fütüwwet-nāmes*.[574] And there is an interesting emphasis, here, on hierarchy, apprenticeship and initiation, which again may be said to resonate intertextually and physically with European rituals of knighthood.[575]

All this is underpinned by Ines Aščerić-Todd, who, while acknowledging the military nature of the *futuwwa* groups organised by the 'Abbasid Caliph al-Nāṣir li-Dīn Allāh,[576] notes the later metamorphosis of the term to designate craftsmen whose honour codes had elements in common with those of the earlier *futuwwa* 'knights'.[577] It is clear from all this that, when we speak of *futuwwa*, we speak of an institution which is multivalent in meaning and which could be secular or spiritual, or both, military or artisan, sufi or non-sufi. 'Islamic chivalry', *futuwwa*, as the sources lucidly show, was multi-faceted and cannot – and should not – be tied to a solitary, portmanteau aspect or definition.

1.6 *Secular and Sacred: Linking the Ways of Perfection*

Both Islam and Christianity speak of perfection in various ways and at various times. The Qur'ān, for example, notes:

> This day have those who
> Reject Faith given up
> All hope of your religion:
> Yet fear them not
> But fear Me.

This day have I
Perfected your religion[578]
For you, completed
My favour upon you,
And have chosen for you
Islam as your religion.
[*Al-yawma akmaltu*
lakum dīnakum
wa atmamtu ʿalaykum
niʿmatī wa raḍītu
lakum al-Islāma
dīnan].[579]

Yusuf Ali comments that the phrase referring to the perfection of religion marked the fact that Muḥammad was drawing near to the end of his life.[580]

In this Qur'ānic verse, it is a question of the perfection or 'completion' of a religion. In the Gospel, however, there is also a dual orientation. Jesus proclaims that he has not 'come to set aside the law and the prophets … but to bring them to perfection'.[581] So, religion, as in the Qur'ānic verse, is to be 'perfected' or 'completed'. But man, too, must perfect himself: 'But you are to be perfect, as your heavenly Father is perfect'.[582] Of the first verse, Benedict T. Viviano comments that 'Matthew's wording … goes beyond a purely legal discussion to a broader Christological perspective',[583] while of the second verse (Matthew 5:48) he says: '*Teleios*, "perfect", is a rare word in the Gospels (found only here and 19:21) … It is common in G[ree]k thought, where it can mean conformity to the divine ideal.'[584] In both the Qur'ān and the Gospels, then, there is an important stress on the idea of perfection.

Now St Thomas Aquinas (AD 1225–74) famously spoke of *quinque viae*, a phrase sometimes translated as 'five proofs for the existence of God';[585] a better and more literal translation might be 'Five Ways'. By analogy, in this chapter we have identified and delineated 'five ways of perfection' – some secular, some sacred, some a mix of both. Our choice is intended to be by no means exclusive or essentialist but merely illustrative and indicative, and to serve as a prolegomenon and context for the entire volume. Our aim has been to adumbrate and disclose these 'Ways' in a manner that discloses various intertextual *links*, models and paradigms; some will be perceived as obvious, others rather less so.

Both secular and sacred paradigms emerge. The pure love of God by the mystic, and God's own pure love for mankind, contrast powerfully with the pure (and sometimes impure) love of the Lady by the Knight in the Courtly Love tradition. The essential components of the *sacred paradigm* are Perfection and the concepts of Perfect Deity and Perfect Man (*al-Insān al-Kāmil*). The essential components of the *secular paradigm* comprise Courtly Love, Knighthood, the Perfect Hero and Ideal/Idealised Woman (contrasting, sometimes, with the imperfect, flawed hero and temptress-woman).

Out of all this, we can establish a third, *colour paradigm*, often founded upon the colour 'green', which is Janus-faced: the Colour Green can be vaunted as *the* mystic colour of perfection (al-Khaḍir, Muḥammad, the green band in *Sir Gawain*, the national flag of Pakistan), but it can also be a symbol of evil (aspects of the Green Man, the Green Knight, Herne the Hunter).

Imbuing much of what we have discussed is the motif and link of chivalry, secular and spiritual, Garter and *futuwwa*; there is a particularly interesting common chivalric thread running through *Sir Gawain and the Green Knight*, *The Merry Wives of Windsor* and *Windsor Castle*. These 'Garter' stories all draw on a common pool of chivalric virtues in their narration which resonate powerfully with what can sometimes be more spiritual arenas, such as the Islamic *futuwwa*.

Then there is a *prosopographical paradigm* which links Elijah, al-Khaḍir, Muḥammad, Sir Gawain and St George. These are all sublime exemplars of secular and sacred virtues, majestic might and mystic or quasi-mystic powers. Elijah is a recipient of revelation and triumphs over the priests of Baal. Al-Khaḍir is the bearer of infused knowledge and exhibits his commanding strength of will and power in the three tests. Muḥammad is the recipient and vehicle of the Divine revelation of the Qur'ān and is the almost bloodless reconqueror of Mecca. Sir Gawain exhibits an almost mystical endurance – and, while he does not receive any Divine revelation as such, he is spiritually strong enough, Joseph-like, to withstand the seductions of the Lady of the Castle. And the myth of St George and the dragon, with all the secular and sacred aspects of that legend, is too well known to require repetition here. All these figures contrast vividly with the antics of such anti-heroes in the chivalric field – though all are knights – as Sir John Falstaff, the adulterous Sir Lancelot and the lustful King Henry VIII.

From all this, we may usefully derive a fifth, overarching and final pattern or paradigm which might be characterised as *the Paradigm of Mystical Salvation* and which seeks to compose the links in composite form between everything which we have thus far surveyed. Diagrammatically, it might look like this:

> Green > Green Man of Paganism > al-Khaḍir/Elijah/St George > Muḥammad > Sir Gawain > European Chivalry/*Futuwwa* > Mystic Ideals of Islam/Christianity > Secular and Sacred *Ways of Perfection*.

It is not suggested here that each of these *topoi* immediately or automatically flows, or even derives, from its predecessor but only that some kind of links *of one kind or another* may be identified and exhibited on the journey from this terrestrial world to the celestial Hereafter. This volume is an attempt to articulate and illustrate the mystic's journey towards the Divine in both Islam and Christianity, a journey whose essential features were adumbrated in the Preface.

It is a journey in which the Islamic and Christian mystics seek knowledge about, and ultimately union with, the Divine, whatever that mystic term 'union' might actually mean. And ultimately, as both religions show, such knowledge can only ever be fragmentary and partial. As Allah Himself says in the Qur'ān, responding to the angels at the time of the creation of Adam:

> I know what ye know not.
> [A'*lamu mā lā ta'lamūna*]. [586]

And the angels respond, uniting in that response, according to Yusuf Ali's translation, two of our key *topoi* of knowledge and perfection:

> Glory to Thee: of knowledge
> We have none, save what Thou
> Hast taught us: in truth it is Thou
> Who art perfect in knowledge and wisdom.[587]

Knowledge of or about the Divine may, in Islam, Christianity and, indeed, Judaism, be linked to revelation; and the chosen place of revelation for these religions, as we shall see, may be a *cave*, as with Elijah and Muḥammad. *Secular space* (for example, the cave of Qur'ānic revelation or the dell in Ainsworth's *Windsor Castle*), which may originally be a *locus* of ignorance, mystery and fear, may be transformed into *sacred space* as a site of knowledge and Divine revelation. The cave, then, and spaces like it, together with all that they represent, become vital 'stations' on the mystic path and the mystic journey.

CHAPTER
2

CAVES, CLOUDS AND MOUNTAINS: THE APOPHATIC TRADITION

2.1 *Caves*

2.1.1 The Cave made Textual: *Sūrat al-Kahf*

In the Qur'ān, God's values, laws and edicts rule. The same goes for the Qur'ānic cave, which represents a *locus* of revelation, safety and Divine protection. The 'physical cave' and the 'textual cave' embrace and disclose the 'hero' or vessel of revelation. In the beginning was the Qur'ānic text, to coin a phrase, and the text bespoke God's salvific, protective and fortifying cave.[1]

Elsewhere, in an analytical study of *Sūrat al-Kahf*,[2] I have identified eight distinct sections as forming the elementary structure of this eighteenth *sūra* of the Qur'ān. Notable among these are 'the Story of the Companions of the Cave (*Aṣḥāb al-Kahf*)' (vv. 9–26) and 'the Story of Mūsā and al-Khaḍir' (vv. 60–82). We have already dealt in some detail with the latter; it is the former story which will concern us here.

In the same study, I also identified five major archetypes which 'clothe or "house" the signs and meanings of the text'.[3] They are: the Sleeper (as epitomised in the Companions of the Cave), the Proto-Muslim (the Companions of the Cave together with the Just Critic of the Vineyard-Owner), the Mystic (al-Khaḍir), the Hero (Mūsā and Dhū 'l-Qarnayn) and the Anti-Hero (Gog and Magog and the Wicked Vineyard-Owner).[4] All are significant in terms of their reality, their symbolism and their archetypical nature. However, it is the first, the sleeper, which will detain us here in view of the associations with that topographical archetype of the Cave.

I have noted elsewhere that this

> is a partly passive, partly active archetype with parallels of one kind or another in many other traditions. One thinks, for example, of the manifold folktales of the Sleeping Beauty,[5] the story of Rip van Winkle,[6] the protagonist in Zakarīyā Tāmir's short story entitled 'Ḥamza',[7] and the Arab philosophers, the Ikhwān al-Ṣafā' (c. AD tenth/eleventh century), who characterised

> themselves, metaphorically, as 'Sleepers in the Cave of our father Adam' (*Kunnā niyāman fī kahf abīnā Ādam*).[8] And, of course, there are the obvious parallels with the Christian tradition of the Seven Sleepers of Ephesus.[9] We might also compare the picaresque adventures of Ibsen's Peer Gynt on awakening, after knocking himself unconscious on a rock in the Rondane Mountains (Act II, Scene IV).[10] The principal *theologeme* to be associated with the archetype of the Sleeper in this *Sūra* is the CAVE.[11] Caves have an immense resonance in early Islamic history: Muḥammad received his first revelation of the Holy Qur'ān in a cave on Mount Ḥirā';[12] during the *hijra* he avoided early capture by hiding in a cave, across the mouth of which a spider spun its web.[13] Early Islamic history thus signals that the cave is a place both of revelation and protection. In a striking parallel, later medieval Scottish history would find the Scottish leader and king, Robert the Bruce (1274–1329), taking refuge in a cave on Rathlin Island off the coast of Antrim, and being inspired by the persistence of a spider.[14]

There is no doubt, then, that within the framework of this *Sūra*

> the cave signifies a place of safety and God's protection,[15] within the shelter of which one may literally sleep. Even their dog co-operates with God in protecting the Sleepers, stretching its limbs across the entrance: it too is a *sign* of the Deity's protection.[16] The function of the Sleeper as archetype is to elicit a manifestation of God's mercy and power[17] and precipitate a test.[18] The former are displayed in abundance throughout the tale; and, unlike Mūsā further on in the *Sūra*, the Sleepers, whose exact number in the Islamic Qur'ānic account is uncertain,[19] appear to pass their test![20]

One of the most powerful messages of *Sūrat al-Kahf* is that it is possible to bring harmony out of chaos. The seemingly chaotic antinomianism of al-Khaḍir is resolved and explained into a satisfactory harmony of logic, as the sage himself explains, while 'the chaos of persecution is resolved by the harmony of sleep in a protecting cave and a waking to an ordered environment'.[21]

2.1.2 Spider, Cave and *Hijra*: The Cave of Unknowing

We have briefly alluded to the fact that the cave in which the Prophet Muḥammad hid during his famous *hijra* from Mecca to Medina in AD 622 may be construed as a place of protection. But this cave has a Janus-face, for it is also a place where the unknown is confronted and human fear is deeply felt.

Muḥammad's enemies in Mecca were many. If we follow the account of Ibn Isḥāq (c. AD 704–c. 767), we learn that

> When the Quraysh became distressed by the trouble caused by the enmity between them and the apostle and those of their people who accepted his teaching, they stirred up against him foolish men who called him a liar, insulted him, and accused him of being a poet, a sorcerer, a diviner and of being possessed. However, the apostle continued to proclaim what God had

> ordered him to proclaim, concealing nothing, and exciting their dislike by contemning their religion, forsaking their idols, and leaving them to their unbelief.[22]

The leading tribe of Mecca, the Quraysh, attack, imprison and beat those who embrace Islam. They deprive the new Muslims of food and drink and expose them to the fierce Meccan sun in an endeavour to turn the young converts from their newly-found faith; some yield, but some resist.[23] At the suggestion of the Prophet Muḥammad, some of his companions make the primary Islamic *hijra* (migration) to Ethiopia, placing their trust in the ruler of that land.[24] Ibn Isḥāq identifies this as the first Islamic *hijra*.[25] This, of course, was the prototype or paradigm of the greater *hijra* of the Prophet himself some time later. And, just as the Medīnans were later to offer the Prophet protection and sanctuary, so, in this earlier *hijra* to Ethiopia by his companions, these are offered the protection and sanctuary of the Negus.[26] And the Qurayshī delegation to the Negus, which attempts to retrieve the Companions of the Prophet from the safety of the Negus, are ignominiously dismissed by that ruler.[27]

The court of the Negus, supreme ruler of Ethiopia, thus metaphorically becomes a 'cave of security and protection' for those first migrants in *actuality*, but, like the later cave inhabited for three days by the Prophet on his own *hijra*, the court was *potentially* a place of fear: it could have been a dead-end trap for the migrants had the Negus not been impressed by the honesty of his new visitors and their total commitment to Islam.[28]

It is the intention not to survey here, in full, the events which precipitated the Prophet's own *hijra* but merely to highlight some analogies which may be drawn with that proto-*hijra* of his followers to Ethiopia, as well as to illustrate examples of the persistent enmity of the Quraysh.

Things eventually came to a head with a plot to assassinate Muḥammad which would avoid any individual clan bearing sole responsibility for the deed; in consequence, blood money would have to be accepted. As Ibn Isḥāq puts it:

> Thereupon Abū Jahl said that he had a plan which had not been suggested hitherto, namely that each clan should provide a young, powerful, well-born, aristocratic warrior; that each of these should be provided with a sharp sword; then each of them should strike a blow at him and kill him. Thus they would be relieved of him, and responsibility for his blood would lie upon all the clans.[29]

But Muḥammad is warned by the angel Jibrīl (Gabriel) not to sleep in his usual bed.[30] What follows is highly significant in the context of one of the *leitmotivs* of this book, namely the emphasis on the colour green. 'Alī b. Abī Ṭālib, later to be the fourth *khalīfa* over the Islamic community, is asked by Muḥammad to be his substitute (*khalīfa*) in Muḥammad's own bed and to wrap himself in the *green* Ḥaḍramī cloak or mantle (*burdī hādhā al-Ḥaḍramī al-akhḍar*).[31] The would-be assassins are duly tricked, and 'Alī remains unharmed, protected by the same green garment which used to cover the Prophet himself. This green cloak is thus a powerful symbol of both the protection of Allah and the former presence of the Prophet.

Certain garments in Islam often have not just a symbolic significance but also a physical potency: in *Sūrat Yūsuf*, Yūsuf (Joseph) sends a shirt to his father Ya'qūb which enables the latter to recover his sight.[32] As Yusuf Ali comments: 'It will be remembered that they [the brothers of Joseph] had covered their crime by taking his shirt, putting on the stains of blood, and pretending that he had been killed by a wolf ... The first shirt plunged Jacob [Ya'qūb] into grief. This one will now restore him.'[33] There is clearly a sublime, and subliminal, preternatural power in the garment in which 'Alī wraps himself on that fateful evening of the *hijra*.

Ibn Iṣḥāq's text deploys the Arabic word *burd*, which may variously be translated as 'garment', 'cloak' or 'mantle' and which is clearly the same as the Arabic *burda*: the *Encyclopaedia of Islam* defines this as 'a piece of woollen cloth used since pre-Islamic times, which was worn as a cloak by day and used as a blanket at night. That of the Prophet has become famous.'[34] The *Encyclopaedia* draws attention to the famous poem by al-Būṣīrī (AD 1212–c. 1294/5) to which the garment gave its name.[35] The 'greenness' of the cloak in the accounts of such authors as Ibn Isḥāq, al-Ṭabarī and Ibn Kathīr resonates powerfully within the context of this volume as a symbol of goodness, power, security and Divine protection, and the garment itself may credibly be said to have intertextual affinities with the healing garment of Yūsuf, to which we have just alluded, bestowed by that prophet on his father Ya'qūb, to cure him of his blindness.

The traditional date given for the start of the *hijra* era (AH: *Anno Hegirae*), according to which Islam begins its calendar, is AD 16 July 622. We are instructed that the *hijra* era does not date from the time of the actual arrival of the Prophet in the city of Medina but rather 'on the first day of the lunar year in which that event took place, which is reckoned to coincide with 16th July 622'.[36] W. Montgomery Watt further reminds us that there is a deeper and more subliminal meaning to the Arabic word *hijra* than just its usual translation of 'emigration' or 'flight': he emphasises that its primary connotation is 'the breaking of the ties of kinship or association'.[37] Watt notes that, when Muḥammad's clan chief, Abū Ṭālib, died in about AD 619, he was replaced by the hostile Abū Lahab.[38] I have noted elsewhere that

> 'Abd al-'Uzzā b. 'Abd al-Muṭṭalib (died c. 3/624) [was the] uncle of the Prophet Muḥammad who vehemently opposed the Prophet. He was called by the name Abū Lahab meaning 'Father of Flame' because he was so good-looking. He may be said to have been one of the catalysts which led to the hijra of Muḥammad from Mecca to Medīna: when the Prophet Muḥammad's uncle Abū Ṭālib, who had been head of the clan of Hāshim, died, Abū Lahab assumed the headship, and the protection of the clan of Hāshim was later withdrawn from Muḥammad. The tension between Muḥammad and Abū Lahab is reflected in *Sūrat al-Masad* of the Qur'ān. Abū Lahab died soon after the Battle of Badr [in AD 624]. His children converted to Islam.[39]

This *Sūra* is the 111th in the Qur'ān. *Al-Masad* may be translated as 'The Palm Fibres'. It is a very short, Meccan *sūra* of only five verses and derives its title from verse five, in which Abū Lahab's wife is portrayed as having palm fibres round her neck. The whole chapter is a magisterial condemnation of Abū Lahab, in view of his profound hostility to Islam, and we are told that his wealth will not preserve him and his wife from the flames of Hell.[40] In the light of all this, it is hardly surprising that the Prophet felt a loosening, if not an actual breaking, of his erstwhile kinship ties, and decided on a *hijra* to the city of Medina.

In the events which follow, the *cave* on Mount Thawr plays a central and significant role. Scholars have drawn attention to an important Qur'ānic verse which might be labelled 'The Verse of the Cave':

> If ye help not (your leader),
> (It is no matter): for God
> Did indeed help him,
> When the Unbelievers
> Drove him out: he had
> No more than one companion:
> They two were in the Cave [*al-ghār*]
> And he said to his companion,
> 'Have no fear, for God
> Is with us': then God
> Sent down His peace upon him,
> And strengthened him with forces
> Which ye saw not, and humbled
> To the depths the word
> Of the Unbelievers.
> But the word of God
> Is exalted to the heights:
> For God is Exalted in might, Wise.[41]

Al-Ṭabarī specifically links the cave mentioned in the Qur'ān here to the *hijra* cave on Mount Thawr.[42] What lies behind this verse is the fact that Muḥammad and his faithful companion (and later *khalīfa*) Abū Bakr have taken refuge from their enemies and pursuers during their *hijra* in a cave on Mount Thawr, a few miles from Mecca. Here they remain for three days.[43] This cave, then, is here a *locus* of refuge but also of fear. It is a 'cave of unknowing', fear, worry and sorrow; the Prophet, as the Qur'ān shows, puts his entire trust in Allah, but his companion, Abū Bakr, cannot know for certain whether they will emerge from the cave alive. For their enemies are all around, and the cave environment, at times, is hostile.[44] But, as the Qur'ānic verse cited above shows, the Prophet endeavours to console Abū Bakr, telling him not to worry or be afraid (literally: 'Don't be sad') for God is definitely with them (*innā Allāha maʿanā*).[45] God sends His protection in the form of a spider, two doves and a tree. The episode does not appear to be recorded in the *Sīra* of Ibn Isḥāq, so it is to such sources as Ibn Kathīr,[46] the fourteenth-century historian and traditionist, and his *al-Sīra al-Nabawiyya* that we now turn.

Ibn Kathīr relates that, once Muḥammad's enemies discover that ʿAlī had impersonated the Prophet in the latter's bed, they attempt to follow his tracks up Mount Thawr. They pass the cave in which the Prophet is hiding but, seeing a spider's web spun across the opening, assume that no one can be within. God also commands a tree to rise up and hide the Prophet, and two wild doves at the entrance to the cave again persuade the searchers that no one can be inside the cave.[47] The Prophet realises that God has sent the two doves for the protection and salvation of himself and Abū Bakr.[48]

The *hijra* was, of course, one of the seminal events in the history of Islam and the life of the Prophet Muḥammad. However, in this section, we have focused not so much on the narrative history as on certain anthropological and semiotic features such as the green *burd* of Muḥammad and the triple protective shield of spider, dove and tree. Above all, our emphasis is on the Cave, its symbolism as a place of 'unknowing' but also of protection, and its contrast with the cave on Mount Ḥirā', the cave of revelation and knowledge, where the Qur'ān was first revealed to the Prophet Muḥammad.

2.2 *Clouds*

2.2.1 *The Cloud of Unknowing*

Muḥammad, the Prophet of Islam, travels, pilgrim-like, towards his destiny and goal in Medina. Like Bunyan's hero in *The Pilgrim's Progress*, he encounters many obstacles on his *hijra*, not the least of which is the three-day sojourn in the cave. As we have seen, this mountain cave has a Janus-face: 'Unknowing', but protective of the Prophet at the same time.

In the text which we shall now encounter, we meet a different kind of 'unknowing'. As with Muḥammad, the anonymous author of *The Cloud of Unknowing* has a considerable trust in God. But *The Cloud*, and *its* way to perfection, is articulated from within a profoundly *apophatic* tradition, whereas the sacred text of Islam, the Qur'ān, conceives of God in both an apophatic and cataphatic or positive sense, a transcendent and an immanent way: on the one hand, it proclaims that there is nothing and no one like Him;[49] on the other, God tells mankind that he is closer to man than his own jugular vein.[50] Comparisons with *The Cloud of Unknowing* are instructive.

The Eastern and Western branches of the Christian Church have long recognised two approaches to what mankind can know about God, especially in the realms of mystical theology. They are the *Via Positiva* or Cataphatic Way, and the *Via Negativa* or Apophatic Way, to which latter tradition, as we have noted, *The Cloud* belongs.[51] A. C. Spearing, in the 'Introduction' to his translation of the *The Cloud*, notes, however, how contrary this was to what prevailed in medieval England:

> The *Cloud* author … draws on a radically different tradition, one that is in many ways opposed to the main stream of medieval English devotion. This tradition is that of the *via negativa* (way of negation), and it focuses not on God's human nature but on his divine nature, seen as totally transcendent, totally beyond the reach of human understanding and human language.[52]

Spearing traces this *via negativa* tradition back to the Neoplatonist author who wrote c. AD 500 whom scholars know as Pseudo-Dionysius[53] and who heavily influenced, directly or indirectly, the author of *The Cloud*.[54]

Rosemary Arthur stresses that Pseudo-Dionysius was definitely a Neoplatonist,[55] draws attention to what she characterises as 'the Dionysian themes of incomprehensibility, ineffability and silence' found both in Pseudo-Dionysius and the Nag Hammadi writings,[56] and, in a section entitled 'The Cloud of Unknowing and the Dazzling Darkness', concludes: 'Christian mystics have always longed to see God and to be united with him, in this life as well as in the life to come. The inseparable themes of the Cloud and the Dazzling Darkness are attempts to explain why we cannot hope to reach a perfect knowledge of God.'[57] Here, in Rosemary Arthur's passages, the references are not to the medieval text of *The Cloud of Unknowing* but to the imagery in the Old Testament Book of Exodus, where 'both cloud and darkness are at the same time the result of the divine glory and a protective device'.[58]

Spearing also draws attention to the *Cloud* author's adaptation of a Dionysian text entitled *Deonise Hid Divinite* or *De Mystica Theologia* (a title translated as *The Mystical Theology of St Denis*), in which the author, in true apophatic fashion, presents a listing of the things that cannot be said about the Deity.[59] For example, chapter 4 of this treatise, entitled 'That he who is the Cause of all that can be perceived by the senses cannot be so perceived', stresses that God is utterly beyond corporeal imagining, lacking in such things as form, weight, location and visibility, and has nothing that can be perceived by the senses, being beyond such things.[60] Chapter 5, which follows under the name 'That he who is the Cause of all that is intelligible is not himself intelligible', then furnishes us with a long string of what God is not: for example, 'he is not number, or order, or greatness, or littleness, or equality, or likeness or unlikeness'; a little further on, we are told 'that he has no power, nor is he power, or light, nor does he live, nor is he life or substance or age or time'.[61] All this is a far cry from St Thomas Aquinas' idea that we can characterise God positively *by analogy* with human characteristics and actions.[62]

The theology of the *Deonise Hid Divinite/De Mystica Theologia* is the same as that of *The Cloud of Unknowing*. The full Middle English title of *The Cloud* is *A Book of Contemplacyon, the Whiche is Clepyd The Clowde of Unknowyng, in the Whiche a Soule is Onyd with God*,[63] a title which appears, when rendered in a modern English translation, as *A Book of Contemplation called The Cloud of Unknowing, in which a soul is made one with God*.[64] Right from the very beginning, then, in the actual title, the idea of union of the soul with God is advanced, despite the seeming paradox that it is a negative theology, the *via negativa*, which will be the *Way* or vehicle by which the aspirant soul will strive to reach a very positive goal, eternal bliss in union with the Deity Himself. Indeed, Phyllis Hodgson suggests that paradox is part of the very fabric and language of the text.[65]

While, as will become apparent, we can learn much about the spirituality and mystical theology of the author of *The Cloud* simply by reading the text, his actual identity remains cloaked in the darkness of a happy, possibly deliberate, anonymity. As Phyllis Hodgson neatly puts it in her 'Introduction': 'Recent and far-reaching research has increased the general understanding of *The Cloud of Unknowing* … but not yet produced the final solution to the problem of authorship. All still remains conjecture.'[66] A. C. Spearing believed that the author went to considerable trouble to hide his real identity.[67] We can say with some certainty that he *was* a priest:

Wolters and other scholars direct us to the very last paragraph of the last chapter of *The Cloud*, chapter 75, in which our author invokes a dual blessing from God *and* himself: '*Farewel, goostly frende, in Goddes blessing and myne!*'[68]

Was he a Carthusian monk? This is a distinct possibility, though by no means proven beyond all doubt.[69] Yet Evelyn Underhill perspicaciously observes that the Carthusian mode of life, in which members of that Order live a mainly eremitical life of solitude and only come together to sing the Divine Office, would not have given the author of *The Cloud* a great deal of opportunity to note and record some of the quirks of life 'of which he gives so amusing and realistic a description in the lighter passages of the *Cloud*'.[70] And the Carthusian Order itself never officially claimed him in any formal medieval document.[71]

Another attribution of authorship, now discarded, was to the Augustinian Walter Hilton (died AD 1396).[72] Evelyn Underhill was splendidly firm in rejecting this possibility, though it would certainly be possible to establish at least an intertext between Hilton's *The Scale of Perfection*, his *Song of the Angels* and *The Cloud*.[73] Hodgson admits that there are still those, following the fifteenth-century Carthusian monk James Greenhalgh, who like to ascribe *The Cloud* to Walter Hilton, but underlines the lack of any real evidence.[74] However, regardless of whether our clerical author was a secular priest or a member of a religious order, it is clear that he was very likely, on the evidence of his mystical theology and general theological scholarship, to have been a graduate of the University of either Oxford or Cambridge.[75]

When we come to look at the author's character, as revealed in his texts, we are on much firmer ground. With Justin McCann, we can certainly agree that the author of *The Cloud* was hugely gifted intellectually, with a considerable literary bent.[76] Underhill admires his sense of humour combined with an acuity of observation and vigorous common sense,[77] while Clifton Wolters lauds a knowledgeable scholar who knew how to express complex matters in a lucid fashion.[78]

Wolters dates *The Cloud* to the second half of the fourteenth century, making it a contemporary, or near-contemporary, text of Chaucer's *Canterbury Tales*.[79] Indeed, Justin McCann characterises this fourteenth century as 'Chaucer's Century'.[80] English mysticism (as Wolters suggests – and McCann and Baker concur) may well have been 'in full flower' with such luminaries as Richard Rolle (AD 1300–49), Walter Hilton (died AD 1396) and Julian of Norwich (AD 1343–1413),[81] but it was also an age of appalling turmoil, unrest, transition and devastation. Wolters puts it like this: 'Medieval Christendom was passing away, and modern nationalism was coming to painful birth'. [82] Its midwives included the Hundred Years War, the Black Death and the 'exile' of the papacy at Avignon.[83] It is little wonder, then, that the mystical tradition should have provided a kind of safe haven and a sure path to perfection and Paradise in the midst of so much turmoil.[84]

Spearing reminds us that it was also an age of perceived heresy, notably in the form of Lollardy, and points to the condemnation of heresy in chapter 56 of *The Cloud*:[85]

> Some there be, that although they be not deceived with this error as it is set here, yet for pride and curiosity of natural wit and letterly cunning leave the common doctrine and the counsel of Holy Church. And these with all their

> favourers lean over much to their own knowing: and for they were never grounded in meek blind feeling and virtuous living, therefore they merit to have a false feeling, feigned and wrought by the ghostly enemy. Insomuch, that at the last they burst up and blaspheme all the saints, sacraments, statutes, and ordinances of Holy Church. Fleshly living men of the world, the which think the statutes of Holy Church over hard to be amended by, they lean to these heretics full soon and full lightly, and stalworthy maintain them, and all because them think that they lead them a softer way than is ordained of Holy Church.[86]

It is clear, then, that *The Cloud* teaches that the way of, and to, perfection is a hard one – and, as Wolters emphasises, even the most advanced contemplatives may leave this path to perfection.[87] In their struggles, they despair of ever achieving the spiritual perfection towards which they aspire: 'Many come as far as this on their spiritual journey, but because their suffering is great and they get no comfort, they go back to the consideration of worldly things'.[88]

The *Way of Perfection*, for the author of *The Cloud*, is difficult but, if the composition of his text is anything to go by, it is also somewhat unstructured. There appears to be no proper 'plan' in the presentation of the text, although Wolters helps us by suggesting that the initial three chapters, with their focus on love of God and His jealous love for man, provide the key to the comprehension of the rest of *The Cloud* and that the remainder of the text, from a total of seventy-five chapters, is actually an exegesis of chapters 1–3.[89]

The author of *The Cloud* speaks as a Master to a disciple, a monastic novice master to a novice[90] or a sufi shaykh to a new *murīd* (novice), and this is not surprising: early in *The Cloud*, in chapter 4, we learn that the person to whom the text is addressed is only 24 years old.[91] Time is passing, time is precious, and it is already too late to make *full* satisfaction to God for past sins: only the future is under the disciple's control, and even that control will be diluted by human weakness unless help is given from on high by the love of Jesus.[92] And God's love for man and the need for man to love God in return is a cardinal *leitmotiv* of the entire text of *The Cloud*.[93]

Wolters has identified five principal themes or motifs: Grace, the Naked Intent which is Longing Love, the Hardness of the Way, Sin, and Contemplation.[94] The present volume will examine *seven* themes (with accompanying illustrations from *The Cloud*), chosen because they have a particular resonance not only with other Christian mystical texts but also with much in the Islamic mystical tradition: (1) *Cloud*; (2) *Self-abnegation*; (3) *Contemplation*; (4) *The Dark Night*; (5) *Perfection*; (6) *Human and Divine Love*; (7) *Union*. These themes are intended to be by no means exclusive but merely indicative of a wider spectrum of mystical experience; several other themes could have easily been chosen. However, they are presented here as being among the most dominant themes of *The Cloud*. At the beginning of our survey and analysis, it is worth noting Hodgson's observation that, in *The Cloud*, the words *contemplation*, *perfection* and *union* are to be regarded as virtual synonyms.[95] Indeed, '*Perfection* signifies the perfect love of God' in the mind and writings of the author of *The Cloud*.[96]

Cloud

The image of the cloud has two aspects: there is 'the cloud of unknowing' which gives the whole work its title, and there is 'the cloud of forgetting'.[97] The image of 'the cloud of unknowing' emerges early in the text of chapter 3:

> Do not give up, then, but work at it till you have this longing. When you first begin, you find only darkness, and as it were a cloud of unknowing. You don't know what this means except that in your will you feel a simple steadfast intention reaching out towards God. Do what you will, this darkness and this cloud remain between you and God, and stop you both from seeing him in the clear light of rational understanding, and from experiencing his loving sweetness in your affection.[98]

A little later, the text stresses that the 'darkness' and the 'cloud' are not like the physical clouds in the sky or the darkness with which one is familiar at home during the night 'when thi candel is oute'.[99] The author is at great pains to emphasise that what he means by 'darkness' is 'a lackyng of knowyng'.[100] And this lack of knowledge of God our author characterises not as a cloud in the air but as 'a cloude of unknowyng that is bitwix thee and thi God'.[101] Only longing love of God appears capable of piercing this dark nimbus cloud of unknowing: 'If thou wilt stonde and not falle, seese never in thin extent, bot bete evermore on this cloude of unknowyng that is bitwix thee and thi God with a sharpe darte of longing love'.[102]

Justin McCann reminds us that 'it is clear that an important part of the disciple's effort, and a condition of its success, is a negative process, a progressive abstraction from sense and sensible things, and from discursive thought, until his activity may be described as a "loving stirring and a blind beholding"'.[103] All this is explicit in our author's reference to a second type of 'cloud', that is, 'the cloud of forgetting': just as 'the cloud of unknowing' is between man and God, so there should be 'a cloude of forgetyng bineth thee, bitwix thee and alle the cretures that ever ben maad'.[104] If we are unconcerned about forgetting the material created world, if there is no 'cloud of forgetting' between man and creation, then the gulf between man and God is immeasurably larger.[105]

The author of *The Cloud* summarily enjoins: 'Alle schuld be hid under the cloude of forgetyng'.[106] Chapter 5, one of the earliest, which embraces all these quotations, is itself given a lengthy title which articulates its contents in a nutshell: 'That in the tyme of this werk alle the cretures that ever have ben, ben now, or ever schal be, and alle the werkes of thoo same creatures, scholen [= shall][107] be hid under the cloude of forgetyng'.[108] Spearing translates this chapter 5 heading in full: 'While this work is being performed, all created beings that have ever existed, exist now or ever shall exist, and all their deeds, must be hidden beneath the cloud of forgetting',[109] while Wolters' rendition of the Middle English original is rather shorter: 'The Cloud of Forgetting must obliterate all things'.[110]

Our attention is drawn[111] to chapter 26, where the author of *The Cloud* admits that it is going to be very hard work to forget the material created world, but it can be done with the help of God's grace and love:

> But wherein then is this travail, I pray thee? Surely, this travail is all in treading down of the remembrance of all the creatures that ever God made, and in holding of them *under the cloud of forgetting* [my emphasis] named before. In this is all the travail; for this is man's travail, with help of grace. And the tother [*sic*] above – that is to say, the stirring of love – that is the work of only God. And therefore do on thy work, and surely I promise thee He shall not fail in His.[112]

All this would clearly resonate with a Muslim mystic or Muslim mystical theologian. For the goal of most of the sufis was the control, indeed the extirpation, of the *nafs*, a multivalent Arabic word used in Islamic mysticism to denote 'selfness' and all that keeps one earthbound in terms of vice, sin and sinful inclinations, rather than its primary Arabic sense of 'soul'. Indeed, Wehr's *Dictionary* definition of *nafs* ranges through a diversity of meanings: '*Nafs* ... soul; psyche; spirit, mind; life; animate being, living creature, human being, person, individual ...; essence, nature; inclination, *liking, appetite, desire* [my emphases]; personal identity, self'.[113]

And, as Dr Javad Nurbakhsh has neatly put it, by meditation the advanced sufi will lose all sense of selfhood, die to that 'selfness' and be brought to life again in God Himself.[114] He will have freed himself from the dictates and the tyranny of the *nafs*.[115]

Self-abnegation

Such ideas link us neatly to our second major *Cloud* theme, which is self-abnegation, a motif common to both the Islamic and Christian mystical traditions. Classically, Islamic sufis interpreted the idea in an extreme sense and deployed the Arabic word *fanā'*, again a multivalent word whose semantic range moves from 'passing away, cessation of being' to 'recedence of the ego, obliteration of the self'.[116] The Persian mystic 'Alī b. 'Uthmān al-Jullābī al-Hujwīrī (died c. AD 1075), in his famous *Kashf al-Maḥjūb* (*The Disclosure of the Concealed*) spoke of 'the eye of annihilation (*fanā'*)': when one looks at creation with this eye, then nothing appears to exist except God.[117] The essence of this *fanā'* is to become conscious of the imperfection of things and to lack any desire for them.[118] This is confirmed by another fellow sufi, Abū Bakr al-Kalābādhī (died AD 990 or 995), who defines *fanā'* as a state in which all passion is spent and the mystic is devoid of all feelings towards everything.[119]

All this links very neatly both with the motif of 'the cloud of forgetting' and with the idea of self-abnegation. In chapter 43 of *The Cloud of Unknowing*, the disciple is urged to empty his mind and will and to focus on God. Knowledge and feeling of, and for, all that is not God is to be similarly disposed of. All must be trodden down 'under the cloude of forgetyng'.[120] Even the knowledge, awareness and feeling of one's own existence is a barrier to perfect contemplation.[121]

Contemplation

This is the third of the seven major motifs which we have singled out for discussion. It is a vital, key word appearing in the full, longer medieval title of the work itself, together with that other key theme of union with God (to which we shall devote some space); its 'idea' infuses the entire text of *The Cloud*.

Wolters reminds us that contemplation has nothing to do with human emotion but, rather, 'it is the awareness of God, known and loved at the core of one's being'.[122] The sublime joy to which contemplation may sometimes give rise is indescribable, but the actual *path* to such contemplation may be articulated in words.[123] Phyllis Hodgson suggests that contemplation's goal could be arcane knowledge of the Divine, united with that Divine in an incomprehensible mystical union.[124] In the Prologue to *The Cloud*, the author makes it clear that the book is intended for the aspirant to the contemplative life and state. Indeed, the whole 'werk' of the book is contemplation.[125]

For the *Cloud* author, Mary, the sister of Martha, whose story is told in the Gospel of Luke,[126] is the model of all contemplatives:[127] and she participated in 'the cloud of unknowing' with a loving heart. The *Cloud* text portrays her as sitting, completely immoveable, full of love and happiness, 'reaching out into that high cloud of unknowing that was between her and God';[128] and she becomes an ineluctable paradigm for every mystic, however far advanced and pure: all must sit in the shadow of this overarching cloud. Within the cloud, Mary's love is articulated and experienced in a variety of different ways, for this cloud represents the highest and most sacred state of earthly contemplation.[129]

The last chapter, 75, stresses that not all are called to the contemplative state or life, but there is no harm in testing oneself. A sign of a real vocation to this life is if, after a period of spiritual aridity, 'he has a burning desire and a deeper passion for contemplation than ever before'.[130]

While the story of Martha and Mary in Luke's Gospel provides some notable images and paradigms for the author of *The Cloud*, their brother Lazarus is not mentioned. Yet, as Esler and Piper observe, the resurrection of Lazarus from the dead which we find in John 11 has made a powerful mark on all who have read this Gospel.[131] Lazarus' tomb may be said to have some affinities with the *hijra* cave of Muḥammad, for it is a tomb of unknowing and finality from which, nonetheless, new (or renewed) life is suddenly born, or reborn: the 'cave' of potential death (in the case of Muḥammad) or actual death (Lazarus) becomes a cave/tomb of new life.[132] It is intriguing that Esler and Piper are at pains to stress that 'in the Johannine narrative (11:38) Lazarus has been laid in a tomb in the form of a cave (*spēlaion*)', that is, a natural or artificial hillside hole.[133]

The Dark Night

The actual terms 'Dark Night' and 'Dark Night of the Soul' are not ones used in *The Cloud of Unknowing*. Indeed, *The Cloud* is happy to admit the possibility of spiritual sweetness as a result of contemplation,[134],so the 'Dark Night' as envisaged by Juan de la Cruz (St John of the Cross, of whom more later) is also somewhat different from the two clouds of 'unknowing' and 'forgetting' which we have encountered in our text. The classical 'Dark Night' is a period of spiritual aridity, darkness and desolation, a feeling of being totally bereft spiritually and cut off from God, whereas the 'cloud of unknowing', while forming a 'barrier' between man and God, also constitutes a 'link' according to the apophatic tradition.

Yet, while the 'Cloud' is not exactly the 'Night' of San Juan de la Cruz, we can still perceive other aspects of the text which do provide analogies to this latter 'Night': Clifton Wolters, in his Introduction to *The Cloud*, notes that the classical 'two nights' paradigm which John adumbrates, that is, the 'Night of the Senses' and the 'Night of the Spirit', are merged into one night by the *Cloud* author; where we do find a much closer parallelism is the picture of Hell in *The Cloud* 'and the feeling of utter despair (chapter 69)'.[135] Wolters continues: 'St John's *toda y nada* is almost the exact echo of *The Cloud*'s "nothing which is the all" (chapter 68). Indeed the similarity of doctrine between the two mystics, English and Spanish, separated as they are by two centuries ... has often been commented on.'[136] So, let us turn here, briefly, to these two chapters to which Wolters directs us.

Chapter 68, in particular, delineates a 'darkness of the soul' very much akin to the mystical spirit of St John. There is an emphasis on achieving a state of physical 'nowhere-ness' in order to be everywhere spiritually: 'For whi nowhere bodely is everywhere goostly'.[137] There may be a complete withdrawal of all spiritual consolation for the bodily senses, for they may think that nothing spiritual is being accomplished, yet the aspirant to perfection, immersed and miserable in this 'dark night', is urged to persist in undertaking this nothing out of pure love of God.[138]

The soul is not to worry if it cannot understand this 'nothing' intellectually; it can be *felt* more easily than seen. Yet its essence is really an excess of spiritual light rather than any real darkness or lack of actual light.[139] In other words, the 'Dark Night', with all its sorrow and feelings of utter spiritual abandonment by God, is by no means what it seems but rather a chastening and purging and refining experience for the advanced mystic who aspires to final perfection and union with the Godhead.

Chapter 69 vividly illustrates those 'feeling[s] of utter despair' to which Clifton Wolters alludes: in it, the author of *The Cloud* describes in vivid detail the impact of what he characterises as 'this nothing' ('this nought'),[140] and which we, in John's terminology, may characterise as 'the Dark Night'. There will be a full recognition and horror of past sins which will so appal the aspirant to perfection that he is overwhelmed by a hellish and despairing recognition that he might never embrace real perfection or peace'.[141] Eventually, however, the realisation will dawn that it *is* possible to purge one's past sins and achieve forgiveness, that his 'hell' will at least become 'purgatory' and that he may even gain some spiritual consolation and delight, though that 'Cloud of Unknowing' will always remain between himself and God.[142] True perseverance and endurance in the horrors of 'the dark night' or 'darkness' can bring 'som hope of perfeccion'.[143] It is to that aspiration of the youthful disciple who is addressed in *The Cloud* that we will now turn.

Perfection

Right at the beginning of *The Cloud*, in the first lines of the first chapter, the author identifies 'foure degrees and fourmes' of the Christian life: these are 'Comoun, Special, Singuler and Parfite'.[144] The first three (common or ordinary, special and solitary) can be commenced and concluded during this earthly life; but the fourth and last, the state of perfection, may well, by God's grace, be started on earth, but it will continue for all eternity in Paradise.[145] And, as we have seen, from its textual content, 'Perfection' is a ubiquitous *leitmotiv* of the whole of *The Cloud*. We do well to remember that it is a virtual synonym of both those other two constant *leitmotivs*, 'Contemplation' and 'Union' '(ME *oneheed* "oneness")',[146] i.e. with the Godhead.

Certain passages stand out and are worthy of note. Chapter 15 draws attention to Christ's injunction in Matthew 5:48 that one is to be perfect according to the example of perfection of one's heavenly Father, or, as *The Cloud* puts it, in its preferred fashion, 'where he biddeth that we schuld be parfite by grace as he hymself is by kynde'.[147]

Chapter 49 urges the aspirant to follow 'this meek steryng of love in thin herte'.[148] Such love is 'nothing but a good will in harmony with God'[149] and, as such, it is 'the substaunce of alle perfeccion'.[150] Elsewhere, *The Cloud* states that the striver for perfection should avoid venial sin insofar as he can, for it can lead to mortal sin, and that he should cultivate the virtue of 'perfect humility'.[151] *The Cloud* makes it clear that this fourth state of perfection will not be achieved without such virtues and attitudes of mind.

In his book, *In the Paradise of the Sufis*, Dr Javad Nurbakhsh emphasises that the goal of Islamic mysticism is 'the realization of the Truth' and that the path to that Truth is by Love. One needs to be perfected because humanity in a state of imperfection cannot know the Truth. To become 'perfected', one must throw off the demands of the *nafs* (self) and follow the spiritual path as a *murīd* or novice, under the guidance of a sufi master.[152] And, just as the anonymous author of *The Cloud of Unknowing* attempts to guide his youthful disciple, so does the author of *In the Paradise of the Sufis*. In both texts, there is an emphasis on self-abnegation, freeing oneself from the material demands of the body and the often sinful inclinations of the soul, and striving for that Perfection in which one may 'become one with the Absolute'.[153]

Human and Divine Love

The theme of Divine love is another of the constant and sublime *leitmotivs* of *The Cloud*, if not the most important one. And it must be reciprocated. Wolters observes'On almost every page the book is concerned with the soul's love for God'.[154] He draws attention to a passage in chapter 7 where the disciple is urged to latch onto a word like 'God' or 'love' and fix it in his heart so that it will function as 'thi scheeld and thi spere, whether thou ridest on pees or on werre'.[155]

God's own love for man is beyond all comprehension:

> [There] is the over-abundant love and the worthiness of God in Himself; in beholding of the which all nature quaketh, all clerks be fools, and all saints and angels be blind. Insomuch, that were it not that through the wisdom of His Godhead He measured their beholding after their ableness in nature and in grace, I defail to say what should befall them.[156]

Chapter 26 speaks of the spiritual consolation or sweetness which may occasionally pierce the cloud of unknowing, and the text deploys the language of fire when it speaks of God's love: 'Than schalt thou fele thine affeccion enflaumid with the fire of his love, fer more then I kan telle thee'.[157]

This kind of spiritual consolation may be welcomed, but the novice is not to depend on it, and one should not really love God for the sake of gaining such spiritual sweetness: that sort of love is neither perfect nor pure. The text of *The Cloud* here makes it clear that God is to be loved for his own sake, regardless of what spiritual joy may or may not accompany that human love for the Divine.[158] The whole of chapter 1 of *The Cloud* is saturated with references to God's love, and it is that which has led the disciple to whom *The Cloud* is addressed from the *common* state of life to the *special* and thence to the *solitary*, whence the first steps towards the *perfect* life are learned.[159]

Union

Our seventh and final *leitmotiv*, one which infuses the full title of *The Cloud of Unknowing*, is that of *union* with the Godhead. However, although 'union' is the heart and very essence of *The Cloud*, in terms of actual definition or even description, *The Cloud* and its related treatises do not have a huge amount to say.[160] Indeed, the text warns: 'For of that work, that falleth to only God, dare I not take upon me to speak with my blabbering fleshly tongue: and shortly to say, although I durst I would do not'.[161] The Beatific Vision, with all that it entails of 'union' with God, is indeed ineffable.

In his book entitled *Secretum sive Mysticum Being an Exposition or Certain Notes upon the Book called The Cloud*, the English Benedictine monk, Augustine Baker (AD 1575–1641), discoursed as follows on 'Aspirations and the Mystic Union':

> The aspirations of which we have spoken are an exercise by which we immediately aspire to a perfect union with God. In the aspirations themselves there is much good love and a kind of union; but there is not in them perfect love or perfect union. The aspirations are a certain greedy longing or thirsting after God out of love; but when the soul is come to be united to him, then do they cease: she being come to enjoy and possess that food which by her aspirations she aspired and tended unto. But such union ceasing – for it doth not always last – she reneweth her aspirations, by them aspiring to a new union. The which perfect union consisteth in the coupling of the powers of the soul by love and affection to the Spirit of God, all images of creatures for the time being driven and held without. And although the perfect felicity of this life doth consist in that perfect union and possession of God, yet is there an imperfect felicity even in those aspirations by which one tendeth and aspireth to that perfect union.[162]

Dom Augustine Baker's *Commentary* on *The Cloud* is notable here for the way in which it weaves together so many of the key motifs of that text into a seamless whole: perfection, union, aspiration, love, felicity, imperfection. All are here in this, one of *The Cloud*'s earliest and most distinguished commentaries. The key, of course, to this Divine 'union' is love, and this is emphasised very early on in *The Cloud* in chapter 4:

> For in the love of Jesus; there shall be thine help. Love is such a power, that it maketh all things common. Love therefore Jesus; and all thing that He hath, it is thine ... Knit [*Knyt*] thee therefore to Him, by love and by belief, and then by virtue of that knot thou shalt be common perceiver with Him, and with all that by love so be knitted [*knittyd*] unto Him ...[163]

As we can see, Underhill's translation here sticks closely to the original Middle English and renders the words *knyt* and *knittyd* literally, whereas Wolters prefers the more modern 'unite' and 'united' respectively.[164] Spearing, however, prefers to translate *knyt* as 'bind' and *knittyd* as 'bound'.[165] Regardless of how the original Middle English words *knyt* and *knittyd* are rendered, however, it is clear that the focus in the original was that 'union' towards which the entire text of *The Cloud* aspired. Again we recall, with Phyllis Hodgson, how so many of the words in the mystic vocabulary – contemplation, perfection, union – merge into one.[166] For the one who has achieved 'union' with the Deity is one who has been perfected and in that state is capable of perfect contemplation.

In Islamic mystical theology, *al-baqā'* is the transcendent opposite of *al-fanā'*. *Baqā'* has been defined as 'remaining, subsistence, abiding, survival, immortality'.[167] It has a technical sense in Islamic Sufism 'to indicate a stage in the mystical experience after *fanā'* … in which the mystic "abides" or "subsists" in God. *Baqā'*, which takes place after death, does not entail a total loss of individuality.'[168] The second edition of the *Encyclopaedia of Islam* suggests that the terms *baqā'* and *fanā'* are 'partly antithetical and partly complementary'.[169] Sufis of most persuasions, 'sober' and (mystically) 'intoxicated', 'have usually categorically denied both the incarnation of God in man and the total mergence of the individual and finite human ego in God'.[170] Just as *fanā'* is quite different from Indian religions' concept of *nirvana*,[171] so *baqā'* is not to be associated with either incarnationism or monism.[172] And F. Rahman is at pains to stress that it is the prophet in Islam, whom he characterises as 'the mystic par excellence', who is best able to participate in this quality of *baqā'*, since the prophet's function is 'to be constantly both with God and with the world, to transmute the course of history through the implementation of the religio-moral divine Truth'.[173]

Normally, the sublime level of *baqā'* will not be attained *until the next life*; but here Rahman seems to indicate that those rare paragons of virtue, the Islamic prophets, may actually be partakers of that transcendent state in this world. Here, we seem to have an interpretation of *baqā'* or 'union' which appears to parallel the states of bliss occasionally achievable in contemplation by some Christian mystics and referred to in *The Cloud of Unknowing*, as we have seen. But it goes beyond the occasional sweetness of spiritual consolation, as articulated in *The Cloud*, since, if I have understood Rahman correctly, the Islamic prophet achieves *baqā'* with message, mission and Divine goal. And the *fruits of baqā'*, *most notably in terms of Divine revelation*, are thus, potentially, for all *on this earth* and not just the individual, isolated, Islamic mystic, in a future life.

Elsewhere, I have drawn attention to what the Persian author 'Alī b. 'Uthmān al-Jullābī al-Hujwīrī (died c. AD 1075) wrote on the subject in his famous *Kashf al-Maḥjūb (The Disclosure of the Concealed)*. His words bear repetition: 'Seeing is of two kinds: he who looks at anything sees it either with the eye of subsistence (*baqá*) or with the eye of annihilation (*faná*). If with the eye of subsistence, he perceives that the whole universe is imperfect in comparison with his own subsistence.'[174]

Abū Bakr al-Kalābādhī (died AD 990 or 995)[175] put it this way: 'Persistence [*al-baqā'*] which follows passing away [*al-fanā'*], means that the mystic passes away from what belongs to himself, and persists through what is God's'.[176]

In all these different ways, then, sufis at different times articulated in different places their understanding of such terms as *baqā'* and 'union'. Sometimes, in doing so, they travelled a parallel path to that portrayed in *The Cloud*, and at other times they diverged from *The Cloud* paradigm quite markedly. The succinct summary of the matter in the words of Javad Nurbakhsh, late master of the Niʿmatullāhiyya *ṭarīqa* in the UK, are instructive; his words not only apply to his own sufi order but also encapsulate the essential message of *The Cloud*, as well as neatly articulating our journey theme: 'Baqa is the beginning of the "journey in God" … Here, God neither veils the creation, nor does the creation veil God.'[177]

2.2.2 The Clouded Soul: The Dark Night of Juan de la Cruz

San Juan de la Cruz (AD 1542–91), or St John of the Cross as he is universally known in English, was born in the small town of Fontiveros, which was situated about mid-way between the major cities of Salamanca and Ávila.[178] His birth name was Juan de Yepes y Álvarez[179] but such were the vicissitudes of his life, ranging from deep friendships to deep imprisonment, that, with the eye of hindsight, he could just as well have been named Joseph after the hero of the narrative in Genesis.[180] For Juan was at times the victim of profound jealousies and much anger.

Alex Kurian reminds us that a huge amount of recent scholarship has been produced on John from a whole variety of perspectives, enabling us to know the man in a way that was not possible before; and Kurian situates him in a 'mystic' Spain, a land which was itself a producer of great mystics.[181] More specifically, of course, as Kathleen Jones notes, Juan lived out his mystic life in parallel with the life and reign (AD 1556–98) of King Philip II of Spain.[182] Of Spain under this Philip, Fernand Braudel (died 1985), the doyen of the *Annales* historians in France, wrote:

> The grandiose ambitions of Carlos I/Charles V [of Spain, *reg.* 1516–56] were doomed by the beginning of Philip's reign … Little by little, the powerful movement towards Catholic reform … was gathering strength and becoming established … it exploded violently in opposition to the Protestant North in the 1580s. It was this movement which pushed Spain into the great struggles of the end of Philip's reign and turned the Spanish king into the champion of Catholicism, the defender of the faith.[183]

In his magisterial *Europe: A History*, Norman Davies provides a fascinating vignette of the Spanish monarch. He draws attention to Philip's deskbound nature in the Escorial Palace, his austerity, tirelessness and his love of penances resulting in a spiritual and regnal 'control freak' whose desire for uniformity was entirely undermined by the variety of empire.[184] The Inquisition indulged in an orgy of *autos-da-fé*; the Armada was defeated in 1588, and 1596 saw Philip II 'formally bankrupt' yet again.[185]

In such a world, it was wise to be careful about the religious beliefs which one held and how they were articulated. For the movement of what is known to religious history as the Counter-Reformation was the backdrop both to the long reign of Philip II of Spain and to Spain's greatest mystic, Juan de la Cruz.

There was another factor as well which threatened the interior spiritual life of any would-be mystic in the Peninsula of Philip II and cast a potential shadow over the reforms of Juan de la Cruz and his co-worker and reformer, Teresa of Ávila. Many theologians, and those in high places in the Church, had become suspicious of 'the tendency to interior prayer', of which Luther was deemed to be a prime exemplar.[186] All mysticism and mystical impulses, not to mention 'visions and raptures', were therefore held to require suppression lest 'the ruin that the Gnostics had begun' was completed.[187] Such people were characterised as *Alumbrados* and *Illuminati*;[188] and, as Juan found to his cost, any suspected of being such were liable to be delated to the Inquisition.[189] The *Alumbrados*, Gerald Brenan tells us, practised two kinds of mystical prayer: *recogimiento* (recollection), which ultimately led to 'the Prayer of Union', and *dejamiento* (letting go), where the passive soul undertook a total surrender 'to the love of God'.[190] All such activities incurred the displeasure of the Inquisition, since they constituted a threat to the strict control which the Church endeavoured to exercise over the faithful in a milieu which was perceived to be gravely threatened by the rise of Lutheranism.[191] For 'Illumination' and the emphasis on experience were regarded as a real threat by a Church already unsettled by the Protestant Reformers.[192] Accusations of adhering to the Quietist heresy, associated with *dejamiento*, were ones from which even Teresa of Ávila was not immune.[193]

In AD 1563, Juan entered the Carmelite novitiate of the Priory of Santa Ana in Medina del Campo, and in 1564 he was professed in the Order, taking the religious name of Brother (Fray) Juan de San Matías.[194] A three-year course at the University of Salamanca followed. Gerald Brenan tells us that, by this time, the university had achieved great fame, being known for its dynamism and the academic disputations between the teachers there.[195] And, given the omnipresent nature of the Inquisition, such disputatiousness could be dangerous![196] Juan's own final-year dissertation consisted of a comparison between contemporary modes of prayer among the illuminists and the earlier ascetic-mystical tradition of the Patristic age.[197] Indeed, it seems that the greatest academic influence on Juan from the official university curriculum at this time was the stress on Biblical and Patristic studies.[198]

And then, soon after ordination in AD 1567, Juan met Teresa de Jesús, who is known universally in the West as Teresa of Ávila (AD 1515–82) in Medina del Campo. This great reforming mystic had arrived there to continue her discalced reform of the Carmelite Order with another convent.[199] This was, indeed, an event of huge significance in the life and work of Juan.[200] Abandoning ideas of transferring to the Carthusian Order, Juan was persuaded by this persistent and tempestuous but saintly nun, twenty-seven years older than himself, to join the Carmelite Reform.[201]

Dicken speculates that the years which followed this encounter must be the most fruitful for all authors who would analyse their spiritual development in view of their lengthy and close proximity.[202] Despite the age gap, Juan would address Teresa as *hija* (daughter), and Teresa would call Juan *mi padre* (my father).[203] It has been suggested that, in terms of spirituality, Juan was the real teacher and Teresa was the actual disciple in the early years of their acquaintance.[204]

It is not the purpose of this section of this book to trace their continued reforming careers together, nor to survey every aspect of their individual lives. Such details are extremely well known and documented in numerous texts elsewhere. Our purpose, in these introductory passages, is to introduce these two great mystical reformers, stress their initial physical and spiritual encounters and then adumbrate Juan's life insofar as it was the vital backcloth against which he developed his doctrine of 'the Dark Night of the Soul'. It is true, however, that the spirituality must be contextualised; hence our earlier references to the *Illuminati* and the shadow of the Inquisition, not to mention the Counter-Reformation. Reform and counter-reform were in the air; heresy seemed to be everywhere; and the mystical impulse could be physically dangerous for those who articulated it in a way which the Inquisition, labouring against the *Illuminati* and the Quietists, might find disagreeable!

What Juan's career illustrates is that his spiritual development was mirrored very often in his 'life's journey': there was very much a 'dark night of the body' as well as the soul, if we pause to reflect upon the vicissitudes of a most turbulent and often upsetting career. From September 1572, for five and a half years, he was the confessor at the Carmelite Convent of the Encarnación in Ávila, a Calced convent where Teresa was prioress for the first eight months of his stay.[205] Brenan considers this to have been 'a period of growth and preparation'.[206] However, the Carmelite Friars of the Ancient Observance, the Calced, became extremely apprehensive about the reform by the Discalced wing of the Order, and events conspired to give them the upper hand at various times: Juan's life was plunged into a maelstrom of kidnappings, arrests, imprisonments and escapes.[207] Emilie Griffin writes of the period of Juan's imprisonment in Toledo in 1577 as follows: 'John was confined to a room measuring six by ten feet. He was severely flogged, fed a diet of bread and water, and held in solitary, common punishments of the time. He was asked to renounce the Teresian way of life, which he refused to do. This time of imprisonment was for John a "dark night".'[208]

Further vicissitudes abounded: the first General-Chapter of the Reformed Carmelites met in Madrid in June 1588 against the historically dramatic backdrop of the preparations for the sailing of the Spanish Armada, which was about to attack England.[209] Juan was appointed the premier of the four definitors and also gained a place on the *consulta* as a councillor, of whom there were six in all.[210] In August 1588, he became prior of the Discalced Carmelite house in Segovia.[211] Brenan suggests that his three years here 'brought him to some new peak of his spiritual ascension'.[212]

Yet it was not to last. None of the primacy in hierarchy that he had painfully achieved within his own reformed Order was allowed to remain. After three years, the General-Chapter of the Order, held in Madrid in June 1591, stripped him of the offices of definitor, member of the *consulta* and the priorship of Segovia.[213] Ill health overtook the mystic and he died on 14 December 1591.[214] *Post mortem*, his sanctity was immediately recognised by huge crowds who fought for *pieces* of his body and clothing.[215] The mountain, whose ascent he had described in one of his most famous mystical texts, *The Ascent of Mount Carmel*, had been conquered; purification and union had been mystically achieved in 'that high state of perfection we here call union of a soul with God'.[216]

The similarities between the mystical theology of *The Cloud of Unknowing* and John's own spirituality and mystical theology have certainly not gone unnoticed.

William Johnston, for example, refers to the *Cloud* author's 'striking similarity to St John of the Cross'.[217] He notes that the *Cloud* author has been characterised 'as a St John of the Cross two centuries before his time' and suggests, perhaps slightly exaggeratedly as we shall see, 'that almost every detail of his doctrine is paralleled in the later Spanish mystic'.[218]

It is, of course, true that there are similarities; but there are differences as well. What must be stressed immediately, as Johnston does, is that both the *Cloud* author and Juan de la Cruz are heirs to, and joyful participants in, a great apophatic tradition,[219] at the heart of which lies Pseudo-Dionysius.[220] J. P. H. Clark concurs; his conclusion is that 'the points of similarity between the *Cloud*, [Walter] Hilton and St John of the Cross are best understood as springing from a comparable experience interpreted in the light of a common tradition of contemplative spirituality ... [where] (for the *Cloud* and St John of the Cross) Pseudo-Dionysius [is] understood in the Latin tradition'.[221]

Constantino S. Nieva, while acknowledging, like so many scholars before and after him, that there are obvious similarities between the works of the *Cloud* author and Juan from a pedagogical and metaphorical perspective, emphasises that there is still no direct proof that Juan ever read *The Cloud of Unknowing*.[222] Thus these similarities should not lead us to suppose that they are necessarily 'using the same categories or describing the same states in the ascent to God'.[223]

It is true, for example, that both texts may stress a desire for 'aloneness',[224] exhibit a Dionysian apophaticism,[225] alert the would-be mystic to the dangers of 'knowledge and memory',[226] and offer a possibly necessary purgation;[227] it is true that both texts may counsel extreme caution in revealing 'the presence of interior experiences',[228] and urge that the spiritual journey be cloaked in 'darkness and concealment'.[229]

But there are profound differences in the articulation of the journey as well: Juan de la Cruz identifies *two* nights, the night of the sense and the night of the spirit, whereas the *Cloud* author does not make this kind of radical distinction; his words are equally applicable to senses and spirit and their gradual cleansing.[230] Johnston suggests that the *Cloud* theology of forgetting, in the sense of 'the rejection of attachment to all creatures', already encapsulates neatly the strict ascetical syllabus of John's *Ascent of Mount Carmel* without any twofold division of 'nights'.[231] For Johnston, the English author's 'alling and noughting'[232] is the obvious, but simpler, ancestor and counterpart of John's '*todo y nada*'.[233] There is a similar 'telescoping of the two nights' in *The Cloud* to be perceived with regard to 'passive purification',[234] and it is clear that, generally, the *Cloud* author has a rather simpler mystical theology than that espoused by Juan de la Cruz.[235]

So, what *is* this 'dark night' to which we have so frequently alluded?

At the heart of John of the Cross's mystical theology of the Dark Night is his sublime Spanish poem, whose first line is *En una noche oscura*.[236] This has been variously rendered as 'On a dark night',[237] 'On a night of darkness'[238] and 'Upon a gloomy night'.[239] The 'real' title, however, is rather longer and runs as follows: *Canciones del alma que se goza de haber llegado al alto estado de la perfección, que es la unión con Dios, por el camino de la negación spiritual*.[240] Roy Campbell translates this title as follows: 'Songs of the soul in rapture at having arrived at the height of perfection, which is union with God by the road of spiritual negation'.[241]

Clark accurately characterises the whole poem as a 'love-poem' and reminds us that two of the key prose works of Juan's *oeuvre*, the *Noche Oscura*[242] (*The Dark Night of the Soul*)[243] and the *Subida del Monte Carmelo*[244] (*Ascent of Mount Carmel*),[245] are in fact commentaries – albeit incomplete[246] – on this poem.[247] And, while there have been many commentaries on *En una noche oscura*,[248] perhaps none is as vivid and dynamic as the poet's own.

Margaret Wilson underlines the fact that diverse critics have identified Juan's night symbolism as the real essence of the poem.[249] It is, indeed, an extremely evocative symbol, with the motif of darkness entirely suffusing the initial three verses, and then, as Wilson shows, with the night metamorphosing from *oscura* [dark] to *dichosa* [happy, lucky] into *amable* [dear, kind, desirable] at the heart of the poem. As she puts it, night becomes 'fully personified as the entity which has actively guided the lovers to their meeting. *Night is much more than an indifferent setting, it is the essential catalyst for the union*.'[250]

The poem functions on two levels: on the literal plane, it portrays a girl creeping out of her silent house one dark night, with a heart filled with love. No one observes her, and her only light and guide is the love which burns within her. Yet the night, too, is a faithful guide, and leads and joins her to the beloved. In the sublime encounter with the beloved, all care ceases.[251] Thus we move through the dark night from the images of the first stanza,

En una noche oscura
Con ansias en amores inflamada,
Oh dichosa ventura!
Salí sin ser notada,
Estando ya mi casa sosegada,[252]

whose sublime cadences have been translated in an almost exultant fashion by Roy Campbell,[253] to

Oh noche que juntaste
Amado con amada
Amada en el Amado transformada![254]

which portrays the night joining the lovers in an ecstasy in which they are transformed into each other.[255]

On the spiritual and mystical plane, of course, the 'dark night' or *noche oscura* is a metaphor for that 'night of the senses' in which external impressions are lost.[256] That all-embracing, circumambient darkness is to be feared, but the soul is able to progress by the light of love which burns within its core and, thus, ultimately, face the dark, which becomes a friend[257] and a guide and leads the soul to the Divine Beloved. On the literal plane, as Margaret Wilson powerfully puts it, 'male and female become one, the soul is transformed into the very substance of God'.[258]

As we have already noted, Juan de la Cruz's own commentaries (incomplete though they be) on this most mystical and majestic of poems, rightly and vividly compared to the *Song of Songs*,[259] are enshrined in two treatises which contain the essence of his thinking in his Dark Night doctrine. They are *The Ascent of Mount Carmel* and *The Dark Night of the Soul*. While having features in common with *The Cloud of Unknowing*, as we have seen, each is much more complex than that earlier English mystical work, though all three breathe the air of the apophatic tradition.[260] We will refer to each of Juan's two treatises briefly in what follows, but our primary reference will be to *The Dark Night of the Soul*.

The structure, doctrine and stages of spiritual progress in *The Ascent* and *The Dark Night* have been treated at length by other scholars, most notably in recent times by E. W. Trueman Dicken;[261] they will not be repeated here in full. Suffice it to stress here, with E. Allison Peers, that the principles which underlie Juan's apophatic mystical theology are to be found in the very first section of *The Ascent*.[262] Peers draws our attention to the twofold division of the latter, where the respective focus is on the 'Active' night and the 'Passive' night. The Active Night receives a further division into the Night of the Sense and the Night of the Spirit. The Passive Night is similarly divided. Peers continues: 'One book is devoted to the Active Night of Sense; two are needed for the Active Night of the Spirit'. But Juan's text remains unfinished: night does not give way to day as the author 'certainly intended to do', and a description of the full symbolism of the Passive Night is absent.[263]

Structurally, its sister treatise and commentary, *The Dark Night*,[264] is somewhat shorter than *The Ascent*, though it represents a continuation of many of *The Ascent*'s principal themes.[265] John Newton neatly summarises the content of *The Dark Night* and compares it with *The Ascent*, which he places, chronologically, as anterior[266] to *The Dark Night of the Soul* treatise:

> In his earlier work he described the active night – first describing the night of sense and then the night of spirit – showing how the individual can deny and purify his or her soul, with the aid of God's ordinary grace, in such a way as to prepare his or her senses and faculties for union with God. In the *Dark Night of the Soul* St John describes the passive night – and again first describes the night of sense and then the night of spirit. Here he tells how those same senses are purged and purified by God in order to the same end, that of spiritual union with the Lord.[267]

After that outline of the key structures and content of these two seminal treatises, we will now examine the text of *The Dark Night*, with some reference also to *The Ascent*, in order to identify, extract and discuss briefly the seven major *topoi* which we detected earlier in *The Cloud*. They were *Cloud*, *Self-abnegation*, *Contemplation*, *The Dark Night*, *Perfection*, *Human and Divine Love*, and *Union*.

Cloud

As will be apparent by now, the 'cloud' imagery of *The Cloud of Unknowing* is transmuted into the 'night' imagery of Juan. This is his preferred image, as diverse authors have testified. E. Allison Peers emphasises its ubiquity in both his prose and his poetry.[268] Colin P. Thompson identifies the 'dark night' as Juan's 'most famous symbol',[269] while for Elizabeth Teresa Howe the originality of his night imagery represents the symbol *par excellence* of his mysticism,[270] on a par with the water images beloved by his co-worker Santa Teresa de Jesús of Ávila.[271] However, San Juan does not eschew the image of the 'cloud' completely. William Johnston draws attention[272] to the following lines in *The Dark Night*: 'A dense and heavy cloud overshadows the soul, distresses it and holds it as if it were far away from God. This is the darkness in which the soul says that it travels in safety'.[273] And, in the same chapter, the author pursues this 'cloud' imagery, stressing this idea that safety is to be found in the darkness, for God is the Guide:[274]

> This is the reason why David said that God made darkness His hiding-place and covert, His tabernacle around Him, dark water in the clouds of the air.[275] *The dark water in the clouds of the air is the dim contemplation and divine wisdom in souls*...when God brings them nearer to Himself.[276]

Such 'cloud' imagery is immensely resonant of that to be found in *The Cloud of Unknowing*, which we considered and analysed earlier. And the 'water' image reflects and resonates with a classic Teresian motif.[277]

Self-abnegation

In our consideration of *The Cloud of* Unknowing, we have already examined this concept, whose essence implies 'denial; renunciation ... self-sacrifice'[278] and self-denial, and whose extreme form in the shape of *fanā'* was articulated by the sufi mystics. Indeed, the whole idea of renouncing oneself for the sake of God is a commonplace in both the Western and Eastern mystical traditions[279] and could incorporate and reflect a Platonic suspicion of the human body.[280] But Colin Thompson emphasises that, for San Juan, it was not only the body that had to be negated, but a purgation of the soul was required as well: the Night of the Spirit was the logical completion of the Night of the Senses.[281] Juan taught that the security which only God can give is bound up with self-mortification.[282] And mortification is the product of spiritual sobriety and temperance: '*La sobriedad y templanza spiritual lleva otro temple muy diferente de mortificación* ...' [283]

The Dark Night emphasises that a certain moderation is to be observed, coupled with obedience, in order to avoid the dangers of 'spiritual gluttony' (*la gula spiritual*): for many beginners on the spiritual path are so exhausted by the sweetness of the Divine consolations which they are initially granted that they indulge in bodily mortifications well beyond what is reasonable, and even endanger their own lives as a result.[284] For Juan, asceticism, properly understood and undertaken in a spirit of humility and moderation, means that one empties oneself of everything that is not God and applies a Divinely inspired *nada* (nothing) to the whole of one's life.[285] To apply a Greek term, it is thus a complete physical and spiritual *kénōsis*, emptying of the self; and here the close affinities to Arabic *fanā'* will be apparent. John's *nada*, Greek *kénōsis* and Arabic mystical *fanā'* can all imply, or have at their root, the obliteration of the ego, the Arabic *nafs*. Alex Kurian draws attention to the danger of becoming a slave to the whims and dictates of the ego; only a profound love of God and resisting the demands of the ego can make one free.[286]

This whole theme of self-abnegation and obliteration of the ego is powerfully adumbrated by San Juan in *The Dark Night*: understanding, mind, intellect (*el entendimiento*), will (*la voluntad*) and memory (*la memoria*) require purification with regard to earthly perceptions, affections, speeches and information; indeed, the very soul must undergo annihilation concerning all these things in fulfilment of Psalm 72:22: *Fui yo aniquilado y no supe*.[287] The Psalmist's words may be translated as: 'I am brought to nothing, and I knew not'[288] or, in an alternative rendering, 'I was all dumbness, I was all ignorance'.[289] Pursuing the theme of 'annihilation', and using the same Spanish verb *aniquilar*, meaning 'to destroy' or 'to annihilate', San Juan stresses that the degree of darkening, emptying and annihilation of the soul with regard to *sus aprensiones y afecciones particulares* (its apprehensions and particular affections), whether they be celestial or terrestrial, is in direct proportion to the greater or lesser purity and simplicity of the Divine light (*divina luz*) as it strikes the soul.[290] It is, of course, what might be characterised as the stubborn 'artefacts of the ego' that are to be annihilated, not the immortal soul itself.

It may be emphasised that Juan de la Cruz was by no means the first to write in detail about self-abnegation.[291] But one of his distinctive merits was to provide a rationale for the syllabus of perfection which he outlined, and also to show that the many who think that, as a result of their bodily renunciations and mortifications, they have already won the longed-for union with the Divine are still a long way short of that sublime goal.[292] Juan's own underlying *leitmotiv* is summed up in the following: 'So many are detached from so much, yet ... they still retain subtle attachments; whereas if they want the All – *todo* – which is God, they must be attached to nothing – *nada*'.[293] Juan's great kenotic lesson with regard to self-abnegation is that *nada* yields *todo*!

Contemplation

Mortification, or self-abnegation leading to extinction of the ego (which the Arabic tradition knew as *fanā'*), is thus seen to be one of the most obvious keys to Divine union in the mystical theology of San Juan. Another is contemplation.

E. W. Trueman Dicken draws attention to the 'unusual' nature of contemplation even if 'it represents the true norm'.[294] What are regarded as '*extra ordinem*' by the Carmelite saints are 'trances, visions, raptures ... levitation, clairvoyance and miracles'.[295] All these, of course, are known to the historian of Eastern and Western mysticism; but, as Dicken stresses, Teresa and Juan did not regard such extraordinary occurrences as vital in the attempt to follow the path of spiritual perfection.[296] And, as Juan insists in *The Dark Night* commentary, there is a purpose to the 'ordinary' contemplative mode of perfection:

> *Esta noche oscura es una influencia de Dios en el alma, que la purga de sus ignorancias e imperfecciones habituales, naturales y espirituales, que llaman los contemplativos contemplación infusa o mística teología, en que de secreto enseña Dios al alma y la instruye en perfección de amor, sin ella hacer nada ni entender cómo.*[297]

> The dark night is a certain inflowing of God into the soul which cleanses it of its ignorances and imperfections, habitual, natural and spiritual. Contemplatives call it infused contemplation, or mystical theology, whereby God

> secretly teaches the soul and instructs it in the perfection of love, without efforts on its own part.[298]

Here, an equation is made between the dark night itself and contemplation in a manner reminiscent of the gnostic knowledge (*ma'rifa*) beloved of the sufi mystics. Elaborating on the phrase in the *Dark Night* poem, in the second stanza, *por la secreta escala, disfrazada*[299] ('By the secret ladder disguised'),[300] Juan characterises contemplation as 'a secret ladder', that is, 'to the union of love' (*a la unión de amor, secreta escala*)[301] and 'secret wisdom' (*sabiduría secreta*).[302]

And, if this sounds difficult and painful for the beginner and would-be aspirant to the mystical path, Juan acknowledges that it is! The unprepared soul, with all its weaknesses and imperfections, is unfitting for the reception of the light of contemplation:[303] the soul is simply not ready for such Divine sweetness, wisdom and light. Transformation, and the desire for such transformation, can be incredibly painful psychologically, and Juan's basic theme here is that 'God is an inflowing God; and his inflow transforms'.[304]

At the end of his magisterial volume, *The Crucible of Love: A Study of the Mysticism of St Teresa of Jesus and St John of the Cross*, E. W. Trueman Dicken devotes an entire concluding chapter to the question 'Is Contemplation for All?' [305] San Juan was a realist as well as a mystic, and he readily acknowledges that contemplation is certainly not within the capacity and reach of all: not even 50 per cent of those who undergo spiritual trials achieve the state of 'perfect contemplation', and the reasons are only known to God.[306] Ultimately, contemplation is a Divinely infused gift,[307] and not all are happy to welcome that gift or even acknowledge its Christian orientation. Colin Thompson, for example, cites the theologian Karl Barth (1886–1968) as holding that we should not think of contemplation as something that is unique to the Christian tradition, since it is common to the mystical articulation of other world religions as well.[308] It is certainly true that contemplative techniques, of one kind or another, and related meditative techniques, are to be found in a wide range of world religions, including Buddhism,[309] Judaism[310] and, of course, Islam. It is instructive to compare Juan's 'contemplation' with *jhana*, a Pali word which, for the Buddhist, represents 'a state of serene contemplation attained by serene meditation. Eight states of *jhāna* are recognized, but only in the highest is utter elimination of [the] idea of "self" attained, and the complete union with Reality (*Samādhi*) experienced.'[311]

The Dark Night

We now come to a consideration of 'the Dark Night' itself in Juan's writings. We have already made much allusion to this mystical phenomenon in what has preceded. Here we will focus, briefly and mainly, on its structure and significance, for we have already surveyed and analysed much of its basic nature.

Contemporary scholarship is fond of endowing Juan with several metaphysical 'doctorates'! For example, he is 'the Doctor of the *Nada*';[312] he is a '*Doctor de Todo*';[313] above all, however, we may stress with the anonymous Benedictine author of Stanbrook Abbey that San Juan is 'the Doctor of the Night'.[314]

J. P. H. Clark and Marie M. Gaudreau draw our attention to the way in which Juan plays numerically with the motif of 'night'; but they both highlight a passage in which a 'tripartite night' is, in fact, to be conceived as a single night:[315] the night of the senses resembles the start of night, when it becomes difficult to see things; the night of faith is like midnight, when one is wrapped in absolute darkness; and the night of God is like the end part of the night, which is close to daylight.[316] Here, we have the classic Juanian Night of the Senses and Night of the Spirit[317] set within a tripartite structure. As Gaudreau demonstrates, the various structures and formulations of the motif of night can become quite complex, since both the *Subida* (*Ascent*) and the *Noche* also talk about active and passive nights![318] And Clark points out that, while chapter 1 of the *Subida* concerns itself with 'the (active) night of the senses', and the following two chapters discuss 'the active night of the spirit', the treatment of the passive night for both the spirit and the senses was never undertaken in the *Subida*: 'Instead, breaking the logical structure of the *Ascent*, a digression on the passive night in both sensory and spiritual aspects is described in the *Dark Night* …'[319]

Other scholars have delved more deeply into Juan's structures of the *noche*,[320] and I do not propose here to examine further the diverse complexities of Juan's motif and doctrinal structure of the *noche*; suffice it to say that there are two broad nights: *the Dark Night of the Senses* and *the Dark Night of the Spirit*. 'When the first night is passed, there usually follows a long time in the Illuminative Way.'[321] It is, however, useful to note Gaudreau's diagrammatic illustration of 'The Tripartite Night of St John of the Cross'. This shows a '*Terminus a quo* (Base of the Mountain)' and a '*Terminus ad quem* (Image Goal)'. The three parts of the *Noche* are respectively characterised as 'Denial of Sensual Desires (= Purgative Way)', 'Faith (= Illuminative Way)', and 'God (= Unitive Way)'.[322]

E. Allison Peers, a former Gilmour Professor of Spanish in the University of Liverpool and one of the twentieth century's most distinguished commentators on San Juan de la Cruz, was clearly moved throughout a long life of studying the thought and doctrines of San Juan. He vaunts the saint's deep psychological acumen displayed in the *Dark Night*,[323] admires the realism in Juan's detailed portrait of the Dark Night of the Senses,[324] and concludes that Juan remains unsurpassed in the vigorous and lively way in which he has presented the Night of the Spirit.[325] The vocabulary is vivid and rich in the extreme as the soul progresses through the various nights, embracing a range of 'hunger, thirst, wound, pain, touch and light'.[326]

In a powerful essay, Ronald Rolheiser, a Canadian Oblate priest, has provided a contemporary interpretation of Juan's *Dark Night*.[327] He argues that the dark night of the soul about which Juan talks so much may be considered in a metaphorical sense as 'paschal transformation'.[328] For him, Juan's dark night represents a purgative and purificatory way whereby the aspirant's life is metamorphosed into another: 'Natural life becomes eschatological life, earthly life becomes eternal life'.[329] For Rolheiser, the Dark Night is not just something primarily rooted in prayer but a transformational 'paschal' paradigm which can affect one's whole life. It reflects a movement from Good Friday's death on the cross to the resurrection on Easter Sunday.[330] Thus, Rolheiser perceives the dark night as best articulated in terms of '*transformation*', a transformation of 'love and service to others' and not just a part of one's prayer life as with Juan.[331]

He extrapolates a paradigm of transformation from Juan's writings which develops as follows:

> 'Pre-Conversion ("Indifference")' > 'Conversion ("Falling in Love" – "The active night of the senses")' > 'First Fervour ("The honeymoon" – "The active night of the senses come to full bloom")' > 'Waning of Fervour ("The death of the honeymoon" – The passive night of the senses)' > 'Proficiency ("The growth of easefulness")' > 'The Final Stage of Growth Towards Transformation ("The Purification of One's Guidance System" – The dark night of the spirit)'.[332]

Rolheiser thus identifies these as six stages in what he characterises as 'paschal transformation', constituting a Juanian/Rolheiser paradigm which reflects the well-known saying of Jesus in the New Testament that new life emerges from the 'dead' grain of wheat in the ground.[333] San Juan de la Cruz focuses on purification via a terror-strewn path through the Dark Nights of Senses and Spirit; Rolheiser extrapolates a paradigm, based on Juan, but which focuses on renewal and transformation as it might affect every area of life and not just the interior life of prayer.

Perfection

The Dark Nights of Juan are, of course, a means to an end, that end being union with God Himself. The Dark Nights are Juan's preferred pathways towards this and the actualisation of the perfection necessary for that sublime encounter. The *Noche Oscura* identifies three states: that of beginners (*estado de principiantes*), that of 'proficients' (*los aprovechantes*) and that of the perfect (*los perfectos*):[334] the latter state is characterised by Juan as that of the soul when it has finally achieved Divine union with the Deity (*la divina unión del alma con Dios*).[335] We shall develop this ultimate theme of Divine Union in a short while; our concentration here is on the related theme of 'perfection'.

In one place, Juan describes 'the path of perfection' (*el camino de perfección*) as the denial of one's own will and one's own pleasure for the sake of God (*la negación de su voluntad y gusto por Dios*).[336] Of course, this is much easier said than done, and human imperfections require 'the passive purgation of the dark night' (*la pasiva purgación de aquella oscura noche*), undertaken by God, in order to become fitted 'for the divine union of perfection in the love of God' (*para la divina unión de perfección de amor*).[337] The path of perfection is thus the path of night, indeed, many nights, of varying degrees of spiritual purification and terror, as the words of Juan, especially in the *Noche* and the *Subida*, amply demonstrate. And Juan is at pains to stress that the perfection of Divine union *must* be preceded necessarily by purgation and purification.[338] That purgation is otherwise envisaged by Juan in all his work as a *necessary* spiritual night.[339] Its end product is that 'divine union of perfection' to which we have referred.

Human and Divine Love

As we have seen, perfect Divine union is bound up ineluctably with love of God and God's love.[340] The *Noche Oscura* does stress the difference between human and Divine love,[341] although we note that Colin Thompson suggests that there is no real difference 'in kind' between the two types of love, since both love the Holy Spirit.[342] He suggests that this is the view of San Juan. While one can see what he means, a close reading of the *Noche Oscura* suggests that, qualitatively, there is always a huge gulf between the sublime and eternal love of God for man and man's feeble and imperfect love for God.

The truly passionate, but painful, love of God which the mystic spirit desires to be enkindled within his or her soul is born of the Dark Night. Commenting on the second line of the first verse of Juan's famous *Dark Night* poem (*Con ansias en amores inflamada*: 'With anxious love inflamed'),[343] Juan observes: 'In this love the soul speaks of the fire of love ... which, in the night of painful contemplation, seizes upon it as material fire on the fuel it burns'.[344] The dark night, bitter as it is to endure, purifies the soul,[345] but there may be occasional sweetness resulting from the *oscura noche de contemplación* (dark night of contemplation).[346]

Intriguingly, a little further on, Juan identifies a 'ladder of secret contemplation' (*escala de contemplación secreta*)[347] and, pursuing a well-worn theme, stresses that 'contemplation is the science of love, which is an infused loving knowledge of God, and which enlightens the soul and at the same time kindles within it the fire of love ... for it is love only that unites the soul and God'.[348] It is to this theme of ultimate union with God that we shall shortly progress.

Following a popular scheme, wrongly and variously attributed to St Bernard of Clairvaux (AD 1090–1153) and St Thomas Aquinas (c. AD 1225–74),[349] Juan then outlines in two major chapters the ten steps on the mystical ladder of Divine love.[350] He concludes that, on achieving the heights of the tenth step, the soul becomes totally absorbed in God. As Zimmerman translates: 'The soul becomes wholly assimilated unto God in the beatific vision which it then immediately enjoys'.[351] And the perfect purification of love undergone by the soul, as it has laboured painfully up the mystic ladder, means that it is spared the pains of Purgatory.[352]

All the above may lead one to suppose, in John McGowan's words, that Juan truly embraced the myth which portrayed him as 'an unbalanced ascetic and a spiritual masochist, someone obsessed with the cross, suffering and the heavy parts of the gospel'.[353] But McGowan holds that this really is a myth: what Juan was fixated upon was consummation and union with the Divine Beloved, and he was genuinely impatient with all else that distracted him from that mystic goal.[354] Thus it is to that key Juanian motif of *union*, the last of our seven major *topoi* (whose presence we detected earlier in *The Cloud of Unknowing* as well), that we will now turn.

Union

We have already made frequent reference to this goal of union. What follows will, therefore, attempt to draw together some of these scattered threads. Primary keys to this state of bliss thus far identified include the two Nights as well as contemplation.

In chapter 5 of book 2 of the *Ascent*, Juan attempts a survey and definition of what it *means* for the soul to achieve union with God. Union for Juan implies the whole transformation of the soul before God, which results from the soul's coming in some ways to resemble God via the motor of love.[355] Indeed, wherever we turn in the *oeuvre* of San Juan, we return to his paramount *leitmotiv* of love. Diagrammatically, the paradigm of Juan which the saint wishes the would-be mystic to embrace may be illustrated as follows:

> Beginners/Meditation/Purgation > Proficients/Contemplation/Illumination > the Perfect/'Divine union with God' (*la divina unión del alma con Dios*).[356]

Colin Thompson emphasises that, in all his writings, Juan must have been aware of the classical divisions in contemporary mystical theology of 'the ways of purgation, illumination and union, for beginners [*principiantes*], proficients [*aprovechantes*] and the perfect [*los perfectos*]'.[357] In both the *Ascent* and the *Dark Night* treatises, Juan uses these divisions to extremely powerful effect as he surveys the difficult rocky journey to Divine union, a mystical union whose Juanian term, *unión con Dios*, as Dicken points out, is directly synonymous with the idea of conformity with God's will.[358] With Dicken too, and most importantly, we may also stress here that, by this mystical term, Juan does not suggest that the very being of the soul's nature is changed.[359] In Juan's mystical doctrine, man never *becomes* God; the two remain totally distinct.[360] The union is primarily one of love.[361]

There is an intertextual resonance here with the sufi concept of *baqā'*, with its literal sense of 'remaining' or 'abiding' (in Allah), which, while not meaning exactly the same thing as Juan does by 'union', nonetheless has some useful parallels which are worth exploring briefly. Related to all this is the sufi concept of *qabḍ* or 'contraction'.

Terry Graham, significantly, has described Juan de la Cruz as 'heir to the mystical intensity of Sufi forebears'.[362] Margaret Wilson suggests that 'the Arabic origin, in whole or in part of [the words *almena*, ramparts, battlements, and *azucenas*, white lilies, towards the end of Juan's seminal *Noche Oscura* poem], gives them a certain exoticism'.[363] And Luce López-Baralt draws attention[364] to the way in which Asín Palacios emphasised the shared symbolism of the soul's dark night in the works of Juan de la Cruz and Muḥammad ibn Ibrāhīm 'Abbād al-Rundī (AD 1333–90).[365] R. P. Scheindlin characterises the mysticism of the latter – known more popularly as Ibn 'Abbād of Ronda (in Spain) – as 'non-ecstatic, stressing chastity, self-abnegation and *qabḍ*, the contraction of the soul'.[366] However, for Julian Baldick, Ibn 'Abbād should be characterised as an extreme reactionary who opposed the bolder articulations of sufi theory and who was more a preacher than an actual sufi.[367] Yet his influence on the development of Sufism, *pace* Baldick, seems to have been considerable.

Miguel Asín Palacios' (1871–1944) essential thesis is that much of the technical vocabulary of the great Carmelite masters like Juan de la Cruz has a sufi origin.[368] Ibn 'Abbād adhered to the Shādhilī sufi tradition, a major feature of whose ascetical theology concerned 'expansion' (*basṭ*) and 'contraction' (*qabḍ*). Asín Palacios explains that the former related to the spiritual joys that the soul might feel, while the latter was 'a state of anguish and desolation that overwhelms the soul with profound sadness and malaise'.[369] The soul's ascent begins with an awareness of sin, which inspires the soul to purgation and privation (*qabḍ*); some spiritual sweetness follows (*basṭ*), only to be followed again by a state of *qabḍ* once more. Only those who have reached a perfect state of 'transforming union' are exempted from the painful alternations of *qabḍ* and *basṭ*.[370]

The parallels with Juan's Dark Night doctrines are clear.[371] In Schimmel's succinct phrase: 'Ibn ʿAbbād, following his predecessors in the Path, compares the *qabḍ* to the night out of which great things will be born'.[372] Asín Palacios draws attention to Ibn ʿAbbād's citation of Abū 'l-Ḥasan al-Shādhilī (AD 1187–1258) as the originator of the comparison between night and day, and *qabḍ* and *basṭ*:[373]

> Abū 'l-Ḥasan says: 'Oppression [*qabḍ*] and expansion [*basṭ*] are two states that rarely fail to affect the servant of God. Both of them occur alternately in the soul like night and day ... Oppression appears to be more like night, as expansion appears to be more like day. If oppression comes to you without your knowing the cause, it means that you are obliged to be in quietness. The quietness must be in three things: in your words, your movements, and your volition. If you do this, very soon the night will disappear with the dawning of your day ... or of a moon to shed light on you ... *The moon is the moon of ecstatic union* ... But if you move in the midst of the darkness of night, rarely will you be free from downfall.'[374]

And God may reveal Himself in 'the night of desolation', teaching that which may not be taught 'in the splendour of the day of consolation'.[375]

A simple question remains: how does one explain the similarities between the work of Ibn ʿAbbād of Ronda and San Juan de la Cruz? Asín Palacios suggests a number of possibilities which include ruling out pure coincidence but acknowledging the possibility 'of imitation of a literary tradition' via Christian converts from Islam, or the *Illuminati*, and the additional possibility of 'cultural restitution' of an oriental Christian or apophatic Neoplatonic tradition.[376] It is impossible to be absolutely definitive on the matter; what is not in any doubt is that both Ibn ʿAbbād of Ronda and San Juan de la Cruz both worked within, and powerfully developed, a major mystical tradition which had a widespread impact on their own and succeeding generations.

In 3 Kings 19:19 and 4 Kings 2:3, Eliseus, Elijah's successor, is invested with, and takes up, the cloak and mantle of his master Elijah. But Eliseus is not to be reckoned the only recipient of Elijah's mantle. Juan de la Cruz, too, may be characterised in every sense as a 'New Elijah'. Whereas Elijah himself represents a pre-Christian paradigm of prophethood and witness, Juan represents the Christian paradigm.

- *Firstly*, both men are ineluctably bound up with Mount Carmel, the Old Testament prophet physically so, as attested in 3 Kings 18 with the prophets of Baal on Mount Carmel, and 'the New Testament prophet', Juan, metaphorically, in the reform of the Carmelite Order.
- *Secondly*, both men endure the 'dark night' not once but throughout their lives. We have surveyed in depth the *noche oscura* of Juan; here, our focus will be briefly upon the dark night of Elijah, that Old Testament paradigm of the

'Dark Night'. Firstly, Elijah withdraws to 'find a hiding-place in the valley of Kerith, that flows to meet the Jordan'.[377] There, he is told, the ravens will feed him, and his thirst will be quenched by the river. And Elijah does as God commands[378] and enters 'the dark night'. As Eileen Bailie reminds us, he is

> totally obedient ... Elijah is sent to a place of solitude, loneliness and abandonment, away from all activity and people ... Elijah meets a darkness linked to the presence of God who, while obviously present, remains hidden ... The wadi, although dark, retains a glimmer of light. It resembles the *dark night of sense* because in this darkness there is still some light – a feeling, still, of the presence of the hidden God. Elijah is made aware of God's presence when God sends the ravens to bring him meat and bread.[379]

Here is a vivid analogy with the 'spiritual consolations' occasionally encountered by the would-be mystic in some of the other mystical texts which we have examined. Later, after the defeat of the prophets of Baal on Mount Carmel, and in flight from the wrath of Jezebel,[380] Elijah has another major 'dark night' experience: as he reaches, in the wilds he has entered, a realisation of his own human frailties, his feelings of utter desolation, abandonment and destruction of all that he has striven for lead him into that *spiritual night* of which Juan was to speak so many centuries later.[381] Eileen Bailie confirms that this *is* his 'dark night of the spirit' and continues, evocatively: 'It is a terrifying darkness – an experience like that of the tomb or the cave. If anyone has ever been in a cave, they will know the depth of blackness. This is total abandonment. And at this stage, God has withdrawn – in order that love for him may grow.'[382]

These are powerful images which resonate intertextually with both *The Cloud* and *Noche Oscura*, as well as with our other multifarious images of caves and mountains to which we have earlier alluded. And, in their exegeses adumbrated above, both McCaffrey and Bailie show that Elijah constitutes a perfect proto-paradigm or precursor for Juan de la Cruz's doctrine of the *Night of the Senses* and *Night of the Spirit*. They are further linked by their lives' profound emphasis on 'justice, solidarity and mystical awareness'.[383]

- *Thirdly*, and finally, both Elijah and Juan may be characterised, from varying perspectives, as 'Green Men' of Carmel and thus linked to what we have surveyed earlier of the 'Green Man' motif. They are, of course, very different from the 'Green Men' of folklore, but they do have what I will term here *green theological affinities* to support these alleged 'green' credentials. Elijah is truly a man of the wilderness, whose character is forged and matured in that wilderness; in appearance he is 'a shaggy fellow ... with a skin girt about his loins'.[384] And in the *Noche Oscura*, 'green' is the symbol of hope: 'Over the white robe of faith the soul puts on forthwith that of the second colour, a green coat [*una almilla de verde*], emblem of the virtue of hope, by which it is delivered and protected from its second enemy, the world'.[385] Juan tells us that God is so pleased with this green robe that it is able to achieve everything that it hopes for from God.[386] One will recall that it was in the green garment of hope that the disguised soul initially ventured forth 'in this secret and dark night' (*por esta oscura y secreta noche*).[387] As Alex Kurian stresses, it is the virtue of hope, 'the green livery of hope', that allows advancement along Juan's difficult way of *nada*.[388] And Elijah is the archetypical prefiguration of the *nada*.

2.3 *Mountain Caves of Knowledge and Revelation*

It is clear from these discussions that certain mountains and caves have a special resonance in the Islamic and Christian mystical traditions. We are told that 'in iconography ... a cave denotes darkness, a place of non-redemption'.[389] But, as the same commentator shows, the cave is also the *locus* of mystical encounter: 'Elijah lodges in a cave on Mount Horeb, like Moses in earlier times; and both encounter the living God'.[390] The cave in which the Prophet Muḥammad hides during his famous *hijra* to Medina is, indeed, a cave of darkness and fear of a possible enemy encounter; but the cave on Mount Ḥirā', in which he encounters the angel Jibrīl, is transformed by the transmission of the Qur'ān from a dark place of solitude, of mere barren *tahannuth*,[391] to one of encounter, dramatic revelation and *da'wa* or mission. The darkness of Lazarus' cave burial is dispelled by the raising to life of Lazarus by Jesus.[392] Finally, for Juan de la Cruz, the cave can be the *locus* of Divine union, as he shows in his *Cantico Espiritual*.[393]

The mountains, too, share in this resonance and intertextuality. Their legacy is 'The Mendicant Rule' or 'Way of Life'. Biblically, they are 'places of divine revelation'.[394] Veronica Corner characterises them as 'symbolic of the ascent to the divinity'[395] – and this kind of imagery was certainly appreciated by San Juan de la Cruz, who, as we have noted, named an entire work *The Ascent of Mount Carmel* and diagrammatically and famously illustrated the 'Mount of Perfection' (*Monte de perfección*).[396]

Mount Carmel is sacred to three world religions: Judaism, Christianity and Islam.[397] From it ultimately sprang the Carmelite Rule via Albert di Vercelli (c. AD 1150–1214), the Patriarch of Jerusalem, a Rule approved with modifications by Pope Innocent IV in 1247.[398] This was the famous '*formula vitae* – "formula of life" or "rule of life" – [originally] written by Albert of Jerusalem between 1206 and 1214 ... based on the "propositum" or "proposal" of the hermits on Mount Carmel'.[399] It was written in the form of a medieval letter and is characterised by an extreme brevity, having (in 1999) only twenty-four paragraph-length chapters.[400]

Mount Ḥirā' has a more specific resonance for the Islamic tradition, being the initial *locus* of the Qur'ānic revelation,[401] the 'Rule of Islam'. By contrast, Sinai is sacred to all three monotheistic faiths: the journeys of both Moses and Elijah end 'in a final theophany or manifestation of God on the same mountain: Sinai, also called Horeb'.[402] In Judaism and Christianity, the mountain is always associated with the giving of the ten commandments.[403] But Mount Sinai has an extra significance for Islam: Moses is called by Allah from the right-hand side of Mount Sinai, called simply *al-Ṭūr* (the Mountain) in Q. 19:52, while in Q. 95:2 the mountain is invoked at the beginning of the *Sūra* by the name *Ṭūr Sīnīna* as one of the classical Qur'ānic oaths.[404]

The Old Testament paradigm of Sinai as a place of thunder, lightning, mist, fire and smoke[405] is replaced, for the Christian New Testament tradition at least, by the blazing light of the transfiguration of Jesus on Mount Tabor, in the company of Moses the lawgiver and Elijah, the 'Father of all Carmelites':[406] 'And he was transfigured in their presence, his face shining like the sun, and his garments becoming white as snow'.[407] The Mountain of Tabor, like several other mountains we have mentioned, has become a mountain of revelation, revelation of the hidden glory of God and the bliss of deceased prophets and saints like Moses and Elijah. Like the desert in Rabbinic literature, the mountain has become a place of freedom, wonder *and danger*![408]

There is another *possible locus*, a final 'cave' or, rather, castle this time, of human design, where our 'green' and chivalric hero (he of many intertextual links and names: Green Man > al-Khaḍir > Elijah > St George > Gawain) is revered – and that is St George's Chapel in Windsor Castle. Here, every year to this day, the celebrations of the Order of the Garter – that mysterious item of apparel whose origins we surveyed earlier – are held.[409] This is the medieval domain, the unlikely spiritual 'cavern' of our past and present 'Green Man'.

We have noted the legend of Herne the Hunter associated with the nearby Windsor Great Park. The green baldric of the *Sir Gawain* story may have become a blue garter.[410] But there is an essential element of 'mystic green' in all the characters of al-Khaḍir, Elijah, Gawain and the Islamic George. Indeed, St George has been characterised, Islamically, as 'a symbol of resurrection and renovation … [whose] festival marks the return of spring' and who is regarded as one who 'makes trees sprout and pillars bear flowers'.[411] Together with the possible identification or, at least, confusion, in Islam of al-Khaḍir and Elias with St George,[412] all this serves to create a composite, highly syncretic, legendary and multi-faceted figure whose far-flung domains reach, geographically, from the Meeting Place of the Two Seas (*Majma' al-Baḥrayn*) through Mount Carmel to the Green Chapel of *Sir Gawain* and St George's Chapel in Windsor Castle itself, and whose diverse incarnations have become the very bedrock of world folklore and Judaic, Christian and Islamic tradition. The 'chivalry' of a George and a Gawain coalesce in the dynamic spirituality of al-Khaḍir and Elijah to form a unique 'composite' being, a 'green hero' of myth and legend, both secular and spiritual. Jane Ackerman makes the links as follows:

> [Al-Khaḍir/al-Khiḍr is] … the green one who wears a green robe or perhaps sits on a green mat. As such, he entered Western iconography as the Green Man, whose verdant face often appears in the carvings on public buildings. While the color is universally associated with life, Muslims also connect it with surrender to God in response to God's revelation.[413]

Our final semiotic link or *leitmotiv* is the mountain, with or without a cave, as the spiritual *locus par excellence*: it is, variously, a site of revelation, inspiration, hope, fear and awe, whether it be Carmel, Sinai/Horeb, Tabor, Ḥirā' or, indeed, Zion itself.[414] Its lofty fruits of mystery, chivalry and Divine immanence are illuminated in the Green Chapel of Gawain and the Garter Chapel of St George at Windsor. And, as William Harrison Ainsworth reminds us in his novel, *Windsor Castle*, which we surveyed and analysed earlier, 'not only does Saint George's Chapel form a house of prayer and a temple of chivalry, but it is also the burial-place of kings'.[415]

CHAPTER

3

THE MYSTIC *TELOS*: CATAPHATIC AND ECSTATIC TRADITIONS

3.1 *Guidebooks to Paradise: A Traveller's Bookshelf Surveyed*

It is a wise precaution on the part of any traveller to consult the guide books written by those who have gone before. Those who omit to do so risk getting lost in well-mapped territory.[1]

With these words, E. W. Trueman Dicken begins chapter 5 ('Contemplation and Spiritual Progress') of his volume *The Crucible of Love*, which surveys and analyses the mystical thought of Juan de la Cruz and Teresa of Ávila. And, Dicken adds, only God can 'teach us to pray'.[2] As we have seen from both *The Cloud* and the *Noche Oscura*, the way is facilitated for the would-be mystic by that mental prayer known as contemplation,[3] generally regarded as the highest form of prayer. This is not for the beginner, however, but, rather a Divine gift[4] for the 'proficient', to use Juan's vocabulary. And, in so much of this type of mystical doctrine, the vocabulary of *the road, the path, the way, the journey, the ṭarīqa*[5] (to deploy the Islamic term) is paramount. Discussing Santa Teresa, Elizabeth Howe cites the saint as admitting 'that the soul advances to God by means of his "*secretos caminos*"' but also suggesting 'that the mystic must follow the example of those who have already traversed these roads'.[6]

The best road to follow, in the view of mystics like Juan de la Cruz and Santa Teresa of Ávila, may very well be the road of the cross;[7] but even these two saints envisage that road in somewhat different ways. Juan's apophatic mystical theology leads to a preference for a road which is 'straight and narrow'; Teresa is 'less rigid' and describes 'the road to union as an *ancho camino y real* [a wide and royal road]'.[8] Howe detects here that Teresa's mystical theology is rather 'less rigid and less ascetical',[9] which contrasts with the severity of Juan's teaching. Thus here, perhaps, in the two saints, we have an apophatic (Juan) and a cataphatic (Teresa) articulation of the mystical path to perfection.

The theme of 'the Path' or 'the Way' is a key *topos* in Christianity: its New Testament origins lie in the famous saying of Christ: 'I am the way; I am truth and life; nobody can come to the Father, except through me'.[10] This is emphasised by the theme of Christ as 'the door'. He says: 'A man will find salvation if he makes his way in through me; he will come and go at will, and find pasture'.[11] The two themes of door or gate and road, whether broad or narrow, are combined in one powerful scriptural verse, Matthew 7:13–14, cited by Juan de la Cruz: 'Make your way in by the narrow gate. It is a broad gate and a wide road that leads on to perdition, and those who go in that way are many indeed; but how small is the gate, how narrow the road that leads on to life, and how few there are that find it!'[12]

As we have seen, Juan expands the theme of 'the Way' by devising a map of the ascent up this narrow path of perfection. As we have also seen, and will continue to see, Islam, too, frequently envisages the striving for perfection and ultimate union, in its mystical theology, as a 'road' or 'path'. Finally, it is worth mentioning here that Buddhism teaches a 'Noble Eightfold Path … which leads to the cessation of suffering'.[13] It is not suggested here that there is a direct equivalence in the Christian concept of Divine union, Islamic *baqā'* and Buddhist Nirvana.[14] There *is*, however, in all three religions a powerful equivalence and emphasis on the image of 'the Way' or 'the Road' which must be undertaken in one form or another in the soul's journey towards perfection, whether that perfection is theistic or a-theistic.

In the previous chapter, we concentrated very much on the apophatic aspects of that Road, envisaged through the spectacles of the author of *The Cloud* and San Juan de la Cruz. If these figures may be considered prime representatives of that tradition, then perhaps it is appropriate to consider Teresa de Jesús, *inter alia*, a representative, as Howe suggests,[15] of a milder, gentler (and more practical!) cataphatic tradition. It is that cataphatic tradition, together with what I will term the ecstatic, which will constitute the substance of this chapter. The powerful contrasts with the apophatic tradition, delineated earlier, will be readily apparent.

In what follows, the choice of individual figures in the surveys of both Muslim and Christian mystics is intended to be indicative rather than exclusive. As with our earlier analyses of cave, cloud, mountain and night, we intend to highlight certain mystical trends using various themes and figures as examples. The coverage is *not* intended to be exclusive, essentialist or all-embracing. Our frequent aim is to make connections, often intertextual connections. What is common, however, to nearly all our selected mystics is that their writings emerge against a backdrop of political or spiritual or religious or intellectual upheaval, even chaos, which may take the diverse forms of the rise of Ismā'īlism, the appearance of the Jansenist heresy, the scourge of the Black Death or the Wars of the Roses.

There can be little doubt that a spiritual path, a way of perfection, offered a way forward, indeed, a 'way out', from an all-too-corruptible, fading, fallible and transient world. One might also say that a certain Platonic dualism of 'idealising' soul and 'earthbound body' was at the root of many of the exemplars that we will survey in the following pages.

3.2 *Islamic*

In a valuable survey and analysis of early Sufism, Ahmet T. Karamustafa has stressed the tendency in modern scholarship to decry attempts at extracting 'mysticism' and 'spirituality' from their historical milieu.[16] In the analyses and three Islamic case studies which follow, as well as in the next three Christian case studies, the authors and their writings will certainly be approached thematically but always with an awareness of the historical milieu in which they wrote. Karamustafa stresses that, to understand the 'mystical and spiritual dimensions' of a religious tradition, one needs to be aware that context is all and that 'the exact content and meaning of these dimensions should not be conceived as unchanging essences'.[17] Thus, as we have already noted, such terms as 'union', *baqā'* and *nirvana* are not coterminous, while sharing some features in common, and they have themselves, individually, varied in meaning within the same religious tradition.

None of this is to deny, however, that there *are* common themes which may be identified within and across the spectrum of religious mystical traditions, though the approaches to, and essence of, those terms *may* be historically and culturally diverse, depending on the milieu in which they were first articulated.

Summarising some of the most important aspects of the early Baghdādī sufis, Karamustafa focuses on the image of the journey towards God, a journey which begins in the individual sufi's realisation that he is weak in all that he does and that the only real one who truly acts in and upon creation is God.[18] It is an unsystematised journey, marked by the terminology of the path or the way (*ṭarīq*/*ṭarīqa*), halting places (*manāzil*), stations (*maqāmāt*) and states (*aḥwāl*).[19] The mystic *telos* of God is variously characterised, but it is never intended to imply that the human becomes Divine.[20] Language, however, particularly the language of metaphor and mysticism, can be slippery, the milieu can be both diverse and hostile, and accusations of heresy are not only possible but omnipresent.[21] Furthermore, as Karamustafa emphasises, trends of renunciation and asceticism may well be beloved in later Sufism, but they were by no means the only catalysts for the initial development and rise of Sufism,[22] especially in the Central Asian regions and the north-eastern areas of Iran.[23]

In what follows, we shall examine briefly the milieu as well as the common themes, aware at all times of the slippery, diverse and variegated nature of both, and the dangers of an unnecessary essentialism. And the Islamic and Christian authors who are discussed are chosen as indicative examples with common themes *between themselves* from different centuries; they are meant to be neither exclusive nor essentialist.

3.2.1 Al-Kalābādhī (died c. AD 990) and *The Doctrine of the Sufis*

The date of death of the Bukhāran Ḥanafī sufi, Abū Bakr Muḥammad ibn Ibrāhīm al-Kalābādhī, is variously given as AD 990 or 995,[24] the 990s[25] and 990 or 994.[26] We know very little about his life[27] although his name shows that he came from a part of Bukhārā called Kalābādh.[28] Karamustafa stresses that his written corpus is little help in understanding 'the local context'.[29] Nonetheless, it is clear from his dates that his life was lived out against a background of dwindling Sāmānid power in

Central Asia, the rise of opposing Turkish commanders, financial crises precipitated by Persian wars and an unsuccessful Ismāʿīlī *daʿwa* in Transoxania during the rule of the Sāmānid ruler Naṣr II (*reg.* AD 914–43). In other words, the background was one of religious, political and financial instability.[30] Was the stability to be sought, therefore, in the mystical tenets and 'certainties' of Sufism? Did the mystic way provide a compensatory solace for the uncertainties of the age?

Al-Kalābādhī's best-known work, the *Taʿarruf*,[31] appears to be 'academic' in style rather than the fruit of experience, and some scholars suggest that parts resemble an *apologia* for Sufism, following the execution of the controversial sufi, al-Ḥallāj, in AD 922.[32] It is actually possible that this may have occurred while al-Kalābādhī was a child, as Arberry suggests.[33] But Karamustafa holds that we should not try to reduce al-Kalābādhī's theological exposition of Sufism to 'mere apologetics'.[34]

Structurally, the *Taʿarruf* is divided into seventy-five chapters (*abwāb*)[35] in which the general definitions and theology of Sufism are surveyed in the first thirty chapters, and such matters as the *aḥwāl* (mystic states),[36] ecstasy and union are dealt with in the remainder. These have been variously analysed by scholars of the sufi tradition,[37] and their analyses will not be repeated here. What we *will* do, briefly, is examine how closely al-Kalābādhī's *Taʿarruf* accords, thematically, with the sevenfold paradigm already identified for *The Cloud* and the *Noche Oscura*. While it would be far too essentialist to contend that there is a universal, perennial mysticism in Islam of which these are the component and ineluctable parts, it would not be untrue to suggest that these seven aspects are at least common *to the principal mystics, Islamic and Christian, whose lives and writings are adumbrated in this volume*. It should also be stressed here, once again, that our sevenfold selection of mystical themes as the components of this paradigm is indicative rather than exclusive. It is a mystical paradigm, moreover, where, in its cataphatic and ecstatic mode, some of the elements become radically altered. There *are* differences even within a single tradition, and it is not the intention of this volume to ignore those differences, much less force a diverse range of material into fitting an artificial and unsuitable paradigm. What we seek is the identification of an intertextual web of resonant links between the authors under discussion.

Cloud

Our first theme, drawn from the preceding discussion of the apophatic tradition, is that of *cloud*. Already in al-Kalābādhī's survey of sufi scholarship, we detect a difference. It is certainly noted and acknowledged that there can be a barrier between the Creator and His creation; but that barrier is articulated, traditionally, through the imagery of the 'veil' and 'veiling' (*al-istitār*) rather than the 'cloud': 'Veiling means that creaturehood prevents thee from seeing the unseen'.[38] It is revelation that raises such veils, even though there may still be some veiling of God's deepest secrets *after* revelation.[39] That said, God may permit or cause a more cataphatic knowledge of Himself.[40] The intellect is unable to know God 'except through God' (*fa-lam yakun li'l-ʿaql an yaʿrif Allāh illā bi-llāh*).[41] But man may be enabled to know God in some sense 'through His self-revelation to him'.[42]

In an important chapter entitled 'The Sciences of the Sufis are the Sciences of the [Spiritual] States' (*'Ulūm al-Ṣūfiyya 'Ulūm al-Aḥwāl*) al-Kalābādhi, having surveyed the views of others, commences with the word *Aqūl* (I say)![43] He goes on to say that the *aḥwāl* can only be the product of right action.[44] In a manner which mirrors the mystical thinking, in a slightly later age, of Abū Ḥāmid al-Ghazālī (AD 1058–1111),[45] al-Kalābādhī stresses that the foundations of real Sufism rest upon the mainstream practices of Islam like *sharī'a* and *fiqh*, prayer and fasting, together with a thorough knowledge of the Qur'ān, *sunna*, and the consensus of the early generations of Muslims (*ijmā' al-salaf al-ṣāliḥ*).[46] In addition, the aspirant or initiate on the sufi path must learn how to avoid evil and satanic temptations. This, says al-Kalābādhī, 'is the science of wisdom' (*hādhā 'l-'ilm 'ilm al-ḥikma*).[47] Only after this come the realms of gnostic knowledge (*'ilm al-ma'rifa*) and then 'the sciences of contemplations [or witnessings] and revelations [or manifestations]' (*'Ulum mushāhadāt wa 'l-mukāshafāt*).[48] And the key to real knowledge of such things is actual mystical experience.[49]

All these promised *aḥwāl* (states) and *maqāmāt* (stations) for the Islamic mystic go beyond the occasional sweetnesses and consolations which may be experienced by the disciple who follows his master in *The Cloud*. A state of ecstasy (*wajd*) may be encountered; and al-Kalābādhī quotes one sufi as defining *wajd* as 'the glad tidings sent by God of the mystic's promotion to the stations of His contemplation'.[50] And the sufi who is 'intoxicated' by the presence of God may even lose all ability to distinguish between the pleasurable and unpleasurable, such will be his immense sense of the debt of gratitude which he owes to God.[51]

The veils to which al-Kalābādhī has alluded *can*, therefore, obviously be breached, and in a much more radical and cataphatic fashion by the advanced Islamic mystic than by the disciple in *The Cloud*. It *is* possible for an Islamic 'Veil of Unknowing' to be a transient phenomenon which may be pierced by the advanced aspirant on the sufi path. This cataphatic trend of states, stations, ecstasy and ultimate 'union' (whatever that might mean and however it might be variously defined) will be elaborated upon in what follows.

Self-abnegation and Contemplation

Self-abnegation is another feature of al-Kalābādhī's mystical path. He quotes a number of sufis, approvingly, who speak highly about humility. In particular, he cites one who claims that 'humility [*al-tawāḍu'*] is taking pride in constriction, adhering to submission, and shouldering the burdens of the people of religion'.[52] It is fostered by a spirit of asceticism, renunciation and abstinence (*zuhd*) where God is the only goal and focus.[53] It is also fostered by the practice of recollection (*dhikr*) which, for the sufi is the counterpart of contemplation as we find it in the writings of Juan de la Cruz and the author of *The Cloud*: 'Real recollection', says al-Kalābādhī, 'consists in forgetting all but the One recollected'.[54] Associated with this is a spirit of detachment and separation.[55]

The Dark Night

Al-Kalābādhī does not espouse a 'dark night doctrine' or image in the same way as Juan de la Cruz or Ibn 'Abbād. There is, however, an equivalent of Juan's 'night of the senses', and that is 'the separation [*tafriqa*] which ... is a state in which the mystic is separated from his carnal resolves, and from the desire for pleasant and pleasurable things ... he knows that this is God's doing, and that God thus chooses him and draws him to Himself' [56].

Perfection

Yet, as in every mystical tradition, the sufi in al-Kalābādhī's text strives for perfection. This may be achieved by such classic paths as repentance (*tawba*),[57] asceticism (*zuhd*),[58] fear of God (*khawf*)[59] and piety (*taqwā*).[60] Al-Kalābādhī cites a certain Muḥammad b. Sinjān as defining *taqwā* as 'leaving all that is not God'.[61] Total 'detachment' from all worldly things is the goal.[62] Al-Kalābādhī uses the Arabic word *tajrīd*, which Arberry translates as 'detachment',[63] but this word here is rather more powerful than just 'detachment': *tajrīd* implies a total stripping away of an outer shell or husk.[64] Al-Kalābādhī's own definition of *tajrīd*, deploying an Aristotelian turn of phrase, is that one should be, outwardly, completely stripped of the accidents (*al-a'rāḍ*), and, interiorly, completely removed from any desire to seek forms of compensation (*al-a'wāḍ*) for what has been given up.[65] Our author quotes the following saying, approvingly: 'Detachment (*al-tajrīd*) means that one does not possess, separation (*al-tafrīd*) means that one is not possessed'.[66] Analogies in all this with the ascetical theology, and the paths to perfection, developed by the author of *The Cloud* and Juan de la Cruz are readily apparent.

Human and Divine Love

Of course, the prime motivation for entering upon the path of perfection, as much for the sufi as for the Christian mystic, is love. The ardent soul feels that it is perishing, dying, because it longs to be near God, yet it is painfully conscious that it has no good deeds which might merit such closeness.[67] Al-Kalābādhī devotes an entire chapter (no. 51) to 'The Sufi View of Love' (*Qawluhum fī 'l-Maḥabba*). Starting with the very simple definition of love by the sufi Abū 'l-Qāsim al-Junayd (died AD 910), that love is just the effortless inclination of our hearts towards God and what pertains to God,[68] al-Kalābādhī goes on to distinguish, via a quotation, between human love of God and God's love for man: man's love for God may be characterised as 'a glorification' or 'exaltation' (*ta'ẓīm*) in the innermost depths of his heart, a 'love' which it does not permit for anyone other than God; the sublime love of God for man is a Divine instrument of testing whereby God renders man unable to focus on anything other than him (*fa-la yaṣlaḥ li-ghayrihi*).[69] God is 'The Beloved' (*al-Maḥbūb*).[70]

Union

The desire for perfection is intimately linked to the love of God in all traditions, and the two lead to that final *telos*, 'union', a theme ineluctably bound up with the technical terminology of *fanā'* and *baqā'*. However, it is clear that sufis down the ages have meant different things at different times by this concept of 'union'. So, what exactly did al-Kalābādhī mean by this term?

At the beginning of an unusually long chapter, at least for al-Kalābādhī (chapter

59: 'The Sufi View of *al-Fanā'* and *al-Baqā'*' / *Qawluhum fī 'l-Fanā' wa 'l-Baqā'*), the author defines *fanā'* as a state in which all passion is spent, while the succeeding state of *baqā'* means that one 'remains' or 'persists' 'through what is God's'.[71] These are clearly slippery and ambiguous definitions, and al-Kalābādhī is well aware of the wide range of sufi opinion on the subject.[72] The sufi 'remains', 'persists' or 'survives' in God's own attributes (*bāqiyan bi-awṣāf al-Ḥaqq*);[73] in other words, having passed away from one's own 'pleasures' (*ḥuẓūẓ*), one 'remains' within the 'pleasures' of another.[74]

The last two key chapters for the doctrine of 'union' (*al-ittiṣāl*) in al-Kalābādhī are chapters 50 and 61. In the first, *al-ittiṣāl* is defined as implying an interior detachment from all that is not God, where God becomes the only object of vision and thought.[75] Chapter 61 is more mystical in tone and orientation: entitled 'The Sufi View of Tawḥīd' (*Qawluhum fī 'l-Tawḥīd*), it identifies seven pillars (*arkān*) of the declaration of the Oneness of Allah (*tawḥīd*)[76] before moving to the citation of a number of mystic utterances by fellow sufis on the subject of the mystic and *tawḥīd*. A. J. Arberry translates *tawḥīd* in the context of this chapter as 'unification'[77] rather than the more traditional rendition of 'the declaration of the oneness of God', and it is clear that this 'unification' sense is the sense intended by the sufis quoted. All their definitions in the chapter, however, manage to avoid identifying man totally with God, but all are clothed in a multivalent mystical terminology.

A common theme appears to be the total abnegation of self in the face or presence of the Divine. As al-Kalābādhī puts it, citing another sufi: '*Tawḥīd* means going out from your whole self'.[78] In sum, 'union' is a 'joining' or a 'finding'[79] but not a 'becoming'. Discussing *fanā'*, Annemarie Schimmel summarises as follows: '[The] veil cannot be lifted completely during one's lifetime. The mystic cannot completely and substantially be annihilated in God, but he may be lost for a while in the fathomless ocean of bewilderment, as it has been defined by Kalābādhī.'[80]

3.2.2 Al-Daylamī (c. 983–1002) and *The Treatise on Mystical Love*

Baldick provides a neat, succinct summary of what he regards as al-Daylamī's principal contribution to Sufism: 'Daylami associated with members of the Greek philosophical tradition and incorporated their ideas in a book of love'.[81] The reference is clearly to his *Kitāb 'Aṭf al-Alif al-Ma'lūf 'alā al-Lām al-Ma'ṭūf*,[82] which Bell and Al Shafie loosely translate as *A Treatise on Mystical Love*,[83] and which Jean-Claude Vadet in his edition renders as *Le Traité d'Amour Mystique d'Al-Daylami*.[84] A much more literal rendition of the Arabic might be the more flowery and rather more awkward *The Book of the Affection of the Beloved Alif for the Beloved Lām*. Bell and Al Shafie prefer *Book of the Conjunction of the Cherished Alif with the Conjoined Lām*,[85] which is equally possible. In neither the latter, nor in my own rendition, however, can the rhyme of the original Arabic adequately be duplicated in English. As Bell and Al Shafie observe, 'the title has been understood and translated in different ways, and precisely because it plays on the various meanings implied by the roots *'–ṭ–f* and *'–l–f*, most of the translations that have been given of it can be justified'.[86]

None of this, however, is *fundamentally* important. What *is* important, and the reason for our inclusion of a section on al-Daylamī at this point, is that 'his *Kitāb 'aṭf al-alif al-ma'lūf 'alā 'l-lām al-ma'ṭūf* is one of the earliest extant treatises on mystical love in Arabic literature'.[87] It thus harmonises with one of the constant *leitmotivs* of this book, which is human and Divine love. Bell and Al Shafie characterise its spirituality as Sunnī but suggest that this is mingled with some traces of Shī'ism in the way that the author expresses himself at times.[88]

We know little about the actual life of al-Daylamī, having neither a date of birth nor death.[89] Bell and Al Shafie conclude that he was alive during the first fifty years of Buyid power in Iraq and western Persia and note that this was the time when this dynasty reigned supreme in the central lands of Islam.[90] His city was the Persian city of Shīrāz.[91]

The theme of his whole work is love; and the shade of Plato and Plato's famous *Symposium* hangs over the whole volume. I have had occasion, elsewhere, to discuss the links between Plato, al-Mas'ūdī's *Arabic Symposium* in his *Murūj al-Dhahab* (*Fields of Gold*) and al-Daylamī.[92] However, we note in particular, here, al-Daylamī's reference to Plato; although the Greek philosopher's *Symposium* is not named, it is clear that this is the origin, directly or indirectly, of al-Daylamī's brief adumbration of the famous *Symposium* story, put into the mouth of Aristophanes, about the creation of humanity: 'Plato said: God Most High created all spirits together in the shape of a ball. Then he divided them amongst all creatures, placing them in the body of whomever he chose in his creation.'[93]

Structurally, the Arabic text divides into twenty-four main chapters (*abwāb*), many of which are subdivided into smaller sections (*fuṣūl*); and this twenty-fourfold division has been observed by the editors of the English and French translations whom we have cited in our notes, Joseph Norment Bell and Hassan Mahmoud Abdul Latif Al Shafie, and Jean-Claude Vadet. The division into twenty-four *abwāb* or chapters is al-Daylamī's own.[94] After some preliminaries about beauty – shades of Plato again! – nearly every following chapter is concerned with the concept of love (*al-maḥabba*, *al-ḥubb*, *al-'ishq*). This is, therefore, a suitable point at which to examine al-Daylamī's text in the light of our sevenfold paradigm which we have previously applied to some other Islamic and Christian mystic authors.

Cloud

As with al-Kalābādhī, there is no 'cloud' as such; al-Daylamī is writing much more within a cataphatic tradition, and the evidence is clear from the encomium of the Divine with which his work begins. It is true that Allah is acknowledged as Hidden (*al-Bāṭin*) as well as Manifest (*al-Ẓāhir*),[95] but equally true that mankind has perceived, in one way or another, actually or metaphorically, 'the radiance of his dazzling loveliness'.[96] He has even made mankind 'witnesses to himself' (*ja'alahum li-nafsihi shāhidan*),[97] a phrase interpreted by Bell and Al Shafie as 'apparently an allusion to the … covenant mentioned in Koran 7:172, which is widely held by Muslim mystical and Neoplatonising writers to refer to a covenant made between God and men's souls prior to the existence of their bodies'.[98] That interpretation is disputed by Abdullah Yusuf Ali.[99] Regardless of that, however, all this with al-Daylamī is a reflection of the immanent Qur'ānic aspect of Allah, rather than the transcendent, sometimes apophatic, side. There seems to be no *cloud* between man and his Creator. Rather, there is knowledge.

We will look at this theme in a moment, but let us note here how strongly the text stresses this immanent aspect. For example, Allah endows His first creation, Adam, with all His own loveliness, and al-Daylamī cites the Prophet Muḥammad as saying: 'God created Adam in his own image' (*khalaqa Allāh Ādam 'alā ṣūratihi*).[100] And the Prophet actually sees Allah in a dream.[101] Indeed, Allah speaks to those who really love Him, during the night in dreams: they converse with Him in that state while actually seeing Him and are emboldened to make requests to Him.[102]

This is certainly not the way *The Cloud of Unknowing* conceives of God: the *cloud* prevents any such felicitous dreams, actual or metaphorical. For the sufi al-Daylamī, knowledge about love is the key, and he will seek it from a diversity of wise and eminent scholars and holy men,[103] including the sufi gnostics (*ahl al-ma'rifa*).[104] 'Love ... is a man's knowledge of God's favors [*sic*] to him and his good will towards him'.[105] Indeed, al-Daylamī believes that there are eight distinct groups of those 'who hold that love is knowledge' (*qālū inna al-maḥabba ma'rifa*).[106]

There is, then, no 'cloud of unknowing' between man and God. There is, however, and not unexpectedly, for some, a *veil* – and there are a few references to this veil in al-Daylamī's work, but they have by no means the prominence of the *cloud* in *The Cloud of Unknowing*; they constitute more an occasional sufi trope or *topos* rather than an overall dynamic attempt on the part of al-Daylamī to convert the basically cataphatic stance of his *Kitāb* into an apophatic one. Furthermore, his book is riddled with quotations – and while he does, at times, confirm his own views with the phrase 'The author of this book said' (*Qāla ṣāḥib al-kitāb*),[107] it is not always clear how much he agrees with the authors whom he actually quotes. It is unlikely, however, that he shares the views of 'those who claim that love is for you to give credence to the followers of all religions and not to embrace a particular faith, since the followers of all religions are seeking God'.[108]

Examples of veil images include the following statements: after noting, Platonically, that 'every beauty is derived from the universal beauty, [which] is near to the Beautiful',[109] al-Daylamī notes that the human perception of beauty may be determined by the material quality of the veil (*sitr*) which overhangs such beauty.[110] But the final veil (*ḥijāb*) through which the lover of God must pass is the veil of self (*ḥijāb dhawātihim*).[111] There is a particular resonance here with Christian texts such as *The Cloud of Unknowing*, which we have earlier studied; and, of course, the fight against the *nafs*, the self, is a constant sufi *leitmotiv* in our own age,[112] as well as in these medieval texts.

We note, too, in al-Daylamī's text, the usage of two distinct Arabic words for 'veil', *sitr* and *ḥijāb*: the former has connotations of 'screening', 'draping' or 'curtaining'[113] and perhaps asks us to envisage a chamber in which the human lover of God is separated from his or her Divine Beloved by a full curtain, as in the Persian poet Farīd al-Dīn 'Attār's famous *Manṭiq al-Ṭayr* (*The Conference of the Birds*);[114] the latter Arabic word *ḥijāb*, while also embracing some of the above meanings of *sitr*, has a primary significance of 'woman's veil'[115] and embraces a theology of the body in its metaphorical relationship in al-Daylamī's text with the *nafs*.

Al-Daylamī goes on to observe that once the veil of the self, the ego, is removed, the branch (= the human lover) is reunited with the trunk (= God, the Beloved]) whence she/he had come in the first place.[116] We shall deal with the theme of mystical union again in a short while; here, we note the theme of 'return' and a likely reference to the idea of the 'pre-existence' of the soul before its corporeal habitation.[117] The theme of the veil can be a potent one here, as in many other sufi texts: al-Daylamī cites a certain Abū Sulaymān al-Darānī (died AD 830) commenting on the lack of joy felt by a wise man (*'āqil*) in the terrestrial world 'as if he were to be veiled from God for a single moment' (*ḥujiba 'an Allāh sā'atan wāḥidatan*)[118] and how horrific it would be to be veiled from the sight and presence of God for all eternity. Such references, however, are to be expected, and they do not mean that al-Daylamī's work should be considered in the category of apophatic rather than cataphatic texts.

Self-abnegation

Al-Daylamī does not have a great deal to say about self-abnegation *per se* in this text, but he is by no means unaware of this key motif. We have noted the need he expresses to rid oneself of the veil of selfhood before proceeding to the final stages of union with the Divine. This is the highest form of abnegation, but al-Daylamī is also aware of those who blame love for some reason or other (*dhamma al-maḥabba li-'illa*) and therefore do not wish to be held in its thrall.[119] They may renounce human love because of their elevated spiritual state and immersion in spiritual love. Zulaykhā says to Joseph: 'When I tasted love for God, love for you left me'.[120] Self-abnegation, and the abnegation of human types of love, are, then, for al-Daylamī, as for so many sufi and Christian mystics, key aspects of the path to salvation.

Contemplation

Another is contemplation. Citing Abū Sa'īd Aḥmad b. Muḥammad b. Ziyād al-'Arābī (AD 860–952), who is characterised as 'one of al-Daylami's most important sources on the theory of love',[121] al-Daylamī notes, among a whole list of spiritual stations (*maqāmāt*), all to be encompassed by the generic term of *hawā* (passion, love, appetite),[122] that contemplation (*ta'ammul*) is the embassy (or mediation) of the home country (*sifārat al-waṭan*) between it and connection (*muwāṣala*).[123] It is a strange but striking definition, which Bell and Al Shafie render more eloquently as 'Contemplation (*ta'ammul*) is the mediation of the homeland between the soul and union'.[124] Elsewhere, however, there is direct reference to what Bell and Al Shafie translate as 'the beatific vision' (*ru'ya*); and al-Daylamī cites those who believe that the depth of one's love of God determines the depths of this vision.[125]

The Dark Night

Al-Daylamī's treatise does not belong in any sense to the apophatic 'dark night' genre of mysticism espoused by its later most notable exponent and adherent, Juan de la Cruz. With Abū Sa'īd, to whom we referred earlier, Al-Daylamī is perhaps much more interested in 'steps, levels, meanings and definitions. Each of its steps has a name, and each of its stations (*maqām*) has a distinguishing sign.'[126] Nonetheless, there is at least one area in the *Kitāb 'Aṭf al-Alif* where al-Daylamī approaches the imagery, if not necessarily the intention, of 'the dark night' of Juan de la Cruz: this occurs in section 4 of chapter 6, which is entitled, long-windedly in Arabic, *Fīmā Dhahabnā ilayhi min al-Qawl fī Nafs al-Maḥabba wa Māhiyyatihā*,[127] a title rendered more briefly and elegantly by Bell and Al Shafie as 'Our Opinion on the Essence and Quiddity of Love'.[128] Here, love is to be defined, essentially, as an entity of light. It is *nūrānī* (luminous).[129] Its original pristine purity became diluted by the gross imperfections of humanity, and pure light became mixed with the dark physicality of the latter. Al-Daylamī gives us an image of entering a dark house holding a lamp – and the surroundings, thus illuminated, are a compound of light and darkness, and neither purely light nor purely dark.[130]

In a clear reference to the Deity, al-Daylamī notes: 'pure light dazzles one's vision, since vision is part of the universal light (*al-nūr al-kullī*)'.[131] And now, in a most significant phrase – perhaps one of the most important in the whole treatise – al-Daylamī proceeds from the motif of light to that of union with the source of light, and explains succinctly what such union means for him: we see, on entering the house with a lamp, a mix of light and darkness, that is, a 'partial' light. But, if the part is joined to the whole Light, the eternal source of light, then a union takes place 'and there remains only one thing. Thus (in pure light) you would not sense that your total being was anything but light. It is to this that our teachers refer when they speak of *the extinction of man in God [fanā' 'l-'abd bi-'l-Ḥaqq] and of the joining of the lover to the beloved [jam' al-muḥibb bi-'l-Maḥbūb]*.'[132] And unbelief (*al-kufr*) is to be equated with darkness.[133]

There is, here, an intertext of classic mystical motifs: in Juan de la Cruz's *Noche Oscura*, the lover *leaves* the house and enters the darkness. But the Beloved is encountered, nonetheless, at the end of the journey. In al-Daylamī's text, the lover *enters* the house, and the realisation, actual or metaphorical, of a partial light leads on to a meditation on the whole Light of God and an ultimate – and much to be desired – union in both al-Daylamī's text and that of Juan. Al-Daylamī bolsters his own light/darkness imagery with an apposite quotation from the Qur'ān, indicating that the light is ultimately a gift from God Himself:

> Depths of darkness, one
> Above another: if a man
> Stretches out his hand,
> He can hardly see it!
> For any to whom God
> Giveth not light,
> There is no light.[134]

Yusuf Ali's commentary completes the intertext: 'The true source of Light in the world of Reality is God, and anyone who cuts himself off from that Light is in utter darkness indeed, for it is the negation of the only true Light, and not merely relative darkness, like that which we see, say, in the shadows of moonlight';[135] nor, we might add, like the partial darkness of the interior of the house so evocatively described in al-Daylamī's text.

Perfection

In this concept, rendered by the Arabic word *kamāl*, we have another very important motif common to the other Islamic and Christian mystics whom we have discussed and will discuss. Al-Daylamī, too, embraces the Way of Perfection.

It is bound up with love: for example, an imperfect knowledge of God's perfection, power and majesty (*bi-kamālihi wa 'aẓamatihi wa qudratihi*) may yield an imperfect love in terms of love's reality (*ḥaqīqat al-maḥabba*).[136] This dual theme of perfection and love is developed to its fullest extent in al-Daylamī's text in chapter 21, entitled simply *Fī Ḥadd Kamāl al-Maḥabba*[137] ('Towards a Definition of Love's Perfection'). Love is incorporated in gnostic knowledge (*al-ma'rifa*) and one becomes a knower (*'ārif*) as well as a lover (*muḥibb*), while the very state (*ḥāl*) of love is elevated to that of a station (*maqām*). And al-Daylamī tells us that this is regarded by gnostics (*ahl al-ma'rifa*), as an extremely noble station (*maqām sharīf jiddan*). Ultimately, the lovers of God achieve union with their Beloved Deity (*ittiḥād bi-'l-Maḥbūb*), to be defined as eternal life, or they gain what is termed 'the station of unification' (*maqām al-tawḥīd*), whose definition is joining the Beloved in such a manner that one realises he is the Reality of all things (*Ḥaqīqa kull shay'*).[138] Here, in this text, we reach the heights of an almost pantheistic notion of Divinity achieved via gnostic knowledge and great love. Knowledge and love, love and knowledge, thus lead to this perfect and perfected spiritual state which is that mystery of *ittiḥād*, union with the Beloved Godhead. This is al-Daylamī's Way of Perfection.

He himself acknowledges the strangeness and mystery behind what he has said.[139] Citing al-Ḥallāj's illustrative verse on his concept of union with God (*ittiḥād*), al-Daylamī quotes:

> I am the one I love, and the one I love is I.
> We are two spirits dwelling in one body.[140]

And the ultimate perfection of love is epitomised in the absolute self-abnegation articulated by 'Amr b. 'Uthmān al-Makkī, where the perfect lover's very names, attributes and traces are wiped off the faces of both Heaven and Earth: only God remains![141]

Human and Divine Love

We turn now in al-Daylamī's text to the themes of human and Divine love, man's love for God and God's love for man. Al-Daylamī considers these topics sufficiently important to address these topics on several different occasions. Very early on in his text, in chapter 2, the author agonises over a specifically semantic point: is it acceptable to apply the word *'ishq* (passionate love, *érōs*) in the two-way traffic of man's love for God and God's for man (*al-'ishq 'alā Allāh wa min Allāh*)?[142] Al-Daylamī notes the wide disparity of views on the subject but is not inclined to eschew the use of *'ishq* in such discussions, since it is simply a synonym for him of the more widely used Arabic word *maḥabba*. His conclusion is that he will use *'ishq* where others do, and *ḥubb* or *maḥabba* when *that* is the preferred usage. Linguistically and semantically, on this point, he will be all things to all men![143] And sometimes al-Daylamī chooses to use both words in the same sentence![144]

However, there are two key chapters in this text on the subject of God's love for man and man's for God. A comparatively lengthy chapter 14 provides an exegesis of the evidence of God's love for man (*Fi Shawāhid Maḥabba Allāh Taʿālā li-ʿAbdihi*).[145] In pride of place, al-Daylamī suggests the idea that the human should love his Creator as he loves the human (*kamā tuḥibbuk*);[146] there should be an almost preternatural equivalence of love! He goes on to adumbrate ten distinct pieces of evidence for God's love for man.[147]

Al-Daylamī's definition of his first sign or evidence of God's love for man, that is, that man should love God as God loves him, is of particular interest because it touches on our next major *topos* of union, a theme already referred to several times in our dissection of this text. Deploying the image of the light of God's love (*nūr maḥabbatihi*), al-Daylamī tells us that man's humanity is absorbed within God's Divinity and unites with God: one can then no longer distinguish between the Divine Beloved and the human lover.[148] None of this, however, can be accomplished without suffering and pain – and, in a passage which resonates with many of the *topoi* of Christian mysticism (we note, for example, the sufferings of the twentieth-century stigmatist Padre Pio),[149] al-Daylamī proclaims that such suffering is a sign of God's love for man and thus a sure path to salvation. It is identified as the sixth sign of God's love for man, a Deity who is a jealous lover and who desires that the human's love should not be distracted away from the Divine by worldly affairs. God's love for man is revealed in the sufferings He inflicts on him, and the love of God is an all-consuming Divine love which brooks no rivals, even from the closest family members.[150]

In the face of such a Divine onslaught, how should man's love for God be articulated? Al-Daylamī adumbrates this in the following chapter 15, which is entitled 'An Exegesis of Human Love for Almighty God' (*Fī Tafsīr Maḥabba al-ʿAbd li-llāh Taʿālā*).[151] Displaying an almost Aristotelian passion for classification, and consciously matching the ten signs outlined in chapter 14 for God's love for man, al-Daylamī, in chapter 15, now adduces ten major signs whereby one might identify a human's love of God.[152] The first is that one should prefer God to anything else that one loves.[153] This symmetrical decade of signs concludes by noting that the end result of embracing all ten signs is 'the state of annihilation' (*ḥāl al-fanā'*);[154] here again, there is a wonderful literary and mystical symmetry with the previous chapter 14, whose first sign is also articulated with reference to *fanā'*.[155]

Fanā', that mystical extinction of self (*nafs*) and all the sins and imperfections which keep the soul earthbound, is thus, in al-Daylamī's text, integral to, and bound up with, the two-way procession of love which he so symmetrically and neatly articulates: God's love for man and man's love for God. And, in Islamic mysticism, *fanā'* is the mysterious and mystical precursor of *baqā'*, that mystical state of somehow 'remaining' eternally in and with God. It is thus to the ramifications of that state as expressed in the concept of *union* and unification that we will now turn; this is the seventh aspect of that sevenfold paradigm or methodology whereby we have chosen to unveil the thought of the mystics surveyed and analysed in this volume.

Union

We have already had occasion to analyse al-Daylamī's doctrine of *union*, and we shall not repeat all this here. It is clear that *ittiḥād*, union,[156] is the ultimate product of God's love for man. And it is 'the people of unification' (*ahl al-tawḥīd*) [157] who may be said, in al-Daylamī's hierarchy, to represent 'the most advanced mystics'.[158] All in all, it is no exaggeration to say that al-Daylamī's text is saturated with the whole notion of 'union'.

The mystical complexities of his elaboration of this notion have not escaped the notice of scholars. Noting that 'the *alif* ... can become the symbol of the spiritually free, the true mystics who have reached union with God', Schimmel, changing track and in reference to al-Daylamī's text, suggests that

> the author proves that *alif* is both one and three, and that therefore Christian ideas of trinity are much closer to Sufism than dualist ideas as defended by the Iranians – a somewhat surprising result, which can, however, be understood, since Sufi terminology is very fond of threefold groupings or of proving the basic unity of lover, beloved, and love ...[159]

Julian Baldick, pursuing a similar theme, identifies a similar triad in al-Daylamī of 'Love, Lover and Beloved'. He continues: 'The Christians, with their Trinity, come close to affirming God's Uniqueness'.[160] As al-Daylamī puts it:

> [Love] consumes its abode in flames and melts away the one who is afflicted with it. It joins the lover [*al-muḥibb*] to his Beloved [*Maḥbūbahā*], and as long as anything identifiable remains of the lover, he may be described with an attribute but if his identity is obliterated by the force of love, then his only attribute is his drunkenness [a kind of ecstasy?], his only strength is love [*al-ḥubb*], and the beloved is his, in his entirety, his might and his act.[161]

It will be noticed how often the theme of 'union', our seventh aspect of the sevenfold sieve, has infiltrated other aspects of that sieve. And at the heart of al-Daylamī's mystical doctrine lies the triad remarked upon by Schimmel and Baldick: Love is one of the eternal attributes of the eternal God; His eternal self-love revealed a single triad of three in One, a Deity who is Lover, Beloved and Love (*al-Muḥibb, al-Maḥbūb wa 'l-Maḥabba*).[162] It is such triads that lead al-Daylamī to suggest that unity is more apparent in a group of three than two and to proclaim that the Trinitarian Christians are closer to the Islamic doctrine of *tawḥīd* by their belief in Trinity (*al-Tathlīth*) than the dualist Zoroastrians.[163]

Thus far, we have applied our chosen sevenfold sieve to the work of al-Daylamī, showing, by and large, that it has concordance, and resonates intertextually, with the works studied earlier of some of the great Christian mystics. But there is an extra, intriguing, dimension – a 'green' dimension in al-Daylamī's text which links it to one of the recurring *leitmotivs* of this whole volume. This is the section devoted to al-Khaḍir/al-Khiḍr, supplemented by additional references to Elijah.

Chapter 24 of al-Daylami's text is entitled 'On the Death of Divine Lovers' (*Fī Dhikr Mawt al-Ilāhiyyīn*).[164] Our author proposes an initial fivefold division of such lovers, and it is the first and the last group which are of particular interest to us here.

The first group is said to include Idrīs, al-Khaḍir, Elijah (Ilyās) and Jesus ('Isā).[165] Love of God has so possessed them that they have become spiritual beings, dwelling with the angels, at once 'celestial and terrestrial, angelic and human'.[166]

The fifth group is movingly characterised by the motif of the veil (*ḥijāb*): these have cut their way through veil after veil until they come finally to the ultimate veil, the veil of self (*ḥijāb dhawātihim*). Throwing off this final veil enables the union of branch and trunk, or, translated another way, limb and origin (*al-far' bi -'l-aṣl*).[167]

In al-Daylamī's narrative, al-Khaḍir and Elijah are two distinct beings. But, intriguingly, al-Khaḍir is identified here with the Old Testament prophet Jeremiah (Irmiyā, also Armiyā): 'Al-Khaḍir's name was Jeremiah son of Ḥilqīyā [Armiyā (*sic*) b. Ḥilqīyā]. He was a prophet, it is said, who was sent to the children of Israel.'[168] Because Irmiyā was given a very long life in the sources, Vajda notes that 'there is a tendency to confuse him with al-Khaḍir'.[169]

Al-Daylamī is aware of the debate as to how exactly al-Khaḍir is to be classified; he is not mentioned by name in the Qur'ān, although, as we have seen, he *is* to be identified with the mysterious gnostic figure who administers the threefold test to an increasingly irritated Moses (Mūsā) in the Qur'ānic *Sūra of the Cave* (*Sūrat al-Kahf*) [18: 65–82]:

> So they found one
> Of Our servants ['*abd min 'ibādinā*]
> On whom We had bestowed
> Mercy from Ourselves
> And whom We had taught
> Knowledge ['*ilm*] from Our own
> Presence. [Q.18:65]

But al-Daylamī, in common with many other Muslim commentators, is not sure whether al-Khaḍir/[Jeremiah] bears the charism of prophethood (*nubuwwa*) or 'sainthood' (*walāya*).[170]

Drawing on the accounts of al-Ṭabarī (as Bell and Al Shafie show),[171] who must, in turn, either at first or second hand, have had access to the Biblical narrative,[172] al-Daylamī narrates an intriguing account of the siege of Jerusalem by the Babylonian King Nebuchadnezzar II (Bukht Naṣṣar) (*reg.* 605–562 BC) in 587/6 BC. In this, an unnamed king of Israel questions al-Khaḍir as to a previous promise (of security?), but al-Khaḍir, honest being that he is, is urged by an angel to invoke God's wrath on the wicked city, whose temple is then incinerated, with the destruction of nine of its gates.[173]

Al-Khaḍir/Jeremiah then displays his 'green' credentials by fleeing into the wilderness, which he inhabits with the wild beasts and where he may sometimes be seen.[174] Al-Daylamī goes on to allude to the famous *topos* which separates out al-Khaḍir from Elijah but has them meeting once a year.[175] The succeeding allusions to Elijah (Ilyās) are brief and restricted to a single paragraph. Al-Daylamī's principal interest here is the 'ascension' of Elijah in front of Elisha on a fiery horse (*faras min nār*),[176] in the manner of the Old Testament Books of Kings.[177] There is no reference here to the prophets of Baal. What al-Daylamī *does* wish to stress is the previously mentioned *leitmotiv* according to which 'Elijah joined the angels and became both human and angelic, terrestrial and celestial'.[178]

In sum, what we have here is the conflation of several accounts – Islamic and Biblical – together with the unusual, but not impossible, conflation of the figures of al-Khaḍir and Irmiyā/Jeremiah. The latter is more an example of extreme love for the Divine rather than a fully fleshed-out theological or historical figure, but it is one who becomes wild and 'green' and who has much intertextual baggage in al-Daylamī's narration.

3.2.3 Al-Qushayrī (986–1072) and *The Sufi Book of Spiritual Ascent*

Abū 'l-Qāsim 'Abd al-Karīm ibn Hawāzin al-Qushayrī was both a mystic and a fiercely Ash'arite theologian.[179] Ahmet T. Karamustafa lauds him as 'a product of the exceptionally-productive period for the combination of Shāfi'ī jurisprudence and Ash'arī *kalām* in Nishapur [Naysābūr]', whose fame in this city led him to be among the four most eminent Ash'arite *'ulamā'* who suffered Saljūq persecution between the years 1053 and 1064.[180] He even suffered imprisonment at the hands of his opponents for a few days or weeks before being rescued at the instigation of those who shared his views.[181] In this imprisonment – albeit brief – we may draw parallels with the similar fate which befell Juan de la Cruz.

Most scholars agree that al-Qushayrī was born in the year AH 376/AD 986 and died in Nishapur in 465/1072,[182] although some place his death in 1074.[183] There is thus some overlap with the life of the great theologian and sufi mystic Abū Ḥāmid al-Ghazālī (AD 1058–1111), but divergence on some key elements of sufi doctrine.[184] Like many Islamic scholars before and after him, al-Qushayrī travelled in search of knowledge,[185] visiting, for example, Ṭūs, Marw and Baghdād; but it is, perhaps, with the city of Nishapur that his name is most associated.[186]

Baldick heralds him as one of the leaders of the Sunnī revival in the mid-eleventh century AD.[187] He is chosen as a case study here, like our other choices, as one who is indicative of a certain type of mysticism in a particular age, not because he is indicative of all types of Islamic mysticism in all ages. We will, however, in what follows, attempt to apply our sevenfold paradigm of themes and evaluate to what extent al-Qushayrī may be said to reflect that paradigm and thus, in his writings, reflect an intertext with the writings of other mystics, Islamic and Christian, studied in this volume.

There *is* an interesting intertextual link with al-Sulamī and some of the medieval Christian and Islamic 'chivalric' authors whose work we assessed earlier. Al-Qushayrī's education included a grounding in *furūsiyya* (chivalry)[188] – and one of the most notable of his sufi shaykhs and teachers, Abū 'Alī al-Ḥasan al-Daqqāq (died c. AD 1015–21),[189] introduced his disciple to Abū 'Abd al-Raḥmān al-Sulamī (died AD 1021).[190] Knysh reminds us that al-Sulamī 'is quoted on almost every page of the *Epistle*'.[191]

Al-Qushayrī lived his life against the background of the Saljūq rise to power and Ghaznavid opposition. It was a fluid and fractious age[192] into which he was born. In August AD 1071, about one year before al-Qushayrī's death, the second ruler of the Turkish Saljūq dynasty, Alp Arslan (*reg.* 1063–72), would defeat the Byzantine Emperor Romanus IV Diogenes at the devastating Battle of Manzikert.[193] And over all loomed the political spectre of the Saljūq vizier, Niẓām al-Mulk (AD 1018–92), appointed by Alp Arslan, the successor of the Saljūq Sultan Tughril Bey (*reg.* AD 1038–63), who had won, lost and won the city of Nishapur as he battled the Ghaznavids and sought to control Khurāsān.[194] Intriguingly, Karamustafa tells us that Niẓām al-Mulk, when young, was a student of al-Qushayrī and studied ḥadīth with him.[195]

It was against this background and milieu – historical, political, religious and intellectual – that the famous *Risāla* [*Epistle* or *Treatise*] of al-Qushayrī was written in AD 1046 or 1045.[196] It has become known down the ages as the *Risāla*,[197] but its full title is *al-Risāla al-Qushayriyya fī ʿIlm al-Taṣawwuf*[198] (lit. *The Qushayriyyan Epistle on the Science of Sufism*). The work has garnered numerous plaudits. Knysh suggests that al-Qushayrī is famous principally because of this mystical treatise and that it was 'probably the most popular Sufi manual ever'.[199] Schimmel concurs, holding that it 'is probably the most widely read summary of early Sufism' and stressing that 'it was analyzed in the West prior to most other books on Sufism'.[200] Halm, in his *Encyclopaedia of Islam* article, cherishes al-Qushayrī's *Risāla* as 'a most important compendium of the principles and terminology of Ṣūfism',[201] where, in this work as elsewhere, al-Qushayrī attempts to reconcile sufi practices, held as suspect by so many of the *ʿulamā'*, with the dictates of Islamic law.[202]

Al-Qushayrī may or may not himself have been conscious that he was producing a syncretic system which was not totally coherent or wholly 'unified', despite 'a considerable degree of theoretical classification';[203] but the *Risāla* was certainly a volume which he believed to be entirely *necessary*: the corruption of the age demanded no less[204] and it was necessary to adumbrate the lives of the sufi masters[205] in a volume whose intention was to fortify those on the mystic journey.[206] Karamustafa summarises by suggesting that al-Qushayrī's *approach* is comparable to that of al-Kalābādhī but his *substance* resembles a well-judged merging of key works by al-Sulamī and al-Sarrāj.[207]

Attention has been drawn to the way in which the great medieval theologian and mystic al-Ghazālī was able to gain acceptance for his own sufi stance by rejecting the idea that the *awliyā'* (lit. 'Friends' of God) had an elitist role as the conveyors of special Divine favours to humanity and, by virtue of their authority as spiritual *pirs* (guides or directors) derived from God himself, articulated a mysticism which was based on their esoteric and gnostic learning.[208] However, while al-Qushayrī incorporated precisely such elements into his own Sufism,[209] al-Ghazālī, his mystic contemporary, was very clear: Sufism, or what al-Ghazālī termed *ʿilm aḥwāl al-qalb* ('the science of the states of the heart'),[210] was a duty incumbent upon all Muslims and not just a select few like the *awliyā'*.[211] For al-Ghazālī, salvation would not be achieved by the infusion of some kind of gnostic 'grace' or Protestant 'justification by faith alone'. Real Islam comprised faith and good works: 'Faith is … action in accordance with the [five] pillars' (*wa 'l-īmān … ʿamal bi 'l-arkān*).[212]

The *linked* duality of faith and works is encapsulated, for al-Ghazālī, in a saying attributed to ʿAlī b. Abī Ṭālib: 'Whoso believes that he will attain his goal without effort is a wishful thinker. And whoso believes he will reach his goal by the expending of effort is presumptuous.'[213] The intrinsic link between faith and works which should not be broken is confirmed by the grandson of the Prophet Muḥammad, al-Ḥasan: 'Seeking the Garden without action is a sin' (*Ṭalab al-Janna bilā ʿamal dhanb*).[214] Tobias Mayer summarises: 'Ghazali here salvages an impeccably Ashʿari doctrine of *sola gratia*: no-one is actually saved by their deeds as such'; and Mayer quotes al-Ghāzalī to the effect that 'the worshipper attains Paradise by the bounty and grace of God the Exalted' (*bi faḍl Allāh Taʿālā wa karamihi*).[215] This comes perilously close to sounding like the mainstream Christian doctrine of grace,[216] and so it is perhaps slightly misleading to translate the Arabic *faḍl* (*inter alia*, 'surplus, favour, merit, desert, benefit, gift, present')[217] by the term 'grace', which has such resonance in Christian doctrine and history and which here produces a conflict of theological registers. Yusuf Ali, in his translation of the Qur'ān, perhaps provides a more acceptable translation of this slippery theological term:

> And they returned
> With Grace and *Bounty* [*faḍl*]
> From God: no harm
> Ever touched them:
> For they followed
> The good pleasure of God:
> And God is the Lord
> Of *bounties* unbounded
> [*Wa-Allāh dhū faḍl ʿaẓīm*].[218]

Al-Qushayrī, however, in his text of the *Risāla*, is very much concerned, at least in the first section, to vaunt the variegated merits of many of the great sufi masters of past ages. Thus it is to the *structure* of his text, and then the *themes*, analysed according to our usual sevenfold template, that we will now turn.

The text of the *Risāla* may not be wholly coherent or totally unified,[219] but it *is* fairly simple from a structural perspective. After al-Qushayrī's Introduction, there are just three major, large sections: a first part which surveys a plethora of eighty-three sufi masters; a second, which explains twenty-seven of the principal technical terms of Sufism; and a third, lengthier one which surveys the mystical states (*aḥwāl*) and stations (*maqāmāt*).[220] It has been pointed out that much of this is derivative;[221] but Karamustafa holds that al-Qushayrī's text achieves 'a happy marriage between Sufism and legal-theological scholarship', which helps to account for the popularity of the *Risāla* down the ages.[222] It is al-Qushayrī's most important text and has tended to overshadow several other important texts of his, even his sufi *Laṭā'if al-Ishārāt* (*Subtle Allusions*), which deserves to be better known.[223]

Cloud

If we move now to the themes of al-Qushayrī's *Risāla*, and follow the sevenfold paradigm adumbrated for several of our mystics above, we come first to the motif of *cloud*. Whereas al-Daylamī eschewed the 'cloud' image of the Christian *Cloud of Unknowing* text in favour of the 'veil' image, al-Qushayrī actually uses both, although the latter does predominate. The Arabic text is replete with a specific vocabulary of concealment and unveiling. It includes such words as *maghfira* (here = veil),[224] *satr* (concealment)[225] and *tajallī* (Divine manifestation),[226] *muḥāḍara* (presence),[227] *kashf* (unveiling),[228] *mukāshafa* (unveiling)[229] and *mushāhada* (witnessing).[230] The nearest the text comes to a proper taxonomy of these terms is in a paragraph which orders the terms as 'presence' followed by 'unveiling' followed by 'witnessing'.[231] The most dramatic phrase in the succeeding passage, at least from an intertextual perspective as we bear in mind the images of *The Cloud of Unknowing*, is the sentence:

> When the sky of the innermost heart is free from the clouds of veiling [*'an ghuyūm al-satr*], the sun of witnessing begins to shine from the Zodiacal sign of nobility [*burj al-sharaf*].[232]

And there is a profound epistemological dimension to 'unveiling' and 'witnessing': piety (*taqwā*) and fearing, or being aware of, God (*murāqaba*) are the keys to unveiling (*kashf*) and witnessing (*mushāhada*).[233] Such unveiling, in turn, is the epistemological key whereby the Qushayrian 'Cloud of Unknowing' is finally pierced: in its various forms,[234] 'unveiling [*al-mukāshafa*] is the beginning of certainty', and it is followed by the direct sight and witness of God Himself (*al-mu'āyana, thumma al-mushāhada*).[235] But, as both the Qur'ān at Q. 7:143 and the ḥadīth show, the true glory and majesty of God can be too much – and utterly dangerous – for mortal man.[236] Considerable spiritual strength, awareness of God and piety are required, and perhaps this is why 'concealment' (*satr*) is the preserve of the common people (*al-'awāmm*) while the Divine manifestation of God (*tajallī*) is ultimately reserved for His special 'friends' (*awliyā'*) or sufis, characterised here as a spiritual 'elite' (*al-khawāṣṣ*).[237]

This, of course, runs counter to al-Ghazālī's view, to which we referred earlier, that all should involve themselves in the mystical dimension of Islam. Ultimately, however, al-Qushayrī agrees that both concealment and manifestation are profound mysteries: as Knysh translates, 'God has made Himself apparent by that which He has manifested, while at the same time concealing Himself by that which He has veiled'.[238]

Self-abnegation

Our next *leitmotiv*, that of self-abnegation, is more speedily considered. Such renunciation of self has a number of diverse but constituent aspects which are scattered through the text. There is, firstly, the classic passing away from, or annihilation of, self (*fanā'*) and all its sinful inclinations, states and sins which keep that 'self' earthbound.[239] The result is 'subsistence' or remaining (*baqā'*) in God. Al-Qushayrī emphasises that *fanā'* from the self and one's own attributes is to be achieved by gaining subsistence within God's own attributes (*Fa 'l-awwal fanā' 'an nafsihi, wa ṣifātihi bi-baqā'ihi bi-ṣifāt al-Ḥaqq*).[240]

The way of self-abnegation or renunciation of self is hard and long and will involve, *inter alia*, the elimination (*maḥw*) of habits of sin and sinful tendencies,[241] the practice of abstinence and asceticism (*zuhd*),[242] humility (*khushū'*),[243] and a general tendency to oppose the evil inclinations of the soul (*mukhālafat al-nafs*).[244]

Vision and epistemology are linked by the bridge of *fanā'*: the witnesser has his *nafs* cancelled as a result of the knowledge he gains of God.[245]

Finally, that initial annihilation from one's own *nafs* and consequent subsistence in God's attributes leads on to two further, and even greater, annihilations: 'Then comes the annihilation (*fanā'*) from the attributes of God in the contemplation (*shuhūd*) of God. Then one is annihilated from the vision of one's own annihilation by being subsumed in the existence of God Himself (*fī wujūd al-Ḥaqq*)'.[246] Knysh here translates *shuhūd* as 'contemplation' – and it is clear that actual 'witnessing' is involved, as in some of al-Qushayrī's previous usages of *mushāhada*.

Contemplation

If we turn now to our third *leitmotiv* of contemplation, as articulated in its classical sense, then we note firstly such statements as that cited from Abū 'Alī al-Ḥasan b. 'Alī al-Juzjānī: God's Friends annihilate their own states as they become caught up in contemplating (*al-mushāhada*) God; they lose all awareness of themselves, and their only residing is with God.[247] Knysh here translates *mushāhada* as 'contemplation', and it is left open to the readers of the Arabic to work out for themselves whether actual 'witnessing' of God is involved or just contemplation in the classical sense of an advanced form of meditative prayer. Perhaps the latter is best, and less ambiguously, identified in al-Qushayrī's writings by examining his usage of the classical Arabic sufi term *dhikr*, usually translated as 'remembrance' or 'recollection'. Schimmel, for example, draws our attention[248] to al-Qushayrī's *Tartīb al-Sulūk fī Ṭarīq Allāh* (*Principles of Wayfaring/Behaviour on the Sufi Path*),[249] 'which contains an impressive description of the overwhelming experience of *dhikr* by which the mystic is completely beyond sleep and rest and lives exclusively in his *dhikr* ...'[250]

In the third of the three major sections of the *Risāla*, al-Qushayrī devotes a whole section to *dhikr*:[251] he grounds this in the classical Qur'ānic injunction that the believers should remember God often.[252] Al-Qushayrī also makes reference to another classical *topos*, which was the division of *dhikr* into two types: 'remembrance or recollection of the tongue' (*dhikr al-lisān*) and 'remembrance of the heart' (*dhikr al-qalb*). The ideal is to combine both.[253] It is true that this differs somewhat from the classical Christian concept of 'contemplation': it is perhaps closer to the litanies or Jesus prayer of the Christian tradition, or the mantra of India,[254] and the Islamic sufi *dhikr* may be silent or articulated.[255] But the *telos* of both *dhikr* and contemplation is enormously similar in 'accessing' the Divine and bringing the soul nearer to God: even ecstasy (*al-wajd*) may be the result![256]

Al-Qushayrī repeats the well-known story of the sufi adept who repeated the name *Allah* over and over again until it was a part of the fabric of his very being. One day, his head was gashed by a branch which fell from a tree. Blood poured from his head, and the words *Allah, Allah* appeared in the blood on the ground.[257] It is not surprising, in the light of such anecdotes, that *dhikr* is considered to be superior to *fikr* (thinking, reflection, meditation).[258] (Here, Knysh confusingly translates *fikr* as 'contemplation' – which *is* semantically possible – but he does qualify it as '[rational] contemplation'.)[259]

The Dark Night

The *Risāla* of al-Qushayrī does not articulate a 'Dark Night of the Soul' doctrine *in the same way* as Juan de la Cruz, but it does have a section devoted to the classical sufi states (*aḥwāl*) of what are translated as 'contraction' (*al-qabḍ*) and 'expansion' (*al-basṭ*).[260] These are states on the sufi spiritual path which may be said to have an analogy with Juan's 'Dark Night' doctrine. One may, for example, feel that God is displeased with one and that some punishment is due. Thus, one's heart will 'contract' with dismay and, perhaps, fear. On the other hand, a feeling of closeness to God and a perception of His loving kindness may engender an 'expansion' of the heart.[261]

These are clearly psychological spiritual states, and their kinship to the 'Dark Night' doctrine may be seen in the words of the great sufi Abū 'l-Qāsim al-Junayd (died AD 910)[262] in which a fear/hope dichotomy engenders precisely these *aḥwāl* of contraction and expansion, and for whom separation from the Divine constitutes a veritable veil and precipitates feelings of abandonment.[263]

There is, however, one passage in al-Qushayrī's *Risāla* which does come remarkably close to the 'Dark Night' doctrine of Juan de la Cruz. It is not elaborated nor remarked upon, but it does exhibit an intertextual link to our Spanish mystic, albeit, perhaps, to a limited degree:

> *And if God wishes to test the aspirant, He will banish him to the wastelands of alienation from Him (fī maṭāriḥ ghurbatihi).*[264]

The imagery is clearly different from that of John – there is no 'dark night' here – but the two authors share an underlying sense of banishment and exile (*ghurba*).

Perfection

Our fifth *leitmotiv* is perfection. This is a constant theme throughout much of the text, in which the aspirant to the sufi path and, indeed, the adept, is urged to perfect him- or herself in a variety of ways as a prelude to, or part of, ascending to a higher *ḥāl* (state) or *maqām* (station). Thus, we are told that perfection in personal and mystical questing (*fī ḥāl sulūkihi*) can be achieved (*wa huwa al-kāmil*) by God's servant if his heart and tongue have the willing ability to undertake remembrance.[265] But such perfection requires effort and striving (*mujāhada*). Nothing will be unveiled on the sufi path to the would-be practitioner if that person does not make a constant effort to advance spiritually.[266] The mystical states (*al-aḥwāl*) are pure gifts (*mawāhib*) from the Divine, bestowed on mystics regardless of intention; but the mystical stations (*al-maqāmāt*) can be earned (*al-maqāmāt makāsib*),[267] and it is abundantly clear from every aspect of al-Qushayrī's text that the mystic path whereby one moves systematically towards perfection from one station (*maqām*) to another is his preferred path *par excellence*.[268]

Human and Divine Love

All this leads to love, human and Divine, which is our sixth motif. Al-Qushayrī, in a section which deals with 'Proximity [*qurb*] and distance [*bu'd*]',[269] cites the famous *ḥadīth qudsī*, which may aptly be termed the 'Divine Love Ḥadīth', as follows:

> [My servant] draws near me through nothing more than that which I have made obligatory for him. My servant [*al-'abd*] never ceases drawing near to me through supererogatory works until he loves Me and I love him. Then, when I love him, I become his sight and hearing through which he hears and sees …[270]

Here, it is love which is powerfully associated with works – supererogatory works (*nawāfil*) – rather than the classical combination of faith (*īmān*) and works. This particular *ḥadīth qudsī* was clearly a favourite of al-Qushayrī's, for it is repeated in a slightly different form elsewhere in his text as well.[271]

Al-Qushayri devotes a whole, lengthy section to the Station (*maqām*) of Love (*al-Maḥabba*).[272] It is preceded by that devoted to the Station entitled *al-Ma'rifa bi-llāh*,[273] which Knysh translates as 'Divine Gnosis',[274] and followed by the Station designated as *al-Shawq* (Longing, Yearning).[275] Al-Qushayrī cites Abū 'l-Ḥasan al-Sarī al-Saqaṭī (died c. AD 865) as proclaiming that, for the gnostic, 'longing' (*al-shawq*) was the most sublime of all the mystical stations when it is effected within him.[276] And, if the sufi adept is to follow the rule laid down by al-Qushayrī whereby one does not move from one station to the next higher one before one becomes proficient in the rules of the first,[277] and *if* al-Qushayrī intended his description of the *maqāms* to be chronological, then it is clear that the sufi path for him advances from Divine Gnosis, through the Station of Love, to Longing. However, it is by no means certain that al-Qushayrī intended a strictly chronological account of the *maqāms*.

The section on love offers numerous definitions, descriptions and anecdotes about love; indeed, the whole of al-Qushayrī's text is replete with scattered references relating to this topic. From these, we gain a clear idea about the ideal sufi concepts of both human and Divine love. For example, deploying the classic medieval Arabic motif of love as a sickness,[278] we are told about a youth whose love of God is so extreme that he has become ill to the point of death.[279] And the sufi gives voice to his longing for the Beloved Deity (*al-Ḥabīb*) in prayerful supplication (*du'ā'*).[280] There is no rest for those in love with God until they become close to Him whom they love so dearly (*illā bi-qurb ḥabībihim*).[281]

We note here this *leitmotiv* of 'closeness to the Divine' already encountered in an entire earlier section.[282] Love brings the devotee closer to God and destroys the veils between God and man – another very common sufi motif.[283] Such was the Arabian prophet Shu'ayb's love of, and longing for, God that he became blind from weeping several times.[284] This story, of course, belongs to the body of extreme examples of the ways in which the human could manifest his love for the Divine, but they all illustrate how all-embracing that love for God was supposed to be. The images of this kind of love are many and varied in al-Qushayrī's *Risāla*, including, as Baldick reminds us, that of gay love as an image of the sufi's love of the Divine.[285]

So much for human love of God. The reverse – God's love for humanity – has already been adumbrated in the *ḥadīth qudsī* cited above. And there are diverse other references in the *Risāla*: al-Qushayrī suggests that, in the Qur'ān, there is a mutual loving relationship between God and man.[286] When God is filled with love for one of his creatures (*al-'abd*), he commands the angel Jibrīl to love that man too.[287]

Union

All this brings us to the final part of our sevenfold mystical paradigm as we apply it to al-Qushayrī, and to the ultimate goals of this mystic, which are union (*jam'*),[288] the union of union (*jam' al-jam'*),[289] and, finally, absolute subsistence in the Divinity (*baqā'*).[290] This may result in ecstasy.[291]

'Union' (*jam'*) is defined as 'the assertion of the Real' (*ithbāt al-Ḥaqq*).[292] It means that one sees absolutely everything through the eyes of God.[293] But 'the Union of Unions' (*jam' al-jam'*) means that one is totally dissolved or consumed within the Godhead.[294] He subsists in God and His attributes[295] and, in an utterly mysterious way, may achieve unity with God and become one with Him.[296]

There are 'green' links in al-Qushayrī's *Risāla* as well: al-Khaḍir/al-Khiḍr appears in the text several times, usually encountered in a mysterious fashion by sufi travellers,[297] and most notably in his traditional Qur'ānic guise with Mūsā.[298] Al-Khaḍir provides water to a man collapsed with thirst in the desert,[299] conjures up much-desired food[300] and proves to be a healer.[301] He is also portrayed as speaking in very laudatory terms about the great jurists of medieval Islam, al-Shāfi'ī (AD 767–820) and Aḥmad b. Ḥanbal (AD 780–855).[302]

Al-Khaḍir is thus lauded in al-Qushayrī's text as a protector of the virtuous and, in his guise as healer and provisioner (especially of water), one with impeccable 'green' credentials. It is interesting that, for Ḥātim al-Aṣamm (died AD 851/2), cited by al-Qushayrī, green is one of the colours of *taṣawwuf*: to embrace the mystic path is to embrace a 'green death' (*mawt akhḍar*) whereby one wears the patched garments (*al-riqā'*) of the sufi adept.[303] And, as the Qur'ān shows,[304] al-Khaḍir is also a leader, *par excellence*, of and among mystics. He may have been classified as a *walī* ('Friend' [of God]) rather than a *nabī* (prophet)[305] but, in the sufi stratosphere of the *awliyā'*, he was – and remains – enormously powerful. This brings us to the role of leader in the eyes of al-Qushayrī and, in particular, the role of the sufi master or shaykh.

Both Baldick and Karamustafa draw particular attention to al-Qushayrī's emphasis on the huge need for proper guidance and training from a proficient master, *shaykh*, for the novice sufi (*murīd*).[306] As Karamustafa reminds us, so important is the motif of obedience by the aspirant to the Master, that the ideal sufi disciple–master relationship is likened to that between al-Khaḍir and Mūsā in the Qur'ān in the famous encounter to which we have already alluded several times.[307] Here, again, we find the ubiquitous figure of al-Khaḍir, the 'Friend of God', who here epitomises the sufi shaykh who must be obeyed, regardless of the request or provocation. In Karamustafa's succinct phrase, 'for Qushayrī, the authority of the training master had virtually no bounds'.[308]

There can be little doubt that, in such emphases and structures, al-Qushayrī was influenced by the impact of his own masters like the Ash'arite sufi shaykh, Abū 'Alī al-Daqqāq (died AD 1015), whose daughter Fāṭima he later married,[309] and the elderly Khurāsānian sufi Abū 'Abd al-Raḥmān al-Sulamī (died AD 1021).[310] Rabia Harris suggests that 'if Daqqaq formed Qushayri as a teacher, Sulami formed him as a writer'.[311]

It is, of course, a truism that leaders – sufi shaykhs or others – cannot lead without those who agree – willingly or unwillingly, under conditions of trial like Mūsā with al-Khaḍir or perfectly voluntarily – to follow them. Among such followers may be the aspirants and sufi *murīdīn* (novices), as well as the fully fledged *ikhwān* (Brethren) of the formal sufi Orders (*Ṭuruq*). There are intertextual links here with what we treated earlier in connection with al-Sulamī and his *Kitāb al-Futuwwa* and Ibn Baṭṭūṭa's encounter with the *fityān*. Schimmel reminds us that al-Qushayrī devotes a whole section of his *Risāla* to the *maqām* or station of *futuwwa*;[312] Knysh translates the latter word as 'chivalry',[313] but Karamustafa suggests that it is a 'spiritualised' *futuwwa*, discussed in the 'abstract' and reduced 'to its core, altruistic self-sacrifice'.[314]

Spiritualised or not, while it is true that al-Qushayrī's text does not vaunt knightly deeds of warfare and valour, it does place a premium on many of the other classical Western and Eastern *topoi* of chivalry such as always serving, or 'looking out for', other people (*fī amr ghayrihi*),[315] treating others with justice while not seeking justice for oneself,[316] maintaining high moral standards,[317] treating everyone equally,[318] exhibiting sensitive good manners in the face of adversity,[319] and abiding by the code of honour demanded by the concept of *futuwwa*.[320]

It is, perhaps, unsurprising that the *maqām* treated by al-Qushayrī after *futuwwa* is that of *firāsa*, which means 'perspicacity, acumen, discernment'[321] but which is translated by Knysh as 'spiritual insight'.[322] Here we learn, right at the beginning of the section, that *al-firāsa* is something that enters the heart and evicts anything it finds there which opposes *firāsa*.[323] Those who have insight see things as God sees them;[324] and al-Qushayrī shows that real insight is one of the gifts of the great sufis (*al-ʿārifīn*).[325] In his perspicacious and much-loved survey of the sufi world of his and past ages, this gift of *firāsa* was also something which he might have claimed for himself.

3.3 *Christian*

In introducing the earlier sections of this chapter, we focused on the motif of the journey towards God. In this final section, we will be no less concerned with this primary theme of the long, hard journey towards the Creator and eternal salvation. It is the mystical equivalent of the much-cited Islamic *riḥla fī ṭalab al-ʿilm* (journey in search of knowledge), with the rider that the 'knowledge', devoutly desired, is *always* that of the Divine.

At the core of William Harmless's book *Mystics*[326] are case studies of six major Christian mystics drawn from over 1,500 years of religious history and experience: Evagrius Ponticus (AD 345–99), Bernard of Clairvaux (AD 1090–1153), Hildegard of Bingen (AD 1098–1179), Bonaventure (AD 1217–74), Meister Eckhart (c. AD 1260–1327) and Thomas Merton (1915–68). In sharp contrast, these are followed by studies of the great medieval Islamic mystical poet Jalāl al-Dīn Rūmī (AD 1207–73) and the Japanese Sōtō Zen founder, Dōgen (AD 1200–53).[327]

Harmless provides specific reasons for his eclectic choices,[328] and these are implicit in the way he characterises his *dramatis personae*: Evagrius Ponticus is 'Mystic as Desert Calligrapher';[329] Bernard of Clairvaux is 'Mystic as Experienced Exegete';[330] Hildegard of Bingen is 'Mystic as Multimedia Artist';[331] Bonaventure is 'Mystic as Cartographer';[332] Meister Eckhart is 'Mystic as Mystagogue';[333] and

Thomas Merton is 'Mystic as Fire Watcher'.[334] The whole volume is written in the light of William James's (1842–1910) 'common core' hypothesis, as elaborated in *The Varieties of Religious Experience*,[335] to the effect 'that mystics speak with a certain unanimity';[336] 'that peak mystical experiences are ultimately the same the world over but are simply experienced differently by different individuals in different religions';[337] and that 'mystics form a sort of worldwide confraternity'.[338] Was William James right to suggest 'that mystics, however diverse their reports, are experiencing the same thing'?[339]

By dint of his meticulous case studies, Harmless finds evidence both in support of, and in opposition to, this 'common core' hypothesis.[340] One simply cannot – must not – generalise, especially in the sensitive arena of comparative mysticism.[341] What Harmless usefully does, also, is draw attention to what he terms 'convergences', for example, 'between Sufism and Christian Mysticism'[342] and, drawing on Steven Katz, the need to 'contextualise' and write in a way that will 'target specific mystics, specific mystical themes, and specific mystical traditions'.[343]

It is not the intention in this book to embrace wholeheartedly a 'common core' hypothesis, despite a plethora of enormously distinguished past adherents to this view who include not just William James but also Aldous Huxley, Mircea Eliade and Ninian Smart.[344] While I do deploy a sevenfold paradigm which I apply to each of the major Islamic and Christian mystics whose writings form the substance of this volume, this is not intended to indicate 'an irreducible common core'[345] in *all* mystics and *all* mysticisms, nor to resort to an apodeictic essentialism which may be perceived in these arenas. It is acknowledged that there are diverse differences between multifarious mystical persons and multifarious mystical traditions, all of which swim in their own individual milieux of time, space, history, culture and religion. *The seven-pronged paradigm adumbrated and deployed in various places in this volume is intended to illuminate only those Islamic and Christian mystics to whom it is applied.* It does not – and cannot – have universal significance, for it is recognised that every mystic and every mystical tradition is an individual product of context, experience, milieu and history.[346] To establish an *intertext*, as I have attempted so often in this work, is *not* to establish total sameness.

William Harmless's approach and choice of mystical figures in his volume has come in for some criticism. Reviewing his book, Lucy Beckett, for example, observes: 'To choose [Hildegard of Bingen] over Julian of Norwich or Teresa of Ávila as the only female subject in *Mystics* seems odd to say the least'.[347] These lacunae *are* rectified in this book of mine in what follows. Beckett finds that 'Harmless's selection and ordering of case studies, six Christians, one Sufi and one Zen Buddhist, confuse as well as clarify his central theme'.[348] It is hoped that the approach and content of what has preceded and what will follow, with its deep emphasis on primary text,[349] will illuminate rather than obfuscate. For *our* central theme is the *mystic journey*, a journey which is as much of the mind as the body, as the sub-editor who titled Beckett's review 'The mind's journey' was well aware.

That journey in Christianity and Islam took diverse forms and was undertaken against a variety of historical and theological backgrounds, by mystics exhibiting vastly different types of lives lived and spiritualities thereby engendered.

On the back cover of a paperback translated edition of the 1608 classic text by Francis de Sales (AD 1567–1622), *Philothea, or An Introduction to the Devout Life*, we find the following blurb: 'As no sensible person would make a long road trip without first consulting a map, so the person intent on gaining Heaven shall first resort to a competent guide to reach that Goal of all goals'.[350] Francis de Sales, aware of both the rise of Calvinism and the admiration for him of the courts of the French kings Henri IV (*reg.* AD 1589–1610) and Louis XIII (*reg.* 1610–43),[351] presents an everyday guide to salvation, addressed to all Christians, which teaches 'that the very height of sanctity and perfection might be attained by any man or woman who, in the fear of God and His Love, fulfils all the duties of the state of life in which his lot has been cast'.[352] Here, in the emphasis on Divine Love and perfection, there is a parallelism in de Sales' work with much of what we have already examined above, as well as a harmony with al-Ghazālī's insistence[353] that, before the mystic path proper is to be embraced, there was to be a perfect fulfilment of the five pillars of the Islamic faith, the *arkān*. The goal of Francis de Sales' text is not the traditional mystical union *per se*, but mystical perfection with the theme of the journey as a constant.[354] It deals with the ordinary virtues and vices of this world, but, in its pursuit of perfection, it is no less a mystical text for all that. Actions and, indeed, body parts like the ear may have a mystical significance.[355]

Philothea is a logical and natural successor to the *De Imitatione Christi* of Thomas à Kempis, which we shall soon analyse in more detail. It also has an intertextual affiliation *in terms of the mystical journey* with that great spiritual travelogue and archetype by John Bunyan (AD 1628–88), published in 1678, under the title of *The Pilgrim's Progress*,[356] although the two texts are articulated in very different ways. Francis de Sales' volume is a work of piety and good counsel while Bunyan's is an allegorical fiction. At the heart of both, however, is the spiritual journey. And, while de Sales' text, by and large, is a highly *practical* primer, it *is* aware of the possibility in this life of 'spiritual consolation', those 'heavenly consolations [which] are as foretastes of the eternity of bliss which God gives to those souls who seek it'.[357]

But it is also aware of Juan de la Cruz's 'Dark Night': 'Such pleasant seasons will not always endure. On the contrary, at times you will be so deprived and destitute of all devout feeling that you will imagine your soul to be a desert, fruitless, sterile land wherein is no path or road leading to God, nor any water-springs of grace which can moisten the dryness that threatens to reduce it to dust.'[358] Here, the theme is of the Road which has ended, unsignposted, in the desert, with the latter image replacing Juan's 'Dark Night' and the 'Cloud' in *The Cloud of Unknowing*.

Francis de Sales concludes as follows: 'The less self-interest we have in the pursuit of virtue, the greater therein will be the purity and brightness of divine love. The child embraces his mother when she gives him sugar, but it is greater sign of love if he embraces her when she has given him wormwood or camomile.'[359] For the initial bestowal of spiritual consolations and later withdrawal of the same are all designed to give the soul 'some foretaste of heavenly joy' and lead that soul 'in the pursuit of divine love'.[360] It is that Divine Love towards which the soul is urged by Francis to travel, however difficult the path.[361] And, as we have seen before, that difficulty may require a guide of some kind. It might be the shaykh or the *pir* of the

Islamic tradition, as, for example, al-Qushayrī's shaykh and teacher; the 'holy guide and conductor' recommended by Francis de Sales;[362] the brave little hoopoe bird of Farīd al-Dīn 'Attār's (died AD 1220) *Conference of the Birds*, who is designated 'our Imām, to bind and to loose';[363] the questing caravans in Naguib Mahfouz's (AD 1911–2006) great novel *The Journey of Ibn Fattouma* (*Riḥlat Ibn Faṭṭūma*);[364] or the Virgin Mary as intercessor, intermediary and guide, as in the spirituality of Louis Marie Grignion de Montfort (AD 1673–1716).[365]

There is, indeed, a certain equivalence of motifs or, put another way, intertextuality, here in the deeply felt need for a spiritual guide. And the same is true of the *leitmotiv* of *pain*, of alienation, again in one form or another, which lies behind so much in the Islamic and Christian mystical traditions, whether it be articulated in the shape of the desert, the veil or the dark night. This can take a physical as well as a psychological form. One of the most notable Christian examples of this was the twentieth-century Capuchin friar of Pietrelcina in Italy, universally known as Padre Pio (AD 1887–1968),[366] who not only suffered the 'dark night of the soul'[367] but was beset by acute ill health as well as the severe pain of the stigmata.[368]

He was by no means alone. Of the Swiss mystic Adrienne Von Speyr (AD 1902–67), her close friend, collaborator, spiritual director and confessor, Hans Urs Von Balthasar, wrote: 'I have mentioned that Adrienne had a wound under her breast dating from the first Marian vision in 1917. She perceived this as a mysterious seal, a reminder and a promise. After her conversion this wound was sharply accentuated and other stigmata were at times manifested along with it.'[369] Her health, too, like Padre Pio's, was a constant physical trial.[370]

Of course, ill health has never been a necessary 'charism', pre-requisite or companion in the mystical life, but it has often been a possible one, especially if the mystic suffered some kind of mystical wounding like the stigmata as well. Francis de Sales, Padre Pio and Adrienne Von Speyr are three extremely different types of the cataphatic mystical tradition. Indeed, the latter two verge on what I can only characterise here as the cataphatic-ecstatic. They are briefly introduced here by way of illustrating the diversity of type of mystic in the Christian tradition – a diversity paralleled in the Islamic: we might compare the life of the notorious al-Ḥallāj (died AD 922), for example, with the more sober al-Qushayrī surveyed above. In the light of all this, we turn now to an analysis of three Christian mystics and their associated texts, bringing to bear once again, by way of illumination, our chosen sevenfold paradigm.

3.3.1 Julian of Norwich (c. 1343–after 1416) and *The Way of the Anchoress*

Scholars differ slightly about Julian's exact *dates*. Nicholas Watson and Jacqueline Jenkins suggest c. AD 1343–after 1416;[371] Andrea Janelle Dickens states definitively AD 1343–1413;[372] while Elizabeth Ruth Obbard gives AD 1342–1420.[373] We know little of her actual *life*, and even her real name is lost to us. What we do know is that she lived as an anchoress and was associated with St Julian's church, Norwich, from which she probably adopted the name by which she is universally known to posterity.[374] Carmel Bendon Davis shows that we can only really know the textual

Julian,[375] though many have envisaged her through the medium of fiction.[376] Above all, as Christopher Abbott stresses, her text, 'in whatever register it is written at any given point – anecdotal, didactic, descriptive, theological, analytical, advisory', is the total product of her own dynamic and personal experience.[377]

It is a text or, rather, as we shall see, a pair of texts, which have been much lauded by scholars. Although not susceptible to easy categorisation in terms of its mysticism,[378] it has won plaudits such as Dickens' description of it as 'a cornerstone of women's mysticism in the middle ages'.[379] Watson and Jenkins hold that it is the product of 'one of the great speculative theologians of the Middle Ages'. For them, Julian is 'an intellectual whose rare ability to pay simultaneous attention to what is true in an abstract sense and to what humans need to be true in a material one gives her writing extraordinary tension and energy'.[380]

Christopher Abbott sees 'her affirmation of the personal' as taking 'the form of a developed incarnational theology'.[381] Such comments rather give the lie to the idea that 'Julian's book is not a manual for contemplatives or a theological treatise'.[382] In its emphasis both on contemplation and on matters theological, it could aptly be described as both.

To say with Elizabeth Ruth Obbard that Julian lived during 'a time of tragedy and unrest'[383] is almost an understatement. Norwich, of course, was a wealthy commercial city,[384] but the plague was the backdrop to Julian's early life.[385] The Hundred Years War was raging with France.[386] Gail Alva Berkeley goes so far as to suggest that Julian's writings were actually a *response* to the woes of the age.[387] Yet, within this discordant orchestra of plague, war and civil unrest, we may detect a few positive notes. One was the increasingly prominent role of women in everyday life[388] and, indeed, in authorship.[389] Notable among these must rank Julian of Norwich.

Illness, indeed near-death, and visionary experiences seem to go hand in hand with Julian. It would be no exaggeration to chararacterise her as an early Adrienne Von Speyr, to whom we have earlier referred and who was also prone to bouts of sickness. Von Speyr's mentor and confessor, Hans Urs Von Balthasar, recalls how, on the evening of 9 August 1945, a very agitated Von Speyr summoned Von Balthasar; he describes how she had been caught in a 'mystical' thunderstorm in which she saw a 'woman with twelve stars around her head … wrapped in fire and stand[ing] on a globe. She was pregnant and was crying out during the entire time.' The globe proves to be the moon, and then a dragon appears which 'had seven heads, ten horns and seven diadems on its heads'.[390] Von Balthasar explains to Von Speyr that she has seen the vision of the Virgin Mary as described in the Book of the Apocalypse.[391]

Julian's own vision is no less terrifying but also has an element of comfort and easing of pain rather than the utter confusion suffered by Adrienne Von Speyr. Lying close to death on 13 May 1373 in Norwich, Julian is about to receive extreme unction for the second time, when the cross in her hand becomes extremely bright, her pain eases and a series of revelations (or 'showings') begin during the remainder of the day and in the night.[392]

In a typically Julianic triadic – one might almost say 'Trinitarian' – format, Julian has earlier requested that she be given three graces:

> I desirede thre graces be the gifte of God. The first was to have minde of Cristes passion. The second was bodelye syekeness. And the third was to have of Goddes gifte thre woundes.[393]

It is not for nothing that Andrea Dickens characterises Julian as a 'Bodily Mystic'[394] and stresses how much of Julian research 'notes how the body plays an important role in her spirituality and theology'.[395] The appalling and ubiquitous spectre of the Black Death can only have increased such a sensitive awareness.[396] Berkeley perceives the use of illness 'throughout the text … as a figure for sin'[397] whereas, for Carmel Davis, the emphasis is more positively on Julian's pain as an analogue of Christ's own redemptive suffering.[398] And the pain of the latter can *take away* the human pain of the former, as witnessed in the disappearance of Julian's 'deathbed' pain while she gazes at the crucifix she has been shown.[399] And, despite much physical and spiritual suffering, Julian, because of her profound mystical love of God which she believed to be reciprocated, remained an optimist! As she herself famously put it:

> But Jhesu, that in this vision enformed me of alle that me neded, answered by this worde and saide: 'Sinne is behovely [= befitting],[400] but alle shalle be wele, and alle shalle be wele, and alle maner of thinge shalle be wel'.[401]

The structure of Julian's revelations is neat, lucid and simple. It consists of two distinct textual versions of the revelations, known to scholars as the 'long text' and the 'short text',[402] covering sixteen 'showings' or revelations,[403] whose longer version comprises eighty-six chapters.[404] All are united by the overarching theme of love, God's love for man and man's love for God.[405] The 'short text' is known as *A Vision Showed to a Devout Woman*, while the longer version goes under the title *A Revelation of Love*.[406] Both are often brought together under the simple title *Revelations of Divine Love*.[407] The two texts are intimately related. Watson and Jenkins identify the dialect in which they were written as 'a northeastern dialect of Middle English' and surmise that they date to a time between the eighth decade of the fourteenth century and Julian's death. They note that they are personal reports of the same vision experienced at the height of Julian's encounter with death at the age of 30.[408]

Both texts, notes Andrea Dickens, are doctrinally similar, as is their content, but the 'long text' is the more stylistic of the two. Furthermore, the latter illustrates the way in which Julian endows with real meaning the revelations she has received.[409] In sum, to use the words of Elizabeth Ruth Obbard, Julian, in both the structure and content of her two texts, 'penetrates the *meaning* of the Christian mystery and elucidates it in an inimitable and original way'.[410] Thus, it is to that 'Christian mystery', *in its mystic garb*, and by means of the sevenfold paradigm which we have previously deployed for both the Islamic and Christian traditions, that we will now turn.

Cloud

Generally speaking, Julian's visions place her firmly within a cataphatic – indeed, ecstatic – mystical tradition rather than the apophatic tradition of *The Cloud of Unknowing*. There is no cloud or veil to hide what she sees, although there were clearly different types of 'seeing': 'And I suddenly saw the red blood trickling down from under the crown of thorns, all hot, freshly, plentifully and vividly …'[411] There is, then, an actual, perceived physical and personal contact with the Deity. Julian herself, in her habitual 'Trinitarian', triadic fashion, confirms the physicality of some of her 'showings' in chapter 73 of the 'long text':

> Alle this blessed teching of oure lorde God was shewde by thre partes: that is to sey, by bodely sight, and by worde formed in mine understonding, and by gostely sighte.[412]

Wolters translates these three modes of vision as 'by physical sight, by words formed in my intellect, and by spiritual sight'[413] and notes that some scholars have tried to trace Julian's division to Augustine's triple division of 'visions' into 'corporeal' (i.e. actually perceived by the senses), 'imaginary' and 'intellectual' ('fed into the soul by the direct action of God').[414] But Wolters believes that Julian's own classification of her visions cannot be straitjacketed in such a rigid manner.[415]

We can say, in conclusion, that, whatever the exact range or type of vision experienced by Julian, there was much that was sensory, visual and physical over which the classical 'cloud of unknowing' did not cast its shadow. As we shall see, Julian may have experienced a form of 'dark night', but that was a sensual or sensory rather than epistemological dimension of her mysticism. For Julian *knows* from personal and physical experience that God exists, feels His absence keenly and yearns to join Him.[416] Denise Nowakowski Baker draws attention to Julian's essential epistemology as expressed in chapter 56 (on her fourteenth *Showing*), where Julian asserts that it is easier to know God than it is to know one's own soul.[417]

Self-abnegation

Reading her texts, we are left in little doubt about the fundamental humility of Julian of Norwich. She describes herself, for example, in chapter 9 of the 'long text', as 'right nought'[418] (= 'really nothing'),[419] and further designates herself as 'a simple creature unletterde',[420] although in the 'long text' there is a considerable dilution, overall, of the self-abasement.[421] Yet this is one whom Watson and Jenkins characterise as 'one of the great speculative theologians of the Middle Ages'.[422] So, is there just a faint possibility that, here at least, Julian protests overmuch and may even be accused of some false humility? Baker indicates that there is a considerable debate over the extent of her learning.[423] Could she read Latin as well as English? Did she forego the services of an amanuensis and both write and revise her own texts?[424]

In the light of her ubiquitous *textual* humility, perhaps the most acceptable conclusion is that she underplayed her own learning out of 'conventional modesty'[425] and that her self-designation as 'a simple creature unletterde' was but one of the 'conventional signals of devotional discourse' deployed by mystics rather than indicators of their actual education.[426]

Contemplation

Julian has an accurate understanding of what contemplation is and the need for it:

> And after this our Lord showed himself to me in even greater glory, it seemed to me, than when I saw him before, and from this revelation I learned that

> each contemplative soul to whom it is given to look for God and seek him, shall see her [the Virgin Mary] and pass on to God through contemplation.[427]

Here, there is a magnificently prescient Marian gloss to Julian's adumbration of the merits of contemplation. Prefiguring such later Catholic saints as Louis Marie Grignion de Montfort,[428] Julian here teaches, in effect, that Mary is a pathway to Jesus. Later, in an extended passage which links both Mary and the Trinity, Julian notes that the soul of man 'sees God, *it contemplates God* and it loves God'.[429]

The Dark Night

Pace Clifton Wolters,[430] other scholars have not been slow to notice that Julian suffers a kind of 'dark night' akin to that adumbrated several centuries later by Juan de la Cruz, but delineated more briefly and in a very different style.[431] Spiritual delights and consolations may be followed by a profound aridity and depression mingled with loneliness.[432] Julian even uses the image of the 'night', albeit in a slightly different way from Juan: 'Thus I saw and understood that our faith is our light in our night, light which is God, our everlasting day.'[433] And it is not only the aridity of the classical 'night' which afflicts her. She is afflicted and tempted in her illness, during the sixteenth showing or revelation, with renewed sickness in which she is beset by demonic images – from which, however, her profound trust in the mercy of God releases her.[434] Julian's 'Dark Night' is unlike Juan's but no less traumatic for all that.

Perfection

One of the key *leitmotivs* in this volume is the search for perfection, both secular and sacred, and an investigation and analysis of its diverse pathways. This theme provides a vital link between our Chapter 1 in which, borrowing a phrase from St Thomas Aquinas, we explored the *quinque viae* of perfection, and the present Chapter 3 in which, via our sevenfold paradigm, we investigate the writings of six Islamic and Christian mystics.

The theme of perfection is no less important in the life and writings of Julian than in any of these other mystics. If one overarching theme of both sets of revelations is love, then another is the constant need to perfect oneself. One is never to cease in one's search for God, and that seeking is to be undertaken 'with faith, hope and charity'.[435] The whole of Julian's text is a primer for such seeking, carving out the ways to perfect the soul, for 'it is Gods will that we seke into the beholding of him, for by that shall he shew us himself of his special grace when he will'.[436] Sin is devoutly to be avoided – and, by the power of the Holy Ghost, we express our sorrow for sin, make a firm purpose of amendment and thereby lessen the wrath of the Creator who loves us and who says: 'My dere darling, I am glad thou arte come to me. In alle thy woe I have ever ben with the, and now seest thou my loving, and we be oned in blisse.'[437]

Julian teaches that we should never cease to seek the ways of perfection. It is recognised that sin is almost inevitable, but 'if through our blindness and our wretchedness we ever fall, we are taught to rise again quickly, recognizing the sweet touch of grace, and *earnestly amend our life* on the basis of Holy Church's teaching according to the grievousness of the sin, and go at once to God in love'.[438]

From these two quotations, then, we see that it is the purpose of amendment that sets the sinful soul once again on the path towards perfection, even if that sublime *telos* is never reached in this life.

Human and Divine Love

All this links us neatly to the final two parts of our sevenfold paradigm, God's love for man and the need for the latter to love Him; and eternal union with Him in the next world.

Now, it is a truism that the whole theme of the 'Showings' is Love.[439] Chivalric notions of romantic love had, of course, been characteristic of society and literature in the early Middle Ages,[440] and so it is no surprise, given the historical backcloth to their lives, that female mystics should have incorporated such notions, in one form or another, into their approach to God.[441] Julian's own deep intimacy with God, however, is to be characterised as 'realist' rather than 'romantic'. Deeply conscious of the capacity for sin in fallen humanity, as we have seen, she shows that it is God's overwhelming *love* for us (and our attempts to love Him) – even as a mother, as is sometimes the case in Julian's vocabulary![442] – that will win us Paradise.

Echoing Augustine's famous dictum that our hearts were made for God and would never rest until they rested in Him,[443] Julian comments on the unsatisfying nature of earthly life and concludes that God is the only satisfactory haven and rest.[444] For God has loved us eternally, even before the beginning of time,[445] and will never cease from doing so.[446] As Wolters puts it, summarising that last, most beautiful, of all the chapters of the 'long text' (chapter 86): 'Above all else, God is love, and all his works, natural or spiritual, are done in love'.[447] As Julian herself put it: 'Wit it wele, love was his mening. *Who shewed it the? Love*.'[448] Spearing translates: 'Know well that love was what he meant. Who showed you this? Love.'[449]

Carmel Bendon Davis comments:

> The answer gives assurance to Julian that Love is all-encompassing and eternal. Love is not confined to body-space but extends infinitely into soul-space. Thus, Love is simultaneously immanent and transcendent. Likewise, Julian's mystical space is an all-encompassing space in which time offers no resistance to the seamless blending of physical and spiritual experience. In her mystical space, Love encloses Julian just as Julian encloses Love and the two medieval postulations of space as a receptacle and that which is contained are reconciled.[450]

Union

The ultimate *telos* and joy for every mystic – Christian or Muslim – is union with the Divine. In some mystical fashion, the soul dwells 'in God', 'unites' with God. We can identify scattered gradations in the way Julian speaks of this union. In Section Four of the 'short text', Julian desires to become a single substance with God without anything-created between them.[451] In chapter 28 of the 'long text', Julian is told by God that all earthly passions will be shattered and she shall be made 'meke and milde, clene and holy, by oning [= uniting][452] to me'.[453] In chapter 54, we are told by Julian that we should feel great happiness in the fact that God lives within our soul, and even more that it lives in Him.[454]

Then, in the same chapter, Julian makes a spectacular and breathtaking leap in her vocabulary of Divine Union which, in the words of Christopher Abbott, 'only just (but also absolutely) stops short of assigning actual divinity to human nature itself';[455] with Abbott, it is worth quoting in full: we shall use here Elizabeth Spearing's translation for clarity:

> Our soul is made to be God's dwelling (= *wonning/wonyng*)[456] place, and the dwelling place of the soul is God, who is not made. It shows deep understanding to see and know inwardly that God, who is our maker, dwells in our soul; and deeper understanding to see and know that our soul, which is made, dwells in God's being; through this essential being – God – we are what we are. And I saw no difference between God and our essential being, it seemed to be all God, and yet my understanding took it that our essential being is in God: that is to say that God is God and our essential being is a creation within God ...[457]

Abbott neatly explains and shows that Julian has not fallen into the morass of pantheism or identification of divinity and humanity: 'God is divine by nature. Humanity is divine by participation.'[458]

In conclusion, we might ask: how *green* was Julian? *This* particular colour does not have a mystical or privileged significance in her text. She does see in her imagination underwater 'hilles and *dales grene* seeming as it were mosse begrowen',[459] but the scene is interpreted as meaning that God's omnipresence, even under the sea, would be sufficient protection for the soul and body of man or woman.[460]

If one had to choose, from admittedly fairly scanty evidence, it would seem that at least two of Julian's favourite colours are *blue* and *white*. God is portrayed in the Parable of the Lord and the Servant as wearing clothing which is 'blew as asure'[461] (= 'blue as azure').[462] Julian tells us that this colour signified the quality of steadfastness.[463] The servant in the same parable wears a *white* tunic and represents Jesus and, through him, Adam and all mankind.[464] The white tunic (= *whit kirtel*)[465] represents the flesh, and Julian's Chalcedonian theology is evident in her statement that 'the single thickness shows that there was nothing at all between the Godhead and the Humanity'.[466] Here are the classical two natures in one Person. Finally, the resurrected Christ is seen by Julian with a glorified body which is represented by Christ's new clothing, which 'is now of fair, semely medolour (= mixture)[467] which is so marvellous that I can it not discrive'.[468] Thus, whereas the figures of al-Khaḍir and Elijah may be associated with mystic *green*, Julian's association must ineluctably be with mystic *blue* and *white*.[469]

3.3.2 Thomas à Kempis (c. 1380–1471) and the *De Imitatione Christi*

Should Thomas à Kempis' renowned spiritual classic, *The Imitation of Christ* (*De Imitatione Christi*),[470] be classified as a mystical text or merely an ordinary primer for prayer and spiritual praxis? I suggest that, in its fervent search for the ways of *perfection*, the answer, *prima facie*, should be the former. As we shall see, there are also other good reasons for a mystical classification of this text.

There is a slight difference of opinion among scholars in dating Thomas à Kempis' life. Leo Sherley-Price gives AD 1380 as his date of birth[471] and 1471 as his date of death,[472] whereas Dennis J. Billy is slightly more cautious, suggesting c. AD 1379–1471.[473] However, despite its somewhat 'hidden' nature, we *are* able to glean a certain amount about his life.[474] His names derives from his place of birth, the village of Kempen, which is near Düsseldorf; after schooling in Deventer, Holland, where he first encountered the Brothers of the Common Life, he moved to Zwolle and entered the contemplative monastery of Mount St Agnes. He was ordained a priest in AD 1413 as a canon of St Augustine. His life there then passed uneventfully. He undertook the offices of sub-prior and Master of Novices, wrote a variety of other spiritual works in addition to his *magnum opus*, the *De Imitatione Christi*, and died in 1471, aged 92. His tomb was discovered in 1672.[475]

This is not the place to enter the debates over the authorship of the *De Imitatione Christi*. While we may acknowledge, with Thomas' translator Leo Sherley-Price, that the authorship has been a matter for considerable dispute down the ages,[476] we will also go with the majority, cited by Sherley-Price, who hold that Thomas most likely *was* the author of this text and that the uncertainty about its authorship was initially precipitated by Thomas' own humility, since the *Imitation* first circulated anonymously.[477] Sherley-Price concludes that, in his own view, 'Thomas' authorship is well nigh indisputable'.[478]

We do not propose, either, to enter here the somewhat sensationalist debate as to whether Thomas à Kempis had the misfortune to be buried alive, as surmised from alleged scratch marks discovered on the inside of his coffin [479]. He himself believed that it was the *text*, rather than the authorial person, that was important [480]. Thus it is to the text itself that we will now turn.

It was probably round about the years of his ordination in AD 1413 that the *De Imitatione Christi* was written,[481] with an initial anonymous circulation[482] and 'the earliest printed edition' appearing in c. 1470.[483] The simplicity and lucidity of its style have been much applauded. John Wesley (AD 1703–91), famed as the founder and father of Methodism, was also particularly fond of this work and, in 1735, published his edition under the title *The Christian's Pattern*. In his Preface to the edition, he lauded its plainness, simplicity and total lack of adornment combined with the singular 'strength, spirit and weight of every sentence'.[484] Yet, for all that, it is a profoundly mystical work.

Dennis Billy reminds us that the spirituality espoused by *The Imitation of Christ* was the inexorable product of its religious and historical milieu.[485] The backcloth was a pre-Reformation Europe, torn by civil war as in the Wars of the Roses in England (AD 1455–85), religious schism as with the Papacy (AD 1378–1417), and with much suffering in Germany, Italy and France.[486] In AD 1453, well within the lifetime of Thomas à Kempis, Constantinople fell to the Ottoman army of Sultan Mehmet II (*reg.* AD 1451–81).[487] The Hundred Years War (AD 1337–1453) also spanned much of Thomas à Kempis' life. In AD 1415, King Henry V of England (*reg.* AD 1413–22) defeated the French at the Battle of Agincourt. Thomas à Kempis must have been aware of at least some of these bloody events in what was an extremely long lifetime.

The structure of *The Imitation of Christ* is easily delineated. It may be said to follow the classical mystical stages of Purgation, Illumination and Union,[488] as has been noticed by several authors.[489] The text divides neatly into four main sections or books (each divided into numerous chapters), the first three of which reflect these classical mystical stages. They have been variously labelled. Book 1, for example, which adumbrates 'The Way of Purgation',[490] has been characterised as 'Counsels on the Spiritual Life',[491] 'Admonitions, Useful for a Spiritual Life'[492] and 'Useful Reminders for the Spiritual Life'.[493] Book 2, which reflects 'The Way of Illumination',[494] has been variously entitled overall as 'Counsels on the Inner Life',[495] 'Admonitions Tending to Things Internal'[496] and 'Suggestions Drawing One toward the Inner Life'.[497] Book 3, which is a kind of 'proto-climax' to the volume and which charts 'The Unitive Way',[498] has been entitled, by way of epitome, 'On Inward Consolation',[499] 'Of Internal Consolation'[500] and 'Of Inner Comfort'.[501]

The *real* climax to the whole work in general, of course, and to 'The Unitive Way' articulated in book 3, in particular, is book 4 of the *De Imitatione Christi*, whose Eucharistic theology is outlined in eighteen chapters under such diverse overall headings as 'On the Blessed Sacrament',[502] 'Concerning the Sacrament'[503] and 'The Book on the Sacrament'.[504] It is here, in book 4, that real terrestrial union with the Divine, through the Eucharist, is celebrated, as opposed to that union which the mystic may enjoy in the Afterlife.

Before the application of our sevenfold paradigm, it is useful to try to evaluate in a nutshell the *kind* of mysticism espoused by Thomas à Kempis. We have already agreed that he *should*, indeed, be treated as a mystic – but it was a very different kind of mysticism from the visionary kind espoused, for example, by Julian of Norwich in her 'Showings'. Kettlewell characterises it as 'Scriptural Mysticism'.[505] Leo Sherley-Price tells us that 'Thomas à Kempis writes in the first place for his fellow-religious, an ascetic for ascetics, *a mystic for those who aspire to mystical union with God* …', but his wise advice has a ubiquitous relevance for all.[506] Sherley-Price commends his realism and practicality and, in this respect, compares him to Teresa of Ávila.[507] And it is this endearingly *practical* element that other scholars have chosen to highlight as well.[508] As Dennis Billy puts it: 'It steers clear of needless speculation so characteristic of the intellectual climate of the day and focuses instead *on the practical exigencies* of leading a holy life in a world beset by trials and constant temptations'.[509] It has been characterised as 'primarily a book of meditations',[510] but it is also much more than that. As a 'lifelong companion on the spiritual journey',[511] whose ultimate *telos* is eternal salvation and union with and in God, the *De Imitatione Christi* may truly be characterised as a work of *practical mysticism*, much nearer to the Way of Teresa of Ávila, perhaps, than to that of Julian.

Cloud

Certainly, the text belongs to the cataphatic (but by no means ecstatic) mystical tradition, rather than the apophatic, of which *The Cloud of Unknowing* is a primary *exemplum*. In Thomas à Kempis' text, there is no ubiquitous cloud or veil between supplicant sinner and the Divine. Indeed, the very first words of book 1, chapter 1 serve to dispel this apophatic notion: '"He who follows Me shall not walk in darkness", says Our Lord'.[512] The whole of book 2 illustrates 'The Way of Illumination' whereby the novice in the paths of perfection 'is gradually illumined by the divine light of the knowledge of God'.[513] In book 3, chapter 23, the disciple prays that Jesus will 'send the brightness of Your light into my mind, and banish all darkness from the sanctuary of my heart'.[514]

Self-abnegation

The reader of the *Imitation* cannot fail to notice the profound humility of Thomas à Kempis.[515] Its companion virtue in the mystical tradition is self-abnegation, a theme on which the *Imitation* has much to say.[516] Thomas teaches that one must deny oneself[517] and directly echoes Christ's words in Matthew 16:24: 'Deny yourself, take up your cross, and follow Me'.[518] For 'complete self-denial is the only road to perfect liberty'.[519]

Contemplation

The *De Imitatione Christi* does not teach a formal method of contemplation. As we have seen, it has been described as 'primarily a book of meditations';[520] but Dennis Billy advises that a contemplative approach to the work is useful.[521] And there are diverse aspects of contemplation itself: Chapter 1 of book 3 discusses 'How Christ speaks inwardly to the Soul';[522] the following chapter is entitled 'How Truth Instructs us in Silence';[523] while, in one of the greatest contemplative prayers in the *De Imitatione Christi*, Thomas proclaims: 'I too wish to be afire with great and holy desires, and to offer myself to You with all my heart. I also offer and present before You the praises, the glowing affections, the raptures, the supernatural revelations and heavenly visions of all devout hearts ...'[524]

This is the nearest that Thomas à Kempis gets to the classical theme of contemplation. With his commentator, we may agree that the *De Imitatione* 'does not treat of the mystical state of union with God, which consists in contemplation and ecstasies, etc., although it is mentioned in ... Book 1, Ch. 11 [and] Book 3, Ch. 31'.[525]

The Dark Night

We will search in vain for the 'Dark Night' of Juan de la Cruz in Thomas' *De Imitatione*. The latter mystic is much more down-to-earth in his approach. As observed above, he is a proponent of a very *practical* type of mysticism which thoroughly eschews the rarefied heights of Juan's mystical theology. That is not to say, however, that we cannot identify the occasional equivalences. Chapter 9 of book 2 is variously labelled 'On the Lack of all Comfort'[526] and 'Of Emptiness'.[527] Billy comments that 'there are times when the experience of intimacy with God leaves us, and we are left to face the trials of life with nothing but faith'.[528] As Thomas à Kempis himself puts it: 'It is a great thing to be able to forego all consolation, human or divine, and for God's sake willingly to endure desolation of heart ...'[529] In this way, the eager soul staggers onwards towards its goal of perfection.

Perfection

This is the fundamental goal, everywhere expressed, of the *De Imitatione*: the need for man to strive for that perfection which every Christian is bound to seek, which will fit him or her for entry to eternal life and Union with the Divine.[530] In particular, chapter 23 of book 3, entitled 'On Four Things that Bring Peace', has a particular resonance for the theme of perfection. The disciple is told that 'the whole secret of perfection' lies in four things: deciding to follow others' will rather than one's own; being abstemious in what one possesses; having the humility to 'take the lowest place, and regard [oneself] as less than others'; and having the constant intention for the perfect fulfilment of God's will within oneself.[531]

Human and Divine Love

Kettlewell is moved to comment on how powerfully the love of God pervades the whole personality of Thomas à Kempis – and this love of God is, of course, strikingly manifest in his *magnum opus*, the *De Imitatione Christi*. We are advised, for example, to give up all earthly loves and love only Jesus.[532] The 'brave and wise lover' of God will exhibit clear proofs of that love: 'A wise lover values not so much the gift of the lover, as the love of the giver'.[533] And the love which man ought to manifest towards the Divine is to be seen most powerfully in his or her yearning for the Eucharist.[534] But, as Wesley himself was only too well aware, such powerful love does not come to man easily, and Wesley alludes to that classical mystical, triple paradigm of purgation, illumination and union through which the eager soul must be sieved before that state of pure love for God is reached.[535]

Chapter 5 of book 3 of Thomas' text is a sublime hymn entitled 'On the Wonderful Effect of Divine Love'. Here, Thomas lauds the great power of love, prays for his own love of God to be strengthened, and concludes: 'My God and my love, You are all mine, and I am Yours'.[536] And Thomas acknowledges that God is the Divine source of love itself. The evidence for this is made manifest in the sacrament of the Eucharist.[537]

Union

It is in this mystical sacrament that union with the Divine is possible, even on this earth. We have already noted that, apart from a couple of casual references,[538] the *De Imitatione Christi* 'does not treat of the mystical state of union with God, which consists in contemplation and ecstasies, etc. ...'[539] Thomas is well aware that, to 'win experience of heavenly contemplation', one requires a spirit of complete self-abnegation – and that is extremely difficult to come by.[540] Thus it is in and by the Eucharist, rather than in or by any advanced techniques of contemplation, that man achieves union with God. In a seminal chapter of book 4, chapter 13, entitled 'How the Devout Soul should Sincerely Desire Union with Christ in his Sacrament', Thomas proclaims:

> For this is my prayer and desire, that I may be wholly united to You, and withdraw my heart from all created things; that through Holy Communion and frequent offering of the Eucharist, I may come to delight in heavenly and

> eternal things more and more. O my Lord and God, when shall I be wholly united to and absorbed into you, and wholly unmindful of myself? ... When my soul is perfectly united to God, my whole being will be filled with joy.[541]

The practice of prayer and devotion via the ordinary Christian virtues, for the would-be *practical* mystic, leads to union with the Divine; and 'union with Christ is consummated in the Holy Eucharist'.[542]

It will be abundantly clear that the mystical Eucharistic theology espoused and adumbrated by the *De Imitatione Christi* is a world away from the mystical theology of Islam in general and, in particular, that of the Muslim mystics whom we surveyed earlier. Where there is a harmony between the two faith traditions is in the insistence by Thomas à Kempis on the ordinary practice of virtues as a preliminary to union with the Divine in the Eucharist. There is some parallelism here with the thought of that great mystic and theologian of Islam, Abū Ḥāmid al-Ghazālī, who stressed that, before one embarked on the mystic path proper, one should fulfil the ordinary five pillars of Islam (*arkān*) to the best of one's ability.[543] There is also an agreed Christian–Islamic *telos*. Thomas puts the following words into the mouth of Christ: 'Consider everything as springing from the supreme Good, since to Myself, as their Source, must all things return'.[544] To parallel this, we find a key text in the Holy Qur'ān to the effect that all things come from God, and all things will return to Him.[545]

In both Thomas à Kempis and the Qur'ān, there is a Neoplatonic-type ethos of outflow and return.[546] And, for both the Christian and the Islamic mystic, it is that 'return' which is of paramount importance. The Islamic mystical concept of *baqā'* or 'remaining in God' in some kind of mystical union is paralleled, in a rather different and 'lighter' manner, in Thomas' advice to the soul that it should 'rest always in the Lord'.[547] In the latter, there are overtones of both Augustine and Julian of Norwich.[548]

We may note, by way of conclusion, that the metaphors of colour, and in particular that of Green, are absent from the *De Imitatione Christi*. There *is* a reference to grass as Thomas cites Isaiah 40:6, in which mortal flesh is compared to grass,[549] and a further Biblical citation of Apocalypse 2:7 with its reference to the Tree of Life.[550] That, however, is the extent of Thomas à Kempis' 'greenness'!

3.3.3 Teresa of Ávila (1515–82), *The Way of Perfection* and *The Interior Castle*

After her death, the following prayer was found in Teresa's prayerbook:

> *Nada te turbe,*
> *nada te espante;*
> *todo se pasa:*
> *Dios no se muda.*
> *La Pacientia todo lo alcanza.*
> *Quien a Dios tiene nada la falta;*
> *Solo Dios basta.*

> Let nothing disturb you,
> Let nothing frighten you;
> All things are passing away:
> God never changes.
> Patience obtains all things.
> Whoever has God lacks nothing;
> God alone suffices.[551]

This prayer encapsulates in a nutshell her patience, tenacity and immense trust in God, as well as her practical bent. What it does not demonstrate is her mysticism. For 'St Teresa the Great was granted a plenitude of mystical favours; [whereas her namesake] St Teresa of Lisieux [whom we will briefly survey below] was not'.[552]

Teresa of Ávila, also called Teresa de Jesús, poured forth numerous writings[553] and her spirituality and mysticism in consequence have many facets. This section will concentrate on her practical mysticism seen through the lens of her two great seminal volumes, *The Way of Perfection*[554] and *The Interior Castle*.[555] In these are united many of the themes we have encountered elsewhere in this volume, most notably the concept of the *mystic way* or *journey*.

The classical 'threefold Way'[556] with its purgative, illuminative and unitive stations or stages[557] is the backdrop against which Teresa writes, especially in *The Interior Castle*. The *purgative* stage is articulated in the second and third mansions of this volume;[558] the *illuminative* stage in the fifth and sixth mansions;[559] and the climactic *unitive* phase in the seventh, the last of the mansions.[560] From this, it is abundantly clear that Teresa de Jesús writes with an awareness of the great classical mystical tradition. However, Deirdre Green reminds us that she is by no means hidebound or restricted by these divisions or their traditional terminology.[561]

In Teresa, we encounter 'a mystic of the highest order'[562] whose mysticism is not just articulated in profound but lucid writings but is experienced in visions as well,[563] like Julian but unlike Thomas à Kempis. Most famous of her visionary experiences – perhaps by virtue of Bernini's sculpture of the 'Ecstasy of St Teresa' in the Church of Santa Maria della Vittoria in Rome[564] – is the Transverberation of the Heart, in which one of the cherubim several times pierces the heart of Teresa with a fiery golden spear.[565]

Peter Bourne notes that such experience of mystical 'wounding' was by no means unique to Teresa. As we have earlier seen, the Swiss mystic Adrienne Von Speyr underwent a similar wounding;[566] and Bourne stresses that the Capuchin stigmatist, known to the world as Padre Pio, was similarly 'wounded'.[567] This mystical experience of transverberation appears to be peculiar to the Christian mystical tradition; there is nothing similar among the Islamic mystics. It is interesting here to set the experiences of Teresa and Padre Pio side by side and appreciate how this mystical 'wounding' links the Carmelite saint of the sixteenth century with the Capuchin of the twentieth:

> It was our Lord's will that I should see this angel in the following way. He was not tall but short, and very beautiful; and his face was so aflame that he appeared to be one of the highest ranks of angels, who seem to be all on

> fire. They must be of the kind called cherubim ... In his hand I saw a great golden spear, and at the iron tip there appeared to be a point of fire. This he plunged into my heart several times so that it penetrated to my entrails. When he pulled it out, I felt that he took them with it, and left me utterly consumed by the great love of God. The pain was so severe that it made me utter several moans. The sweetness caused by this intense pain is so extreme that one cannot possibly wish it to cease, nor is one's soul then content with anything but God.[568]
>
> I was suddenly terrorized by the sight of a celestial person who presented himself to my mind's eye. He had in his hand a sort of weapon like a very long sharp-pointed steel blade which seemed to emit fire. At the very instant I saw all this, I saw that person hurl the weapon into my soul with all his might. I cried out with difficulty and felt I was dying ... Even my entrails were torn and ruptured by the weapon, and nothing was spared. From that day on I have been mortally wounded.[569]

Perhaps the biggest difference between the two accounts is that, whereas Teresa is content with the 'sweetness' of the pain, Padre Pio constantly feels the transverberation as an open wound in his soul and asks Padre Benedetto whether this is 'not a new punishment inflicted upon me by divine justice?'[570]

It is salutary, but I hope not cynical, to note that Teresa,[571] like Julian of Norwich,[572] Padre Pio[573] and Adrienne Von Speyr,[574] suffered throughout her life from much ill health. Bernard Ruffin reminds us of Evelyn Underhill's observation that ill health was often a common factor in the lives of mystics and cites her suggestion that its cause might be 'the immense strain which exalted spirit puts upon a body which is adapted to a very different form of life'.[575]

Yet, despite her frequent bouts of profound ill health, scholars have also commented on Teresa's dominant personality. For Bárbara Mujica, she and her disciples are 'tough, determined managerial types'.[576] Peter Bourne suggests that 'she was a born leader, courageous ...'[577] She certainly aroused strong emotions. One of her enemies, the papal nuncio Felipe Sega no less, described her as 'a restless, disobedient, stubborn, gad-about female!'[578] By utter contrast, she endearingly characterised herself as a 'picaresque heroine on a series of road adventures'.[579]

The details of her life are very well known. Not only did she leave us an autobiography,[580] written at the command of her spiritual directors,[581] which narrates her life up to the age of 50,[582] but also she was a voluminous letter-writer.[583] She is as famous for her reform of the Carmelite Order[584] and her fruitful association with her pupil and mentor, Juan de la Cruz,[585] as for her mysticism.

Born into a large family on 28 March 1515 in Ávila, she had both Christian and Jewish blood running in her veins, due to a formerly Jewish grandfather.[586] She entered the Carmelite Order at the Convent of La Encarnación, just outside Ávila, in 1536, aged about 21,[587] but did not begin her famous reform movement until after the age of 40. She encountered numerous difficulties in her attempts at making new foundations, reform and her growing desire to separate the Calced and Discalced Carmelite Orders.[588] Eventually, in AD 1581, King Philip II of Spain issued a short decree formally separating the two branches of the Order – and with this, one might say, with Mujica, 'The Reform had triumphed'.[589]

Throughout the latter part of her life, Teresa felt much bolstered in her reforming mission by the companionship of Juan de la Cruz,[590] whose own mysticism and spirituality we have already analysed in some depth. When Juan was abducted, together with Fray Germán, and imprisoned, she wrote an impassioned letter to King Philip, pleading for the release of her friars. Whether the king actually read the letter or not is a moot point. There was no answer, and Juan escaped from his prison in August 1578.[591]

By the time Teresa achieved her goal of the separation of the two branches of the Carmelites, age had crept up on her and she was ill.[592] But the theme of the mystic journey, on which she had laboured for so long and so practically through so many trials and travels, was omnipresent. Two days before her death on 4 October 1582, she is recorded as exclaiming: 'My Lord, it is time to set out; may the journey be a propitious one …'[593]

We have already mentioned the classical mystical tradition which formed a backdrop to Teresa's life. Of her own reading, with regard to the intellectual milieu of the day, we are told that she read little, at least in terms of what is considered 'great literature', but she *was* very familiar with Augustine's *Confessions* and the *De Imitatione Christi*.[594] Intriguingly, she tells us that, like her mother, from whom she caught the habit, she was fond of works of chivalry.[595] Later, she would become God's own mystical chevalier. Here, then, there is a direct literary link between the court traditions of the early and high Middle Ages and the Reformation and Counter-Reformation historical milieu in which Teresa grew up and lived in sixteenth-century Spain. Indeed, Bourne equates *The Interior Castle* with the chivalric romances of her youth. He characterises it as being 'in its own way a love story, a romance in the tradition of her own times'.[596]

Mujica portrays a Spain where, although the Catholic monarchs Ferdinand and Isabella had triumphed in AD 1492, there was still much residual anti-semitism, persecution of the Jews, trial by inquisition and profound suspicion of the *Alumbrados* or *Illuminati*.[597] Indeed, the latter became equated with Lutherans and incurred the wrath of the Inquisition.[598] In Ávila itself, Jews and *conversos* (Jews who had converted to Catholicism) accused of murder were publicly executed in AD 1491.[599] And that 'Teresa Sánchez Cepeda y Ahumada', whom we now know as Teresa of Ávila, 'was born in Ávila in 1515, the daughter of a *converso* silk and woollens merchant'.[600]

It comes as no surprise, then, that at least one scholar, Deirdre Green, has detected profoundly Jewish mystical roots at the heart of *The Interior Castle*.[601] Others, however, look to an Islamic sufi paradigm and antecedent.[602] Green acknowledges the possibility of the latter.[603] Ultimately, it is impossible to define precisely if and how Teresa was influenced in *The Interior Castle* by either Jewish mysticism, Islamic Sufism or even both.[604] Both traditions certainly have some overlap with Christian mysticism, especially the Islamic, as was recognised, for example, by Thomas Merton (AD 1915–68), that twentieth-century Cistercian (and Carthusian manqué!) mystic of the Abbey of Our Lady of Gethsemani in Kentucky,[605] who, according to

Harmless, 'had a knack for getting the mystical to speak to the modern',[606] and who proclaimed jokingly: 'I am the biggest Sufi in Kentucky'.[607]

We now turn to our two major Teresan texts, *The Way of Perfection* and *The Interior Castle*, to which we have hitherto briefly alluded, and which we shall now examine in more depth through the sieve of our sevenfold paradigm. The structures of the two texts differ profoundly.

The Way of Perfection was written in two versions, the first between 1562 and 1566, and the second after 1569.[608] As its structure makes clear, it was a book of counsels directed at Teresa's nuns in her new St Joseph's (San José) Convent in Ávila;[609] this was the first of her 'Reformed' convents.[610] The book's structure is loose, and it ranges in subject matter in its initial chapters from the need to keep the rule, the need for confessors to be well instructed, and spiritual love, to perfect contemplation, consolation in prayer, and recollection. Only in the later chapters do the words of the *Pater Noster* provide a framework for the text and its manifold counsels to the sisters.[611] And one central chapter deploys the image of water as a particularly striking metaphor for the spiritual life.[612]

The Interior Castle, written in AD 1577,[613] illustrates the return of the soul to God, to be accomplished by both human effort and Divine grace, that is, faith *and* works.[614] There is no Protestant Reformation justification by faith alone here. The text is much more rigorously structured and sophisticated than *The Way of Perfection*, focusing on seven sets of mansions which may be linked to the classical mystical stages of purgation, illumination and union. Teresa's own preferred title for her work was *Castillo Interior*, but it is known in Spain by her chapter headings of *Las Moradas* (Mansions, Dwelling Places), each of which have several rooms (*aposentos*).[615]

Cloud and Self-abnegation

For Teresa, there is neither cloud nor veil between herself and the Godhead. She actually has visionary experiences, not only of angels, as in the Transverberation of the Heart, but of Jesus Himself.[616] And, in communion, she tells us that she knows that the Lord is within her.[617] Yet, despite the great spiritual favours she is granted, she is acutely aware of the need, both in herself and her sisters, for *self-abnegation* and humility.[618] Indeed, her own humility has been characterised by some scholars as 'excessive', forgetting that she wrote in the omnipresent shadow of the fearsome Inquisition.[619] However, Inquisition or not, Mujica stresses that 'For Teresa, humility was more than a rhetorical ploy; it was an essential element of the way of perfection'.[620] It was also empowering.[621]

Contemplation

Thomas Merton held that 'contemplation, far from being opposed to theology, is in fact the normal perfection of theology'.[622] Deploying a favourite water image, Teresa suggests, while discussing the four stages of prayer, that those who are mere novices in prayer are like 'those who draw the water up out of the well'.[623] The heights of contemplation, however, are analogous to 'heavy rain, when the Lord waters [the garden] Himself without any labour of ours'.[624] But Teresa holds that all Carmelites are called to contemplation,[625] while others may not be apt for this advanced state.[626] The beginnings of contemplation are characterised as the 'prayer of quiet' by Teresa and, pragmatically, likened to 'a kind of interior and exterior stupor'.[627] It is this early aspect of contemplation that McLean identifies as being 'the connecting bond between active and passive prayer'.[628]

The Dark Night

The 'Dark Night' is one of the most famous of all mystical *topoi* and one much associated with the mystical theology of Juan de la Cruz, as we saw earlier. And it is by no means unique to him, but suffered to a greater or lesser degree by many in the Christian mystical tradition. Padre Pio, for example, that Capuchin friar and stigmatist of Pietrelcina in Italy to whom we have earlier referred, suffered acute periods of the 'Night'.[629] For example, he writes, poignantly, to his spiritual director, Padre Benedetto, on 24 January 1918: 'My soul is continually enveloped in darkness which is becoming deeper as time goes on. The temptations against faith are increasing all the time. I am therefore living in constant darkness.'[630]

The Way of Perfection acknowledges that God tests most those whom He loves most.[631] Spiritual ascesis is necessary to cleanse the soul, but this may result in dryness and distraction in prayer.[632] It can be a time of disheartenment and torment.[633] It is in the third mansion of *The Interior Castle* that glimmerings of the classical 'Dark Night' are to be encountered, the Dark Night of the Senses:[634] 'Those who do not receive ... consolations may feel a despondency that is uncalled for, since perfection does not consist in consolation but in greater love'.[635]

But it is in the sixth mansion that the worst trials are adumbrated. Here, we truly encounter the horrors of the dark night of the soul.[636] The experience is described in vivid terms in *The Interior Castle*:

> Prayer makes no difference as far as comforting the heart, which no consolation can enter, nor can the mind even grasp the meaning of the words of vocal prayer: mental prayer is out of the question at such a time, since the faculties are unequal to it. Solitude harms the soul, yet society or conversation is a fresh torment.[637]

Perfection; Human and Divine Love

Of course, the *telos* of the whole mystical journey through purgation and illumination is the perfection of one's human nature to fit the mystic for the final stage of mystical union. The theme is encapsulated in the very title of *The Way of Perfection*. As Teresa shows so frequently in her works, prayer is the key to perfection. Indeed, vocal prayer may even engender perfect contemplation![638] And all is for the sake of love of God and the drawing down of Divine Love. As we have seen, 'perfection does not consist in consolation but in greater love'.[639]

For the mystic, 'God is love'[640] – and this concept in one form or another constitutes a *leitmotiv* in all Teresa's writings. *The Way of Perfection* urges a great love of God which will mirror God's great love for man.[641] Teresa proclaims in *The Interior Castle*, in the fourth mansion, that 'it is not so essential to *think* as much as to *love* much'.[642] Thus we are prepared for the sixth mansion, which 'is a land of intimate communications of divine love'.[643] The depths of that Divine love for man are laid bare in the opening words of the *Pater Noster*.[644] And, while there is no cloud or veil which interposes between Teresa and her knowledge and love of God, and His reciprocal love for her, she does acknowledge in one striking passage that 'the splendour of Him Who is revealed in the vision resembles an infused light, as of the sun, *covered with a veil* as transparent as a diamond …'[645]

Union

In all this, union with the Divine is the ultimate aim. Teresa tells us, in the sixth mansion of *The Interior Castle*, that 'in one sort of rapture, … the soul being thus purified, God unites it to Himself in a way known only to Him and the Spirit …'[646] But it is the seventh mansion which is the climax, both of her *Interior Castle*, and her life itself. It is in this that we find her doctrine of *Divine Union*.[647] In her *Vida*, she states that union occurs in the fourth, most advanced, stage of prayer, though she confesses an inability to define such technical terms, which, she is aware, belong to the realms of mystical theology and which are beyond her.[648]

Discussing Teresa's Prayer of Union (*Oración de Unión*),[649] Deirdre Green suggests that *her* general references to union do not refer to that classical 'final ultimate achievement of oneness with God'. Her preferred term for the latter is the Spiritual Marriage.[650] The seventh mansion of *The Interior Castle* is replete with references to this idea: for example, 'when His Majesty deigns to bestow on the soul the grace of these divine nuptials, He brings it into His presence chamber … He then unites it to Himself, as also during the prayer of union'.[651] In this Spiritual Marriage, God is joined to the adoring soul as powerfully as two people who have just married; and Teresa assures us that God will never separate Himself from such a soul.[652] That soul becomes one with God in the Spiritual Marriage.[653]

Colours as symbols do not figure prominently in the three Teresan works to which we have had reference, the *Libro de la Vida*, the *Camino de Perfección* and the *Castillo Interior*. What we *do* find is a simple delight in water and gardening images – and these *may* be bound up with colour, as in the sentence 'Everything appears to be dry and there is no water to keep things green'.[654]

It is this kind of simplicity, perhaps, rather than the high-flown symbolism of other mystics, which provides a neat link to that nineteenth-century French Carmelite known as Thérèse of Lisieux (AD 1873–97);[655] her 'Little Way' (*Petite Voie*)[656] was vastly different in content and execution from *The Way of Perfection* and *The Interior Castle*. However, her life, in just as passionate a fashion, mirrored and embraced many of the great mystical themes such as the Dark Night,[657] the fire of Divine Love,[658] and the striving for perfection.[659] And Thérèse of Lisieux, too, was afflicted by ill health,[660] dying eventually of tuberculosis.[661]

Above all, it is perhaps a searching for a *Way of Perfection* which links these two very different Carmelite Teresas. For Thérèse of Lisieux was acutely conscious that she could in no fashion emulate her sublime Spanish predecessor.[662] But perfection might still be sought in another fashion, in what she called her 'Little Way'. Monica Furlong summarises: 'The Little Way meant trying to get on with life as it actually was, living it with kindness, unselfishness, detailed care – "always doing the tiniest thing right, and doing it for love'".[663] What links Teresa of Ávila and Thérèse of Lisieux in a particularly profound way is the theme of love: 'My Little Way is all love'.[664] But, by contrast with the mystical theology of Teresa of Ávila, articulated in such sublime works as *The Interior Castle*, Thérèse wishes 'to seek the means of going to heaven by a little way (*par une petite voie*) that is very straight, very short, a completely new little way'.[665]

Teresa of Ávila and Thérèse of Lisieux are linked indirectly to al-Khaḍir/al-Khiḍr in his Christian garb as Elijah/Elias. On the day of her profession as a sister of Carmel, Thérèse tells us that her 'union with Jesus was made … in the midst of a *gentle whisper*, like the one our father Elijah had on the mountain [1 Kings 19:11–13] …'[666] Teresa of Ávila, in *The Interior Castle*, wonders whether the soul should 'remain quiescent in … aridity, waiting, as did our father Elias, for fire to descend from heaven to consume the sacrifice which it makes of itself to God?'[667]

Elijah/Elias is the ancestral Father of all Carmelites and, in his identification with al-Khaḍir, becomes a figure with a profound resonance in the two great monotheistic traditions of Islam and Christianity. He is thus a mystical link between Carmel and the Qur'ān, *not* by virtue of the colour green, but by virtue of a common search for the *Ways of Perfection*, even when, as in the Qur'ānic figure of al-Khaḍir, it is clear that God's ways are not man's ways.

CHAPTER

4

JOURNEY'S END: TOWARDS AN ANTHROPOLOGY OF THE WAY

Everything signifies. The Qur'ān vividly proclaims: *Sa-nurīhim āyātinā fī 'l- āfāq wa fī anfusihim*[1] ('We shall show them Our signs on the horizons and in their very souls [or selves]'). Colour itself, of course, signifies in a very real and dynamic way. In this final chapter we shall draw together the semiotic threads of our previous discussions by highlighting *three* realms of signification which have been of particular importance in many of our mystical authors. These are: (1) *the Realm of Mystic Colour*; (2) *the Realm of al-Khaḍir/Elijah and the Mystic Journey*; and (3) *the Realm of the Mystic Telos*. Together, these realms constitute our *Anthropology of the Way*.

4.1 *The Realm of Mystic Colour*

Physically, 'the colour of many natural objects derives from transformational shifts happening within their atomic structures'.[2] Literary historians have noted how colour might be used by their objects of study 'to encode the authorial intent of [the] narratives. The symbolic use of color, as a component of medieval visual imagery, takes on an emblematic importance in heraldry as it does in religious representation.'[3] Such symbolism could have a sacral, mystical and/or alchemical significance.[4] It is no surprise, therefore, that certain colours might be associated with certain mystics, as, for example, in the taxonomy of the Iranian Kubrāwī sufi 'Alā' al-Dawla Simnānī (AD 1261–1336): here, the seven prophets Adam, Noah, Abraham, Moses, David, Jesus and Muḥammad are associated, respectively, with the colours grey-black, blue, red, white, yellow, luminous black and emerald green.[5]

The Christian mystical tradition has also deployed diverse colours to powerful, and often symbolic, effect. We note the *blue* garb of the Virgin in the Wilton Diptych and at Avignon;[6] in the Julian parable of the Lord and the Servant, God also wears *blue*.[7] In the same parable, the Servant-Jesus figure wears a *white* tunic,[8] while Teresa of Ávila's vision of Christ possesses a 'soft whiteness'.[9] The colour *red*, as Reichert reminds us, may be used 'as a signal to the reader that [the] protagonists are embarking on a spiritual journey and search for Divine knowledge'.[10] *Black* may be the colour of one of the Four Horsemen of the Apocalypse[11] and thus a sign of menace and disaster; but Christianity also knows a very substantial cult of *Black Madonnas* or *Vierges Noires*.[12]

In the light of such diversity, one has some sympathy with Michael Taussig's remark that 'Categories collapse and the first to do so is that of color, specifically the color green, like the green of the sea'.[13] Certainly, at the very least, we can say that *green* has no fixed, universally agreed, significance but may very well have a specific, localised significance, as in Islam.

A global examination of the significance of the colour *green* is instructive and fascinating in its diversity but, ultimately, can seem confusing. It can signal both good and bad, the serious and the comical, as well as a value-free and neutral place in between those extremes. It is not *necessarily* a sign of hope, mystic good or perfection.

For the Chinese, green is regarded as an 'evil' colour. In 2008, a Chinese performance artist named Zhao Bandi decided to sue the *Kung Fu Panda* film (Dreamworks, 2008), holding that the film was an insult to the Chinese nation because of its green eyes. Zhao was quoted as saying: 'A panda with green eyes has the feeling of evil'.[14] By contrast, 'it seems that both Molière and his wife liked the colour green, since numerous costumes were mainly green. Also, green was known as the colour of fools.'[15]

In the Christian tradition, green was a notable liturgical colour for priestly vestments at mass representing hope;[16] and we have noted the incidence of 'green men' in church architecture, with all the diverse interpretations attached to such figures. Interestingly, Clare Church near Sudbury in Suffolk boasts a 'green woman' as well as a 'green man' in the porch.[17] Reichert reminds us of the paradoxical dual significance of green in Christianity, where it can be artistically associated both with Lucifer and with the cross in crucifixion scenes.[18] Green could also be associated with dress and heraldry in the Arthurian tradition,[19] as well as alchemy and hermeticism.[20]

In his seminal cultural, anthropological and literary study of the colour, focusing on the period AD 1575–1700, entitled *The Key of Green*, Bruce R. Smith shows how 'the colour green was curiously prominent and resonant in English culture of the sixteenth and seventeenth centuries'.[21] Smith echoes Taussig, stressing that '"Green" has power to upset. For a start, it lacks an easily fixable meaning.'[22]

Of course, as we have seen in diverse places in this volume, the Islamic tradition was no stranger to the colour green. Smith emphasised that 'to experience green, you need space, time, and a human body, but not necessarily words'.[23] By contrast, the Qur'ān, as the textual 'words' *par excellence* of the Islamic tradition, presents a word picture of the Paradise reserved for the blessed which combines the textual, spiritual and material:

> For them [the righteous] will be Gardens
> Of Eternity; beneath them
> Rivers will flow: they will

Be adorned therein
With bracelets of gold,
And they will wear
Green garments of fine silk.[24]

Yusuf Ali, in his footnote commentary, suggests that 'green is the colour mentioned, because it is the most refreshing to the eye, and fits in well with the Garden'.[25]

As we have noted earlier, green was the favourite colour of the Prophet Muḥammad; and it has a widespread use in traditional Islamic architecture, both Sunnī and Shī'i. Hasan Ali Khan, for example, notes that the monument of the medieval Ḥasan Kabīr al-Dīn, who is identified as a great-grandson of Shams, an Ismā'īlī dā'ī, is a building near the Indus valley town of Uch which has been coated in white and green paint 'to give an overall orthodox Islamic effect'.[26]

It is abundantly clear from all this that the colour green has a multivalent applicability in both the Islamic and Christian traditions. Above all, however, it is the colour associated with al-Khaḍir whose identification with Elijah and, indeed, St George we have had occasion to note in various parts of this book.[27]

4.2 *The Realm of al-Khaḍir/Elijah and the Mystic Journey*

For the Islamic and Christian traditions, al-Khaḍir and Elijah, respectively, are sublime models of the Way of Perfection and of a successful Journey to the Divine. They are heroes – incarnate paradigms – for those who came afterwards: on the Islamic side, al-Kalābādhī, al-Daylamī and al-Qushayrī; on the Christian, John of the Cross and the two Teresas in particular, and even Julian of Norwich, though she does not explicitly mention Elijah. The Journey or Way of Perfection may be fraught with the apophatic (as with the author of *The Cloud of Unknowing*), cataphatic (as with Thomas à Kempis and Thérèse of Lisieux) or even ecstatic (as with Julian and Teresa of Ávila). It may involve sublime mystical stations as adumbrated in the works of diverse sufi mystics, mysterious mansions as with Teresa of Ávila, or a 'Little Way' as espoused by her Carmelite namesake, Thérèse of Lisieux, or as provided by Abū Ḥāmid al-Ghazālī in his injunction to practise the Five Pillars of Islam thoroughly, as a first stage on the mystic path.[28]

There is a diversity of journeys to the Divine, and the Ways of Perfection are many. What unites all, however, is that each Way of Perfection, Islamic and Christian, is a path of love towards an ultimate union of some kind with the Divine Beloved, the Mystic *Telos* or Goal. It was concerning that unimaginable *telos* that St Paul famously observed that no eye had seen nor ear heard nor human heart possibly conceived the wonders that God had in mind for his faithful believers and lovers.[29] And the sentiment is echoed in the Islamic ḥadīth literature.[30]

4.3 *The Realm of the Mystic* Telos

It is the sacred anthropology of that mystic *telos* that we will now finally explore. In an important passage, Victor Turner wrote as follows:

> Van Gennep himself defined *rites de passage* as 'rites which accompany every change of place, state, social position and age' ... [He] has shown that all rites of passage are marked by three phases: separation, margin (or *limen*, signifying 'threshold' in Latin), and aggregation. The first phase (of separation) comprises symbolic behaviour signifying the detachment of the individual or group either from an earlier fixed point in the social structure, from a set of cultural conditions (a 'state'), or from both. During the intervening 'liminal' period, the characteristics of the ritual subject ... are ambiguous; he passes through a cultural realm that has few or none of the attributes of the past or coming state. In the third phase (reaggregation or reincorporation), the passage is consummated.[31]

This taxonomy of rites of passage was neatly adopted by Carmel Bendon Davis in her magisterial volume *Mysticism and Space*: she suggests that the three stages in rites of passage of separation, liminality and reaggregation are all 'identifiable in [her chosen] mystics' approaches, as presented in their texts', but she denies that they are 'intended to have any relationship with the frequently posited stages of mystical life: illumination, purgation and union'.[32] Thus, Julian and the *Cloud* author *separate* from the world,[33] the first via pain and illness[34] as well as the life of an anchoress, albeit one who was much consulted.[35] The mystic journey of Julian and the *Cloud* author represents the liminal phase.[36] Christ is the model for *imitation* on the way of, and to, perfection.[37] The third stage of reaggregation is marked, for Julian and the *Cloud* author, by a 'return to society', Julian of Norwich sharing her spiritual insights with others while the author of the *Cloud* presents his work for the benefit of other would-be contemplatives.[38]

The 'return' to a society from which they have initially fled is accompanied by the 'added value' of several spiritual gifts – wisdom, illumination, spiritual writing, gleaned and developed in the liminal phase – which enhances the rediscovered 'space' of that secular society.[39] They have, classically, according to Van Gennep's tripartite model, transformed their position in society and made a 'transition from body-space to soul-space on behalf of their fellows'.[40]

Davis applies Van Gennep's categories to three mystics, Richard Rolle (c. AD 1300–49),[41] the *Cloud* author and Julian of Norwich, together with their *texts*. But we may go a step further and apply it to *process* as well. *Pace* Davis,[42] there is no reason why the three classical mystical stages of purgation, illumination and union should not be equated with Van Gennep's tripartite categorisation of separation, liminality or 'threshold', and union: in the stage of *purgation*, the novice mystic seeks to *separate* him- or herself from the imperfections, sins and bonds of the flesh; the 'unstructured' soul in a *communitas*[43] of strivers becomes sufficiently *enlightened* to embark on one of the diverse paths to the *thresholds* of perfection; while the *reaggregation* or *reincorporation* is a return to, and *union* with, the Godhead who created that soul, rather than to society in which, perforce, it has lived on earth.

Van Gennep's categories are also adaptable in another direction and may be applied to the sevenfold paradigmatic model or typology which we have deployed throughout this volume in treating a selected number of Christian and Islamic mystics. In this model lies an entire sacred Anthropology of the Way to the *Telos* or final Divine Goal. To avoid essentialism, it is not suggested that this anthropology is applicable to all mystics, Christian and Islamic, at all times in all ages. It is, however, certainly applicable to the principal mystics whose lives and writings we have studied in this volume.

Thus, the *separation* implicit in the *cloud* and *veil* image, underpinned by *self-abnegation* and humility, gives way to types of prayer and *contemplation* whose *liminal* phase may incorporate a species of *dark night* at the *thresholds* of the Divine, and 'liminality is frequently likened to death'.[44] *Reaggregation* or *reincorporation* is achieved as the need and striving for *perfection* is recognised, and it reaches its full flowering in the rays of *Divine Love* and *Mystical Union*.[45] Unknowingness and the apophatic are born of separation and a liminality and *communitas* unpierced by illumination; the cataphatic and knowledge of the Divine are born of a liminality and *communitas* whose boundaries are transcended; and reincorporation with the Divine is achieved in ecstasy, Divine union and, ultimately, Paradise. This paradigm is as applicable to al-Kalābādhī, al-Daylamī and al-Qushayrī as it is to Julian of Norwich, the *Cloud* author, Juan de la Cruz and the two Carmelite Teresas.

There is, finally, a golden *Mystic Web of Intertextual Reading* which we may identify, at least with reference to some of the authors whom we have discussed. To illustrate, we know that Teresa of Ávila read both the *Confessions* of St Augustine and the *De Imitatione Christi*.[46] Her *Interior Castle* may very well have been influenced by Islamic sufi or Judaic mystical texts read in translation. Thérèse of Lisieux was familiar both with the writings of Juan de la Cruz and with the *De Imitatione*.[47] The works of the Islamic mystics are, of course, soaked in the Qur'ān and ḥadīth – but we note, for example, al-Kalābādhī's and al-Qushayrī's considerable familiarity with the work of the sufi writer Abū Naṣr 'Abdallāh al-Sarrāj (died AD 988).[48] Al-Khaḍir is a frequent *leitmotiv*, and the colour *green* makes an occasional appearance in the texts which we have studied. It is not only the Qur'ānic colour of Paradise (where the denizens of *al-Janna*, the Paradise Garden, are garbed in green);[49] but also, as we have seen, this colour plays a prominent role in the Christian tradition, secular and sacred). One text yields another. This volume presents an *intertextual roadmap* of mystic *theologemes*[50] for some of the mystics on their Islamic and Christian journeys.

NOTES

Chapter 1: Exploring the Mystical Imagination

1. Annemarie Schimmel, [Poem entitled] 'At the End of the ACLS Lectures, 1980' in idem, *Nightingales Under the Snow: Poems by Annemarie Schimmel* (London and New York: Khaniqahi Nimatullahi Publications, 1994), p. 42. The mystical poetry of Schimmel deserves to be better known.
2. Idem, *Mystical Dimensions of Islam* (Chapel Hill: University of North Carolina Press, 1975, 1978).
3. See Franklin D. Lewis, *Rumi: Past and Present, East and West: The Life, Teaching and Poetry of Jalâl al-Din Rūmī* (Oxford: Oneworld, 2000) for a magisterial evaluation of Rūmī.
4. Q.31:27: trans. Abdullah Yusuf Ali, *The Holy Qur'ān: Text, Translation and Commentary* (Kuwait: Dhāt al-Salāsil, 1984) [hereafter referred to as Yusuf Ali (trans.), *Qur'ān*], p. 1,087. See also Michel Chodkiewicz, *An Ocean without Shore: Ibn 'Arabî, The Book and the Law* (Albany, NY: State University of New York Press, 1993), pp. 19ff.
5. J. B. Sykes (ed.), *The Concise Oxford Dictionary of Current English*, 6th edn (Oxford: Clarendon Press, 1976, 1979), p. 721 s.v. *mystic*.
6. Schimmel, *Mystical Dimensions*, p. 4.
7. Ibid.; see also p. 23.
8. Ibid., p. xvii.
9. Jalāl al-Dīn Rūmī, *Mathnawī-i ma'nawi (Masnavi-ye ma'navi)*, ed. and trans. Reynold A. Nicholson, E. J. W. Gibb Memorial Series, n. s. 4 (London: Luzac & Co., 1925–33), vol. 3, lines 1,259–68, cited in Schimmel, *Mystical Dimensions*, p. 3; see also M. A. Shaban, *Islamic History: A New Interpretation 2: AD 750–1055 (AH 132–448)* (Cambridge: Cambridge University Press, 1976), p. viii.
10. See Knut Tranøy, 'Thomas Aquinas' in D. J. O'Connor (ed.), *A Critical History of Western Philosophy*, Free Press Textbooks in Philosophy (New York: The Free Press/London: Collier Macmillan, 1964), p. 98; Alexander Broadie, 'Aquinas, St Thomas' in Ted Honderich (ed.), *The Oxford Companion to Philosophy* (Oxford and New York: Oxford University Press, 1995), p. 43.
11. Annemarie Schimmel, 'There is No Love' in idem, *Nightingales Under the Snow*, p. 40.
12. Idem, *Mystical Dimensions*, p. 3.

13. H. G. Liddell (ed.), *An Intermediate Greek–English Lexicon*, Founded Upon the Seventh Edition of Liddell and Scott's *Greek–English Lexicon* (Oxford: Clarendon Press, 1968), p. 523.
14. D. P. Simpson, *Cassell's New Latin-English/English-Latin Dictionary*, 3rd edn (London: Cassell, 1964), p. 386.
15. Margaret Smith, *The Way of the Mystics: The Early Christian Mystics and the Rise of the Sufis* (London: Sheldon Press, 1976, repr. of 1931 edn), p. 1. (The 1931 edn was entitled *Studies in Early Mysticism in the Near and Middle East.*)
16. R. A. S. Seaford, 'The mysteries of Dionysos at Pompeii' in H. W. Stubbs (ed.), *Pegasus: Classical Essays from the University of Exeter* (Exeter: University of Exeter, 1981), p. 59, cited in Ian Richard Netton, 'The mysteries of Islam' in G. S. Rousseau and Roy Porter (eds), *Exoticism in the Enlightenment* (Manchester and New York: Manchester University Press, 1990), p. 40 n. 1. See Richard Seaford, '1 Corinthians XIII:12' in *The Journal of Theological Studies* (Notes and Studies), New Series, vol. 35:1 (April 1984), pp. 117–20. (I am most grateful to Professor Seaford, Professor of Greek in the University of Exeter, for bringing this article to my attention and for generously supplying me with an offprint.)
17. See Netton, 'Mysteries', p. 23; Seaford, 'Mysteries of Dionysos', esp. pp. 52–8; idem, '1 Corinthians XIII:12', pp. 117–20.
18. Trans. R. Knox, *The Holy Bible: The New Testament* (London: Burns & Oates/Macmillan, 1960) [hereafter referred to as Knox (trans.), *Bible: New Testament*].
19. *The Holy Bible* (Oxford: Oxford University Press/London: Geoffrey Cumberlege, n.d.), p. 826.
20. See Seaford, 'Mysteries of Dionysos'; idem, '1 Corinthians XIII:12', pp. 117–20.
21. John S. Kselman and Ronald D. Witherup, 'Modern New Testament Criticism' in Raymond E. Brown, Joseph A. Fitzmyer and Roland E. Murphy (eds), *The New Jerome Biblical Commentary*, 2nd edn (London: Geoffrey Chapman, 1989, repr. 1990) [hereafter referred to as *New Jerome*], pp. 1,136–7.
22. Richard L. Gordon, 'Mysteries' in Simon Hornblower and Antony Spawforth (eds), *The Oxford Classical Dictionary*, 3rd edn (Oxford: Oxford University Press, 1999), p. 1,017.
23. Ibid., p. 1,018.
24. Ibid., p. 1,017.
25. Ibid.
26. Ibid.; see also Kevin Clinton, 'Eleusis' in Hornblower and Spawforth (eds), *Oxford Classical Dictionary*, p. 520.
27. Gordon, 'mysteries', p. 1,017.
28. Smith, *Way of the Mystics*, p. 1.
29. Clinton, 'Eleusis', p. 520.
30. Smith, *Way of the Mystics*, p. 1.
31. See Giovanni Filoramo, *A History of Gnosticism*, trans. Anthony Alcock (Cambridge, MA/Oxford: Blackwell, 1990, 1992); for remarks on cults like the Dionisiac, and the 'mysteries', see pp. 27–8.
32. Ninian Smart, *Dimensions of the Sacred: An Anatomy of the World's Beliefs* (London: HarperCollins, 1996), p. 111; see also p. 105.
33. Reynold A. Nicholson, *The Mystics of Islam* (London and Boston: Routledge & Kegan Paul, 1975; repr. of 1914 edn published by London: George Bell & Sons Ltd), p. v.
34. A. J. Arberry, *Sufism: An Account of the Mystics of Islam*, Ethical and Religious Classics of East and West, no. 2 (London: George Allen & Unwin, 1968), p. 7.
35. Ibid., p. 11.
36. Geoffrey Parrinder, 'Foreword' in Smith, *Way of the Mystics*, p. ix.
37. Smith, *Way of the Mystics*, p. 2.

38. Alexander D. Knysh, 'Ṣūfism and the Qur'ān' in Jane Dammen McAuliffe (ed.), *Encyclopaedia of the Qur'ān, vol. Five Si–Z* (Leiden and Boston: E. J. Brill, 2006) [hereafter referred to as *EQ*], p. 137.
39. Julian Baldick, *Mystical Islam: An Introduction to Sufism* (London: I. B. Tauris, 1989), p. 3.
40. Ibid.
41. Seyyed Hossein Nasr, *Sufi Essays* (London: Allen & Unwin, 1972), p. 17.
42. Ibid., p. 32.
43. Carl W. Ernst, *Words of Ecstasy in Sufism*, SUNY Series in Islam (Albany, NY: State University of New York Press, 1985), p. 1.
44. Ibid.
45. Nicholson, *Mystics of Islam*, p. 8.
46. Schimmel, *Mystical Dimensions*, p. 10.
47. Baldick, *Mystical Islam*, p. 2 (my emphases).
48. Knysh, 'Ṣūfism and the Qur'ān', p. 138.
49. Q.17:1, trans. Yusuf Ali, *Qur'ān*, p. 693. See B. Schricke, 'Isrā'' in H. A. R. Gibb and J. H. Kramers (eds), *Shorter Encyclopaedia of Islam* (Leiden: E. J. Brill/London: Luzac, 1961) [hereafter referred to as *EIS*], p. 183; R. Paret, 'Al-Burāq' in H. A. R. Gibb et al. (eds), *Encyclopaedia of Islam*, 2nd edn (Leiden: E. J. Brill, 1960) [hereafter referred to as *EI*²], vol. 1, pp. 1,310–11; al-Bukhārī, *Ṣaḥīḥ: The Translation of the Meanings of Sahîh al-Bukhārī*, Arabic–English, vol. 5, trans. Muhammad Muhsin Khan (Riyadh: Dār al-Salām, 1997) [hereafter referred to as al-Bukhārī, trans. Khan, vol. 5], Book 63: *Kitāb Manāqib al-Anṣār*, *Bāb* 42, p. 132; J. Horovitz, 'Mi'rādj', *EIS*, pp. 381–4.
50. See al-Bukhārī, trans. Khan, vol. 5, Book 63: *Kitāb Manāqib al-Anṣār*, *Bāb* 42, Ḥadīth no. 3,888, p. 137.
51. Schricke, 'Isrā'', *EIS*, p. 138; Paret, 'Al-Burāq', *EI*², vol. 1, p. 1,310. For a general survey, see al-Bukhārī, trans. Khan, vol. 1, Book 8: *Kitāb al-Ṣalāt*, *Bāb* 1, Ḥadīth no. 349, pp. 237–9; and ibid., vol. 5, Book 63: *Kitāb Manāqib al-Anṣār*, *Bāb* 41, 42, 43, Ḥadīth nos 3,886–7, pp. 131–7.
52. See Horovitz, 'Mi'rādj', *EIS*, p. 383.
53. W. Montgomery Watt, *Companion to the Qur'an* (London: Allen & Unwin, 1967), p. 244.
54. Daniel A. Madigan, 'Revelation and Inspiration' in *EQ vol. Four P-Sh* (Leiden and Boston: E. J. Brill, 2004), p. 441.
55. Ibid.
56. See al-Bukhārī, trans. Khan, vol. 1, Book 8: *Kitāb al-Ṣalāt*, *Bāb* 1, Ḥadīth no. 349, pp. 237–9; ibid., vol. 5, Book 63: *Kitāb Manāqib al-Anṣār*, *Bāb* 42, pp. 135–6. Compare Genesis 18:22–3.
57. Q.53:5, trans Yusuf Ali, *Qur'ān*, p. 1,443.
58. See David Waines, 'Tree(s)' in *EQ vol. Five*, p. 360.
59. Q.53:13–16, trans. Yusuf Ali, *Qur'ān*, pp. 1,444–5.
60. Yusuf Ali (trans.), *Qur'ān*, p. 1,444 n. 5,092.
61. Watt, *Companion*, p. 244.
62. See al-Bukhārī, trans. Khan, vol. 1, Book 8: *Kitāb al-Ṣalāt*, *Bāb* 1, Ḥadīth no. 349, p. 239.
63. Ibid., vol. 5, Book 63: *Kitāb Manāqib al-Anṣār*, *Bāb* 42, Ḥadīth no. 3,887, p. 135.
64. Q.94:1–4, trans. Yusuf Ali, *Qur'ān*, p. 1,755.
65. Ibid., n. 6,188.
66. Watt, *Companion*, p. 313.
67. For Ḥalīma, see W. Montgomery Watt, 'Ḥalīma Bint Abī Dhu'ayb', *EI*², vol. 3, p. 94.
68. See Michael Edwardes (ed.), *Ibn Ishaq: The Life of Muhammad, Apostle of Allah*, trans. Edward Rehatsek (London: Folio Society, 1964, 2003), pp. 19–20. This is 'the first known

English version of Ibn Ishaq's biography' (ibid., p. 12). The translator, Edward Rehatsek (AD 1819–91), completed his translation shortly before he died, and the manuscript was given to the London Royal Asiatic Society in 1898 (see ibid., p. 13). For the original Arabic text, see Ibn Isḥāq/Ibn Hishām, *Al-Sīra al-Nabawiyya li-Ibn Hishām*, ed. Muṣṭafā al-Saqqā et al., vol. 1, 2nd edn, Turāth al-Islām (Cairo: al-Bābī al-Ḥalabī, 1955), p. 166.

69. Al-Bukhārī, trans. Khan, vol. 1, Book 8: *Kitāb al-Ṣalāt*, *Bāb* 1, Ḥadīth no. 349, p. 237. A variation on this narrative occurs in ibid., vol. 5, Book 63: *Kitāb Manāqib al-Anṣār*, *Bāb* 42, Ḥadīth no. 3,887, p. 132.
70. W. Madelung, ''Iṣma', *EI*², vol. 4, p. 182.
71. Ibid.; see also Paul E. Walker, 'Impeccability', *EQ vol.Two E–I* (Leiden and Boston: E. J. Brill, 2002), p. 505.
72. Madelung, ''Iṣma', p. 183.
73. Walker, 'Impeccability', pp. 505–6.
74. See above n. 72.
75. Trans. Yusuf Ali, *Qur'ān*, p. 1,109.
76. Claude Addas, *Ibn 'Arabī: The Voyage of No Return*, trans. David Streight, Muslim Personalities Series (Cambridge: Islamic Texts Society, 2000), p. 21.
77. H. Ritter, ''Abd al-Karīm, Ḳuṭb al-Dīn B. Ibrāhīm al-Djīlī', *EI*², vol. 1, p. 71; R. Arnaldez, 'Al-Insān al-Kāmil', *EI*², vol. 3, p. 1,240. See also R. W. J. Austin (trans.), *Ibn al-'Arabi: The Bezels of Wisdom*, Classics of Western Spirituality (Ramsey, NJ: Paulist Press, 1980), pp. 34–41.
78. See n. 77 above, and Reynold Alleyne Nicholson, 'The Perfect Man' [ch. 2] in his *Studies in Islamic Mysticism* (Richmond: Curzon Press, 1994, repr. of CUP edn of 1921), p. 78; see also Vincent J. Cornell, *Realm of the Saint: Power and Authority in Moroccan Sufism* (Austin: University of Texas Press, 1998), pp. 206–9.
79. Nicholson, *Studies in Islamic Mysticism*, p. 87; see 'Abd al-Karīm b. Ibrāhīm al-Jīlī, *al-Insān al-Kāmil fī Ma'rifat al-Awā'il wa'l-Awākhir* (Cairo: Maktaba al-Thaqāfa al-Dīniyya, 2004), vol. 2, pp. 115–26, esp. p. 115.
80. Nicholson, *Studies in Islamic Mysticism*, p. 87. Little notes: 'Even the most Perfect Man, Muḥammad, is only *a* logos, not *the* Logos, which is [a broader entity characterised as] the Reality of Muḥammad' (John T. Little, '*Al-Insān al-Kāmil*: The Perfect Man According to Ibn al-'Arabi', *The Muslim World*, vol. 77:1 (January 1987), p. 53).
81. Nicholson, *Studies in Islamic Mysticism*, p. 87.
82. Ibid., pp. 77–8.
83. Ibid., p. 108; see al-Jīlī, *al-Insān al-Kāmil*, vol. 1, p. 59.
84. Cornell, *Realm of the Saint*, p. 209; see al-Jīlī, *al-Insān al-Kāmil*, vol. 1, p. 178.
85. Arnaldez, 'Al-Insān al-Kāmil', p. 1,239.
86. Ibid., p. 1,240.
87. Ibid.
88. Austin (trans.), *Bezels*, p. 272; for the original Arabic, see Ibn al-'Arabī, *Fuṣūṣ al-Ḥikam*, ed. Abū 'l-'Alā 'Afīfī (Beirut: Dār al-Kitāb al-'Arabī, 1946), pt 1, p. 214.
89. Q.53:5–10; trans. Yusuf Ali, *Qur'ān*, pp. 1,443–4.
90. Al-Bukhārī, trans. Khan, vol. 1, Book 8: *Kitāb al-Ṣalāt*, *Bāb* 1, Ḥadīth no. 349, p. 238; idem, vol. 5, Book 63: *Kitāb Manāqib al-Anṣār*, *Bāb* 42, Ḥadīth no. 3,887, pp. 133–6.
91. See above n. 56.
92. The full reference provided by Meier is Muḥammad b. 'Alī al-Sanūsī, *al-Manhal al-Rawī 'l-Rā'iq fī Asānīd al-'Ulūm wa-Uṣūl al-Ṭarā'iq* in *al-Majmu'a al-Mukhtara* (Beirut, 1968), p. 49. See Fritz Meier, 'A Resurrection of Muḥammad in Suyūṭī' in *Essays on Islamic Piety and Mysticism*, trans. John O'Kane, ed. Bernd Radtke (Leiden, Boston, Köln: E. J. Brill, 1999), p. 540 n. 98.

93. A. J. Wensinck, 'Al-Khaḍir (al-Khiḍr)', *EI*², vol. 4, p. 905, citing Ibn Ḥajar, *Kitāb al-Iṣāba* [*A Biographical Dictionary of Persons who Knew Mohammad*] (4 vols, Calcutta: Printed by T. J. M'Arthur, Bishop's College Press, 1856–88), vol. 1, pp. 899ff.
94. Wensinck, 'Al-Khaḍir (al-Khiḍr)', p. 902.
95. E.g. see Meier, 'A Book of Etiquette for Sufis' in idem, *Essays*, p. 63.
96. Ibn al-'Arabī, *Shajarat al-Kawn*, ed. Riyāḍ al-'Abdallāh (Beirut: al-Markaz al-'Arabī li 'l-Kitāb, 1984) [hereafter referred to as *Shajarat*]; Interpreted by Shaykh Tosun Bayrak al-Jerrahi al-Halveti, *Ibn 'Arabi: The Tree of Being: Shajarat al-Kawn: An Ode to the Perfect Man* (Cambridge: Archetype, 2005) [hereafter referred to as *Tree of Being*, trans. al-Halveti]. The translations in my text *cite and reflect the interpretations by al-Halveti of the Arabic*.
97. *Tree of Being*, trans. al-Halveti, p. 85.
98. Ibid., pp. 85–6.
99. Q.14:24; trans Yusuf Ali, *Qur'ān*, p. 626.
100. Q.14:25–6; trans. Yusuf Ali, *Qur'ān*, pp. 626–7.
101. John 1:1.
102. *Tree of Being*, trans. al-Halveti, p. 108; Ibn al-'Arabī, *Shajarat*, p. 57.
103. *Tree of Being*, trans. al-Halveti, p. 110; Ibn al-'Arabī, *Shajarat*, p. 59.
104. *Tree of Being*, trans. al-Halveti, pp. 110–11; Ibn al-'Arabī, *Shajarat*, p. 59.
105. *Tree of Being*, trans. al-Halveti, p. 146; Ibn al-'Arabī, *Shajarat*, p. 87.
106. *Tree of Being*, trans. al-Halveti, pp. 147–8; Ibn al-'Arabī, *Shajarat*, p. 88.
107. *Tree of Being*, trans. al-Halveti, p. 148; Ibn al-'Arabī, *Shajarat*, p. 88.
108. *Tree of Being*, trans. al-Halveti, p. 149; Ibn al-'Arabī, *Shajarat*, p. 89.
109. *Tree of Being*, trans. al-Halveti, pp. 162–76; Ibn al-'Arabī, *Shajarat*, pp. 94–101.
110. *Tree of Being*, trans. al-Halveti, p. 162; Ibn al-'Arabī, *Shajarat*, p. 94.
111. *Tree of Being*, trans. al-Halveti, pp. 162–4; Ibn al-'Arabī, *Shajarat*, p. 95.
112. *Tree of Being*, trans. al-Halveti, pp. 174–5; Ibn al-'Arabī, *Shajarat*, p. 101.
113. Q.53:10; trans. Yusuf Ali, *Qur'ān*, p. 1,444; *Tree of Being*, trans. al-Halveti, p. 175; Ibn al-'Arabī, *Shajarat*, p. 101.
114. *Tree of Being*, trans. al-Halveti, Appendix, p. 180.
115. Sir Thomas Malory, *Le Morte Darthur: The Winchester Manuscript*, ed. with Introduction by Helen Cooper, Oxford World's Classics (Oxford: Oxford University Press, 1998), 'Introduction', pp. x, xxxi. See also Sir Thomas Malory, *Le Morte Darthur or The Hoole Book of Kyng Arthur and of His Noble Knyghtes of The Rounde Table*, Authoritative Text, Sources and Backgrounds, Criticism, ed. Stephen H. A. Shepherd, A Norton Critical Edition (New York and London: W. W. Norton & Co., 2004), p. xxvi.
116. Beverly Kennedy, *Knighthood in the Morte Darthur*, 2nd edn (Cambridge: D. S. Brewer, 1992), p. 4.
117. Ibid., p. 5.
118. Ibid., p. 57.
119. Marlé Hammond, 'He Desires Her? Situating Nazhun's *Muwashshah* in an Androgynous Aesthetic of Courtly Love' in Ed Emery (ed.), *Muwashshah! Proceedings of the International Conference on Arabic and Hebrew Strophic Poetry and Its Romance Parallels, School of Oriental and African Studies [SOAS], London, 8–10 October 2004*, Research Papers on Arabic and Jewish Strophic Poetry (London: SOAS, 2006), p. 142. See Hammond's references to Frings and Peter Dronke in ibid., p. 155 n. 7, viz. Theodor Frings, *Minnesinger und Troubadours* (Berlin, 1949) and Peter Dronke, *Medieval Latin and the Rise of European Love Lyric*, 2nd edn (Oxford: Clarendon Press, 1968), vol. 1.
120. Roger Boase, *The Origin and Meaning of Courtly Love: A Critical Study of European Schol-*

arship (Manchester: Manchester University Press/Totowa, NJ: Rowman & Littlefield, 1977), p. 1. See also Pamela Porter, *Courtly Love in Medieval Manuscripts* (London: British Library, 2003), pp. 5–6.
121. Boase, *Origin and Meaning*.
122. Ibid.
123. C. S. Lewis, *The Allegory of Love: A Study in Medieval Tradition* (Oxford and New York: Oxford University Press, repr. 1985).
124. Ibid., p. 2.
125. Bernard O'Donaghue, *The Courtly Love Tradition*, Literature in Context 5 (Manchester: Manchester University Press/Totowa, NJ: Barnes & Noble, 1982), p. 2.
126. Boase, *Origin and Meaning*; see esp. pp. 21, 63, 65, 68.
127. O'Donaghue, *Courtly Love Tradition*, p. 4.
128. Boase, *Origin and Meaning*, p. 123; see also O'Donaghue, *Courtly Love Tradition*, p. 1.
129. Boase, *Origin and Meaning*, p. 129.
130. Guillaume de Lorris and Jean de Meun, *The Romance of the Rose*, trans. and ed. Frances Horgan, Oxford World's Classics (Oxford: Oxford University Press, 1999), p. 65. See also O'Donaghue, *Courtly Love Tradition*, p. 201.
131. Boase, *Origin and Meaning*, pp. 129–30.
132. Lewis, *Allegory of Love*, pp. 2, 12–13.
133. O'Donaghue, *Courtly Love Tradition*, p. 14.
134. Maurice Hussey, 'Introduction' in idem (ed.), *The Merchant's Prologue and Tale, From the Canterbury Tales by Geoffrey Chaucer* (Cambridge: Cambridge University Press, 1966, repr. 2005), p. 6.
135. O'Donaghue, *Courtly Love Tradition*, p. 3 (my emphases).
136. Ibid., p. 12 (my emphases).
137. Boase, *Origin and Meaning*, pp. 1, 5.
138. See Geraldine Heng, 'Enchanted Ground: The Feminine Subtext in Malory' in Shepherd (ed.), *Le Morte Darthur*, pp. 838–9.
139. O'Donaghue, *Courtly Love Tradition*, p. 192; Porter, *Courtly Love*, p. 28.
140. O'Donaghue, *Courtly Love Tradition*, p. 192; Porter, *Courtly Love*, p. 28.
141. Porter, *Courtly Love*, p. 28.
142. Ibid., p. 29; see also O'Donaghue, *Courtly Love Tradition*, p. 192; see Horgan (trans. and ed.), *The Romance of the Rose*; see also Guillaume de Lorris, *Le Roman de la Rose*, ed. Stephen G. Nichols (New York: Appleton-Century-Crofts, 1967).
143. Porter, *Courtly Love*, p. 29.
144. Lewis, *Allegory of Love*, p. 157.
145. O'Donaghue, *Courtly Love Tradition*, p. 7.
146. Ibid.
147. Translation supplied on leaflet (p. 1) by Faye Newton (soprano) and Hazel Brooks (vielle) at a concert by them given during the International Medieval Congress, University of Leeds, in St Chad's Church, Leeds, on 7 July 2008, entitled *Duo Trobairitz*.
148. Chrétien de Troyes, *Lancelot, le Chevalier à la Charrette* in idem, *Romans de la Table Ronde*, ed. Jean-Pierre Foucher, Collection Folio (Paris: Éditions Gallimard, 1970, 1975), pp. 147–244; Chrétien de Troyes, *Lancelot, The Knight of the Cart*, trans. Burton Raffel (New Haven and London: Yale University Press, 1997).
149. Lewis, *Allegory of Love*, p. 29, see also p. 225; see also Boase, *Origin and Meaning*, pp. 21, 124; O'Donaghue, *Courtly Love Tradition*, p. 5.
150. *Lancelot*, trans. Raffel, p. 147; *Lancelot*, ed. Foucher, p. 216.
151. *Lancelot*, trans. Raffel, p. 149; *Lancelot*, ed. Foucher, p. 218.

152. Boase, *Origin and Meaning*, p. 67.
153. Ibid., see also pp. 65, 124, 129.
154. Horgan (tran. and ed.), *The Romance of the Rose*, p. 66.
155. For the archetype of such *majālis* in the Greek world, see Plato, *The Symposium*, trans. Walter Hamilton (Harmondsworth: Penguin Books, 1972).
156. Trans. Paul Lunde and Caroline Stone, *The Meadows of Gold: The Abbasids*, by al-Mas'ūdī (London and New York: Kegan Paul International, 1989), pp. 109–10; for the original Arabic, see al-Mas'ūdī, *Murūj al-Dhahab* (Beirut: Dār al-Andalus, 1996), pt 3, p. 371.
157. Lunde and Stone (trans.), *Meadows of Gold*, p. 112; al-Mas'ūdī, *Murūj al-Dhahab*, pt 3, p. 373.
158. See above n. 154.
159. Boase, *Origin and Meaning*, p. 31.
160. Ibid., pp. 30–1.
161. See ibid., pp. 62, 72–3.
162. Ibid., p. 73.
163. Sykes (ed.), *Concise Oxford Dictionary*, p. 174 s.v. *chivalry*.
164. See Lewis, *Allegory of Love*, p. 72.
165. See Kennedy, *Knighthood in the Morte Darthur*, p. 5.
166. *Le Morte Darthur*, ed. Cooper, 'Introduction', p. xiii.
167. See Lewis, *Allegory of Love*, pp. 158, 279.
168. Kennedy, *Knighthood in the Morte Darthur*, p. 3.
169. See above nn. 116, 117. See also Kennedy, *Knighthood*, pp. 4–5, 57, 83.
170. *Le Morte Darthur*, ed. Cooper, 'Introduction', p. xvi.
171. Ibid.
172. For both original text and translation, see Gerard J. Brault (ed.), *The Song of Roland: An Analytical Edition, vol. 2: Oxford Text and English Translation* (University Park and London: Pennsylvania State University Press, 1978). For an extensive Introduction and commentary, see idem (ed.), *The Song of Roland: An Analytical Edition, vol. 1: Introduction and Commentary* (University Park and London: Pennsylvania State University Press, 1978).
173. Kennedy, *Knighthood in the Morte Darthur*, p. 104.
174. Ibid., p. 105.
175. See ibid., p. 222.
176. Brault (ed.), *The Song of Roland vol. 2*, pp. 126–7 (l. 2,066 French text).
177. Ibid., pp. 66–7 (l. 1,053 French text). See also pp. 70–1, 74–5; see vol. 1, pp. 183–4.
178. Ibid., vol. 2, pp. 110–11 (ll. 1,785–8); see vol. 1, p. 219.
179. Ibid., vol. 1, pp. 6, 4.
180. Ibid., p. 1.
181. Ibid., p. 9.
182. See ibid., p. 10.
183. Ibid., pp. 28–9.
184. Ibid., pp. 42–3.
185. For the original text, see Larry D. Benson (ed.), *The Riverside Chaucer*, 3rd edn (Oxford: Oxford University Press, 1988); a popular verse translation was undertaken by David Wright, *Geoffrey Chaucer, The Canterbury Tales*, Oxford World's Classics (Oxford: Oxford University Press, 1998).
186. See Benson, 'The Canon and Chronology of Chaucer's Work' in *The Riverside Chaucer*, p. xxv; Wright (trans.), *The Canterbury Tales*, p. xxvii.
187. Lewis, *Allegory of Love*, p. 161.

188. See Kennedy, *Knighthood in the Morte Darthur*, p. 2.
189. *The Riverside Chaucer*, p. 24.
190. Wright (trans.), *The Canterbury Tales*, p. 2.
191. *The Riverside Chaucer*, p. 24 n. 72 on l. 72.
192. Ibid., p. 24.
193. Ibid.
194. Ibid.
195. Ibid.
196. Ibid.
197. See Helen Cooper, *The Canterbury Tales*, 2nd edn, Oxford Guides to Chaucer (Oxford: Oxford University Press, 1996), pp. 61–91.
198. J. A. Burrow, 'The *Canterbury Tales* 1: romance' in Piero Boitani and Jill Mann (eds), *The Cambridge Companion to Chaucer*, 2nd edn (Cambridge: Cambridge University Press, 2007), p. 154.
199. *The Riverside Chaucer*, pp. 6–7.
200. Burrow, '*Canterbury Tales* 1: romance', p. 158. For an evaluation of the whole of *The Knight's Tale*, see Cooper, *The Canterbury Tales*, pp. 61–91.
201. Cooper, *Canterbury Tales*, p. 73.
202. See Horgan (trans. and ed.), *The Romance of the Rose*, pp. 19, 32, 288. For the original French, see *Le Roman de la Rose*, ed. Nichols, pp. 52, 79.
203. Gerald Morgan, *Sir Gawain and the Green Knight and the Idea of Righteousness*, Dublin Studies in Medieval and Renaissance Literature (Dublin: Irish Academic Press, 1991), p. 62.
204. Ibid.
205. J. Speirs, 'Sir Gawain and the Green Knight', *Scrutiny*, vol. 16 (1949), pp. 274–90 and idem, in D. Fox (ed.), *Twentieth Century Interpretations of Sir Gawain and the Green Knight* (Englewood Cliffs, NJ: Prentice-Hall, 1968), pp. 79–94 (p. 83): cited in Morgan, *Sir Gawain*, p. 61 and n. 3.
206. Francis Ingledew, *Sir Gawain and the Green Knight and the Order of the Garter* (Notre Dame, IN: University of Notre Dame Press, 2006), p. 80; see also pp. 93–4.
207. *Sir Gawain and the Green Knight*, trans. Brian Stone, 2nd edn (London: Penguin Books, 1974), p. 9. For a more recent translation, see Simon Armitage (trans.), *Sir Gawain and the Green Knight* (London: Faber & Faber, 2007). For the original text, see J. J. Anderson (ed.), *Sir Gawain and the Green Knight, Pearl, Cleanness, Patience*, The Everyman Library (London: J. M. Dent/North Clarendon, VT: Tuttle Publishing, 2005) [hereafter referred to as ME [Middle English] Text].
208. See Yusuf Ali (trans.), *Qur'ān: Sūra* 18, pp. 728–59; Wensinck, 'Al-Khaḍir (al-Khiḍr)', pp. 902–5; Ian Richard Netton, 'Towards a Modern *Tafsīr* of *Sūrat al-Kahf*: Structure and Semiotics', *Journal of Qur'anic Studies*, vol. 2:1 (2000), pp. 67–87; J. Meri, *The Cult of the Saints: Muslims and Jews in Mediaeval Syria* (Oxford: Oxford University Press, 2002); E. S. Wolper, 'Khidr, Elwan Celebi and the conversion of sacred sanctuaries in Anatolia', *Muslim World*, vol. 90:iii–iv (2000), pp. 309–22.
209. Wensinck, 'Al-Khaḍir (al-Khiḍr)', p. 902.
210. *Sir Gawain*, trans. Stone #7–9, pp. 26–7; ME Text, pp. 173–5.
211. For the brilliant green clothing worn by al-Khaḍir, see Mercia MacDermott and Ruth Wylie, *Explore Green Men* (Loughborough: Explore Books, Heart of Albion Press, 2003), pp. 14–15. But MacDermott points out that, like Sir Gawain's Green Knight, al-Khaḍir/al-Khiḍr 'lacks the foliage' – 'despite the greenness of his robes' – which she insists is 'an essential feature of Green Men' (ibid., p. 15).

212. Wensinck, 'Al-Khaḍir (al-Khiḍr)', p. 905.
213. Ibid.
214. Brian Stone, 'The Common Enemy of Man' in *Sir Gawain*, trans. Stone, pp. 116, 117.
215. Q.18:60–82. See also John Renard, 'Khaḍir/Khiḍr' in *EQ vol. Three J–O*, pp. 81–4.
216. *Sir Gawain*, trans. Stone ('Introduction'), p. 14.
217. Ibid. #81, p. 97; ME Text, p. 254.
218. Ibid. #84, p. 99; ME Text, p. 258.
219. Ibid. #7; p. 26 (my emphases); ME Text, p. 173.
220. Ibid. #20, p. 37; ME Text, p. 186.
221. Ibid. #52–#75, pp. 70–91; ME Text, pp. 221–47.
222. Genesis 39:7–12.
223. Q.12:23–9.
224. R. W. V. Elliott, *The Gawain Country*, Leeds Texts and Monographs, New Series no. 8 (Leeds: University of Leeds School of English, 1984), p. 43. For theories about the actual topographical locations of this chapel, on the assumption that the poet was writing from actual life, see ibid., pp. 43–52; *Sir Gawain*, trans. Armitage, 'Introduction', p. vi.
225. *Sir Gawain*, trans. Stone, #94, p. 108; ME Text, p. 269.
226. *Sir Gawain*, trans. Stone, #93–101, pp. 107–15; ME Text, pp. 267–77.
227. *Sir Gawain*, trans. Armitage, 'Introduction', p. ix.
228. Ibid., p. vii.
229. Iris Murdoch, *The Green Knight* (London: Chatto & Windus, 1993); see the remarks of Fran Doel and Geoff Doel, *The Green Man in Britain* (Stroud: Tempus/Charleston, SC: Arcadia 2001), pp. 113–14.
230. Murdoch, *The Green Knight*, p. 93; Doel and Doel, *Green Man*, p. 113.
231. Murdoch, *The Green Knight*, p. 101.
232. Ibid., p. 103.
233. Ibid., p. 104.
234. For a general orientation, see, *inter alia*, MacDermott and Wylie, *Explore Green Men*; Doel and Doel, *Green Man*; Kathleen Basford, *The Green Man* (Ipswich: Brewer, 1978); John Satchell, 'Green Man in Cumbria', *Folklore*, vol. 110 (1999), pp. 98–9.
235. *Sir Gawain*, trans. Armitage, p. vii.
236. See Roger Bullen et al. (eds), *Complete Flags of the World*, 5th edn (London and New York: Dorling Kindersley, 2008), p. 197 s.v. *Pakistan*.
237. Ibid., p. 181 s.v. *Saudi Arabia*.
238. See Colin Waters, *A Dictionary of Pub, Inn and Tavern Signs* (Newbury: Countryside Books, 2005), p. 67 s.v. *Green*. The entry is more descriptive than explanatory, in answer to the question 'Why green?', but does suggest that 'The Green Man' symbolises life springing from death (see ibid.). See Doel and Doel, *Green Man*, p. 34.
239. Frank Viviano and Michael Yamashita, 'China's Great Armada', *National Geographic*, vol. 208:1 (July 2005), p. 36; for a full biography of Zheng He, see Edward L. Dreyer, *Zheng He: China and the Oceans in the Early Ming Dynasty, 1405–1433*, Library of World Biography Series (New York and London: Pearson Longman, 2007). The latter volume was reviewed by Jonathan Mirsky in the *Times Literary Supplement* (26 January 2007) under the heading 'Tribute, Trade and some Eunuchs', but neither the book nor the review discusses the colour *green*.
240. Viviano and Yamashita, 'China's Great Armada', p. 36.
241. See Hugo Williams, 'Freelance', *Times Literary Supplement*, 17 March 2006, p. 14.
242. See Doel and Doel, *Green Man*, pp. 35–6; compare, for example, the rubric for vestments

to be worn on the Third Sunday after the Epiphany, which specifies 'Green', with that for Easter Sunday, where 'White' is decreed (J. Dukes (reviser), *The Daily Missal and Liturgical Manual*, Leeds: Laverty & Sons, n.d. [1960], pp. 260, 629).

243. Alison Roberts, *Hathor Rising: The Serpent Power of Ancient Egypt* (Totnes: Northgate Publishers, 1995), p. 15.
244. See A. R. Williams, 'Nile Style', *National Geographic* (July 2008), vol. 214: 1.
245. See *Sir Gawain*, trans. Stone, pp. 184–5 n. 2,516; for a much more involved – and bold – attempt to associate the Order of the Garter with the *Sir Gawain* poem, see Ingledew, *Sir Gawain*, passim.
246. For more on 'greenness' and al-Khaḍir, see Hasmik Tovmayan, 'St Sargis and al-Khadir: A Common Saint for Christians and Muslims', *ARAM*, 20 (2008), p. 198, citing al-Bukhārī, *Ṣaḥīḥ al-Bukhārī*, vol. 3 (Beirut, 1987): 1248. For the 'green' miracles of al-Khaḍir, see Marlène Kanaan, 'Legends, Places and Traditions Related to the Cult of St George in Lebanon' in ibid., p. 210.
247. M. A. Hall, 'An Ivory Knife Handle from the High Street, Perth, Scotland: Consuming Ritual in a Medieval Burgh', *Medieval Archaeology: Journal of the Society for Medieval Archaeology*, vol. 45 (2001), p. 179. See also Clive Hicks, *The Green Man: A Field Guide* (Fakenham: Compassbooks, 2000), pp. v, x.
248. Hall, 'Ivory Knife'.
249. Ibid., p. 181, referring to *Sir Gawain*, trans. Stone ('The Common Enemy of Man'), p. 123, from which the last quotation is taken.
250. Hall, 'Ivory Knife', p. 179, citing Basford, *Green Man*, p. 21.
251. *Sir Gawain*, trans. Stone ('The Common Enemy of Man'), pp. 116–17.
252. Hall, 'Ivory Knife', pp. 186–7.
253. J. J. G. Alexander (ed.), *The Master of Mary of Burgundy: A Book of Hours for Engelbert of Nassau (The Bodleian Library, Oxford)* (New York: George Braziller, 1970), plate 72.
254. Basford, *Green Man*, p. 7.
255. Ibid., p. 9.
256. Ibid., p. 19.
257. Ibid.
258. Ibid., pp. 19–20; see Doel and Doel, *Green Man*, p. 19 plate 6, p. 134; MacDermott, *Explore Green Men*, pp. 106–7.
259. Basford, *Green Man*, p. 20.
260. Ibid. See also William Anderson and Clive Hicks, *Green Man: The Archetype of Our Oneness with the Earth* (London and San Francisco: HarperCollins, 1990), p. 97; Hicks, *Green Man*, pp. 8, 15.
261. Satchell, 'Green Man in Cumbria', p. 98.
262. Ibid., pp. 98–9.
263. Ibid., p. 99; see Anderson and Hicks, *Green Man*, p. 99.
264. Satchell, 'Green Man in Cumbria', p. 99.
265. Anderson and Hicks, *Green Man*, p. 14.
266. Ibid.
267. Ibid., p. 33.
268. Ibid., p. 163.
269. Ibid., p. 34.
270. Ibid., p. 14.
271. Hicks, *Green Man*, p. v.
272. Ibid., pp. 2–3.
273. We note, especially, its deployment in church and cathedral architecture.

274. Hicks, *Green Man*, p. 1; see MacDermott and Wylie, *Explore Green Men*, p. 193.
275. See Doel and Doel, *Green Man*, p. 50.
276. Hicks, *Green Man*, p. 9.
277. See above n. 258. See also Hicks, *Green Man*, p. 69.
278. See, for example, Anderson and Hicks, *Green Man*, pp. 140–1.
279. Ibid., p. 31.
280. William Shakespeare, *The Merry Wives of Windsor*, ed. Giorgio Melchiori, The Arden Shakespeare (London: Thomson Learning, 2000), pp. 257 n. 26, 15 n. 4.
281. Wendy Macphee, *Programme Notes for Theatre Set-Up in William Shakespeare's The Merry Wives of Windsor* (London: Theatre Set-Up, 2004), col. 3 ('Myths, Legends, Magic and Celtdom'). For Cernunnos (Cernnunos or Cernunnus), see Eric L. Fitch, *In Search of Herne the Hunter* (Chieveley: Capall Bann Publishing, 1994), pp. 61–72, 121, 137–9, 157 and MacDermott, *Explore Green Men*, pp. 9–10.
282. Shakespeare, *Merry Wives*, ed. Melchiori, pp. 10–18.
283. See ibid., pp. 9, 15, 18–30 esp. p. 19. See especially the speech by Mistress Quickly in Act V, Scene V, ll. 55–75 with its references to the twenty-four choir stalls reserved for the Knights of the Garter in St George's Chapel, Windsor Castle, its reference to the Garter insignia ('the Garter's compass'), and its quotation of the Garter motto *Honi soit qui mal y pense* (Shakespeare, *Merry Wives*, ed. Melchiori, pp. 280–1 nn. 61, 66, 69.
284. Ibid., p. 1.
285. See ibid., p. 105, plate 11 for a portrait of Anthony Quayle in the role of Falstaff, standing in front of Herne's Oak.
286. William Shakespeare, *The Merry Wives of Windsor*, Act IV, Scene IV in Peter Alexander (ed.), *William Shakespeare: The Complete Works*, The Players' Edition (London and Glasgow: Collins, 1951, repr. 1961), p. 76.
287. See MacDermott, *Explore Green Men*, p. 9.
288. See Shakespeare, *Merry Wives*, ed. Melchiori, p. 258 n. 48.
289. Ibid., p. 257 n. 34.
290. See *Merry Wives*, Act V, Scene V.
291. Ibid.
292. Ibid.
293. See Macphee, *Programme Notes … The Merry Wives of Windsor*, col. 3.
294. *Merry Wives*, Act V, Scene V, l. 232; see *Merry Wives*, ed. Melchiori, p. 291 n. 232.
295. See Stephen James Carver, *The Life and Works of the Lancashire Novelist William Harrison Ainsworth, 1805–1882*, Studies in British Literature, vol. 75 (Lewiston, Queenston, Lampeter: The Edwin Mellen Press, 2003).
296. William Harrison Ainsworth, *Windsor Castle: An Historical Romance* (London: Milner & Co. Ltd, n.d.; orig. publ. in 3 vols, London: Henry Colburn, 1843).
297. Carver, *Life and Works*, pp. xvii–xviii.
298. Ibid., p. xx; see also p. xxi.
299. See ibid., p. xxi.
300. Ibid., p. 287.
301. Ibid., p. 344.
302. Ibid., p. 287.
303. Ibid., p. xx.
304. Ibid., pp. 288–9.
305. Ibid., p. 289.
306. Ibid., p. 290. See Ainsworth, *Windsor Castle*, pp. 167–77. That does not seem to have prevented some authors from making very full use of Ainsworth's account, even while

acknowledging that this account is mainly fictitious. See Fitch, *In Search of Herne the Hunter*, pp. 1–7, 145.

307. Carver, *Life and Works*, p. 293; Macphee, *Programme Notes … Merry Wives*, col. 3.
308. Carver, *Life and Works*, p. 293.
309. Rachel Storm, *Myths and Legends of the Ancient Near East* (London: The Folio Society, 2003), p. 638 (my emphases).
310. Carver, *Life and Works*, p. 295.
311. For associations of *green men* with oak trees, see Doel and Doel, *Green Man*, pp. 97–104.
312. Ainsworth, *Windsor Castle*, p. 6.
313. Ibid.
314. Ibid.
315. Ibid.
316. Ibid., p. 9.
317. Ibid.
318. Ibid., p. 256. See Carver, *Life and Works*, pp. 295–6.
319. Carver, *Life and Works*, p. 296.
320. See David Starkey, *Six Wives: The Queens of Henry VIII* (London: Chatto & Windus, 2003), p. 107: 'For the young Henry, devouring *Le Morte d'Arthur* in Caxton's printed edition of 1485 and listening spell-bound to [the Earl of] Ormond's reminiscences, the real and hero-kings became one. He would be another Henry V, another Arthur: brave in war and peace, generous, bold and gallant'; see also Ainsworth, *Windsor Castle*, pp. 248–52.
321. Ainsworth, *Windsor Castle*, pp. 39–42.
322. Ibid.; see also pp. 66–8.
323. Ibid., p. 76.
324. Ibid., pp. 93–5.
325. Ibid., p. 154.
326. Ibid., p. 219.
327. Ibid., p. 226.
328. Ibid., p. 235.
329. Ibid., p. 254.
330. Ibid.
331. Ibid., p. 256.
332. See Leah Bronner, *The Stories of Elijah and Elisha as Polemics against Baal Worship*, Pretoria Oriental Series, vol. vi (Leiden: E. J. Brill, 1968).
333. See Russell Gregory, 'Irony and the Unmasking of Elijah' in Alan J. Hauser and Russell Gregory, *From Carmel to Horeb: Elijah in Crisis*, Journal for the Study of the Old Testament Supplement Series, 85, Bible and Literature Series, 19 (Sheffield: Almond Press/Sheffield Academic Press, 1990), p. 102.
334. Aharon Wiener, *The Prophet Elijah in the Development of Judaism: A Depth-Psychological Study*, The Littman Library of Jewish Civilization (London, Henley and Boston: Routledge & Kegan Paul, 1978), p. 6.
335. Ibid., pp. 174ff. But see also Gregory, 'Irony', pp. 150–2.
336. Peter J. Leithart, *1 and 2 Kings*, SCM Theological Commentary on the Bible (London: SCM Press, 2006), p. 126; see also pp. 141–2, 172; Philip Satterthwaite and Gordon McConville, *Exploring the Old Testament: Volume 2: The Histories* (London: SPCK, 2007), p. 163; J. R. Porter, *The Illustrated Guide to the Bible* (New York: Oxford University Press, 1995), p. 96.
337. Leithart, *1 and 2 Kings*, p. 130.

338. Ibid., p. 128.
339. Older Roman Catholic texts of the Bible (e.g. the translation by Ronald Knox, *The Holy Bible*, London: Burns & Oates/Macmillan: 1960) refer to the first two Books of Samuel as the First Book of Kings and the Second Book of Kings, and designate the First and Second Books of Kings Third and Fourth (see Knox, trans., *Holy Bible*, pp. 227–38). This is changed in *The Jerusalem Bible*: see *The New Jerusalem Bible*, ed. Henry Wansbrough (London: Darton, Longman & Todd, 1985), pp. 356–505. *The nomenclature of two Books of Samuel, followed by only two Books of Kings, is mostly adopted here in my book*. For a general orientation for Elijah, see first 1 Kings 17 to 2 Kings 2:1–18; Jerome T. Walsh and Christopher T. Begg, '1–2 Kings' in Brown, Fitzmyer and Murphy (eds), *New Jerome*, pp. 160–185; Art. 'Elijah' in Scott B. Noegel and Brannon M. Wheeler, *Historical Dictionary of Prophets in Islam and Judaism*, Historical Dictionaries of Religions, Philosophies and Movements, n. 43 (London/Lanham, Maryland: The Scarecrow Press, 2002), pp. 99–101. See also Jane Ackerman, *Elijah: Prophet of Carmel* (Washington, DC: ICS Publications, 2003), passim.
340. See Wiener, *Prophet Elijah*, p. 7.
341. See Gregory, 'Irony', p. 102; see also Bronner, *Stories*, pp. 20–1.
342. See *The Holy Bible: Old Testament*, trans. Knox, pp. 302–12.
343. See A. J. Wensinck and G. Vajda, 'Ilyās', *EI*[2], vol. 3, p. 1,156; Q.6:85, Q.37:123. Yusuf Ali (trans. *Qur'ān*, pp. 312 n. 905, 1,208 n. 4,112) also identifies Elias with the Old Testament Elijah; see also Roberto Tottoli, 'Elijah' in *EQ*, *vol. Two E–I*, pp. 12–13.
344. Wiener, *Prophet Elijah*, p. 1.
345. Satterthwaite and McConville, *Exploring the Old Testament*, p. 161; Porter, *Illustrated Guide*, p. 95 gives slightly different regnal dates: Ahab (869–850 BC) and Ahaziah (850–849 BC).
346. Satterthwaite and McConville, *Exploring the Old Testament*, p. 159; see Hauser, 'Yahweh Versus Death – The Real Struggle in 1 Kings 17–19' in Hauser and Gregory, *From Carmel to Horeb*, p. 12; Wiener, *Prophet Elijah*, p. 5.
347. Wiener, *Prophet Elijah*, pp. 15–16, 18.
348. Bronner, *Stories*, pp. 7, 8–9, 14–15.
349. Wiener, *Prophet Elijah*, p. 5.
350. Wansbrough (ed.), *The New Jerusalem Bible*, p. 458: 1 Kings 17:1.
351. See Wiener, *Prophet Elijah*, pp. 174ff.; Leithart, *1 and 2 Kings*, pp. 128ff.; Hauser, 'Yahweh Versus Death', pp. 13ff.
352. 1 Kings 17:6, trans. Wansborough (ed.), *The New Jerusalem Bible*, p. 458.
353. 1 Kings 17:7.
354. 1 Kings 17:17–24.
355. 1 Kings 18:20–40; see Wiener, *Prophet Elijah*, pp. 10–12; Hauser, 'Yahweh Versus Death', pp. 11, 48–54, 56–7.
356. 1 Kings 19:1–4. See Wiener, *Prophet Elijah*, p. 13.
357. See Anderson, *Green Man*, pp. 10–11.
358. 1 Kings 19:4–5.
359. 1 Kings 19:6–8.
360. 1 Kings 19:6–18.
361. 1 Kings 21:18–29.
362. 2 Kings 2:1–18. For Elijah's ascent into Heaven, see Wiener, *Prophet Elijah*, pp. 16–17, Leithart, *1 and 2 Kings*, pp. 175–7. For the cloak, see Wiener, *Prophet Elijah*, p. 17; Leithart, *1 and 2 Kings*, pp. 169, 174–5, 191.
363. Porter, *Illustrated Guide*, p. 96.

364. See, for example, Ackerman, *Elijah*, pp. 60, 87, 89, 93, 97–8. However, Ackerman does point out that the Arab historian al-Ṭabarī (c. AD 839–923) does regard Elijah and al-Khaḍir/al-Khiḍr as separate figures (see ibid., p. 88).
365. See MacDermott, *Explore Green Men*, p. 9.
366. Wiener, *Prophet Elijah*, p. 6 (my emphases).
367. Q.18:65; trans. Yusuf Ali, *Qur'ān*, pp. 748–9.
368. See Yusuf Ali (trans.), *Qur'ān*, p. 748 n. 2,411.
369. Ibn 'Arabī, *The Wisdom of the Prophets (Fusus al-Hikam)*, trans. Titus Burckhardt and Angela Culme-Seymour (Aldsworth: Beshara Publications, 1975), p. 103 n. 28.
370. Tottoli, 'Elijah', p. 13; see also Wensinck and Vajda, 'Ilyās', p. 1,156.
371. W. Montgomery Watt, *Companion to the Qur'ān* (London: Allen & Unwin, 1967), p. 141.
372. J. Spencer Trimingham, *The Sufi Orders in Islam* (Oxford: Clarendon Press, 1971), p. 158; '[The Qur'ānic Ilyās] Elias is the same as Elijah': Yusuf Ali (trans.), *Qur'an*, p. 312 n. 905, p. 1,208 n. 4,112.
373. Wiener, *Prophet Elijah*, p. 152. See also pp. 153, 157, 179. Wiener (ibid., p. 153) cites a number of medieval Arabic authors who identified al-Khaḍir and Elijah as the same person.
374. Wiener, *Prophet Elijah*, p. 157.
375. '[The *Alexander Romance* was] a fantastic historical novel, probably dating from a generation or two after Alexander's death. It is of no use as history, though it does occasionally support conclusions drawn from the other historians' (Richard Stoneman, *Alexander the Great*, 2nd edn (London and New York: Routledge, 2004), p. 4; see also passim). See also idem, *The Greek Alexander Romance* (London: Penguin Books, 1991), esp. pp. 2, 7, 29.
376. See Wiener, *Prophet Elijah*, pp. 157, 55.
377. Wensinck, 'Al-Khaḍir (al-Khiḍr)', pp. 903, 902.
378. Wiener, *Prophet Elijah*, p. 55.
379. Ibid.
380. Ibid. Cf. Isaiah 55:8–9.
381. Brannon M. Wheeler, *Moses in the Quran and Islamic Exegesis*, RoutledgeCurzon Studies in the Quran (London: RoutledgeCurzon, 2002), pp. 10, 19–26.
382. Ibid., p. 24.
383. Wiener, *Prophet Elijah*, p. 157.
384. Schimmel, *Mystical Dimensions*, p. 202; see also Noegel and Wheeler, 'Khidr' in idem, *Historical Dictionary*, p. 185.
385. Eszter Spät, *The Yezidis* (London: Saqi Books, 2005, first published in 1985), p. 63.
386. See Ibn Kathīr, *Qiṣaṣ al-Anbiyā'*, ed. Muṣṭafā 'Abd al-Wāḥid, 2 pts (Cairo: Dār al-Kutub al-Ḥadītha, 1968), pt 2, pp. 214ff.; idem, *Stories of the Prophets*, trans. Rashad Ahmed Azami, 2nd rev. edn (Riyadh and Jeddah: Maktaba Dar-us-Salam, 2003), pp. 464–70, 474–6; al-Kisā'ī, *Qiṣaṣ al-Anbiyā'/Vita Prophetarum*, ed. Isaac Eisenberg (Leiden: E. J. Brill, 1922), pp. 230–3, 243–50; W. M. Thackston (trans.), *The Tales of the Prophets of al-Kisā'ī*, Library of Classical Arabic Literature, vol. 2 (Boston: Twayne Publishers, G. K. Hall & Co., 1978), pp. 247–50, 262–9; see also Storm, *Myths and Legends*, p. 405.
387. Wheeler, Brannon M. (trans.), *Prophets in the Qur'an* (London and New York: Continuum, 2002), p. 46 (citing al-Bukhārī). See Wiener, *Prophet Elijah*, p. 152 and also G. Vajda, 'Idrīs', EI^2, vol. 3, pp. 1,030–1.
388. See Noegel and Wheeler, *Historical Dictionary*, p. 84; G. Vajda, 'Dhū 'l-Kifl', EI^2, vol. 2, p. 242.

389. See Wensinck, 'Al-Khaḍir (al-Khiḍr)', p. 904; Anderson, *Green Man*, pp. 29, 75; Doel and Doel, *Green Man in Britain*, pp. 53–6 ('Green George' customs); Storm, *Myths and Legends*, p. 405; see also Kanaan, 'Legends, Places and Traditions', pp. 204–12; Zvi Uri Ma'oz, 'En-Nebī Khader (Khouder) at Bāniyās (Dan-Caesarea-Philippi-Paneas) in *ARAM*, 20 (2008), p. 95; Osman Eravşar, 'Miniature Paintings of Prophet Elijah (Ilyas) and Al Khodor (Hidir) in the Ottoman Period' in ibid., p. 146; Hasmik Tovmayan, 'St Sargis and Al-Khiḍr: A Common Saint for Christians and Muslims' in ibid., p. 199.
390. H. A. R. Gibb (trans.), *The Travels of Ibn Baṭṭūṭa AD 1325–1354* (Cambridge: Cambridge University Press for the Hakluyt Society, 1958), vol. 1, p. 123.
391. See ibid.; Ibn Baṭṭūṭa, *Riḥlat Ibn Baṭṭūṭa* (Beirut: Dār Ṣādir/Dār Bayrūt, 1964), p. 87.
392. Gibb (trans.), *Travels*, vol. 1, p. 123 n. 203.
393. Ibn Baṭṭūṭa, *Riḥlat Ibn Baṭṭūṭa*, pp. 599–600; H. A. R. Gibb and C. F. Beckingham (trans.), *The Travels of Ibn Baṭṭūṭa AD 1325–1354* (London: The Hakluyt Society, 1994), vol. 4, pp. 854–5.
394. E.g. Ibn Baṭṭūṭa, *Riḥlat Ibn Baṭṭūṭa*, pp. 319, 326, 553.
395. H. A. R. Gibb (trans.), *The Travels of Ibn Baṭṭūṭa AD 1325–1354* (Cambridge: Cambridge University Press for the Hakluyt Society, 1962), vol. 2, p. 466 n. 193.
396. Tim Mackintosh-Smith, *Travels with a Tangerine: A Journey in the Footnotes of Ibn Battutah* (London: Pan Macmillan, Picador, 2002), p. 321.
397. Harry Schnitker, 'England's Patron Saint and the Crusaders: St George', *Catholic Life* (April 2009), p. 8.
398. Wheeler, *Moses in the Qur'an*, pp. 24, 33.
399. Ibid.
400. Spät, *Yezidis*, p. 63.
401. See Richard Stoneman, *Alexander the Great: A Life in Legend* (New Haven and London: Yale University Press, 2008), p. 32, see also p. 147. See Eravşar, 'Miniature Paintings', pp. 143–4
402. Stoneman, *Alexander the Great: A Life in Legend*, p. 159; see also pp. 146, 161–2.
403. Ibid., p. 155 Plate 29.
404. Ibid., p. 30; see also pp. 142–3. For a general overview of the Greek, Syriac, Arabic, Persian and other Alexander traditions, with source references, see pp. 230–45.
405. See Andrew Jotischky, *The Carmelites and Antiquity: Mendicants and Their Pasts in the Middle Ages* (Oxford: Oxford University Press, 2002), pp. 1, 8 and passim.
406. Ibid., pp. 1, 56, 191; John Welch, *The Carmelite Way: An Ancient Path for Today's Pilgrim* (Leominster: Gracewing, 1996), pp. 7, 37, 52–5, 154, 172.
407. See *Sūrat Maryam* in the *Qur'ān*; see Welch, *Carmelite Way*, pp. 55–8, 172.
408. The reference is to Philip Ribot's (died AD 1391) *Liber de Institutione Primorum Monachorum*, considered today to be 'the second most important document in the [Carmelite] order, after the Rule …' (Welch, *Carmelite Way*, p. 52).
409. Welch, *Carmelite Way*, p. 56.
410. See Simon Schama, *A History of Britain: At the Edge of the World? 3000 BC–AD 1603* (London: BBC, 2000, 2002), pp. 220–1; M. H. Keen, *England in the Later Middle Ages: A Political History* (London: The Folio Society, 1997), p. 95. For a general orientation regarding the reign of King Edward III, see W. M. Ormrod, *The Reign of Edward III: Crown and Political Society in England 1327–1377* (New Haven and London: Yale University Press, 1990); Scott L. Waugh, *England in the Reign of Edward III* (Cambridge: Cambridge University Press, 1991); J. S. Bothwell (ed.), *The Age of Edward III* (York: York Medieval Press/Woodbridge, Suffolk: Boydell Press, 2001).
411. Christopher Lee, *This Sceptred Isle* (London: Penguin Books, 1998; first published by

London: BBC Books, 1997), p. 117.

412. Ibid. See Ormrod, *Reign of Edward III*, pp. 7, 10.
413. Schama, *History of Britain*, pp. 222–73; Lee, *This Sceptred Isle*, pp. 123–6; Philip Ziegler, *The Black Death* (London: The Folio Society, 1997).
414. Schama, *History of Britain*, p. 222; see also Michael Bennett, 'Isabelle of France, Anglo–French Diplomacy and Cultural Exchange in the Late 1350s' in Bothwell (ed.), *Age of Edward III*, p. 215.
415. Bennett, 'Isabelle of France', p. 215.
416. Lee, *This Sceptred Isle*, p. 123. See also Waugh, *England in the Reign of Edward III*, pp. 85–93; Ormrod, *Reign of Edward III*, pp. 21–2.
417. Bennett, 'Isabelle of France', p. 221.
418. Schama, *History of Britain*, pp. 224–5.
419. See Keen, *England in the Later Middle Ages*, p. 124; see Waugh, *England in the Reign of Edward III*, p. 17.
420. See Keen, *England in the Later Middle Ages*, p. 100; see also Waugh, *England in the Reign of Edward III*, pp. 130, 191, 231; Ormrod, *Reign of Edward III*, p. 19.
421. Hugh E. L. Collins, *The Order of the Garter 1348–1461: Chivalry and Politics in Late Medieval England*, Oxford Historical Monographs (Oxford: Clarendon Press, 2000), p. 1.
422. Collins, *Order of the Garter*, p. 39.
423. Peter J. Begent and Hubert Chesshyre, *The Most Noble Order of the Garter: 650 Years* (London: Spink, 1999), p. 13.
424. Ibid., pp. 10, 8–9.
425. See ibid., p. 15.
426. Ibid.; see Collins, *Order of the Garter*, p. 12. Lee (*This Sceptred Isle*, p. 123) seems to adhere to the traditional account, as does Keen (*England in the Later Middle Ages*, p. 133).
427. Keen, *England in the Later Middle Ages*, p. 133; see also Waugh, *England in the Reign of Edward III*, pp. 18, 130.
428. Begent and Chesshyre, *Most Noble Order*, p. 17.
429. See ibid., p. 8; see Collins, *Order of the Garter*, pp. 39–44.
430. Collins, *Order of the Garter*, p. 39.
431. Waugh, *England in the Reign of Edward III*, p. 129.
432. Collins, *Order of the Garter*, pp. 20–1. For St George, see Jonathan Good, *The Cult of St George in Medieval England* (Woodbridge: Boydell Press, 2009), esp. with reference to the Garter: pp. 19, 63–73, 94. For George as 'a patron of agriculture', see pp. 32, 140.
433. We note the symbolism of 'three', perhaps mirroring, in a hagiographical fashion, the Trinity itself.
434. Collins, *Order of the Garter*, p. 20; Begent and Chesshyre, *Most Noble Order*, p. 17.
435. Act IV, Scene IV: see Anthony Hammond (ed.), *King Richard III*, The Arden Shakespeare (London: Thomson Learning, 2006), p. 291.
436. See ibid., p. 291 n. 366.
437. Schama, *History of Britain*, pp. 244–5 (my emphases). Waugh (*England in the Reign of Edward III*, p. 130) agrees: 'He inspired comparisons with Arthurian legend'.
438. Hicks, *Green Man*, p. 17.
439. Begent and Chesshyre, *Most Noble Order*, p. 17.
440. Ibid.
441. Henry Sebastian Bowden and Donald Attwater, *Miniature Lives of the Saints* (London: Burns & Oates, 1959), pp. 179–80.

442. Ibid., p. 180.
443. Ibid.
444. Begent and Chesshyre, *Most Noble Order*, p. 17.
445. See above n. 415.
446. See Begent and Chesshyre, *Most Noble Order*, p. 17; see also Wensinck, 'Al-Khadir (al-Khidr)', p. 904; Doel and Doel, *Green Man in Britain*, pp. 53–6.
447. See *Sir Gawain*, trans. Stone, p. 115.
448. Ibid., p. 185. See also Carolyne Larrington, 'Knight Wear': Review of Francis Ingledew, *Sir Gawain and the Green Knight and the Order of the Garter*, in *Times Literary Supplement*, 21 July 2006, p. 9.
449. See *Sir Gawain*, trans. Stone, p. 115.
450. Ibid., pp. 184–5.
451. Begent and Chesshyre, *Most Noble Order*, p. 149.
452. Ibid., p. 157.
453. Francis Ingledew, *Sir Gawain and the Green Knight and the Order of the Garter* (Notre Dame, IN: University of Notre Dame Press, 2006).
454. Ibid. Back cover of paperback edn, quotation by Christopher Baswell, UCLA.
455. Ibid., p. 3, see pp. 6, 22.
456. Ibid., pp. 66, 123–4, 143–5.
457. Ibid., p. 152.
458. Ibid., p. 153.
459. Ibid.
460. Ibid., p. 66. See Larrington, 'Knight Wear', p. 9.
461. Ingledew, *Sir Gawain*, p. 154; see Larrington, 'Knight Wear', p. 9.
462. *Sir Gawain*, trans. Stone, p. 93 # 77. Simon Armitage translates: 'His blue robe flowed as far as the floor' (*Sir Gawain and the Green Knight*, trans. Armitage, p. 88).
463. *Sir Gawain*, trans. Stone, p. 181 n. on line 1,928.
464. Ingledew, *Sir Gawain*, p. 155.
465. Larrington, 'Knight Wear', p. 9.
466. Ibid.
467. Ingeldew, *Sir Gawain*, p. 12.
468. Giorgio Melchiori, *Shakespeare's Garter Plays: Edward III to Merry Wives of Windsor* (Newark: University of Delaware Press/London and Toronto: Associated University Presses, 1994), p. 77.
469. Ibid., p. 78.
470. Ibid., p. 92; see also Melchiori (ed.), *The Merry Wives of Windsor*, pp. 18–30.
471. Melchiori, *Shakespeare's Garter Plays*, p. 93.
472. Ibid.
473. Melchiori (ed.), *The Merry Wives of Windsor*, pp. 19, 22; see Melchiori, *Shakespeare's Garter Plays*, pp. 95, 103–6.
474. See *Merry Wives*, Act V, Scene V, lines 55–76.
475. Melchiori (ed.), *The Merry Wives of Windsor*, p. 65: Act V, Scene V, lines 65–76.
476. Ainsworth, *Windsor Castle*, pp. 5–6.
477. Ibid., p. 7.
478. bid., p. 10.
479. Ibid., p. 17; see also pp. 16ff.
480. Ibid., p. 27.
481. R. H. Horne, A *New Spirit of the Age* (London: Smith, Elder & Co., 1944), vol. 2 pp. 219–20, cited in Carver, *Life and Works*, p. 29 n. 65.

482. Ainsworth, *Windsor Castle*, p. 31.
483. Ibid.
484. Ibid., pp. 32–3; see Begent and Chesshyre, *Most Noble Order*, p. 187.
485. See *Windsor Castle*, p. 30.
486. See ibid., p. 34.
487. Ibid., p. 35.
488. Ibid., pp. 121–4.
489. Ibid., p. 121.
490. Ibid.
491. Ibid., p. 123.
492. Ibid., p. 236.
493. Ibid., p. 240.
494. Ibid., p. 256.
495. See Matthew 23:27.
496. Hans Wehr, A *Dictionary of Modern Written Arabic*, 2nd printing (Wiesbaden: Otto Harrassowitz/London: George Allen & Unwin, 1966), p. 696 s.v. *futuwwa*.
497. Ibid. For a magisterial survey of *futuwwa* (Persian: *jawanmardi*), with particular reference to Iran, see Lloyd Ridgeon, *Morals and Mysticism in Persian Sufism*, Routledge Sufi Series (London and New York: Routledge, forthcoming 2011).
498. Cl. Cahen and Fr. Taeschner, 'Futuwwa', *EI*[2], vol. 2, p. 961.
499. Ibid.
500. Ibid.
501. Ibid. (my emphases).
502. Ibid., pp. 961–2.
503. Ibid., p. 962.
504. Ibid.
505. Ibid., p. 963.
506. Schimmel, *Mystical Dimensions*, p. 246.
507. Julian Baldick, *Mystical Islam: An Introduction to Sufism* (London: I. B. Tauris, 1989), pp. 23, 91–2.
508. Ibid., p. 92.
509. Alexander Knysh, *Islamic Mysticism: A Short History*, Themes in Islamic Studies, vol. 1 (Leiden: E. J. Brill, 2000), p. 12.
510. Ibid., p. 97.
511. Ibid., p. 198.
512. See Cahen and Taeschner, 'Futuwwa', p. 965; G. Böwering, 'al-Sulamī [Muḥammad b. al-Ḥusayn]', *EI*[2], vol. 9, pp. 811–12.
513. Al-Sulamī, *The Book of Sufi Chivalry: Lessons to a Son of the Moment*, trans. Tosun Bayrak al-Jerrahi al-Halveti (New York: Inner Traditions International, 1983) [hereafter referred to as Sulamī, trans. Halveti]. A brief extract from the Arabic appears in Franz Taeschner, 'As-Sulami's Kitāb al-Futuwwa' in *Studia Orientalia Ioanni Pedersen* (Hauniae: Einar Munksgaard, 1953), pp. 348–51. The entire Arabic text of *Kitāb al-Futuwwa* is printed in Naṣr Allāh Pūrjawādī (ed.), *Majmū'-yi āšār-i Abū 'Abd al-Raḥmān Sulamī* (2 vols, Tehran: Markaz-i Nashr-i Dānishgāhī, 1980–3), vol. 2. (This Arabic text is edited by Sulaymān Ateş.) However, *the Arabic references in this volume of mine will be to*: al-Sulamī, *Kitāb al-Futuwwa*, ed. Aḥmad Farīd al-Mizyadī (Beirut: Dār al-Kutub al-'Ilmiyya, 2009) [hereafter referred to as Sulamī, *Futuwwa*].
514. Knysh, *Islamic Mysticism*, pp. 125, 127.
515. Ibid., p. 125.

516. Ibid.
517. Ibid., pp. 125–6.
518. Ibid., p. 126.
519. Baldick, *Mystical Islam*, p. 57.
520. Ibid., p. 62.
521. Ibid., p. 57.
522. Sulamī, trans. Halveti, p. 16 ('Introduction').
523. Ibid., p. 15 ('Foreword').
524. Ibid., pp. 33–4; Sulamī, *Futuwwa*, p. 13.
525. Sulamī, trans. Halveti, p. 34; idem, *Futuwwa*, p. 13.
526. Sulamī, trans. Halveti, p. 36; idem, *Futuwwa*, p. 14.
527. Al-Nawawī, *Matn al-Arba'īn al-Nawawiyya/An-Nawawi's Forty Hadith*, trans. Ezzedin Ibrahim and Denys Johnson-Davies, 3rd edn (Damascus: Holy Koran Publishing House, 1977), p. 60 (English trans.), p. 61 (Arabic text): [Ḥadīth no. 15].
528. Sulamī, trans. Halveti, p. 80; idem, *Futuwwa*, p. 62.
529. Sulamī, trans. Halveti, p. 90; idem, *Futuwwa*, p. 68.
530. Sulamī, trans. Halveti, p. 99; idem, *Futuwwa*, p. 84.
531. Reynold A. Nicholson, *The Mystics of Islam* (London and Boston: Routledge & Kegan Paul, 1975; repr. of London: George Bell & Sons, 1914 edn), p. 46; see also, for the same story, Schimmel, *Mystical Dimensions*, p. 169.
532. Schimmel, *Mystical Dimensions*, p. 56.
533. Sulamī, trans. Halveti, p. 49; idem, *Futuwwa*, p. 31.
534. See John Main, *The Way of Unknowing* (London: Darton, Longman & Todd, 1989).
535. Sulamī, trans. Halveti, p. 36; idem, *Futuwwa*, p. 14.
536. Sulamī, trans. Halveti, p. 75; idem, *Futuwwa*, p. 58.
537. Sulamī, trans. Halveti, pp. 41, 55, 56, 59; idem, *Futuwwa*, pp. 20, 35–40, 41, 43.
538. Sulamī, trans. Halveti, p. 43; idem, *Futuwwa*, p. 23.
539. Sulamī, trans. Halveti, p. 42; idem. *Futuwwa*, p. 21.
540. Sulamī, trans. Halveti, p. 58; idem, *Futuwwa*, p. 43.
541. Sulamī, trans. Halveti, pp. 55, 70; idem, *Futuwwa*, pp. 35–40, 53.
542. Sulamī, trans. Halveti, pp. 66, 105; idem, *Futuwwa*, pp. 49, 78.
543. Sulamī, trans. Halveti, p. 78; idem, *Futuwwa*, p. 60.
544. Sulamī, trans. Halveti, p. 37; idem, *Futuwwa*, p. 15.
545. Sulamī, trans. Halveti, p. 41; idem, *Futuwwa*, pp. 20–1.
546. Sulamī, trans. Halveti, p. 107; idem. *Futuwwa*, p. 78.
547. Sulamī, trans. Halveti, pp. 40, 91; idem, *Futuwwa*, pp. 19–20, 68–9.
548. Sulamī, trans. Halveti, p. 77; idem, *Futuwwa*, p. 53.
549. Sulamī, trans. Halveti, pp. 85–7; idem, *Futuwwa*, pp. 65–6.
550. Sulamī, trans. Halveti, p. 86n.
551. Ibid., pp. 86–7; Sulami, *Futuwwa*, pp. 65–6.
552. Sulamī, trans. Halveti, p. 45; idem, *Futuwwa*, p. 25.
553. Sulamī, trans. Halveti, p. 47; idem, *Futuwwa*, p. 30.
554. Sulamī, trans. Halveti, pp. 96, 110; idem, *Futuwwa*, pp. 72, 80.
555. Sulamī, trans. Halveti, pp. 52, 78–9 (my emphases); idem, *Futuwwa*, pp. 33–4, 61.
556. Sulamī, trans. Halveti, p. 54; idem, *Futuwwa*, p. 35.
557. For Ibn Baṭṭūṭa, see, *inter alia* Ian Richard Netton, 'Ibn Baṭṭūṭa' in idem, *A Popular Dictionary of Islam* (Richmond: Curzon, 1992, 1997), p. 111; A. Miquel, 'Ibn Baṭṭūṭa', *EI²*, vol. 3, pp. 735–6; Ian Richard Netton, *Seek Knowledge: Thought and Travel in the House of Islam* (Richmond: Curzon Press, 1996), pp. 103–53.

558. Cahen and Taeschner, 'Futuwwa', p. 961.
559. Ibid.
560. See Ibn Baṭṭūṭa, *Riḥlat Ibn Baṭṭūṭa*, pp. 284–5; Gibb (trans.), *Travels of Ibn Baṭṭūṭa*, vol. 2, pp. 417–19.
561. Gibb (trans.), *Travels of Ibn Baṭṭūṭa*, vol. 2, p. 418.
562. Ibid., p. 417 n. 23.
563. Ibid., pp. 417–18 n. 23.
564. Ibid., p. 419 n. 29.
565. Ibid., p. 419; Ibn Baṭṭūṭa, *Riḥlat Ibn Baṭṭūṭa*, p. 285.
566. Gibb (trans.), *Travels of Ibn Baṭṭūṭa*, vol. 2, p. 419; Ibn Baṭṭūṭa, *Riḥlat Ibn Baṭṭūṭa*, p. 285.
567. Gibb (trans.), *Travels of Ibn Baṭṭūṭa*, vol. 2, p. 420; Ibn Baṭṭūṭa, *Riḥlat Ibn Baṭṭūṭa*, p. 286.
568. Ibn Baṭṭūṭa, *Riḥlat Ibn Baṭṭūṭa*, p. 285; Gibb (trans.), *Travels of Ibn Baṭṭūṭa*, vol. 2, p. 419.
569. Ibn Baṭṭūṭa, *Riḥlat Ibn Baṭṭūṭa*, p. 285.
570. Ibid., p. 286.
571. Gibb (trans.), *Travels of Ibn Baṭṭūṭa*, vol. 2, p. 421; Ibn *Baṭṭūṭa*, *Riḥlat Ibn Baṭṭūṭa*, pp. 286–7.
572. Ibn Baṭṭūṭa, *Riḥlat Ibn Baṭṭūṭa*, p. 285; Gibb (trans.), *Travels of Ibn Baṭṭūṭa*, vol. 2, p. 419 n. 28.
573. Ines Aščeric-Todd, 'The Noble Traders: The Islamic Tradition of "Spiritual Chivalry" (*futuwwa*) in Bosnian Trade-guilds (16th–19th centuries)', *The Muslim World*, 97:2 (April 2007), pp. 159–73.
574. Cahen and Taeschner, 'Futuwwa', pp. 967ff.; see also Sulamī, trans. Halveti, p. 20 ('Introduction'), also pp. 25–6 n. 5.
575. Ibid.
576. See Ronald Paul Buckley, 'Al-Nasir, Ahmad B. al-Mustadi, Abu'l-ʿAbbas (AD 1180–1225)' in Ian Richard Netton (ed.), *Encyclopedia of Islamic Civilisation and Religion* (London and New York: Routledge, 2008), pp. 482–3.
570. Aščeric-Todd, 'Noble Traders', pp. 160–1.
578. My emphases.
579. Q.5:4; trans. Yusuf Ali, *Qur'ān*, p. 240.
580. Yusuf Ali (trans.), *Qur'ān*, p. 240 n. 696; see Watt, *Companion*, p. 73; see also Ikhwān al-Ṣafā', *Rasā'il Ikhwān al-Ṣafā'* (Beirut: Dār Ṣādir/Dār Bayrūt, 1957), vol. 4, p. 25.
581. Matthew 5:17, trans. Knox, *Holy Bible: New Testament*, p. 4.
582. Matthew 5:48, trans. Knox, *Holy Bible: New Testament*, p. 5.
583. Benedict T. Viviano, 'The Gospel According to Matthew' in Brown et al. (eds), *New Jerome*, p. 641.
584. Ibid., p. 644.
585. See, for example, Knut Tranøy, 'Thomas Aquinas' in D. J. O'Connor (ed.), *A Critical History of Western Philosophy* (New York: The Free Press/London: Collier Macmillan, 1964), p. 109.
586. Q.2:30, trans. Yusuf Ali, *Qur'ān*, p. 24.
587. Q.2:32, trans. Yusuf Ali, *Qur'ān*, pp. 24–5.

Chapter 2: Caves, Clouds and Mountains

1. See Ian Richard Netton, 'Towards a Modern *Tafsīr* of *Sūrat al-Kahf*: Structure and Semiotics', *Journal of Qur'anic Studies*, 2: 1 (2000), pp. 67–87.
2. See ibid.
3. Ibid., pp. 72ff.

4. Ibid.
5. Ibid., p. 83 n. 54.
6. Ibid., n. 55.
7. Ibid., n. 56.
8. Ibid., n. 57.
9. Ibid., n. 58.
10. Ibid., n. 59.
11. Ibid., n. 60. For a definition of a *theologeme*, see Ian Richard Netton, *Allāh Transcendent: Studies in the Structure and Semiotics of Islamic Philosophy, Theology and Cosmology* (London and New York: Routledge, 1989; repr. Richmond: Curzon Press, 1994), pp. 79–80.
12. Netton, 'Towards a Modern *Tafsīr*', p. 84 n. 61.
13. Ibid., n. 62.
14. Ibid., n. 63.
15. Ibid., n. 64.
16. Ibid., n. 65.
17. Ibid., n. 66.
18. Ibid., n. 67.
19. Ibid., n. 68.
20. Ibid., pp. 72–3.
21. Ibid., p. 79.
22. A. Guillaume (trans.), *The Life of Muhammad: A Translation of Isḥāq's Sīrat Rasūl Allāh*, 20th imp. (Karachi: Oxford University Press, 2006), p. 130 [hereafter referred to as Guillaume, *Life*]; Ibn Isḥāq/Ibn Hishām, *al-Sīra al-Nabawiyya*, 2nd edn (Cairo: al-Halabi, 1955) [hereafter referred to as Ibn Isḥāq, *Sīra*], vol. 1, p. 289.
23. Ibn Isḥāq, *Sīra*, p. 317; Guillaume, *Life*, p. 143.
24. Ibn Isḥāq, *Sīra*, pp. 321ff.; Guillaume, *Life*, pp. 146ff.
25. Guillaume, *Life*, p. 146; Ibn Isḥāq, *Sīra*, p. 322.
26. Ibn Isḥāq, *Sīra*, p. 335; Guillaume, *Life*, p. 151.
27. Ibn Isḥāq, *Sīra*, p. 338; Guillaume, *Life*, p. 153.
28. Ibn Isḥāq, *Sīra*, p. 336; Guillaume, *Life*, p. 151.
29. Guillaume, *Life*, p. 222; Ibn Isḥāq, *Sīra*, p. 482; see also al-Ṭabarī, *Ta'rīkh al-Rusul wa 'l-Mulūk/Annales* ed. M. J. de Goeje (Leiden: E. J. Brill, 1882–5), Prima Series, vol. 3, p. 1,231 [hereafter referred to as Ṭabarī, *Ta'rīkh*, vol. 3]; trans. W. Montgomery Watt and M. V. McDonald, *The History of al-Ṭabarī (Ta'rīkh al-rusul wa'l-mulūk): Volume VI: Muhammad at Mecca*, Bibliotheca Persica, SUNY Series in Near Eastern Studies (Albany, NY: State University of New York Press, 1988) [hereafter referred to as Watt and McDonald, *History of al-Ṭabarī, vol. VI*]; Ibn Kathīr, *al-Sīra al-Nabawiyya*, ed. Muṣṭafā 'Abd al-Wāḥid (Beirut: Dār al-Ma'rifa, 1976) [hereafter referred to as Ibn Kathīr, *Sīra*], vol. 2, p. 229; Trevor Le Gassick (trans.), *[Ibn Kathir's] The Life of the Prophet Muhammad, Volume 2: Al-Sīra al-Nabawiyya*, Great Books of Islamic Civilization (Reading: Garnet, 1998, 2000) [hereafter referred to as Le Gassick, *Life*], pp. 152–3. This plot to kill Muḥammad is covered in the secondary literature, *inter alia*, in: Martin Lings, *Muhammad: His Life Based on the Earliest Sources* (London: George Allen & Unwin/The Islamic Texts Society, 1983), pp. 116–17; W. Montgomery Watt, 'Hidjra', *EI*², vol. 3, p. 366; idem, *Muhammad at Mecca* (Oxford: Clarendon Press, 1953, 1972), p. 150; idem, *Muhammad Prophet and Statesman* (London: Oxford University Press, 1967), p. 90.
30. Ibn Isḥāq, *Sīra*, p. 482; Guillaume, *Life*, p. 222.
31. Ibn Isḥāq, *Sīra*, pp. 482–3; Guillaume, *Life*, pp. 222–3; see also al-Mas'ūdī, *Murūj al-Dhahab*: C. Barbier de Meynard (ed.), *Macoudi: Les Prairies d'Or*, Texte et Traduction (Paris:

L'Imprimerie Nationale, 1914), vol. 4, p. 138 [Arabic with French trans.]; al-Ṭabarī, *Ta'rīkh*, vol. 3, p. 1,232; Watt and McDonald, *History of al-Ṭabarī, vol. VI*, pp. 142–3; Ibn Kathīr, *Sīra*, vol. 2, p. 229; Le Gassick, *Life*, p. 153; Watt, *Muhammad Prophet and Statesman*, p. 90; Lings, *Muhammad*, p. 117.

32. Q.12:93–6.
33. Yusuf Ali (trans.), *Qur'ān*, p. 584 n. 1,769; see also Muhammad Abdel Haleem, *Understanding the Qur'an: Themes and Style* (London and New York: I. B. Tauris, 1999), p. 150.
34. G. S. Colin, 'Burda', *EI*², vol. 1, pp. 1,314–15.
35. Ibid., p. 1,314; see C. E. Bosworth, 'al-Būṣīrī' in Julie Scott Meisami and Paul Starkey (eds), *Encyclopedia of Arabic Literature* (London and New York: Routledge, 1998), vol. 1, p. 163; Ed. [= C. E. Bosworth et al.], 'al-Busiri', *EI*² Supp. Fascs. 3–4 (Leiden: E. J. Brill, 1981), pp. 158–9.
36. Watt, 'Hidjra', p. 367.
37. Ibid., p. 366; see also Watt, *Muhammad Prophet and Statesman*, p. 91; J. G. Hava, *Al-Farā'id Arabic-English Dictionary* (Beirut: Dār al-Mashriq, 1970), p. 816 s.v. *hijra* (= 'estrangement ...').
38. Watt, 'Hidjra', p. 366.
39. Ian Richard Netton, *A Popular Dictionary of Islam* (Richmond: Curzon Press/Atlantic Highlands, NJ: Humanities Press, 1992, 1997), pp. 14–15 s.v. *'Abd al-'Uzza b. 'Abd al-Muṭṭalib*; see also s.v. *Badr, Battle of* (p. 49) and *al-Masad* (p. 164).
40. Ibid., p. 164 s.v. *al-Masad*.
41. Q.9:40, trans. Yusuf Ali, *Qur'ān*, p. 452; see, for example, ibid., p. 452 n. 1,302.
42. Al-Ṭabarī, *Ta'rīkh*, vol. 3 p. 1,236; see Watt and McDonald, *History of al-Ṭabarī, vol. VI*, p. 146, which gives the Q. reference of Q.9:40 in n. 231.
43. See Yusuf Ali (trans.), *Qur'ān*, p. 452 n. 1,302; Watt, 'Hidjra', p. 366; idem, *Muhammad at Mecca*, p. 151; idem, *Muhammad Prophet and Statesman*, p. 91; Lings, *Muhammad*, pp. 118–19. For the cave in the Arabic sources, see, *inter alia*, Ibn Isḥāq, *Sīra*, p. 486; Guillaume, *Life*, p. 224; al-Ṭabarī, *Ta'rīkh*, vol. 3, pp. 1,234–7; Watt and McDonald, *History of al-Ṭabarī, vol. VI*, pp. 144–6; Ibn Kathīr, *Sīra*, vol. 2, pp. 235–47; Le Gassick, *Life*, pp. 155–63; al-Bukhārī, *Mukhtaṣar Ṣaḥīḥ al-Bukhārī* [dual Arabic–English], Islamic Library Project (English) edn, trans. Muhammad Muhsin, comp. Zayn al-Dīn al-Zubaydī (Riyadh: Maktaba Dār al-Salām [1994]), *Kitāb Faḍā'il Aṣḥāb al-Nabī*, p. 748.
44. See Ibn Kathīr, *Sīra*, p. 238; Le Gassick, *Life*, p. 158.
45. See ibid. and Q.9:40.
46. See R. Irwin, 'Ibn Kathīr (c. 700–74/c. 1300–73)' in Julie Scott Meisami and Paul Starkey (eds), *Encyclopedia of Arabic Literature* (London and New York: Routledge, 1998), vol. 1, p. 341.
47. Ibn Kathīr, *Sīra*, pp. 239–41; Le Gassick, *Life*, pp. 158–60; see also Lings, *Muhammad*, pp. 118–19.
48. Ibn Kathīr, *Sīra*, p. 241; Le Gassick, *Life*, p. 160.
49. Q.42:11.
50. Q.50:16.
51. Clifton Wolters (trans.), *The Cloud of Unknowing and Other Works* (Harmondsworth: Penguin Books, 1983) [hereafter referred to as Wolters, *Cloud*], 'Introduction', pp. 16–17.
52. A. C. Spearing (trans.), *The Cloud of Unknowing and Other Works* (London: Penguin Books, 2001) [hereafter referred to as Spearing, *Cloud*], 'Introduction', p. xvi.
53. Ibid., pp. xvi–xvii. For pseudo-Dionysius, see Rosemary A. Arthur, *Pseudo-Dionysius as Polemicist: The Development and Purpose of the Angelic Hierarchy in 6th Century Syria*, Ashgate New Critical Thinking in Religion, Theology and Biblical Studies (Aldershot: Ashgate, 2008).

54. See Augustine Baker (Commentary) and Justin McCann (ed.), *The Cloud of Unknowing and Other Treatises*, 6th rev. edn (London: Burns & Oates, 1952) [hereafter referred to as Baker and McCann, *Cloud*], pp. xi–xv; Wolters, *Cloud*, pp. 15–17, 20; Evelyn Underhill (ed.), *A Book of Contemplation the Which is Called The Cloud of Unknowing, in the Which a Soul is Oned with God*, 6th edn (London: John M. Watkins, 1956) [hereafter referred to as Underhill, *Cloud*], pp. 5–7; Spearing, *Cloud*, pp. xvi–xvii; Phyllis Hodgson (ed.), *The Cloud of Unknowing and Related Treatises on Contemplative Prayer* [Original Middle English Texts] (Salzburg: Institut für Anglistik und Americanistik, Universität Salzburg/Exeter: Catholic Records Press, 1982) [hereafter referred to as Hodgson, *Cloud*], pp. xli–xlv.
55. Arthur, *Pseudo-Dionysius*, p. 1.
56. Ibid., p. 11.
57. Ibid., p. 73.
58. Ibid.
59. Spearing, *Cloud*, 'Introduction', pp. xvii–xviii, 1; for the trans. text, see 'The Mystical Theology of St Denis' (ch. 5) in Spearing, *Cloud*, pp. 8–9. For the original text, see *Deonise Hid Divinite* in Hodgson, *Cloud*, pp. 127–8.
60. Spearing, *Cloud*, p. 8; *Deonise Hid Divinite* in Hodgson, *Cloud*, p. 127.
61. Spearing, *Cloud*, pp. 8–9; *Deonise Hid Divinite* in Hodgson, *Cloud*, pp. 127–8.
62. See Tranøy, 'Thomas Aquinas', pp. 109ff., esp. p. 112.
63. Hodgson, *Cloud*, p. 1.
64. Spearing, *Cloud*, p. 11; see also Wolters, *Cloud*, p. 49; Underhill, *Cloud*, pp. title page, 35; Baker and McCann, *Cloud*, p. 1.
65. Hodgson, *Cloud*, p. lvii.
66. Ibid., p. ix; see also Baker and McCann, *Cloud*, pp. viii–ix; Underhill, *Cloud*, p. 7; Wolters, *Cloud*, pp. 11–12.
67. Spearing, *Cloud*, p. x.
68. Hodgson, *Cloud*, p. 74; see Wolters, *Cloud*, pp. 12, 152; Spearing, *Cloud*, p. 10.
69. Hodgson, *Cloud*, pp. xi–xii; Spearing, *Cloud*, p. x; Wolters, *Cloud*, p. 12; Baker and McCann, *Cloud*, p. viii.
70. Underhill, *Cloud*, p. 7.
71. Hodgson, *Cloud*, p. xi.
72. Spearing, *Cloud*, pp. x, xiv; Baker and McCann, *Cloud*, p. viii.
73. See Underhill, *Cloud*, p. 8.
74. Hodgson, *Cloud*, pp. ix, xi.
75. Ibid., p. x.
76. Baker and McCann, *Cloud*, p. x.
77. Underhill, *Cloud*, p. 9.
78. Wolters, *Cloud*, p. 12.
79. Ibid., p. 13 esp. n. 1; see Spearing, *Cloud*, p. ix.
80. Baker and McCann, *Cloud*, p. vii.
81. Wolters, *Cloud*, p. 9; Baker and McCann, *Cloud*, p. vii. For a good introduction to Julian of Norwich, see Clifton Wolters (trans.), Julian of Norwich, *Revelations of Divine Love* (Harmondsworth: Penguin Books, 1984).
82. Wolters, *Cloud*, p. 10.
83. Ibid., p. 9. For the Hundred Years War, see, *inter alia*, M. H. Keen, *England in the Later Middle Ages* (London: Folio Society, 1997), pp. 111–30; for the Black Death, see Philip Ziegler, *The Black Death* (London: Folio Society 1997); for the Avignon Papacy, see, firstly, Geoffrey Barraclough, *The Medieval Papacy* (London: Thames & Hudson, 1968, 1992), pp. 140ff.

84. Wolters, *Cloud*, p. 10.
85. Spearing, *Cloud*, p. xxvi.
86. Underhill, *Cloud*, pp. 218–19. For the original Middle English (ME) text, see Hodgson, *Cloud*, pp. 57–8. See also Spearing, *Cloud*, p. 81; Wolters, *Cloud*, p. 128; Baker and McCann, *Cloud*, pp. 76–7.
87. Wolters, *Cloud*, p. 42.
88. Ibid., p. 143; for the ME text, see Hodgson, *Cloud*, p. 68.
89. Wolters, *Cloud*, p. 35.
90. Spearing, *Cloud*, p. xx.
91. Hodgson, *Cloud*, p. 11.
92. Hodgson, *Cloud*, pp. 11–12 (ME text); see Wolters, *Cloud*, p. 64; Spearing, *Cloud*, p. 24; Underhill, *Cloud*, p. 69; Baker and McCann, *Cloud*, p. 11.
93. See esp. ch. 50 of *The Cloud* on 'Pure Love'; Hodgson, *Cloud*, pp. 51–2; see ibid., pp. xxxix–xli; Wolters, *Cloud*, pp. 38–40.
94. Wolters, *Cloud*, pp. 37–48.
95. Hodgson, *Cloud*, p. xxi.
96. Ibid.
97. Ibid., p. xxvii.
98. Wolters, *Cloud*, pp. 61–2; for the original ME, see Hodgson, *Cloud*, p. 9.
99. Hodgson, *Cloud*, p. 13; see Wolters, *Cloud*, p. 66; Spearing, *Cloud*, p. 26.
100. Hodgson, *Cloud*, p. 13; see Wolters, *Cloud*, p. 66; Spearing, *Cloud*, p. 26.
101. Ibid.
102. Hodgson, *Cloud*, p. 21; see Wolters, *Cloud*, p. 76; Spearing, *Cloud*, p. 35. Some of these quotations in my text from the ME text of Hodgson are slightly adapted for readability, e.g. ME Þ > th and u > v.
103. Baker and McCann, *Cloud*, p. xvii.
104. Hodgson, *Cloud*, p. 13; Wolters, *Cloud*, p. 66; Spearing, *Cloud*, p. 26.
105. Ibid.
106. Hodgson, *Cloud*, p. 13; Wolters, *Cloud*, p. 67; Spearing, *Cloud*, p. 27.
107. Hodgson, *Cloud*, 'Glossary', p. 221 s.v. *schal*.
108. Hodgson, *Cloud*, 'A table of the chapitres', p. 2; Wolters, *Cloud*, p. 53; Spearing, *Cloud*, p. 13.
109. Spearing, *Cloud*, p. 13.
110. Wolters, *Cloud*, p. 53.
111. Ibid., p. 41.
112. Underhill, *Cloud*, p. 139. For the original ME, see Hodgson, *Cloud*, p. 34. See also Wolters, *Cloud*, p. 94; Spearing, *Cloud*, p. 51; Baker and McCann, *Cloud*, p. 42.
113. Wehr, *Dictionary of Modern Written Arabic*, p. 985 s.v. *nafs*.
114. Javad Nurbakhsh, *In the Paradise of the Sufis*, 3rd edn (New York and London: Khaniqahi-Nimatullahi Publications, 1989), p. 81.
115. Ibid., p. 13.
116. Wehr, *Dictionary*, p. 729 s.v. *fanāʾ*.
117. Al-Hujwīrī, *Kashf al-Maḥjūb*, ed. V. A. Zhukovski (Leningrad: Dār al-ʿUlūm Ittiḥād Jamāhīr Shūrawī Sūsiyālīstī, 1926), p. 231; Reynold A. Nicholson (trans.), *The Kashf al-Maḥjūb: The Oldest Persian Treatise on Sufism, by ʿAlī B. ʿUthmān al-Jullābī al-Hujwīrī*, trans. from the text of the Lahore edn, E. J. W. Gibb Memorial Series, vol. 17 (London: Luzac, repr. 1970), pp. 185–6.
118. Al-Hujwīrī, *Kashf*, p. 313; Nicholson (trans.), *The Kashf al-Maḥjūb*, p. 243.
119. Al-Kalābādhī, *Kitāb al-Taʿarruf li-Madhhab Ahl al-Taṣawwuf*, ed. ʿAbd al-Ḥalīm Maḥmūd

and Ṭāhā 'Abd al-Bāqī Surūr (Cairo: al-Ḥalabī, 1960), p. 123; ibid., ed. Maḥmūd al-Nawāwī, 2nd edn (Cairo: Maktaba al-Kulliyāt al-Azhariyya, 1980), p. 147. *All Arabic textual references henceforth are to the 1980 edition.* There is a trans. by A. J. Arberry, *The Doctrine of the Sufis (Kitāb al-Ta'arruf li-Madhhab Ahl al-Taṣawwuf* (Cambridge: Cambridge University Press, 1977, repr. of 1935 CUP edn), p. 120.

120. Hodgson, *Cloud*, p. 44; Wolters, *Cloud*, p. 110; Spearing, *Cloud*, p. 66.
121. Hodgson, *Cloud*, p. 46; Wolters, *Cloud*, p. 111; Spearing, *Cloud*, p. 66.
122. Wolters, *Cloud*, p. 46.
123. Ibid., pp. 46–8 and text, passim.
124. Hodgson, *Cloud*, p. xxx.
125. Ibid., pp. 1–2; Wolters, *Cloud*, pp. 51–2; Spearing, *Cloud*, pp. 11–12.
126. See Luke 10:38–42.
127. Hodgson, *Cloud*, pp. 26–7: 'For by Mary is understonden alle contemplatyves'; Wolters, *Cloud*, p. 84; Spearing, *Cloud*, p. 42.
128. Wolters, *Cloud*, p. 83; see also Spearing, *Cloud*, pp. 41–2. For the original ME text, see Hodgson, *Cloud*, p. 26.
129. Ibid.
130. Wolters, *Cloud*, pp. 150–1; Spearing, *Cloud*, pp. 100–1; for the original ME text, see Hodgson, *Cloud*, pp. 73–4.
131. Philip F. Esler and Ronald A. Piper, *Lazarus, Mary and Martha: A Social-Scientific and Theological Reading of John* (London: SCM Press, 2006), p. 1.
132. See ibid., pp. 131ff., 146ff.
133. Ibid., p. 135.
134. E.g. see Wolters, *Cloud*, pp. 83, 95; Spearing, *Cloud*, pp. 42, 52; Hodgson, *Cloud*, pp. 26, 34.
135. Wolters, *Cloud*, p. 126.
136. Ibid., pp. 26–7.
137. Hodgson, *Cloud*, p. 67; Wolters, *Cloud*, p. 142; Spearing, *Cloud*, p. 93.
138. Hodgson, *Cloud*, p. 68; Wolters, *Cloud*, p. 142; Spearing, *Cloud*, p. 93.
139. Hodgson, *Cloud*, p. 68; Wolters, *Cloud*, p. 143; Spearing, *Cloud*, p. 94.
140. Ibid.
141. Wolters, *Cloud*, p. 143; Spearing, *Cloud*, p. 94. For the original ME text, see Hodgson, *Cloud*, p. 68.
142. Hodgson, *Cloud*, pp. 68–9; Wolters, *Cloud*, p. 144; Spearing, *Cloud*, pp. 94–5.
143. Hodgson, *Cloud*, p. 68; Wolters, *Cloud*, p. 144; Spearing, *Cloud*, p. 94.
144. Hodgson, *Cloud*, p. 7; Wolters, *Cloud*, p. 59; Spearing, *Cloud*, p. 20.
145. Ibid.
146. Hodgson, *Cloud*, 'Introduction', p. xxi.
147. Hodgson, *Cloud*, p. 24; Wolters, *Cloud*, p. 81 see n. 1; Spearing, *Cloud*, pp. 39, 148 n. 37.
148. Hodgson, *Cloud*, p. 51; Wolters, *Cloud*, p. 119; Spearing, *Cloud*, p. 73.
149. Spearing, *Cloud*, p. 73; Wolters, *Cloud*, p. 119. For the original ME text, see Hodgson, *Cloud*, p. 51.
150. Hodgson, *Cloud*, p. 51; Wolters, *Cloud*, p. 119; Spearing, *Cloud*, p. 73.
151. Hodgson, *Cloud*, pp. 21, 23; Wolters, *Cloud*, pp. 76, 79; Spearing, *Cloud*, pp. 35, 37.
152. Nurbakhsh, *In the Paradise of the Sufis*, pp. 12–13.
153. Ibid., p. 13.
154. Wolters, *Cloud*, p. 40.
155. Hodgson, *Cloud*, p. 15; Wolters, *Cloud*, p. 69; Spearing, *Cloud*, p. 29.
156. Underhill, *Cloud*, p. 101; for the original ME text, see Hodgson, *Cloud*, p. 22; see also

Wolters, *Cloud*, p. 78; Spearing, *Cloud*, p. 37.
157. Hodgson, *Cloud*, p. 34; Wolters, *Cloud*, p. 95; Spearing, *Cloud*, p. 52.
158. Hodgson, *Cloud*, pp. 51–2; Wolters, *Cloud*, pp. 120–1; Spearing, *Cloud*, p. 74. See also ch. 24: Hodgson, *Cloud*, pp. 32–3; Wolters, *Cloud*, pp. 91–2; Spearing, *Cloud*, p. 49; and ch. 20: Hodgson, *Cloud*, p. 29; Wolters, *Cloud*, p. 87; Spearing, *Cloud*, p. 45.
159. Hodgson, *Cloud*, pp. 7–8; Wolters, *Cloud*, p. 59; Spearing, *Cloud*, p. 20.
160. Hodgson, *Cloud*, p. xxxiii.
161. Underhill, *Cloud*, p. 140; for the original ME text, see Hodgson, *Cloud*, pp. xxxiii, 34; see also Wolters, *Cloud*, p. 95 and Spearing, *Cloud*, p. 52.
162. Baker and McCann, *Cloud* ('Commentary on the Cloud'), p. 166.
163. Underhill, *Cloud*, pp. 69–70. For the original ME text, see Hodgson, *Cloud*, p. 12.
164. Wolters, *Cloud*, p. 64.
165. Spearing, *Cloud*, p. 25.
166. Hodgson, *Cloud*, p. xxi.
167. See Netton, *Popular Dictionary of Islam*, p. 51 s.v. *Baqā'*.
168. Ibid.
169. F. Rahman, 'Baḳā' wa-Fanā'', *EI*[2], vol. 1, p. 951.
170. Ibid.
171. Ibid.
172. Ibid.
173. Ibid.
174. Al-Hujwīrī, *Kashf al-Maḥjūb*, p. 231; Nicholson (trans.), *The Kashf al-Maḥjūb*, pp. 185–6. See Ian Richard Netton, *Ṣūfī Ritual: The Parallel Universe* (London: Curzon Press, 2000), p. 177.
175. See Arberry (trans.), *Doctrine*, p. xi.
176. Al-Kalābādhī, *Ta'arruf*, p. 147; Arberry (trans.), *Doctrine*, p. 120; see Netton, *Ṣūfī Ritual*, p. 178.
177. Nurbakhsh, *In the Paradise of the Sufis*, p. 24 (my emphases).
178. Gerald Brenan, *St John of the Cross: His Life and Poetry* (Cambridge: Cambridge University Press, 1973), p. 3; E. Allison Peers, *Spirit of Flame: A Study of St John of the Cross* (London: SCM Press, 1943, 1979), p. 13; E. W. Trueman Dicken, *The Crucible of Love: A Study of the Mysticism of St Teresa of Jesus and St John of the Cross* (London: Darton, Longman & Todd, 1963), p. 15; Emilie Griffin (ed.), *John of the Cross: Selections from The Dark Night and Other Writings*, Foreword by Ron Hansen, Translation by Kieran Kavanaugh, HarperCollins Spiritual Classics (New York: HarperCollins, Harper San Francisco, 2004), p. ix ('Introduction').
179. Brenan, *St John*, p. 3; Peers, *Spirit of Flame*, p. 14; Dicken, *Crucible*, p. 15; Griffin (ed.), *John of the Cross*, p. x.
180. See Genesis, chapters 37ff.
181. Alex Kurian, *Ascent to Nothingness: The Ascent to God According to John of the Cross*, ed. Andrew Tulloch (London and Maynooth: St Pauls Publishing, 2000), pp. 25, 27.
182. Kathleen Jones (trans.), *The Poems of St John of the Cross*, Spanish and English text (London: Burns & Oates, 1993, 2001), p. 7.
183. Fernand Braudel, *The Mediterranean and the Mediterranean World in the Age of Philip II*, trans. Siân Reynolds, abridged by Richard Ollard (London: HarperCollins, 1992), p. 481.
184. Norman Davies, *Europe: A History* (London: Pimlico, 1997), pp. 531–2.
185. Ibid., p. 534.
186. Brenan, *St John*, p. 21.
187. Ibid.

188. Ibid.
189. See ibid., pp. 77, 89, 96–8.
190. Ibid., pp. 96–7.
191. Ibid., pp. 97–8.
192. Ibid., p. 98.
193. Dicken, *Crucible*, p. 493.
194. Brenan, *St John*, pp. 6, 228; Peers, *Spirit of Flame*, pp. 15–16; Griffin (ed.), *John of the Cross*, p. ix; Dicken, *Crucible*, p. 16; Jones (trans.), *Poems*, p. 7.
195. Brenan, *St John*, pp. 7–8, 228.
196. Ibid., p. 7.
197. Ibid., p. 8.
198. Ibid.
199. Ibid., pp. 9, 228.
200. Ibid., p. 9.
201. Ibid., pp. 9, 228; Dicken, *Crucible*, pp. 16–19.
202. Dicken, *Crucible*, p. 18.
203. Ibid., pp. 18–19.
204. Crisógono de Jesús Sacramentado, *San Juan de la Cruz, su obra científica y su obra literaria* (Ávila, 1929), p. 437 cited in Dicken, *Crucible*, pp. 18, 19 n. 17.
205. Brenan, *St John*, pp. 24, 228.
206. Ibid., p. 24.
207. Ibid., pp. 26–38, 228–9; Dicken, *Crucible*, p. 22; Peers, *Spirit of Flame*, pp. 36–53.
208. Griffin (ed.), *John of the Cross*, pp. xi–xii ('Introduction').
209. Brenan, *St John*, pp. 64, 229.
210. Ibid.
211. Ibid.
212. Ibid., p. 65.
213. Ibid., pp. 71, 229.
214. Ibid., pp. 78–81, 229.
215. Ibid., pp. 82–3.
216. Griffin (ed.), *John of the Cross*, p. xii ('Introduction').
217. William Johnston, *The Mysticism of The Cloud of Unknowing: A Modern Interpretation* (New York, Rome, Tournai, Paris: Desclée Co., 1967), p. 11, see also pp. 52, 53, 177, 266; see also J. P. H. Clark, 'The "Cloud of Unknowing", Walter Hilton and St John of the Cross: A Comparison', *Downside Review* (1978), vol. 96, pp. 281, 296–7.
218. Johnston, *Mysticism*, p. 11.
219. Ibid.
220. See Arthur, *Pseudo-Dionysius*, p. 11.
221. Clark, '"Cloud"', p. 298.
222. Constantino S. Nieva, '*The Cloud of Unknowing* and St John of the Cross', *Mount Carmel*, 27: 4 (Winter, 1979), p. 186.
223. Ibid., p. 190.
224. See Johnston, *Mysticism*, p. 42.
225. See Nieva, '*Cloud*', p. 185; Clark, '"Cloud"', pp. 281, 285, 287.
226. Johnston, *Mysticism*, pp. 37, 162–6.
227. Nieva, '*Cloud*', p. 189.
228. Ibid., p. 190.
229. Johnston, *Mysticism*, pp. 185–6.
230. Ibid., pp. 177–8.

231. Ibid., p. 178.
232. Ibid., p. 164. The words are taken from another work by the *Cloud* author entitled *The Epistle of Privy Counsel*. They have been rendered in more modern English as 'this exalting of God' (> 'this high alling of God') and 'this great act of total self-denial' (> 'this noble noughting of itself'): see Wolters, *Cloud* (*The Epistle of Privy Counsel*), p. 176.
233. Johnston, *Mysticism*, pp. 178, 164, 166.
234. Ibid., p. 178.
235. Ibid., p. 179; see also Nieva, '*Cloud*', pp. 183–4, 186, 188.
236. Juan de la Cruz, *Obras Completas*, Maestros Espirituales Carmelitas, no. 3 (Burgos: Editorial Monte Carmelo, 1982), pp. 21–2.
237. Jones (trans.), *Poems*, p. 19.
238. Brenan, *St John*, p. 145 (trans. of poetry by Lynda Nicholson).
239. Roy Campbell (trans.), *The Poems of St John of the Cross* (Glasgow: Collins Fount Paperbacks, 1983), p. 11.
240. *Obras Completas*, p. 21.
241. Campbell (trans.), *Poems*, p. 11.
242. Juan de la Cruz, *Noche Oscura* in idem, *Obras Completas* [hereafter referred to as Juan, *Noche*], pp. 541–727.
243. Idem, *The Dark Night of the Soul*, ed., trans. and intro. by John Newton and Benedict Zimmerman, Baronius Press Classics (London: Baronius Press, 2006; re-edn of London: Thomas Baker, 1916 edn) (hereafter referred to as Zimmerman, *Dark Night*).
244. Idem, *Subida del Monte Carmelo* in idem, *Obras Completas*, pp. 127–539 [hereafter referred to as Juan, *Subida*].
245. Idem, *Ascent of Mount Carmel*, trans. and ed. E. Allison Peers (London and New York: Burns & Oates, 1983) [hereafter referred to as Peers, *Ascent*].
246. Margaret Wilson, *San Juan de la Cruz: Poems*, Critical Guides to Spanish Texts, no. 13 (London: Grant and Cutler, in association with Tamesis Books, 1975), pp. 47–8.
247. Clark, '"Cloud"', p. 281.
248. See, for example, Wilson, *Poems*, pp. 46–51; Emilie Griffin (ed. with intro.) and Kieran Kavanaugh (trans.), *John of the Cross: Selections from The Dark Night and Other Writings*, HarperCollins Spiritual Classics (New York: HarperCollins, 2004), pp. 1–15.
249. Wilson, *Poems*, p. 47.
250. Ibid. (my emphases).
251. *Noche*, pp. 21–2.
252. Ibid., p. 21.
253. See Campbell (trans.), *Poems*, p. 11.
254. *Noche*, p. 22.
255. See Campbell (trans.), *Poems*, p. 13.
256. Wilson, *Poems*, p. 48.
257. Ibid., p. 49.
258. Ibid., p. 50.
259. Clark, '"Cloud"' p. 281.
260. For more on this tradition of negativity, see Marie M. Gaudreau, *Mysticism and Image in St John of the Cross*, European University Papers, Series xxiii Theology: vol. 66 (Bern: Herbert Lang/Frankfurt am Main: Peter Lang, 1976), pp. 97–124, 125–69.
261. See Dicken, *Crucible*, pp. 215–67.
262. E. Allison Peers, 'The Rede Lecture for 1932' in idem, *St John of the Cross and Other Lectures and Addresses, 1920–1945* (London: Faber & Faber, 1946), p. 27. See Juan *Subida*, pp. 186–245; Peers, *Ascent*, pp. 17–62.

263. Peers, *Ascent* ('Introduction'), p. 2.
264. Juan, *Noche*, pp. 541–727; see Zimmerman, *Dark Night*.
265. John Newton, 'Preface' to Zimmerman, *Dark Night*, p. ix.
266. Ibid. For comments on the chronology and dating of *The Ascent* and *The Night*, see Dicken, *Crucible*, p. 217; Clark, '"Cloud"', p. 283; Peers, *Ascent*, pp. xxxiv–xxxv ('General Introduction').
267. Newton, 'Preface' to Zimmerman, *Dark Night*, p. ix.
268. Peers, *St John of the Cross*, p. 22.
269. Colin P. Thompson, *The Poet and the Mystic: Study of the Cántico Espiritual of San Juan de la Cruz* (Oxford: Oxford University Press, 1977), p. 97.
270. Elizabeth Teresa Howe, *Mystical Imagery: Santa Teresa de Jesús and San Juan de la Cruz*, American University Studies, series 2. Romance Languages and Literature: vol. 76 (New York, Bern, Frankfurt am Main, Paris: Peter Lang, 1988), p. 3.
271. Ibid., p. 12; see also pp. 48, 110.
272. Johnston, *Mysticism*, p. 53.
273. Zimmerman, *Dark Night*, p. 129; for the original Spanish text, see Juan, *Noche*, p. 688.
274. Zimmerman, *Dark Night*, p. 133; Juan, *Noche*, p. 691.
275. As the editor points out, the reference is to Psalm 17:12: Zimmerman, *Dark Night*, p. 134 n. 10. In Knox's trans., vv. 10–12 read: 'He bade heaven stoop, and came down to earth, *with a dark cloud at his feet*; he came, cherub-mounted, borne up on the wings of the wind, *shrouded in darkness, canopied with black rain-storm and deep mist*' (my emphases) (Knox (trans.), *Holy Bible: Old Testament*, p. 484).
276. Zimmerman, *Dark Night*, p. 134 (my emphases); Juan, *Noche*, p. 692.
277. Ibid., pp. 134–6; Juan, *Noche*, pp. 692–4. See also Notes to Chapter 3, n. 623.
278. Sykes (ed.), *Concise Oxford Dictionary*, p. 3 s.v. *abnegation*.
279. See Thompson, *The Poet and the Mystic*, p. 10.
280. Ibid.; see also Plato, *Phaedo*, 64B–66E; Ikhwān al-Ṣafā', *Rasā'il Ikhwān al-Ṣafā'* (Beirut: Dār Ṣādir, 1957), vol. 3, p. 49.
281. Thompson, *The Poet and the Mystic*, p. 160.
282. Juan, *Noche*, p. 688; Zimmerman, *Dark Night*, pp. 129–30.
283. Juan, *Noche*, p. 602; Zimmerman, *Dark Night*, p. 28. See also Juan, *Subida*, bk 1, ch. 5, pp. 202–8; Peers, *Ascent*, pp. 28–33.
284. Juan, *Noche*, p. 599; Zimmerman, *Dark Night*, p. 24.
285. Kurian, *Ascent to Nothingness*, p. 124; see also pp. 129–30.
286. Ibid., p. 205.
287. Zimmerman, *Dark Night*, p. 94; Juan, *Noche*, p. 657.
288. Zimmerman, *Dark Night*, p. 94.
289. Knox (trans.), *Holy Bible: Old Testament*, p. 507.
290. Juan, *Noche*, p. 657; Zimmerman, *Dark Night*, p. 94.
291. See A Benedictine of Stanbrook Abbey, *Mediaeval Mystical Tradition and Saint John of the Cross* (London: Burns & Oates, 1954), p. 149.
292. Ibid.
293. Ibid.
294. Dicken, *Crucible*, pp. 117, 118.
295. Ibid., p. 118.
296. Ibid.
297. Juan, *Noche*, p. 643.
298. Zimmerman, *Dark Night*, p. 76.
299. Juan, *Noche: Canciones del Alma: 'En una noche oscura'*, p. 580.

300. Zimmerman, *Dark Night*, p. 137.
301. Ibid.; Juan, *Noche*, p. 695.
302. Zimmerman, *Dark Night*, p. 142; Juan, *Noche*, p. 700.
303. See Juan, *Noche*, pp. 666, 644; Zimmerman, *Dark Night*, pp. 104, 76–77.
304. Iain Matthew ODC, 'John and daily life' in John McGowan (ed.), *A Fresh Approach to St John of the Cross* (Slough: St Pauls, 1993), p. 148. See also Dicken, *Crucible*, p. 124.
305. *Crucible*, pp. 483–514.
306. Zimmerman, *Dark Night*, p. 40; Juan, *Noche*, p. 613.
307. Thompson, *The Poet and the Mystic*, p. 11.
308. Ibid., p. 168.
309. See Sue Hamilton, *Indian Philosophy: A Very Short Introduction* (Oxford: Oxford University Press, 2001), pp. 42, 102–3; Damien Keown, *Buddhism: A Very Short Introduction* (Oxford: Oxford University Press, 2000), pp. 21–2, 54–5, 84–96; Michael Carrithers, *Buddha: A Very Short Introduction* (Oxford: Oxford University Press, 2001), esp. pp. 29–31, 33–4, 36–7, 39–45.
310. See Lavinia Cohn-Sherbok and Dan Cohn-Sherbok, *A Popular Dictionary of Judaism* (Richmond: Curzon Press, 1995), pp. 37, 111 s.v. *Devekut*, *Meditation*.
311. Christmas Humphreys, *A Popular Dictionary of Buddhism* (London: Curzon Press, 1984), p. 99 s.v. *Jhāna*.
312. A Benedictine, *Mediaeval Mystical Tradition*, p. 155.
313. Howe, *Mystical Imagery*, pp. 10, 27 n. 16 citing Gabriel Celaya, *Exploración de la poesía* (Barcelona: Seix Barra, 1964); see pp. 158, 176.
314. A Benedictine, *Mediaeval Mystical Tradition*, p. 154.
315. Clark, '"Cloud"', pp. 282–3; Gaudreau, *Mysticism and Image*, p. 187 and n. 91.
316. Juan, *Subida*, Bk 1, ch. 2, para. 5, pp. 191–2; Peers, *Ascent*, pp. 20–1.
317. See Juan, *Noche*, Bk 1, ch. 8, paras 1 and 2, p. 605; Zimmerman, *Dark Night*, p. 32; Juan, *Subida*, Bk 1, ch. 1, para. 2, p. 188; Peers, *Ascent*, p. 18.
318. Gaudreau, *Mysticism and Image*, p. 187.
319. Clark, '"Cloud"', p. 283; see Dicken, *Crucible*, pp. 218–19.
320. See n. 322 below.
321. A Benedictine, *Mediaeval Mystical Tradition*, p. 154; see also pp. 151–5.
322. Gaudreau, *Mysticism and Image*, p. 193, Figure 1. See Figure III in ibid., p. 195 for a diagrammatic illustration of the Active and Passive dimensions of the *noche* with sense and spirit. The structures of the *noche* are vastly elaborated in Dicken, *Crucible*, pp. 144–69 ('The Passive Night of the Senses'), 215–44 ('Structure and Doctrine in the *Ascent* and the *Night*') and 245–68 ('Stages of Spiritual Progress in the *Ascent* and in the *Night*').
323. Peers, *St John of the Cross*, p. 34.
324. Ibid.
325. Ibid.
326. Howe, *Mystical Imagery*, p. 200.
327. Ronald Rolheiser, 'John and Human Development: The Dark Night of the Soul … A Contemporary Interpretation' in McGowan (ed.), *Fresh Approach*, pp. 31–60.
328. Ibid., p. 60.
329. Ibid., p. 33.
330. Ibid.
331. Ibid., p. 35.
332. Ibid., pp. 36–45.
333. Ibid., p. 43; see John 12:24.
334. Juan, *Noche*, Bk 1, ch. 1, para. 1, p. 584; Zimmerman, *Dark Night*, p. 6.

335. Juan, *Noche*, Bk 1, ch. 1, para. 1, pp. 584–5; Zimmerman, *Dark Night*, p. 6.
336. Juan, *Noche*, Bk 1, ch. 7, para. 2, p. 603; Zimmerman, *Dark Night*, p. 30.
337. Juan, *Noche*, Bk 1, ch. 3, para. 3, pp. 592–3; Zimmerman, *Dark Night*, pp. 15–16.
338. Juan, *Noche*, Bk 2, ch. 3, para. 4, p. 638; Zimmerman, *Dark Night*, p. 70.
339. Ibid.
340. See above n. 337.
341. Juan, *Noche*, Bk 1, ch. 4, paras 7–8, pp. 596–7; Zimmerman, *Dark Night*, p. 21.
342. Thompson, *The Poet and the Mystic*, p. 167.
343. Line trans. thus by Zimmerman, *Dark Night*, p. 110.
344. Ibid.; Juan, *Noche*, Bk 2, ch. 11, para. 1, p. 670.
345. Juan, *Noche*, Bk 2, ch. 12, para. 1, p. 674; Zimmerman, *Dark Night*, p. 115.
346. Juan, *Noche*, Bk 2, ch. 13, para. 1, p. 678; Zimmerman, *Dark Night*, p. 119.
347. Juan, *Noche*, Bk 2, ch. 18, para. 5, p. 702; Zimmerman, *Dark Night*, p. 145.
348. Zimmerman, *Dark Night*, p. 145; Juan, *Noche*, Bk 2, ch. 18, p. 702.
349. See Juan, *Noche*, p. 702 n. 2.
350. Ibid., Bk 2, chs 19 and 20, pp. 702–10; Zimmerman, *Dark Night*, pp. 146–54.
351. Zimmerman, *Dark Night*, p. 153; Juan, *Noche*, Bk 2, ch. 20, para. 5, p. 709.
352. Ibid.
353. 'The man, the myth and the truth' in McGowan (ed.), *Fresh Approach*, p. 23.
354. Ibid.
355. Peers, *Ascent*, pp. 75–6; Juan, *Subida*, Bk 2, ch. 5, para. 3, p. 262.
356. Juan, *Noche*, Bk 1, ch. 1, para. 1, pp. 584–5; Zimmerman, *Dark Night*, p. 6.
357. Thompson, *The Poet and the Mystic*, p. 9; Juan, *Noche*, p. 584.
358. See Dicken, *Crucible*, pp. 352ff.
359. Ibid., p. 353.
360. Ibid.
361. Ibid., pp. 355ff. for a magisterial elaboration of this kind of union of love.
362. Terry Graham, 'Christian Mysticism and Sufism' in *Sufi*, no. 74 (Winter 2007), p. 42.
363. Wilson, *Poems*, pp. 50–1.
364. Luce López-Baralt, *Islam in Spanish Literature from the Middle Ages to the Present*, trans. Andrew Hurley (Leiden/New York/Köln: E. J. Brill/San Juan: Editorial de la Universidad de Puerto Rico, 1992), pp. 42, 183; see idem, *San Juan de la Cruz y el Islam. Estudio sobre la filiación semítica de su poesía mística* (Colegio de México/Universidad de Puerto Rico, 1985; repr. Madrid: Hiperión, 1990).
365. See R. P. Scheindlin, 'Ibn ʿAbbād al-Rundī (733–92/1333–90)' in Meisami and Starkey (eds), *Encyclopedia of Arabic Literature*, vol. 1, p. 301.
366. Ibid. For Ibn ʿAbbād, see John Renard (trans.), *Ibn ʿAbbād of Ronda: Letters on the Ṣūfī Path*, Classics of Western Spirituality (New York/Mahwah, NJ/Toronto: Paulist Press, 1986) as suggested by Scheindlin; see also Paul Nwyia, 'Ibn ʿAbbād', *EI*², vol. 3, pp. 670–1; idem, *Ibn ʿAbbād de Ronda (1332–1390): un mystique prédicateur à la Qarawīyīn de Fes*, Recherches publiées sous la direction de L'Institut de Lettres Orientales de Beyrouth, Tome XVII (Beirut: Imprimerie Catholique, 1961). See also Ibn ʿAbbād, *al-Rasā'il al-Sughrā/Lettres de Direction Spirituelle*, ed. Paul Nwyia, Recherches publiées sous la direction de L'Institut de Lettres Orientales de Beyrouth, Tome VII (Beirut: Imprimerie Catholique, 1958).
367. Baldick, *Mystical Islam*, p. 104.
368. Miguel Asín Palacios, *Saint John of the Cross and Islam*, trans. Howard W. Yoder and Elmer H. Douglas (New York: Vantage Press, 1981; first published as *Un Precursor Hispano-Musulman de San Juan de la Cruz*, Al-Andalus, 1 (Madrid, 1933), pp. vii–viii, 12, 24–7.

369. Ibid., p. 13.
370. Ibid.
371. Ibid., pp. 13–14.
372. Schimmel, *Mystical Dimensions*, p. 253; see Ibn ʿAbbād al-Rundī, *Sharḥ al-Shaykh Muḥammad b. Ibrāhīm al-Maʿrūf bi-Ibn ʿAbbād al-Nafzī al-Rundī ʿalā Kitāb al-Ḥikam li … Ibn ʿAṭāʾ Allāh al-Sakandarī* (2 vols in 1, Cairo: al-Ḥalabī, 1939) [hereafter referred to as *Sharḥ*], vol. 1, pp. 68–9, cited in Nwyia (ed.), *Ibn ʿAbbād de Ronda*, p. 34 n. 3.
373. Asín Palacios, *Saint John*, pp. 26, 80 n. 4. For al-Shādhilī, see, *inter alia*, Lloyd Ridgeon, 'Al-Shadhili (1187–1258)' in Netton (ed.), *Encyclopedia of Islamic Civilisation and Religion*, p. 589; P. Lory, 'Al-Shādhilī', *EI*², vol. 9, pp. 170–2.
374. 'Some Maxims (*Ḥikam*) of Ibn Aṭā Allāh with Commentary (*Sharḥ*) by Ibn ʿAbbād': Maxim 91 (my emphases) cited in Asín Palacios, *Saint John*, pp. 36–8. For the original Arabic, see Ibn ʿAbbād, *Sharḥ*, vol. 1, pp. 68–9, cited (with a different Arabic reference) in Asín Palacios, *Saint John*, p. 39; see also p. 54.
375. Ibn ʿAbbād, 'Some Maxims …': Maxim 159, cited in Asín Palacios, *Saint John*, p. 53.
376. Asín Palacios, *Saint John*, pp. 28–31.
377. 3 Kings 17:3–4, trans. Knox, *Holy Bible: Old Testament*, p. 302.
378. 3 Kings 17:4–7 (Knox nomenclature).
379. Eileen Bailie, 'Travelling with Elijah: A Journey into Darkness', *Mount Carmel [Special Issue: Elijah and the Rule]*, vol. 56:2, Pillars of Carmel 1 (April–June 2008), p. 41 (my emphases).
380. 3 Kings 19:3 (Knox nomenclature).
381. James McCaffrey, 'The Prophet Elijah: Man of Prayer and Action', *Mount Carmel [Special Issue: Elijah and the Rule]*, pp. 12–13 (my emphases).
382. Bailie, 'Travelling with Elijah', p. 43.
383. Miceál O'Neill, 'A Prophet for the Church and the World: The Mission of Elijah for Today', *Mount Carmel [Special Issue: Elijah and the Rule]*, pp. 65–6.
384. 4 Kings 1–8, trans. Knox, *Holy Bible: Old Testament*, p. 311. See Jane Ackerman, *Elijah, Prophet of Carmel* (Washington, DC: ICS Publications, 2003), pp. 46, 54, 87, 102, 105.
385. Zimmerman, *Dark Night*, p. 157; Juan, *Noche*, Bk 2, ch. 21, para. 6, p. 712.
386. Zimmerman, *Dark Night*, p. 158; Juan, *Noche*, Bk 2, ch. 21, para. 8, p. 713.
387. Zimmerman, *Dark Night*, p. 158; Juan, *Noche*, Bk 2, ch. 21, para. 9, p. 713.
388. Kurian, *Ascent to Nothingness*, p. 156.
389. Veronica Corner, 'An Icon of Elijah: A Gradual Revelation', *Mount Carmel [Special Issue: Elijah and the Rule]*, p. 24.
390. Ibid., p. 23. See 3 Kings 19:9 (Knox); see also Jotischky, *Carmelites and Antiquity*, p. 9.
391. 'Some sort of devotional practice': see W. Montgomery Watt, *Muhammad at Mecca* (Oxford: Clarendon Press, 1953, repr. 1972), pp. 44, 40.
392. John 11:43–4.
393. See 'Canciones entre el alma y el esposo' in Juan, *Obras Completas*, p. 754; trans. (with Spanish text) Campbell, *Poems*, pp. 26–7; for commentary, see Howe, *Mystical Imagery*, pp. 274–5.
394. Jotischky, *Carmelites and Antiquity*, p. 83.
395. Corner, 'An icon of Elijah', p. 24.
396. See Peers, *Ascent*, pp. xiii, xxxii–xxxiii; Juan, *Subida*, p. 176; see Kurian, *Ascent to Nothingness*, pp. 70–3.
397. McCaffrey, 'Prophet Elijah', p. 17; Jotischky, *Carmelites and Antiquity*, pp. 8–9.
398. Bruce Baker and Gregory L. Klein (eds), *The Carmelite Rule* ('Introduction') (New Jersey: Catholic Book Publishing Co., 2000), p. 12 [The 'Introduction' is by Joseph Chalmers].

399. Joseph Chalmers, 'Prayer and Contemplation: In the Spirit of the Carmelite Rule (1)', *Mount Carmel [Special Issue: Elijah and the Rule]*, p. 27, see also ibid., pp. 28–35. See also Craig Morrison, 'The Carmelite Rule: A Lectio Divina by Albert of Jerusalem (1)' in ibid., pp. 44–51.
400. See Baker and Klein (eds), *The Carmelite Rule*, passim; Christopher O'Donnell O.Carm. (rev. trans.), *The Rule of St Albert, as approved by Innocent IV (1247)*, Leaflet, circulated with the Carmelite Order Secular Newsletter, September 2003; Hugh Clarke and Bede Edwards, *The Rule of Saint Albert*, Vinea Carmeli, 1 (Aylesford: Carmelite Priory/Kensington: Carmelite Priory, 1973). This contains the Latin text of *The Rule of Saint Albert/Regula Sancti Alberti*, ed. with an English trans. by Bede Edwards, pp. 73–93, which was divided by the editor, contrary to tradition, into '20 numbered paragraphs'. Compare *Rule of Saint Linus*, MS Lambeth 192, fol. 46, discussed in a paper by Michelle M. Sauer at the International Medieval Congress, University of Leeds, 2007. I am most grateful to Rev. Dr J. Alban O.Carm. for confirming and clarifying the numbering in the Rule of St Albert. In an e-mail dated 3 August 2008, he wrote: 'The new agreed numbering ... was settled in 1999 between the two General Councils, O.Carm. and OCD. This system is documented officially in *Analecta Ordinis Carmelitarum*, vol. 50 (1999), pp. 147–65.' It comprises twenty-four very short chapters.
401. See Yāqūt, *Mu'jam al-Buldān* (Beirut: Dār Ṣādir, 1977), vol. 2, pp. 233–4.
402. McCaffrey, 'Prophet Elijah', p. 19.
403. Cf. Exodus 19:20 to 20:21.
404. For more on 'Oaths and Adjurations in the Qur'ān', see Yusuf Ali (trans.), *Qur'an*: Appendix XIV, pp. 1,784–7.
405. Cf. Exodus 19:16–18.
406. James McCaffrey, 'Focus', *Mount Carmel [Special Issue: Elijah and the Rule]*, p. 5. See also idem, 'Prophet Elijah', pp. 18–19.
407. Matthew 17:2–3ff.; Mark 9:1–7; Luke 9:28–36.
408. Tziona Grossmark, 'The Desert in Talmudic Travelers' Tales – Reality and Imagination': unpublished paper presented on 8 July 2008 at the International Medieval Congress, University of Leeds (7–10 July 2008).
409. See John and Caitlín Matthews, *King Arthur: History and Legend* (London: Folio, 2008), p. 225.
410. Ibid; see also pp. 196–8.
411. See B. Carra de Vaux, 'Djirdjis', *EI*², vol. 2, p. 553.
412. Ibid.
413. Ackerman, *Elijah*, p. 94.
414. See ibid., p. 126.
415. *Windsor Castle*, new edn illustrated by George Cruikshank and Tony Johannot (London: Henry Colburn, 1843), p. 154.

Chapter 3: The Mystic Telos

1. Dicken, *Crucible*, p. 116 (my emphases).
2. Ibid.
3. Ibid., p. 117.
4. Ibid., pp. 117–18.
5. See I. R. Netton, 'Ṭarīḳ', *EI*² vol. 12 (=Supp.) (Leiden: E. J. Brill, 2004), pp. 794–5; compare E. Geoffroy et al., 'Ṭarīḳa', *EI*², vol. 10, pp. 243–57.
6. Howe, *Mystical Imagery*, p. 246.

7. Ibid., p. 249.
8. Ibid., pp. 246–9. See Juan, *Subida*, Bk 2, ch. 7, para. 2 cited by Howe, *Mystical Imagery*, p. 247; Teresa of Ávila [Teresa de Jesús], *Libro de la Vida*, xxxv, 13–14 [hereafter referred to as Teresa, *Vida*] (5th edn Madrid: Editorial de Espiritualidad, 2000, pp. 244–5), cited by Howe, *Mystical Imagery*, p. 247.
9. Howe, *Mystical Imagery*, p. 248.
10. John 14:6; trans. Knox, *Holy Bible: New Testament*, p. 104.
11. John 10:9 in ibid., p. 99.
12. Trans. Knox, *Holy Bible: New Testament*, p. 6; see Juan, *Subida*, Bk 2, ch. 7, para. 2 [p. 272] cited in Howe, *Mystical Imagery*, p. 247.
13. Keown, *Buddhism*, pp. 54–6.
14. For this concept, see ibid., pp. 44–5, 52–4.
15. Howe, *Mystical Imagery*, p. 248.
16. Ahmet T. Karamustafa, *Sufism: The Formative Period*, The New Edinburgh Islamic Surveys (Edinburgh: Edinburgh University Press, 2007), p. vii.
17. Ibid.
18. Ibid., p. 19.
19. Ibid.
20. Ibid., pp. 19–20.
21. See ibid., p. 20.
22. Ibid., p. 173.
23. Ibid., p. 172.
24. Baldick, *Mystical Islam*, p. 55; Arberry (trans.), *Doctrine*, p. xi.
25. Karamustafa, *Sufism*, p. 69.
26. P. Nwyia, 'Al-Kalābādhī', EI^2, vol. 4, p. 467.
27. Arberry (trans.), *Doctrine*, p. x; Nwyia, 'Al-Kalābādhī', p. 467; Karamustafa, *Sufism*, p. 69.
28. Nwyia, 'Al-Kalābādhī', p. 467.
29. Karamustafa, *Sufism*, p. 69.
30. See W. Barthold and R. N. Frye, 'Bukhārā', EI^2, vol. 1, p. 1,295; C. E. Bosworth, 'Sāmānids', EI^2, vol. 8, pp. 1,027–8; idem, *The New Islamic Dynasties* (Edinburgh: Edinburgh University Press, 1996), pp. 170–1; Richard Nelson Frye, *Bukhara: The Medieval Achievement* (Costa Mesa, CA: Mazda Publishers, 1996); idem (trans. and ed.), *The History of Bukhārā*, trans. from the Persian abridgement of the Arabic original by Muḥammad ibn Jaʿfar Narshakhī (Princeton, NJ: Markus Wiener Publishers, 2007); Muḥammad ibn Jaʿfar Narshakhī, *Tārīkh Bukhārā* (Tehran: Bunyād-i Farhang-i Īran, 1351 = 1972); idem, *Tārīkh Bukhārā* (Cairo: Dār al-Maʿārif, 1965).
31. *Kitāb al-Taʿarruf li-Madhhab Ahl al-Taṣawwuf*, loosely trans. by A. J. Arberry as *The Doctrine of the Sufis*, is perhaps more closely rendered by Karamustafa (*Sufism*, p. 69), as *Introducing the Way of the People of Sufism*, although the word *taʿarruf* can equally well be rendered as 'acquaintance', 'exploration', 'study' or 'knowledge' (Wehr, *Dictionary*, p. 606 s.v. *taʿarruf*).
32. See Karamustafa, *Sufism*, pp. 69–70; Nwyia, 'Al-Kalābādhī', p. 467.
33. Arberry (trans.), *Doctrine*, p. xiv.
34. Karamustafa, *Sufism*, p. 71.
35. See *Taʿarruf*, passim.
36. For the contrast between *aḥwāl* (mystic states) and *maqāmāt* (mystic stations), see Lloyd Ridgeon, 'Aḥwāl' in Netton, *Encyclopedia*, pp. 32–3.
37. E.g. see Arberry (trans.), *Doctrine*, pp. xv–xvii; Baldick, *Mystical Islam*, p. 56; Karamustafa, *Sufism*, pp. 70–1.

38. Arberry (trans.), *Doctrine*, p. 119; for the original Arabic, see al-Kalābādhī, *Ta'arruf*, p. 146.
39. Ibid.
40. Al-Kalābādhī, *Ta'arruf*, pp. 78–81; Arberry (trans.), *Doctrine*, pp. 46–50.
41. Arberry (trans.), *Doctrine*, p. 50; al-Kalābādhī, *Ta'arruf*, p. 81.
42. Arberry (trans.), *Doctrine*, p. 50; al-Kalābādhī, *Ta'arruf*, p. 82.
43. Al-Kalābādhī, *Ta'arruf*, p. 104.
44. Ibid.
45. See al-Ghazālī, *Iḥyā' 'Ulūm al-Dīn* (5 vols, Beirut: Dār al-Ma'rifa, n.d.), passim; W. Montgomery Watt, *Muslim Intellectual: A Study of al-Ghazali* (Edinburgh: Edinburgh University Press, 1971), esp. pp. 163, 176.
46. Al-Kalābādhī, *Ta'arruf*, p. 104.
47. Ibid., p. 105; Arberry (trans.), *Doctrine*, p. 75; Karamustafa, *Sufism*, p. 71.
48. Al-Kalābādhī, *Ta'arruf*, p. 105; Arberry (trans.), *Doctrine*, p. 76.
49. Al-Kalābādhī, *Ta'arruf*, p. 105.
50. Arberry (trans.), *Doctrine*, p. 107; al-Kalābādhī, *Ta'arruf*, p. 135.
51. Al-Kalābādhī, *Ta'arruf*, pp. 138–40; Arberry (trans.), *Doctrine*, pp. 110–12.
52. Arberry (trans.), *Doctrine*, p. 88; al-Kalābādhī, *Ta'arruf*, p. 116.
53. Al-Kalābādhī, *Ta'arruf*, p. 112.
54. Arberry (trans.), *Doctrine*, p. 95; al-Kalābādhī, *Ta'arruf*, p. 123.
55. Arberry (trans.), *Doctrine*, pp. 104–5; al-Kalābādhī, *Ta'arruf*, pp. 133–4.
56. Arberry (trans.), *Doctrine*, pp. 114–15; al-Kalābādhī, *Ta'arruf*, p. 143.
57. Al-Kalābādhī, *Ta'arruf*, p. 111.
58. Ibid., p. 112.
59. Ibid., p. 116.
60. Ibid., p. 117.
61. Ibid. (my trans.).
62. Ibid., p. 133.
63. Arberry (trans.), *Doctrine*, p. 104.
64. Wehr, *Dictionary*, p. 119 s.v. *jarada*.
65. Al-Kalābādhī, *Ta'arruf*, p. 133; Arberry (trans.), *Doctrine*, p. 104.
66. Arberry (trans.), *Doctrine*, p. 105; al-Kalābādhī, *Ta'arruf*, p. 133.
67. Al-Kalābādhī, *Ta'arruf*, p. 129; Arberry (trans.), *Doctrine*, p. 100.
68. Al-Kalābādhī, *Ta'arruf*, p. 130; Arberry (trans.), *Doctrine*, p. 102.
69. Al-Kalābādhī, *Ta'arruf*, p. 131.
70. Ibid., p. 132.
71. Arberry (trans.), *Doctrine*, p. 120; al-Kalābādhī, *Ta'arruf*, p. 147.
72. See al-Kalābādhī, *Ta'arruf*, pp. 147–57 and Baldick, *Mystical Islam*, p. 56.
73. Al-Kalābādhī, *Ta'arruf*, p. 148.
74. Ibid., p. 149.
75. Ibid., pp. 129–30.
76. Ibid., p. 160.
77. Arberry (trans.), *Doctrine*, pp. 135–7.
78. Al-Kalābādhī, *Ta'arruf*, p. 161.
79. See ibid., p. 162.
80. Schimmel, *Mystical Dimensions*, p. 143.
81. Baldick, *Mystical Islam*, p. 57.
82. Abū 'l Ḥasan 'Alī b. Muḥammad al-Daylamī, *Kitāb 'Aṭf al-Alif al-Ma'lūf 'alā 'l-Lām al-Ma'ṭūf*, ed. J. C. Vadet, Textes et Traductions d'Auteurs Orientaux, vol. 20 (Cairo:

Imprimerie de l'Institut Français d'Archéologie Orientale, 1962) [hereafter referred to as al-Daylamī, *Kitāb*]. See the remarks on this text by Bell and Al Shafie (trans.), *Treatise on Mystical Love* (cited below), p. lxix.

83. Abū 'l-Ḥasan 'Alī b. Muḥammad al-Daylamī, *A Treatise on Mystical Love*, trans. Joseph Norment Bell and Hassan Mahmood Abdul Latif Al Shafie, Journal of Arabic and Islamic Studies Monograph Series 1 (Edinburgh: Edinburgh University Press, 2005) [hereafter referred to as al-Daylamī, *Treatise*].
84. Jean-Claude Vadet (trans.), *Le Traité d'Amour Mystique d'Al-Daylami*, Hautes Études Orientales, vol. 13 (Geneva: Librairie Droz/Paris: Librairie Champion, 1980) [hereafter referred to as al-Daylamī, *Traité*].
85. Al-Daylamī, *Treatise*, p. 1.
86. Ibid. ('Introduction'), p. lvii.
87. Ibid., p. xi.
88. Ibid.
89. Ibid., *Treatise* ('Introduction'), pp. xii–xiii, xxi.
90. Ibid., p. xiv.
91. Ibid., pp. xii, xvi, xviii; al-Daylamī, *Traité* ('Introduction'), pp. 4–6.
92. See my article 'Majlis Readings in the Golden Age of Islam: Text and Intertext' in Robert Gleave (ed.), *Books and Bibliophiles: Studies in the Bio-Bibliography of the Muslim World in Honour of Paul Auchterlonie* [forthcoming].
93. Al-Daylamī, *Treatise*, p. 64; idem, *Kitāb*, p. 40, # 144, 81a–82b; idem, *Traité*, p. 83; see Plato, *Symposium* [dual Greek-English text], ed. with an introduction, trans. and commentary by C. J. Rowe, Aris and Phillips Greek Philosophy Series (Warminster: Aris & Phillips, 1998), 189–93: pp. 48–56 (Greek text), pp. 49–57 (English trans); al-Mas'ūdī, *Murūj al-Dhahab* (Beirut: Dār al-Andalus, 1966), vol. 3, p. 373.
94. Al-Daylamī, *Kitāb*, p. 3.
95. Ibid., p. 1; idem, *Treatise*, p. 2.
96. Idem, *Treatise*, p. 1; idem, *Kitāb*, p. 1.
97. Ibid.
98. Idem, *Treatise*, p. 1 n. 2.
99. Yusuf Ali (trans.), *Holy Qur'ān*, p. 393 n. 1,146.
100. Al-Daylamī, *Treatise*, pp. 13, 12; idem, *Kitāb*, p. 8.
101. Idem, *Kitāb*, p. 9; idem, *Treatise*, p. 13.
102. Idem, *Kitāb*, p. 86; idem, *Treatise*, p. 129.
103. Idem, *Kitāb*, p. 2; idem, *Treatise*, p. 3.
104. Ibid.
105. Idem, *Treatise*, p. 56; idem, *Kitāb*, p. 35.
106. Idem, *Kitāb*, pp. 51–2; idem, *Treatise*, pp. 81–2.
107. Idem, *Kitāb*, p. 34; idem, *Treatise*, p. 55.
108. Idem, *Treatise*, p. 82; idem, *Kitāb*, p. 52.
109. Idem, *Treatise*, p. 164; idem, *Kitāb*, p. 110.
110. Ibid.
111. Idem, *Kitāb*, p. 125; idem, *Treatise*, p. 185.
112. See, for example, Javad Nurbakhsh, *The Psychology of Sufism (Del wa Nafs)* (London and New York: Khaniqahi-Nimatullahi Publications, 1992), pp. 11–67.
113. See Wehr, *Dictionary*, p. 397 s.v. *sitr*.
114. See Farīd al-Dīn Muḥammad b. Ibrāhīm 'Aṭṭār, *Manṭiq al-Ṭayr*, 3rd edn (Tehran and Tabriz: Kitabfroushi-ye Tehran, 1968); idem, *The Conference of the Birds*, trans. C. S. Nott (London: Routledge & Kegan Paul, 1974).

115. Wehr, *Dictionary*, p. 156 s.v. *ḥijāb*.
116. Al-Daylamī, *Kitāb*, p. 125; idem, *Treatise*, p. 185.
117. Compare al-Mas'ūdī, *Murūj al-Dhahab*, vol. 3, pp. 373–4.
118. Al-Daylami, *Kitāb*, p. 85; idem, *Treatise*, p. 128.
119. Idem, *Kitāb*, p. 72; idem, *Treatise*, p. 109.
120. Idem, *Treatise*, p. 112; idem, *Kitāb*, p. 74.
121. Idem, *Treatise* ('Introduction'), p. lxi.
122. Idem, *Treatise*, p. 29; idem, *Kitāb*, p. 19.
123. Idem, *Kitāb*, p. 19.
124. Idem, *Treatise*, p. 28.
125. Idem, *Kitāb*, p. 49; idem, *Treatise*, p. 79.
126. Idem, *Treatise*, p. 27; idem, *Kitāb*, p. 18.
127. Idem, *Kitāb*, p. 45.
128. Idem, *Treatise*, p. 73.
129. Idem, *Kitāb*, p. 45; idem, *Treatise*, p. 73.
130. Idem, *Kitāb*, p. 46; idem, *Treatise*, p. 74.
131. Idem, *Treatise*, p. 74; idem, *Kitāb*, p. 46.
132. Ibid. (my emphases).
133. Idem, *Kitāb*, p. 46; idem, *Treatise*, p. 74.
134. Q.24:40, trans. Yusuf Ali, *Holy Qur'ān*, p. 910; al-Daylamī, *Kitāb*, p. 46; idem, *Treatise*, p. 74.
135. Yusuf Ali (trans.), *Holy Qur'ān*, p. 910 n. 3,015.
136. Al-Daylamī, *Kitāb*, p. 51; idem, *Treatise*, p. 81.
137. Idem, *Kitāb*, pp. 110–13; idem, *Treatise*, pp. 166–9.
138. Idem, *Kitāb*, p. 111; see idem, *Treatise*, pp. 166–7.
139. Idem, *Kitāb*, p. 112.
140. Idem, *Treatise*, p. 168; idem, *Kitāb*, p. 112.
141. Idem, *Kitāb*, p. 113; idem, *Treatise*, p. 169.
142. Idem, *Kitāb*, pp. 5–6; idem, *Treatise*, pp. 8–9.
143. Ibid.
144. Idem, *Kitāb*, p. 32; idem, *Treatise*, p. 51.
145. Idem, *Kitāb*, pp. 89–94; idem, *Treatise*, pp. 135–41.
146. Idem, *Kitāb*, p. 89; idem, *Treatise*, p. 135.
147. Idem, *Kitāb*, pp. 89–94; idem, *Treatise*, pp. 135–41.
148. Idem, *Kitāb*, p. 90; idem, *Treatise*, p. 135.
149. See below.
150. Al-Daylamī, *Kitāb*, p. 92; idem, *Treatise*, p. 138.
151. Idem, *Kitāb*, pp. 94–100; idem, *Treatise*, pp. 142–50.
152. Ibid.
153. Idem, *Kitāb*, p. 94; idem, *Treatise*, p. 142.
154. Ibid.
155. Idem, *Kitāb*, p. 90; idem, *Treatise*, p. 135.
156. See idem, *Kitāb*, p. 90; idem, *Treatise*, p. 135.
157. Idem, *Kitāb*, p. 2; idem, *Treatise*, p. 3.
158. Idem, *Treatise*, p. 3 n. 7.
159. Schimmel, *Mystical Dimensions*, p. 418.
160. Baldick, *Mystical Islam*, p. 57.
161. Al-Daylamī, *Treatise*, pp. 72–3; idem, *Kitāb*, p. 45.
162. Idem, *Kitāb*, pp. 36–7; idem, *Treatise*, p. 59.

163. Idem, *Kitāb*, p. 38; idem, *Treatise*, p. 62.
164. Idem, *Kitāb*, p. 125; idem, *Treatise*, p. 185.
165. Ibid.
166. Idem, *Treatise*, p. 185; idem, *Kitāb*, p. 125.
167. Idem, *Kitāb*, p. 125; idem, *Treatise*, p. 185.
168. Idem, *Treatise*, p. 187; idem, *Kitāb*, p. 126; see 'The Prophecy of Jeremias' in Knox (trans.), *Holy Bible: Old Testament*, pp. 680–731; see also 'The Lamentations of the Prophet Jeremias' in ibid., pp. 732–6.
169. G. Vajda, 'Irmiyā', *EI²*, vol. 4, p. 79.
170. Al-Daylamī, *Kitāb*, p. 126.
171. Idem, *Treatise*, p. 188 nn. 14, 15, 16.
172. See 2 Paralipomena 36:1–24 in Knox (trans.), *Holy Bible: Old Testament*, pp. 393–4.
173. See al-Daylamī, *Kitāb*, p. 126; idem, *Treatise*, p. 188.
174. Idem, *Kitāb*, p. 127; idem, *Treatise*, p. 188.
175. Ibid.
176. Idem, *Kitāb*, p. 127; idem, *Treatise*, p. 189.
177. See 4 Kings 2:11–12: Knox (trans.), *Holy Bible: Old Testament*, p. 312.
178. Al-Daylamī, *Treatise*, p. 189; idem, *Kitāb*, p. 128.
179. See H. Halm, 'Al-Ḳushayrī', *EI²*, vol. 5, pp. 526–7.
180. Karamustafa, *Sufism*, p. 97.
181. See Halm, 'Al-Ḳushayrī', p. 526; Abū 'l-Qāsim al-Qushayrī, *Al-Qushayri's Epistle on Sufism, Al-Risala al-qushayriyya fi 'ilm al-tasawwuf*, trans. Alexander D. Knysh, Great Books of Islamic Civilization (Reading: Garnet, 2007) [hereafter referred to as al-Qushayrī, *Epistle*], p. xxii [Translator's Introduction]. This Knysh translation omits the use of diacritics; see ibid., p. xx.
182. See e.g., Halm, 'Al-Ḳushayrī', p. 526; Jamil M. Abun-Nasr, *Muslim Communities of Grace: The Sufi Brotherhoods in Islamic Religious Life* (London: Hurst & Co., 2007), p. 47; Karamustafa, *Sufism*, p. 66; al-Qushayrī, *Epistle* [Translator's Introduction], p. xxii; Abū 'l-Qāsim al-Qushayrī, *Sufi Book of Spiritual Ascent (Al-Risala al-Qushayriyya)*, abridged trans. by Rabia Harris, ed. Laleh Bakhtiar (Chicago: ABC Group International/Kazi Publications, 1997) [hereafter referred to as al-Qushayrī, *Sufi Book*], pp. v, xiv.
183. E.g. Schimmel, *Mystical Dimensions*, pp. 88, 486; Baldick, *Mystical Islam*, p. 62.
184. Abun-Nasr, *Muslim Communities of Grace*, pp. 46–7.
185. Halm, 'Al-Ḳushayrī', p. 526 citing al-Subkī, *Ṭabaqāt*, ed. al-Ḥulw and al-Ṭanāhī (Cairo, 1386/1967), vol. 5, p. 158.
186. Halm, 'Al-Ḳushayrī', p. 526.
187. Baldick, *Mystical Islam*, p. 62.
188. Halm, 'Al-Ḳushayrī', p. 526; al-Qushayrī, *Sufi Book* [Translator's Introduction], p. v; idem, *Epistle* [Translator's Introduction], p. xxi.
189. For the alternative dates, see Schimmel, *Mystical Dimensions*, p. 477.
190. Al-Qushayrī, *Epistle* [Translator's Introduction], p. xxi; idem, *Sufi Book*, pp. viii–ix.
191. Ibid. See idem, *Sufi Book* [Translator's Introduction], p. ix.
192. See Halm, 'Al-Ḳushayrī', p. 526; al-Qushayrī, *Sufi Book*, pp. v–vi, iv–xv.
193. See Carole Hillenbrand, *Turkish Myth and Muslim Symbol: The Battle of Manzikert* (Edinburgh: Edinburgh University Press, 2007).
194. See al-Qushayrī, *Sufi Book* [Translator's Introduction], pp. x–xv.
195. Karamustafa, *Sufism*, p. 153.
196. Schimmel, *Mystical Dimensions*, p. 88; Halm, 'Al-Ḳushayrī', p. 527.
197. Karamustafa, *Sufism*, p. 98; see Annabel Keeler, 'Ṣūfī *tafsīr* as a Mirror: al-Qushayrī the

murshid in his *Laṭā'if al-ishārāt*', *Journal of Qur'anic Studies*, 8:1 (2006), p. 3.
198. Al-Qushayrī, *al-Risāla al-Qushayriyya fi 'Ilm al-Taṣawwuf* (Beirut: Dār al-Khayr, 1993) [hereafter referred to as al-Qushayrī, *Risāla*].
199. Al-Qushayrī, *Epistle* [Translator's Introduction], p. xxiv; see Abun-Nasr, *Muslim Communities of Grace*, p. 47.
200. Schimmel, *Mystical Dimensions*, p. 88; Keeler, 'Ṣūfī *tafsīr*', p. 3.
201. Halm, 'Al-Ḳushayrī', p. 527.
202. Ibid.
203. Baldick, *Mystical Islam*, p. 63.
204. Al-Qushayrī, *Risāla*, p. 38; idem, *Epistle*, p. 3.
205. Ibid.
206. Idem, *Epistle*, p. 4; idem, *Risāla*, p. 38. See Abun-Nasr, *Muslim Communities of Grace*, p. 79.
207. Karamustafa, *Sufism*, p. 98.
208. Abun-Nasr, *Muslim Communities of Grace*, p. 46.
209. Ibid., pp. 46–7.
210. Al-Ghazālī, *Letter to a Disciple/Ayyuhā 'l-Walad*, English–Arabic edn, trans. Tobias Mayer (Cambridge: Islamic Texts Society, 2005), pp. xx, 59 (Arabic text), p. 58 (English trans.).
211. Ibid.
212. Ibid., p. 11 (Arabic text), p. 10 (English trans.), see n. A on p. 10.
213. Ibid., p. 12 (English trans), see p. 13 for Arabic text.
214. Ibid.
215. Ibid., pp. xxx–xxxi ('Introduction'), p. 10 (English trans), p. 11 (Arabic text).
216. See J. N. D. Kelly, *Early Christian Doctrines*, 5th rev. edn (London: Adam & Charles Black, 1980), pp. 344–74.
217. Wehr, *Dictionary*, p. 718 s.v. *faḍl*.
218. Q.3:174, trans. Yusuf Ali, *Holy Qur'ān*, p. 168 (my emphases).
219. Baldick, *Mystical Islam*, p. 63.
220. Karamustafa, *Sufism*, pp. 98–9; al-Qushayrī, *Epistle*, p. xxv (Translator's Introduction).
221. Ibid.
222. Ibid., p. 99; see also pp. 102, 104, 106.
223. See Keeler, 'Ṣūfī *tafsīr*', pp. 2–3.
224. E.g. al-Qushayrī, *Risāla*, p. 75.
225. E.g. ibid., p. 74.
226. E.g. ibid.
227. E.g. ibid., p. 75.
228. E.g. ibid., p. 189.
229. E.g. ibid., pp. 75, 180.
230. E.g. ibid., p. 75.
231. Ibid.; see also idem, *Epistle*, p. 97.
232. Idem, *Epistle*, p. 98; idem, *Risāla*, p. 75.
233. Idem, *Risāla*, p. 189; idem, *Epistle*, p. 203.
234. Idem, *Risāla*, p. 180; idem, *Epistle*, pp. 194–5.
235. Idem, *Risāla*, p. 179; idem, *Epistle*, p. 193.
236. See Q.7:143 cited by al-Qushayrī, *Risāla*, p. 72 and the ḥadīth on p. 75.
237. Al-Qushayrī, *Risāla*, p. 74.
238. Idem, *Epistle*, p. 234; idem, *Risāla*, p. 316.
239. Idem, *Risāla*, pp. 67–9.

240. Idem, *Epistle*, p. 91; idem, *Risāla*, p. 69.
241. Idem, *Risāla*, pp. 73–4.
242. Ibid., pp. 115–19.
243. Ibid., pp. 144–51.
244. Ibid., pp. 151–4.
245. Idem, *Epistle*, p. 98; idem, *Risāla*, p. 75.
246. Idem, *Epistle*, p. 91; idem, *Risāla*, p. 69. See Baldick's comments on this in *Mystical Islam*, p. 63.
247. Al-Qushayrī, *Epistle*, pp. 271–2; idem, *Risāla*, p. 262.
248. Schimmel, *Mystical Dimensions*, p. 173 n. 71.
249. For the Arabic text with German translation, see Fritz Meier (ed.), 'Qušayrī's Tartīb as-suluk', *Oriens*, 16 (1963), pp. 1–39 cited in Schimmel, *Mystical Dimensions*, p. 173 n. 71, and Halm, 'Al-Ḳushayrī', p. 527.
250. Schimmel, *Mystical Dimensions*, p. 173.
251. Al-Qushayrī, *Risāla*, pp. 221–6.
252. Q.33:41; al-Qushayrī, *Risāla*, p. 221.
253. Al-Qushayrī, *Risāla*, p. 221.
254. See Netton, *Ṣūfī Ritual*, p. 47.
255. Ibid.
256. Al-Qushayrī, *Risāla*, p. 223.
257. Ibid., p. 226.
258. Ibid., p. 223.
259. Idem, *Epistle*, p. 234.
260. Idem, *Risāla*, pp. 58–61. For concise definitions of *basṭ* and *qabḍ*, see idem, *Epistle*, pp. 417, 422 (Glossary).
261. Idem, *Risāla*, pp. 58–61.
262. For al-Qushayrī's own biography of him, see al-Qushayrī, *Epistle*, pp. 43–5.
263. Idem, *Risāla*, pp. 59–60.
264. Idem, *Epistle*, p. 408 (my emphases); idem, *Risāla*, p. 383.
265. Idem, *Epistle*, p. 232; idem, *Risāla*, p. 221.
266. Idem, *Risāla*, p. 98.
267. Ibid., p. 57.
268. Ibid., p. 56.
269. Idem, *Epistle*, pp. 103–5; idem, *Risāla*, pp. 80–2.
270. Trans. Knysh in al-Qushayrī, *Epistle*, p. 103; see idem, *Risāla*, p. 80.
271. See, for example, al-Qushayrī, *Risāla*, p. 318.
272. Ibid., pp. 317–29.
273. Ibid., pp. 311–17.
274. Idem, *Epistle*, p. 319.
275. Idem, *Risāla*, pp. 329–33.
276. Ibid., p. 332.
277. Ibid., p. 56.
278. See al-Mas'ūdī, *Murūj al-Dhahab*, vol. 3, p. 373.
279. Al-Qushayrī, *Risāla*, p. 307.
280. Ibid., p. 270.
281. Ibid., p. 305.
282. See ibid., pp. 80–2.
283. See ibid., p. 324.
284. Ibid., p. 333.

285. See Baldick, *Mystical Islam*, p. 63; see al-Qushayrī, *Epistle*, pp. 333, 411.
286. Al-Qushayrī, *Risāla*, p. 318.
287. See ibid.
288. Ibid., p. 64.
289. Ibid., p. 65.
290. Ibid., p. 67.
291. Ibid., p. 61.
292. Idem, *Epistle*, p. 87; idem, *Risāla*, p. 65.
293. Idem, *Risāla*, p. 66.
294. Ibid.; idem, *Epistle*, p. 88.
295. Idem, *Risāla*, p. 68.
296. Ibid., p. 302.
297. E.g. ibid., pp. 405, 104, 166.
298. Q.18:65–82. See al-Qushayrī, *Risāla*, pp. 333, 357.
299. See al-Qushayrī, *Epistle*, p. 385.
300. Ibid., p. 391.
301. Ibid., p. 387.
302. Idem, *Risāla*, p. 405.
303. Ibid., p. 394.
304. Q.18:65–82.
305. Al-Qushayrī, *Risāla*, p. 357; idem, *Epistle*, p. 363 and n. 711, where 'some Muslim scholars consider al-Khaḍir to be a prophet'.
306. Baldick, *Mystical Islam*, p. 63; Karamustafa, *Sufism*, pp. 116–19; al-Qushayrī, '*Al-Waṣiyya li-l-Murīdīn*' in his *Risāla*, pp. 378–85.
307. Q.18:65–82; Karamustafa, *Sufism*, pp. 118–19. See al-Qushayrī, *Risāla*, pp. 333–4.
308. Karamustafa, *Sufism*, p. 119.
309. See Halm, 'Al-Ḳushayrī', p. 526; al-Qushayrī, *Epistle* [Translator's Introduction], p. xxi; idem, *Sufi Book*, pp. vii–viii.
310. See al-Qushayrī, *Sufi Book* [Translator's Introduction], pp. viii–ix; idem, *Epistle* [Translator's Introduction], p. xxi.
311. Idem, *Sufi Book* [Translator's Introduction], p. viii.
312. Schimmel, *Mystical Dimensions*, p. 246; see al-Qushayrī, *Risāla*, pp. 226–31.
313. Al-Qushayrī, *Epistle*, p. 237.
314. Karamustafa, *Sufism*, p. 66.
315. Al-Qushayrī, *Risāla*, p. 226.
316. Ibid., p. 227.
317. Ibid.
318. Ibid.
319. Ibid., p. 229.
320. Ibid.
321. Wehr, *Dictionary*, p. 704 s.v. *firāsa*.
322. Al-Qushayrī, *Epistle*, p. 242; see idem, *Risāla*, pp. 231–41.
323. Al-Qushayrī, *Epistle*, p. 242; see idem, *Risāla*, p. 231.
324. Al-Qushayrī, *Risāla*, pp. 231, 232.
325. Ibid., p. 235.
326. William Harmless SJ, *Mystics* (Oxford: Oxford University Press, 2008).
327. Ibid., pp. xiii, 159–88, 189–223.
328. See ibid., pp. xi–xii.
329. Ibid., p. 135.

330. Ibid., p. 41.
331. Ibid., p. 59.
332. Ibid., p. 79.
333. Ibid., p. 107.
334. Ibid., p. 19.
335. See *The Varieties of Religious Experience: a Study in Human Nature* [Being the Gifford Lectures on Natural Religion Delivered at Edinburgh in 1901–1902] (London: Folio Society, 2008).
336. Harmless, *Mystics*, p. 17.
337. Ibid., pp. xii–xiii.
338. Ibid., p. 185.
339. Ibid., p. 254.
340. See, for example, ibid., pp. xiii, 186, 222–3.
341. Ibid., p. 223.
342. Ibid., p. 186.
343. See ibid., pp. 255–357; Steven Katz (ed.), *Mysticism and Philosophical Analysis* (New York: Oxford University Press, 1979); idem (ed.), *Mysticism and Language* (New York: Oxford University Press, 1992); idem (ed.), *Mysticism and Religious Traditions* (New York: Oxford University Press, 1983); idem (ed.), *Mysticism and Sacred Scriptures* (New York: Oxford University Press, 2000).
344. See Harmless, *Mystics*, p. 298 n. 4.
345. Ibid., p. 17.
346. See ibid., p. 226.
347. Lucy Beckett, 'The mind's journey': [Review of] Harmless, *Mystics*, in *Times Literary Supplement*, 8 August 2008, p. 27. See also Edward Howells, [Review of] Harmless, *Mystics*, in *Eckhart Review*, no. 18 (2009), pp. 70–2.
348. Beckett, 'The mind's journey', p. 27.
349. See Howell's critique in his Review of Harmless, *Mystics*, in *Eckhart Review*, pp. 71–2.
350. Francis de Sales, *Philothea, or An Introduction to the Devout Life* (Rockford, IL: Tan Books & Publishers, 1994: paperback repr. of New York: Joseph Wagner, 1923/ Philadelphia: Peter Reilly Co., 1942), back cover. For the original French text, see *Introduction à la vie dévote* in Saint François de Sales, *Oeuvres*, ed. André Ravier and Roger Devos, Bibliothèque de la Pléiade (Paris: Éditions Gallimard, 1969), pp. 1–317.
351. John C. Reville, 'Introduction' to De Sales, *Philothea*, pp. xii–xiii.
352. Ibid., p. xvi.
353. See above n. 45.
354. See De Sales, *Philothea*, pp. 3–4; idem, *Introduction*, p. 33.
355. Idem, *Philothea*, p. 230; idem, *Introduction*, pp. 236–7.
356. See John Bunyan, *The Pilgrim's Progress*, ed. W. R. Owens, Oxford World's Classics (Oxford: Oxford University Press, 2003).
357. De Sales, *Philothea*, pp. 271–9, esp. p. 276; idem, *Introduction*, pp. 276–83, esp. p. 280.
358. Idem, *Philothea*, pp. 279–80; idem, *Introduction*, p. 283.
359. Idem, *Philothea*, p. 285; idem, *Introduction*, p. 288.
360. Idem, *Philothea*, pp. 287–8; idem, *Introduction*, p. 290.
361. Idem, *Philothea*, pp. 311–12; idem, *Introduction*, pp. 311–12.
362. Idem, *Philothea*, pp. 9–12; idem, *Introduction*, pp. 38–40.
363. Farīd al-Dīn 'Aṭṭār, *The Conference of the Birds (Mantiq ut-Tair)*, trans. C. S. Nott (London: Routledge & Kegan Paul, 1974), p. 46. For the original Persian text, see *Manṭiq al-Ṭayr*, p. 106.

364. Najīb Maḥfūẓ, *Riḥlat Ibn Faṭṭūma* (Cairo: Dār Miṣr li 'l-Ṭibā'a, n.d.); trans. Denys Johnson-Davies, *Naguib Mahfouz: The Journey of Ibn Fattouma* (New York and London: Doubleday, 1992).
365. Louis-Marie de Montfort, *Treatise on the True Devotion to the Blessed Virgin* (4th edn, England: Fathers of the Company of Mary, 1957); see also Gabriel Denis, *The Reign of Jesus Through Mary* (6th edn, England: Montfort Fathers, [1958]).
366. See C. Bernard Ruffin, *Padre Pio: The True Story*, rev. and expanded edn (Huntington, IN: Our Sunday Visitor Publishing Division, 1991).
367. Ibid., pp. 103–15.
368. Ibid., pp. 155, 360, 370. Much of Padre Pio's intense mystical spirituality is laid bare in three thick volumes of letters: Padre Pio of Pietrelcina, *Letters, Volume 1: Correspondence with His Spiritual Directors (1910–1922)*, ed. Melchiorre of Pobladura and Alessandro of Ripabottoni; English version ed. Gerardo di Flumeri (2nd edn, San Giovanni Rotondo: Edizioni/Editions Pio da Pietrelcina, 1984); idem, *Letters, Volume 2: Correspondence with Raffaelina Cerase, Noblewoman (1914–1915)*, ed. Melchiorre of Pobladura and Alessandro of Ripabottoni; English version ed. Gerardo di Flumeri (3rd edn, San Giovanni Rotondo: Edizioni/Editions Padre Pio da Pietrelcina, 2002); idem, *Letters, Volume 3: Correspondence with his Spiritual Daughters (1915–1923)*, ed. Melchiorre of Pobladura and Alessandro of Ripabottoni; English version, 2nd edn ed. Gerardo di Flumeri (San Giovanni Rotondo: Edizioni/Editions Padre Pio da Pietrelcina, 2001).
369. Hans Urs Von Balthasar, *First Glance at Adrienne Von Speyr*, trans. Antje Lawry and Sergia Englund (San Francisco: Ignatius Press, 1986), p. 94.
370. See, for example, ibid., pp. 21, 24–6, 44. For Von Speyr's theology and spirituality, see, for example, her *Handmaid of the Lord*, trans. E. A. Nelson (San Francisco: Ignatius Press, 1985); idem, *The World of Prayer*, trans. Graham Harrison (San Francisco: Ignatius Press, 1985); idem, *Mary in the Redemption*, trans. Helena M. Tomko (San Francisco: Ignatius Press, 2003); idem, *The Mystery of Death*, trans. Graham Harrison (San Francisco: Ignatius Press, 1988).
371. Nicholas Watson and Jacqueline Jenkins (eds), *The Writings of Julian of Norwich: A Vision Showed to a Devout Woman and A Revelation of Love* [dual English–Middle English edn], Medieval Women: Texts and Contexts, vol. 5 (Turnhout: Brepols, 2006) [hereafter referred to as Watson and Jenkins (eds), *Writings*], p. ix ('Preface').
372. Andrea Janelle Dickens, *The Female Mystic: Great Women Thinkers of the Middle Ages*, International Library of Historical Studies, vol. 60 (London and New York: I. B. Tauris, 2009), p. 133.
373. Elizabeth Ruth Obbard (ed.), *Medieval Women Mystics* (rev. edn, Hyde Park, NY: New City Press, 2007), p. 119.
374. Ibid.
375. Carmel Bendon Davis, *Mysticism and Space: Space and Spatiality in the Works of Richard Rolle, The Cloud of Unknowing Author, and Julian of Norwich* (Washington, DC: The Catholic University of America Press, 2008), p. 214; see also Julian of Norwich, *Revelations of Divine Love*, trans. Clifton Wolters (Harmondsworth: Penguin Books, 1966, 1984) [hereafter referred to as Julian, *Revelations*/Wolters], p. 14 ('Introduction'); Denise N. Baker (ed.), *Julian of Norwich: Showings: Authoritative Text, Contexts, Criticism*, A Norton Critical Edition (New York and London: W. W. Norton & Co., 2005) [hereafter referred to as Julian, *Showings*/Baker], p. ix ('Introduction'); Denise Nowakowski Baker, *Julian of Norwich's Showings: From Vision to Book* (Princeton, NJ: Princeton University Press, 1997), p. 3.
376. Dr Sarah Salih of King's College, University of London (sarah.salih@kcl.ac.uk) presented

a fascinating list of 'a selection of fictions featuring Julian of Norwich or aspects of her' in a paper entitled 'Julian's Afterlives' at the International Medieval Congress, University of Leeds on 7 July 2008. From her list, we note, *inter alia*, Dana Bagshaw, *Cell Talk: A Duologue between Julian of Norwich and Margery of Kempe* (London: Radius, 2002); James Janda, *Julian: A Play Based on the Life of Julian of Norwich* (New York: The Seabury Press, 1984); Ralph Milton, *Julian's Cell: The Earthly Story of Julian of Norwich* (Kelowna, BC: Northstone, 2002); and Jack Pantaleo, *Mother Julian and the Gentle Vampire* (Roseville: Dry Bones Press, 1999). In the same list, Dr Salih suggests that three of Iris Murdoch's novels were influenced or inspired by the story of Julian (*The Bell*, London: Chatto & Windus, 1958; *The Black Prince*, London: Chatto & Windus, 1973; *Nuns and Soldiers*, London: Chatto & Windus, 1980).

377. Christopher Abbott, *Julian of Norwich: Autobiography and Theology*, Studies in Medieval Mysticism, vol. 2 (Cambridge D. S. Brewer, 1999).
378. Dickens, *Female Mystic*, p. 146.
379. Ibid., p. 133.
380. Watson and Jenkins (eds), *Writings*, p. ix ('Preface').
381. Abbott, *Julian of Norwich*, p. 46.
382. Julian of Norwich, *A Revelation of Love*, ed. Marion Glasscoe (rev. edn, Exeter: University of Exeter Press, 2003), p. xix.
383. Obbard (ed.), *Medieval Women Mystics*, p. 119.
384. Julian of Norwich, *Revelations of Divine Love (Short Text and Long Text)*, trans. Elizabeth Spearing, intro. and notes by A. C. Spearing (London: Penguin Books, 1998) [hereafter referred to as Julian, *Revelations*/Spearing], p. x ('Introduction').
385. Obbard (ed.), *Medieval Women Mystics*, pp. 119–20; Dickens, *Female Mystics*, p. 135.
386. Obbard (ed.), *Medieval Women Mystics*, p. 119 says '30 Years War'!
387. Gail Alva Berkeley, *Julian of Norwich: The Rhetoric of Revelation*, PhD Diss., Princeton University, 1982, p. 315.
388. See Obbard (ed.), *Medieval Women Mystics*, p. 7.
389. See Dickens, *Female Mystics*, p. 1.
390. Von Balthasar, *First Glance*, pp. 90–1.
391. Ibid., p. 92; see Book of the Apocalypse 11:19–12:3.
392. See Baker, *Julian of Norwich's Showings: From Vision to Book*, p. 15. For Julian's own account, in trans., see Julian, *Revelations*/Spearing, pp. 5ff. (short text), 44ff. (long text); for the original text, see Watson and Jenkins (eds), *Writings*, pp. 65ff. (short text), 129ff. (long text).
393. Watson and Jenkins (eds), *Writings*, p. 63 (short text), see also p. 125 (long text); Julian, *Revelations*/Spearing, pp. 3, 42.
394. Dickens, *Female Mystic*, p. 133.
395. Ibid., p. 145.
396. See ibid., p. 135.
397. Berkeley, *Julian of Norwich*, p. 135.
398. Davis, *Mysticism and Space*, p. 219.
399. Ibid., p. 226; see Watson and Jenkins (eds), *Writings*, pp. 65–7 (short text), 131–3 (long text); Julian, *Revelations*/Spearing, pp. 6 (short text), 45 (long text).
400. Trans. of *behovely* in Julian, *Revelations*/Spearing, p. 79.
401. See Julian, *Revelations*/Spearing, pp. 1, 39; idem, *Revelations*/Wolters, p. 13.
402. Watson and Jenkins (eds), *Writings*, p. 209.
403. Obbard (ed.), *Medieval Women Mystics*, p. 120; Watson and Jenkins (eds), *Writings*, passim; Julian, *Revelations*/Spearing, passim; idem, *Revelations*/Wolters, passim, esp. pp.

28–9. In ch. 1 of the 'long text' Julian outlines the sixteen revelations or 'showings': see Watson and Jenkins (eds), *Writings*, pp. 123–5; Julian, *Revelations*/Spearing, pp. 41–2; idem, *Revelations*/Wolters, pp. 61–3 (where the sixteen 'showings' are usefully linked by chapter reference and page to the chapters). See also Baker (ed.), *Julian of Norwich: Showings: Authoritative Text, Contexts and Criticism*, pp. 8–125, which also links the sixteen revelations to the eighty-six chapters by means of page headings.

404. See ibid.
405. Obbard (ed.), *Medieval Women Mystics*, p. 120.
406. See Watson and Jenkins (eds), *Writings*, pp. 1, 61, 121.
407. See, for example, the two Penguin editions by Wolters and Spearing which we have frequently cited.
408. Watson and Jenkins (eds), *Writings*, p. 1.
409. Dickens, *Female Mystic*, p. 136; see also Baker, *Julian of Norwich's Showings: From Vision to Book*, p. 140.
410. Obbard (ed.), *Medieval Women Mystics*, p. 123.
411. Julian, *Revelations*/Spearing, p. 6.
412. Watson and Jenkins (eds), *Writings*, p. 351, See Julian, *Revelations*/Wolters, pp. 30, 191; idem, *Revelations*/Spearing, p. 161.
413. Julian, *Revelations*/Wolters, p. 191.
414. Ibid., p. 30.
415. Ibid., pp. 30–1.
416. See Watson and Jenkins (eds), *Writings*, p. 323; Julian, *Revelations*/Spearing, p. 148.
417. Baker, *Julian of Norwich's Showings: From Vision to Book*, p. 107; Watson and Jackson (eds), *Writings*, p. 301.
418. Watson and Jackson (eds), *Writings*, p. 155.
419. Julian, *Revelations*/Spearing, p. 54.
420. Watson and Jenkins (eds), *Writings*, pp. 125, ix.
421. Ibid., p. 7.
422. Ibid., p. ix ('Preface').
423. Baker, *Julian of Norwich's Showings: From Vision to Book*, pp. 8–11.
424. Ibid., p. 11.
425. Ibid., p. 9.
426. Ibid., p. 11. See also Julian, *Revelations*/Wolters, p. 19; Berkeley, *Julian of Norwich*, pp. 128–9.
427. Trans. Spearing in Julian, *Revelations*/Spearing, p. 20; see, for original text, Watson and Jenkins (eds), *Writings*, p. 91.
428. See above n. 365.
429. (My emphases.) Trans. Spearing in Julian, *Revelations*/Spearing, p. 105; see, for the original text, Watson and Jenkins (eds), *Writings*, p. 259. For an understanding of contemplation and meditation in the age of Julian, see Baker, *Julian of Norwich's Showings: From Vision to Book*, pp. 28–35, esp. p. 29.
430. Julian, *Revelations*/Wolters, pp. 39–40 ('Introduction').
431. E.g. see Frances Beer, *Julian of Norwich: Revelations of Divine Love [and] The Motherhood of God*, Library of Medieval Women (Cambridge: D. S. Brewer, 1998), p. 16 n. 10.
432. See Watson and Jenkins (eds), *Writings*, pp. 175, 247.
433. Trans. Spearing in Julian, *Revelations*/Spearing, p. 177; for the original text, see Watson and Jenkins (eds), *Writings*, p. 377.
434. Watson and Jenkins (eds), *Writings*, pp. 331–5; see Julian, *Revelations*/Spearing, pp. 151–3.
435. Watson and Jenkins (eds), *Writings*, p. 161.

436. Ibid.
437. Ibid., p. 243.
438. (My emphases.) Julian, *Revelations*/Spearing, p. 126; for the original text, see Watson and Jenkins (eds), *Writings*, p. 291.
439. See, for example, Obbard (ed.), *Medieval Women Mystics*, p. 120.
440. See ibid., p. 9.
441. Ibid., p. 10.
442. See, for example, Watson and Jenkins (eds), *Writings*, pp. 311–17.
443. *Fecisti nos ad te et inquietum est cor nostrum, donec requiescat in te*: Augustine, *Confessions, Books 1–8* [dual Latin–English edn], trans. William Watts, The Loeb Classical Library (Cambridge, MA/London: Harvard University Press, repr. 1999), bk 1:1, pp. 2 (Latin), 3 (English trans.). See also Augustine, *Confessions*, trans. Henry Chadwick (Oxford: Oxford University Press, 1991), bk 1:1, p. 4.
444. Watson and Jenkins (eds), *Writings*, pp. 141, 207.
445. Ibid., p. 379.
446. Ibid.
447. Julian, *Revelations*/Wolters, p. 32; Watson and Jenkins (eds), *Writings*, pp. 379–81.
448. Watson and Jenkins (eds), *Writings*, p. 379 (my emphases).
449. Julian, *Revelations*/Spearing, p. 179.
450. Davis, *Mysticism and Space*, p. 247.
451. Watson and Jenkins (eds), *Writings*, p. 69.
452. Julian, *Revelations*/Spearing, p. 81.
453. Watson and Jenkins (eds), *Writings*, p. 213.
454. (My emphases.) Julian, *Revelations*/Spearing, p. 130. For the original text, see Watson and Jenkins (eds), *Writings*, p. 297.
455. Abbott, *Julian of Norwich*, p. 115.
456. Watson and Jenkins (eds), *Writings*, p. 297; Abbott, *Julian of Norwich*, p. 115.
457. Julian, *Revelations*/Spearing, p. 130; for the original text, see Watson and Jenkins (eds), *Writings*, p. 297.
458. Abbott, *Julian of Norwich*, p. 115.
459. Watson and Jenkins (eds), *Writings*, p. 159 (my emphases).
460. Ibid.
461. Ibid., p. 279. For this very important Julianic parable, see Julian of Norwich, *Showing of Love*, trans. Julian Botton Holloway (Collegeville, MN: Liturgical Press, 2003), p. xvi; Abbott, *Julian of Norwich*, pp. 90–104; Julian, *Revelations*/Spearing, pp. xxviii–xxxi; Baker, *Julian of Norwich's Showings: From Vision to Book*, pp. 83–106.
462. Julian, *Revelations*/Spearing, p. 118.
463. Watson and Jenkins (eds), *Writings*, p. 281; Julian, *Revelations*/Spearing, p. 119.
464. Watson and Jenkins (eds), *Writings*, pp. 281, 283; Julian, *Revelations*/Spearing, pp. 120–1.
465. Watson and Jenkins (eds), *Writings*, p. 285.
466. Julian, *Revelations*/Spearing, p. 122; Watson and Jenkins (eds), *Writings*, p. 285.
467. Julian, *Revelations*/Spearing, p. 124.
468. Watson and Jenkins (eds), *Writings*, p. 287.
469. Holloway (*Julian of Norwich: Showing of Love*, p. xvii) draws attention to 'the iconography of the Virgin' at Avignon and in the Wilton Diptych where the Virgin is clad in blue.
470. For various editions see: Thomas à Kempis, *The Imitation of Christ* (London: Burns & Oates, n.d.); idem, *The Imitation of Christ*, trans. with an intro. by Leo Sherley-Price (London: Penguin Books, 1952, repr. 1980); idem, *The Imitation of Christ*, trans. Anthony Hoskins (London: Folio Society, 2008: rev. edn of Oxford: Oxford University Press, 1903

edn). *Textual references below are made to the Penguin edn, which is the most accessible.*
471. *Imitation*, trans. Sherley-Price, p. 20 ('Introduction').
472. Ibid., pp. 22–3.
473. Dennis J. Billy, *The Imitation of Christ [of] Thomas à Kempis: A Spiritual Commentary and Reader's Guide*, Christian Classics (Notre Dame, IN: Ave Maria Press, 2005) [hereafter referred to as Billy, *Commentary*], p. 6.
474. See Samuel Kettlewell, *Thomas à Kempis and the Brothers of Common Life* (London: Kegan Paul, Trench & Co., 1885; repr. Whitefish, MT: Kessinger Publishing, Rare Reprints, n.d.), p. v ('Preface') and passim.
475. These details of his life are taken from *Imitation*, trans. Sherley-Price, pp. 20–3 ('Introduction'); Vincent Scully, 'Thomas à Kempis' in *The Catholic Encyclopedia*, vol. 14 (New York: Robert Appleton Company, 1912); Billy, *Commentary*, pp. 6–7; Howard G. Hageman, 'Thomas à Kempis' in Mircea Eliade (ed.-in-chief), *The Encyclopedia of Religion* (New York: Macmillan/London: Collier Macmillan, 1987), vol. 14, p. 484; P. Mulhern, 'Thomas à Kempis' in Thomas Carson and Joann Cerrito (project eds), *New Catholic Encyclopedia* (2nd edn, Detroit and New York: Thomson-Gale, in assoc. with Catholic University of America, Washington, DC, 2003), vol. 14, pp. 12–13.
476. *Imitation*, trans. Sherley-Price, p. 23 ['Introduction'].
477. Ibid., p. 25.
478. Ibid. See also the remarks of Billy, *Commentary*, p. 8.
479. See Robert Wilkins, *Death: A History of Man's Obsessions and Fears* (New York: Barnes & Noble Books, 1996), p. 16.
480. See *Imitation*, trans. Sherley-Price, bk 1, ch. 5, p. 33; see also p. 23; Billy, *Commentary*, p. 8.
481. *Imitation*, trans. Sherley-Price, p. 22.
482. Billy, *Commentary*, p. 8.
483. Thomas à Kempis, *Imitation*, Folio edn, p. iv (back of title page).
484. See John Wesley, 'Introduction' in ibid., p. xv.
485. Billy, *Commentary*, p. 268.
486. Kettlewell, *Thomas à Kempis*, p. vi.
487. For the fall of Constantinople, see, *inter alia*, John Freely, *Istanbul: The Imperial City* (London: Viking, Penguin Books, 1996), pp. 164–78; Lord Kinross, *The Ottoman Empire* (London: The Folio Society, 2003; repr. of 1977 edn of London: Jonathan Cape), pp. 85–98.
488. See Beer, *Julian of Norwich: Revelations of Divine Love*, p. 5.
489. See Thomas à Kempis, *Imitation*, trans. Sherley-Price, pp. 14–16 ('Introduction'); idem, *Imitation* (London: Burns & Oates, n.d.), pp. 598, 602, 605; Billy, *Commentary*, pp. 8, 11, 19, 73, 101.
490. Billy, *Commentary*, p. 19.
491. Thomas à Kempis, *Imitation*, trans. Sherley-Price, p. 27.
492. *Imitation*, Folio edn, p. 1.
493. Billy, *Commentary*, p. 19.
494. Ibid., p. 73.
495. Thomas à Kempis, *Imitation*, trans. Sherley-Price, p. 67.
496. Ibid., Folio edn, p. 53.
497. Billy, *Commentary*, p. 73.
498. Ibid., p. 101.
499. Thomas à Kempis, *Imitation*, trans. Sherley-Price, p. 91.
500. Ibid., Folio edn, p. 83.

501. Billy, *Commentary*, p. 101.
502. Thomas à Kempis, *Imitation*, trans. Sherley-Price, p. 183.
503. Idem, Folio edn, p. 203.
504. Ibid., p. 225.
505. Kettlewell, *Thomas à Kempis*, p. 279, see also pp. 281–2.
506. (My emphases.) Thomas à Kempis, *Imitation*, trans. Sherley-Price, p. 11 ('Introduction').
507. Ibid., p. 12.
508. See Billy, *Commentary*, pp. 6–7.
509. Ibid., p. 7 (my emphases).
510. Ibid., p. 11.
511. Ibid., p. 17.
512. *Imitation*, trans. Sherley-Price, bk 1, ch. 1, p. 27 citing John 8:12.
513. Ibid., p. 15 ('Introduction').
514. Ibid., bk 3, ch. 23, p. 125.
515. See Kettlewell, *Thomas à Kempis*, p. 367; see Thomas à Kempis, *Imitation*, trans. Sherley-Price, bk 3, ch. 8, pp. 103–4; bk 4, Ch. 15, pp. 211–13.
516. For a summary, see Thomas à Kempis, *Imitation* (London: Burns & Oates, n.d.), pp. 622–4.
517. Idem, *Imitation*, trans. Sherley-Price, bk 2, ch. 11, pp. 83–4.
518. Ibid., bk. 2, ch.12, p. 84.
519. Ibid., bk. 3, ch. 32, p. 137.
520. Billy, *Commentary*, p. 11.
521. Ibid.
522. *Imitation*, trans. Sherley-Price, p. 91.
523. Ibid., pp. 92–3.
524. Ibid., bk 4, ch. 17, p. 215.
525. *Imitation* (London: Burns & Oates, n.d.), pp. 605–6.
526. Idem, *Imitation*, trans. Sherley-Price, p. 78.
527. Billy, *Commentary*, p. 89.
528. Ibid., p. 88.
529. Thomas à Kempis, *Imitation*, trans. Sherley-Price, bk 2, ch. 9, p. 78.
530. See Wesley, 'Introduction' in Thomas à Kempis, *Imitation*, Folio Society edn, pp. xv–xvi, xviii; idem, *Imitation* (London: Burns & Oates, n.d.), pp. 597–8, 606, 620, 622–6.
531. Thomas à Kempis, *Imitation*, trans. Sherley-Price, pp. 124–5.
532. Ibid., bk 2, ch. 7, p. 75; Kettlewell, *Thomas à Kempis*, p. 18.
533. *Imitation*, trans. Sherley-Price, bk 3, ch. 6, p. 99.
534. Ibid., bk 4, ch. 17, p. 214.
535. Wesley, 'Introduction' in *Imitation*, Folio edn, p. xvii; see also p. xxiii.
536. *Imitation*, trans. Sherley-Price, pp. 97–8.
537. Ibid., bk 4, ch.2, p. 189.
538. See bk 1, ch. 11 and bk 3, ch. 31 cited in *Imitation* (London: Burns & Oates, n.d.), pp. 605–6.
539. Ibid.
540. *Imitation*, trans. Sherley-Price, bk 1, ch. 11, p. 38; see also bk 3, ch. 31 in ibid., p. 136.
541. Ibid., pp. 209–10.
542. Ibid., p. 13; see pp. 11–12, 16 ('Introduction').
543. See above n. 45.
544. *Imitation*, trans. Sherley-Price, bk 3, ch. 9, p. 105.
545. See Q.2:156.
546. For example, see Plotinus, *Enneads*, III.8.7 in A. H. Armstrong (ed. and trans.), *Plotinus:*

Ennead III [dual Greek–English text], The Loeb Classical Library (Cambridge, MA/ London: Harvard University Press, 1993), pp. 380, 382, 384 (Greek text), 381, 383, 385 (English trans.).

547. *Imitation*, trans. Sherley-Price, bk 3, ch. 21, p. 120.
548. See ibid., p. 12 ('Introduction').
549. Ibid., bk. 2, ch. 7, p. 76.
550. Ibid., bk. 2, ch. 9, p. 80.
551. Cited in *The Tablet*, 13 October 2007, p. 23; see also Peter Bourne, *St Teresa's Castle of the Soul: A Study of the Interior Castle* (Long Beach, CA: Wenzel Press, 1995), p. 14.
552. A Benedictine, *Mediaeval Mystical Tradition*, p. 154.
553. Dickens, *Female Mystic*, p. 184.
554. A Discalced Carmelite (trans.), *The Way of Perfection* (London: Baronius Press, 2006); repr. of Glasgow: Sands & Co., 1942 edn [hereafter referred to as Teresa, *Perfection*]. For the original Spanish text, see Teresa de Jesús, *Camino de Perfección*, ed. Daniel de Pablo Maroto, 7th edn, Logos vol. 58 (Madrid: Editorial de Espiritualidad, 2009) [hereafter referred to as Teresa, *Perfección*].
555. Teresa of Ávila, *The Interior Castle* (London: HarperCollins, Fount Paperbacks, 1995), trans. Anon. Stanbrook Benedictine nuns, rev. by Benedict Zimmerman OCD, intro. by Robert van de Weyer [hereafter referred to as Teresa, *Interior Castle*]; for the original Spanish text, see Teresa de Jesús, *Castillo Interior o Las Moradas*, ed. José Vicente Rodríguez, 8th edn, Logos vol. 35 (Madrid: Editorial de Espiritualidad, 2006) [hereafter referred to as Teresa, *Castillo*]; see also Julienne McLean, *Towards Mystical Union: A Modern Commentary on the Mystical Text* The Interior Castle *by St Teresa of Ávila* (London: St Pauls, 2003); Ruth Burrows, *Interior Castle Explored: St Teresa's Teaching on the Life of Deep Union with God* (3rd edn, London: Burns & Oates, Continuum Imprint, 2007); Bourne, *St Teresa's Castle of the Soul*; Aniano Alvarez Suárez, *Castillo Interior: Camino hacia el encuentro con Dios con Santa Teresa de Jesús*, Colección 'Karmel' (Burgos: Editorial Monte Carmelo, 2002).
556. See McLean, *Towards Mystical Union*, pp. 27–56.
557. Ibid., p. 27.
558. Ibid., p. 40.
559. Ibid., p. 51.
560. Ibid., p. 52.
561. Deirdre Green, *Gold in the Crucible: Teresa of Ávila and the Western Mystical Tradition* (Longmead, Shaftesbury: Element Books, 1989), pp. 40–2.
562. Teresa, *Perfection*, p. ix ('Preface').
563. See Dickens, *Female Mystic*, pp. 189–91, see also pp. 180, 184–5; Jean-Jacques Antier, *Teresa of Ávila: God Alone Suffices*, trans. Claire Quintal (Boston: Pauline Books & Media, 2007), pp. 95–115; Teresa of Ávila, *The Life of Saint Teresa of Ávila by Herself*, trans. J. M. Cohen (London: Penguin Books, 1957) [hereafter referred to as Teresa, *Life*], pp. 187–95, 283; for the original Spanish of the *Life*, see Santa Teresa de Jesús, *Libro de la Vida*, ed. P. Enrique Llamas Martínez, 5th edn (Madrid: Editorial de Espiritualidad, 2000) [hereafter referred to as Teresa, *Vida*], pp. 167–76, 264–5; Teresa, *Interior Castle*, pp. 142–7; McLean, *Towards Mystical Union*, pp. 273–87; Bourne, *St Teresa's Castle of the Soul*, pp. 73–85, 120–32; Green, *Gold in the Crucible*, pp. 51–64.
564. See Green, *Gold in the Crucible*, p. 45, Plate 7 facing p. 46.
565. Ibid., p. 45; see Teresa, *Life*, ch. 29, p. 210; idem, *Vida*, pp. 190–1; Bárbara Mujica, *Teresa de Ávila: Lettered Woman* (Nashville: Vanderbilt University Press, 2009), pp. 32–3; Bourne, *St Teresa's Castle of the Soul*, pp. 67–8.

566. See above n. 369.
567. Bourne, *St Teresa's Castle of the Soul*, p. 68; see Antonio del Gaudio, 'The Transverberation', *The Voice of Padre Pio*, 38:4 (July–August 2008), pp. 5–8; Padre Pio, *Letters*, vol. 1, p. 1,186, also cited on p. 7 of del Gaudio, 'Transverberation'.
568. Teresa, *Life*, ch. 29, p. 210; idem, *Vida*, pp. 190–1.
569. Padre Pio, *Letters*, vol. 1, letter no. 500: 'Padre Pio to Padre Benedetto', p. 1,186.
570. Ibid.
571. See Teresa, *Life*, pp. 33–8, 42–4, 14 ('Introduction'), 17 ('Introduction'); idem, *Vida*, pp. 15–21, 25–7; Dickens, *Female Mystic*, p. 180; Green, *Gold in the Crucible*, pp. 7, 13.
572. See above n. 392.
573. See Ruffin, *Padre Pio*, pp. 81–4, 92–4, 127–8, 134–5, 349–50, 370–3.
574. See above n. 369.
575. Ruffin, *Padre Pio*, p. 92; Evelyn Underhill, *Mysticism: A Study in the Nature and Development of Man's Spiritual Consciousness*, University Paperbacks (London: Methuen, 1960; repr. from London: Methuen, 1911), p. 59, cited in Ruffin, *Padre Pio*, p. 92. For hints at a possible relation between illness and visionary experience, see Robert A. Scott, *Miracle Cures: Saints, Pilgrimage and the Healing Powers of Belief* (Berkeley, Los Angeles, London: University of California Press, 2010), p. 60.
576. Mujica, *Teresa de Ávila*, p. 1.
577. Bourne, *St Teresa's Castle of the Soul*, p. 1.
578. Green, *Gold in the Crucible*, p. 153.
579. Mujica, *Teresa de Ávila*, p. x.
580. Teresa, *Life*, passim; idem, *Vida*, passim.
581. Teresa, *Life*, p. 11 ('Introduction').
582. Ibid.
583. See Mujica, *Teresa de Ávila*, passim; for the actual letters see Teresa de Ávila, *Epistolario*, ed. Luis Rodríguez Martínez and Teófanes Egido (Madrid: Espiritualidad, 1984); trans. available in Teresa of Ávila, *The Collected Letters of St Teresa of Ávila*, trans. Kieran Kavanaugh (2 vols, Washington, DC: Institute of Carmelite Studies, 2001, 2007).
584. See Teresa de Ávila, *Libro de las Fundaciones* (Buenos Aires: Espasa-Calpe, 1951), passim.
585. See Mujica, *Teresa de Ávila*, pp. 39, 90–2, 188, 230, 232; Antier, *Teresa of Ávila*, pp. 201–13.
586. Teresa, *Life*, p. 17 ('Introduction').
587. Idem, ch. 4, p. 33; idem, *Vida*, p. 16.
588. See idem, *Life* ('Introduction'), pp. 17–18. For fuller, brief surveys of her life, see Mujica, *Teresa de Ávila*, pp. 13–43 and Green, *Gold in the Crucible*, pp. 1–35.
589. Mujica, *Teresa de Ávila*, pp. 43, 101.
590. Teresa, *Life*, p. 18 ('Introduction').
591. Mujica, *Teresa de Ávila*, pp. 90–3.
592. Ibid., p. 102.
593. Green, *Gold in the Crucible*, p. 31.
594. Teresa, *Life*, p. 11 ('Introduction').
595. Ibid., pp. 26, 11–12 ('Introduction'); idem, *Vida*, pp. 7–8.
596. Bourne, *St Teresa's Castle of the Soul*, p. 30.
597. Mujica, *Teresa de Ávila*, pp. 13–25, 33, 56.
598. Ibid., p. 33.
599. Ibid., p. 21.
600. Ibid., p. 13.
601. E.g. Green, *Gold in the Crucible*, pp. 77–119.

602. See Luce López-Baralt, *Islam in Spanish Literature from the Middle Ages to the Present*, trans. Andrew Hurley (Leiden/New York/Köln: E. J. Brill/San Juan: Editorial de la Universidad de Puerto Rico, 1992), pp. 42–3, 91–142.
603. See Green, *Gold in the Crucible*, pp. 109, 196 n. 74.
604. See López-Baralt, *Islam in Spanish Literature*, p. 142.
605. See Terry Graham, 'Sufism: the "Strange Subject": Thomas Merton's Views on Sufism', *Sufi*, no. 75 (Summer 2008), pp. 39–47. For Thomas Merton, see his autobiography *The Seven Storey Mountain*, 50th Anniversary edn (New York: Harcourt Brace, 1998; first published 1948); Morgan C. Atkinson (ed.), with Jonathan Montaldo, *Soul Searching: The Journey of Thomas Merton* (Collegeville, MN: Liturgical Press, 2008); see also Harmless, *Mystics*, p. 38; Rob Baker and Henry Gray (eds), *Merton and Sufism: The Untold Story: A Complete Compendium* (Louisville, KY: Fons Vitae, 1999); see esp. Bernadette Dieker, 'Merton's Sufi Lectures to Cistercian Novices, 1966–68' in ibid., pp. 130–62; Rasoul Sorkhabi, 'Thomas Merton's Encounter with Sufism', *Interreligious Insight*, 6:4 (October 2008), pp. 22–32; Agnes Wilkins, 'Louis Massignon, Thomas Merton and Mary Kahil', *ARAM*, 20 (2008), pp. 355–73, esp. pp. 363–6.
606. Harmless, *Mystics*, p. 18.
607. Wilkins, 'Louis Massignon', p. 364.
608. Dickens, *Female Mystic*, p. 182; see Antier, *Teresa of Ávila*, p. 316, who gives 1567 for the second version of *The Way of Perfection*. But Mujica, *Teresa de Ávila*, p. 38 gives 1566 for *both* versions of *The Way of Perfection*, so there is a clear lack of scholarly agreement on the dating of the two versions.
609. Teresa, *Life*, p. 17 ('Introduction'); Mujica, *Teresa de Ávila*, pp. 35–8; Dickens, *Female Mystic*, p. 182; Antier, *Teresa of Ávila*, pp. 174–90, 303–4; Teresa, *Perfection*, p. xi; for the original Spanish, see Teresa, *Perfección*, p. 13.
610. See Teresa, *Perfection*, p. xi; idem, *Perfección*, p. 13.
611. Idem, *Perfection*, passim; idem, *Perfección*, passim.
612. Idem, *Perfection*, pp. 70–9; idem, *Perfección*, pp. 109–19; see Green, *Gold in the Crucible*, p. 181.
613. Green, *Gold in the Crucible*, p. 28; Antier, *Teresa of Ávila*, p. 317.
614. Dickens, *Female Mystic*, p. 186, see also pp. 187–9.
615. Bourne, *St Teresa's Castle of the Soul*, pp. 4, 25.
616. Teresa, *Life*, ch. 28, pp. 196–7ff.; idem, *Vida*, pp. 177–8ff.
617. Idem, *Life*, ch. 9, p. 67; *Vida*, p. 50.
618. See, for example, idem, *Perfection*, pp. 43–7, 128–33; idem, *Perfección*, pp. 75–80, 184–90; idem, *Interior Castle*, pp. 34, 39–40; idem, *Castillo*, pp. 51–52, 58.
619. Green, *Gold in the Crucible*, pp. 34, 172.
620. Mujica, *Teresa de Ávila*, p. 57; see also pp. 56, 137.
621. Ibid., p. 67.
622. Harmless, *Mystics*, p. 36 citing Thomas Merton, *New Seeds of Contemplation* (New York: New Directions, 1962), pp. 254–5.
623. Teresa, *Life*, ch. 11, p. 79; idem, *Vida*, ch. 11, p. 62.
624. Idem, *Life*, ch. 11, p. 78; idem, *Vida*, ch. 11, p. 62.
625. Idem, *Interior Castle*, p. 67; idem, *Castillo*, p. 90; see Burrows, *Interior Castle Explored*, p. 36; Bourne, *St Teresa's Castle of the Soul*, p. 139.
626. Teresa, *Perfection*, p. 62; idem, *Perfección*, p. 98.
627. Idem, *Perfection*, pp. 120–1; idem, *Perfección*, pp. 175–6; see idem, *Life*, ch. 15, pp. 104–11; idem, *Vida*, pp. 85–92. See also Bourne, *St Teresa's Castle of the Soul*, pp. 52–3; McLean, *Towards Mystical Union*, pp. 220–6.

628. McLean, *Towards Mystical Union*, p. 220.
629. See Ruffin, *Padre Pio*, pp. 105–15, 149–51, 237–8; Padre Pio, *Letters*, vol. 1, pp. 137–64.
630. Padre Pio, *Letters*, vol. 1, no. 461, pp. 1,102–3.
631. Teresa, *Perfection*, p. 66; idem, *Perfección*, p. 103.
632. See McLean, *Towards Mystical Union*, pp. 155–8.
633. See, for example, Teresa, *Interior Castle*, pp. 25–6; idem, *Castillo*, pp. 42–3.
634. See McLean, *Towards Mystical Union*, pp. 175–97; Bourne, *St Teresa's Castle of the Soul*, p. 44.
635. Teresa, *Interior Castle*, p. 40; idem, *Castillo*, p. 59.
636. See McLean, *Towards Mystical Union*, p. 251; see also pp. 252–87.
637. Teresa, *Interior Castle*, p. 99; idem, *Castillo*, p. 128. See also McLean, *Towards Mystical Union*, pp. 254–5.
638. Teresa, *Perfection*, p. 97; idem, *Perfección*, p. 145.
639. See above n. 635.
640. Burrows, *Interior Castle Explored*, p. 27.
641. See Teresa, *Perfection*, pp. 23–7 esp. p. 27, 27–32; idem, *Perfección*, pp. 49–54 esp. p. 54, pp. 55–61.
642. Idem, *Interior Castle*, p. 48; idem, *Castillo*, p. 67.
643. Burrows, *Interior Castle Explored*, p. 90 (my emphases).
644. Teresa, *Perfection*, pp. 104–5; idem, *Perfección*, pp. 154–5.
645. (My emphases.) Idem, *Interior Castle*, p. 149; idem, *Castillo*, pp. 185–6. For the exact nature of her visions, see Teresa, *Life*, ch. 28, p. 197; see idem, *Vida*, ch. 28, p. 178.
646. Idem, *Interior Castle*, p. 116; idem, *Castillo*, p. 145.
647. See McLean, *Towards Mystical Union*, pp. 289–305.
648. Teresa, *Life*, ch. 18, pp. 122–3; idem, *Vida*, ch. 18, pp. 102–4.
649. For the advanced stages of prayer, see idem, *Life*, ch. 18, pp. 117–27; idem, *Vida*, ch. 18, pp. 98–108.
650. Green, *Gold in the Crucible*, p. 42.
651. Teresa, *Interior Castle*, p. 171; idem, *Castillo*, pp. 207–8.
652. Teresa, *Interior Castle*, p. 175; idem, *Castillo*, p. 214.
653. Ibid.
654. Teresa, *Life*, ch. 14, p. 101; idem, *Vida*, ch.14, p. 84.
655. See Thomas R. Nevin, *Thérèse of Lisieux: God's Gentle Warrior* (Oxford: Oxford University Press, 2006); Monica Furlong, *Thérèse of Lisieux* (London: Darton, Longman & Todd, 2001); Thérèse de Lisieux, *Histoire d'une âme*, nouvelle éd. critique par Conrad de Meester (Paris: Presses de la Renaissance, 2005; first published 1898); idem, *The Story of a Soul*, trans. and ed. Robert J. Edmonson (Brewster, MA: Paraclete Press, 2007); Ida Friederike Görres, *The Hidden Face: A Study of St Thérèse of Lisieux*, trans. Richard Winston and Clara Winston (San Francisco: Ignatius Press, 2003).
656. Thérèse of Lisieux, *Story*, pp. xvi–xvii, 230–1; idem, *Histoire*, pp. 278–9; Catholic Truth Society, *The Little Way of St Thérèse of Lisieux from the Saint's Own Writings* (London: CTS, 2005); Aloysius Rego, 'Understanding The "Little Way": Thérèse's Gift to the Church', *Mount Carmel*, 57:3 (July–September 2009), pp. 24–9.
657. See Thérèse, *Story*, pp. 235–8; idem, *Histoire*, pp. 283–4; Görres, *Hidden Face*, pp. 222–9; Catholic Truth Society, *The Little Way*, p. 27; James McCaffrey, 'Focus', *Mount Carmel [St Thérèse Issue Welcoming Her Relics]*, 57:3 (July–September 2009), pp. 5–6; Stephanie-Thérèse, 'Living by Love: Thérèse of Lisieux at Prayer' in ibid., pp. 67–8.
658. Thérèse of Lisieux, *Story*, p. 205; idem, *Histoire*, p. 253; compare Teresa of Ávila, *Life*, ch. 30, p. 221; idem, *Vida*, ch. 30, p. 201.

659. Thérèse of Lisieux, *Story*, pp. 229–30; idem, *Histoire*, pp. 277–8; see Catholic Truth Society, *The Little Way*, p. 7; Görres, *Hidden Face*, pp. 347–86.
660. E.g. see Thérèse of Lisieux, *Story*, p. 234; idem, *Histoire*, p. 282.
661. See Nevin, *Thérèse of Lisieux*, pp. 249–86.
662. See Görres, *Hidden Face*, pp. 326–7; Thérèse of Lisieux, *Story*, pp. 224–5, 181; idem, *Histoire*, pp. 366–7, 232.
663. Furlong, *Thérèse*, p. 96.
664. Vernon Johnson, 'The Little Way' in Bro. Francis Mary F.I. (ed.), *St Thérèse: Doctor of the Little Way* (New Bedford, MA: Franciscan Friars of the Immaculate, 1997), p. 2.
665. Thérèse of Lisieux, *Story*, p. 230; idem, *Histoire*, p. 278; see Rego, 'Understanding the "Little Way"', p. 25. See also Brian J. Nolan, 'Theatre of a Saint: The Plays of Thérèse of Lisieux', *Mount Carmel*, 58:3 (2010), pp. 24–9. The theme of humility in the Theresian theatre is discussed on pp. 25–6.
666. Thérèse of Lisieux, *Story*, p. 187; idem, *Histoire*, pp. 235–6.
667. Teresa of Ávila, *Interior Castle*, p. 138; idem, *Castillo*, p. 172.

Chapter 4: Journey's End

1. Q.41:53.
2. Victoria Finlay, *Colour: Travels Through the Paintbox* (London: The Folio Society, 2009), p. xii.
3. Michelle Reichert, *Between Courtly Literature and al-Andalus: Matière d'Orient and the Importance of Spain in the Romances of the Twelfth-Century Writer Chrétien de Troyes*, Studies in Medieval History and Culture (New York and London: Routledge, 2006), p. 27.
4. Ibid.
5. Schimmel, *Mystical Dimensions*, p. 379; Tom Cheetham, *Green Man, Earth Angel: The Prophetic Tradition and the Battle for the Soul of the World*, SUNY Series in Western Esoteric Traditions (Albany, NY: State University of New York Press, 2005), pp. 69–70.
6. See above, Notes to Chapter 3 n. 469.
7. See above, Notes to Chapter 3 nn. 461, 462.
8. See above, Notes to Chapter 3 n. 464; see also Reichert, *Between Courtly Literature*, pp. 27, 61–2, 64–5, 92, 97, 236.
9. Teresa of Ávila, *Life*, ch. 28, p. 197; idem, *Vida*, ch. 28. p. 178.
10. Reichert, *Between Courtly Literature*, p. 91; see also pp. 27, 64, 90–1, 230, 236.
11. Ibid., p. 92. See also pp. 99, 100, 102, 236.
12. See Ean Begg, *The Cult of the Black Virgin* (London: Arkana, 1985). For the world-famous Black Virgin of Montserrat (Our Lady of Montserrat), known as 'La Moreneta' (lit. 'the dark one'), whose shrine is in the monastery church of Montserrat outside Barcelona, and who is revered as the symbol of Catalonia, see Maria Pilar Queralt and Jaume Balanyà, *Montserrat* (Montserrat/Barcelona: Triangle Postals, n.d.), esp. pp. 11–12, 98–9 (plate). It is intriguing, from the perspective of this book of mine, that St George is also the patron saint of Catalonia (see ibid., p. 9)! Here is another intertextual link.
13. Michael Tausig, *What Color is the Sacred?* (Chicago and London: University of Chicago Press, 2009), p. 65. See also his citation of Roland Barthes's disparaging remarks about colour (p. 18).
14. *The Independent*, Saturday 19 July 2008, p. 23. For more on 'Chinese' green, see Finlay, *Colour*, pp. 228–61.
15. See Molière, *The Misanthrope, Tartuffe and Other Plays*, trans. Maya Slater, Oxford World's Classics (Oxford: Oxford University Press, 2001), p. 358 n. 208; see also p. 361 n. 269. For

the original French of these and other plays by Molière, see Molière, *Oeuvres complètes* (Paris: Gallimard, 1971).
16. See *The Roman Catholic Daily Missal 1962* (Kansas City, MO: Angelus Press, 2004), p. 131.
17. See David Hatton, *Clare, Suffolk: An Account of the Historical Features of the Town, Its Priory and Its Parish Church* (Clare: SOS Free Stock, 1994); idem, *Clare, Suffolk: Book IV: Clare Parish Church*, www.clare-uk.com/Hatton_Book/Clare_Book_IV.pdf, pp. 2, 13; idem, *The Church of SS Peter and Paul, Clare*, www.clare-uk.com/Hatton_Book/Summary_church.pdf, p. 1.
18. Reichert, *Between Courtly Literature*, p. 95.
19. See ibid., pp. 65, 231. For Arthur, see N. J. Higham, *King Arthur: Myth-Making and History* (London and New York: Routledge, 2002, 2009).
20. Reichert, *Between Courtly Literature*, p. 173; see also Nicholas Goodrick-Clarke, *The Western Esoteric Tradition: A Historical Introduction* (Oxford: Oxford University Press, 2008), esp. pp. 71–85, 3–9.
21. Bruce R. Smith, *The Key of Green: Passion and Perception in Renaissance Culture* (Chicago and London: University of Chicago Press, 2009), inside front jacket and pp. 1–2, 3.
22. Ibid., p. 1.
23. Smith, *Key of Green*, p. 5.
24. (My emphases.) Q.18:31; trans. Yusuf Ali, *Holy Qur'an*, pp. 738–9; see also Reichert, *Between Courtly Literature*, pp. 95–6.
25. Yusuf Ali, *Holy Qur'an*, p. 739, n. 2,373.
26. Hasan Ali Khan, *Shi'a-Ismaili Motifs in the Sufi Architecture of the Indus Valley, 1200–1500 AD*, unpublished PhD diss., London University (SOAS), 2009, pp. 229, 235.
27. See also Tom Cheetham, *The World Turned Inside Out: Henry Corbin and Islamic Mysticism* (Woodstock, CT: Spring Journal Books, 2003), pp. 104ff.; idem, *Green Man, Earth Angel*, pp. 122, 109, 113.
28. See above, Notes to Chapter 3 n. 45.
29. 1 Corinthians 2:9–10; see Knox (trans.), *Holy Bible: New Testament*, p. 165.
30. See A. J. Wensinck, *Concordance et Indices de la Tradition Musulmane* (Leiden: E. J. Brill, 1962), vol. iv, p. 451.
31. Victor Turner, 'Liminality and communitas' in Michael Lambek (ed.), *A Reader in the Anthropology of Religion*, Blackwell Anthologies in Social and Cultural Anthropology, no. 2 (Malden, MA/Oxford: Blackwell Publishing, 2002), p. 359; see Victor Turner, *The Ritual Process: Structure and Anti-Structure* (Chicago: Aldine Publishing, 1969); Arnold Van Gennep, *The Rites of Passage*, trans. Monika B. Vizedom and Gabrielle L. Caffee (London: Routledge & Kegan Paul, 1960; first published 1908).
32. Davis, *Mysticism and Space*, pp. 65, 65 n. 8, 79–98.
33. Ibid., p. 80.
34. Ibid., pp. 86–7.
35. See ibid., pp. 92, 94–5, 98–9.
36. Ibid., pp. 87–9ff.
37. Ibid., p. 90.
38. Ibid., pp. 95–6, 98.
39. See ibid., p. 97.
40. Ibid., p. 80; see pp. 97–8.
41. See Richard Rolle, *The Fire of Love*, trans. Clifton Wolters (London: Penguin Books, 1972).
42. Davis, *Mysticism and Space*, p. 65 n. 8.
43. See Turner, 'Liminality and communitas', pp. 360–1, 365, 368, 370–3.

44. Ibid., p. 359.
45. See Davis, *Mysticism and Space*, p. 87, who notes: 'The mystics may be viewed as individuals standing for all Christians whose ultimate aim is to attain everlasting union with God'.
46. Teresa of Ávila, *Life*, p. 11 ('Introduction').
47. Nevin, *Thérèse of Lisieux*, pp. 193, 204; Thérèse, *Story*, pp. 202–3; idem, *Histoire*, p. 250.
48. See Karamustafa, *Sufism*, pp. 69, 98–9.
49. Q.18:31.
50. For the coinage, uses and development of the term *theologeme*, see above, Notes to Chapter 2 n. 11.

BIBLIOGRAPHY OF WORKS CITED

Primary Sources

Arabic, English, French, Greek, Hebrew, Latin, Medieval French, Middle English, Italian, Persian and Spanish Primary Sources are listed here. Translations from these texts are also included in this section.

Ainsworth, William Harrison, *Windsor Castle: An Historical Romance* (London: Milner & Co. Ltd, n.d.; orig. publ. in 3 vols (London: Henry Colburn, 1843).

Alexander, J. J. G. (ed.), *The Master of Mary of Burgundy: A Book of Hours for Engelbert of Nassau (The Bodleian Library, Oxford)* (New York: George Braziller, 1970).

Alexander (ed.), Peter *see* Shakespeare, William

Ali, Abdullah Yusuf (trans.), *see Qur'ān*.

Analecta Ordinis Carmelitarum, vol. 50 (1999).

'Aṭṭār, Farīd al-Dīn Muḥammad b. Ibrāhīm, *Manṭiq al-Ṭayr*, 3rd edn (Tehran and Tabriz: Kitabfroushi-ye Tehran, 1968).

'Aṭṭār, Farīd al-Dīn Muḥammad b. Ibrāhīm, *The Conference of the Birds (Mantiq ut-Tair)*, trans. C. S. Nott (London: Routledge & Kegan Paul, 1974).

Augustine, *Confessions, Books 1–8* [dual Latin–English edn], trans. William Watts, The Loeb Classical Library (Cambridge, MA/London: Harvard University Press, repr. 1999).

Augustine, *Confessions*, trans. Henry Chadwick (Oxford: Oxford University Press, 1991).

Benson, Larry D. (ed.), 'The Canon and Chronology of Chaucer's Work' in Chaucer, *The Riverside Chaucer*.

Brault, Gerard J. (ed.), *The Song of Roland: An Analytical Edition: 1. Introduction and Commentary; 2: Oxford Text and English Translation* (University Park and London: Pennsylvania State University Press, 1978).

al-Bukhārī, *Mukhtaṣar Ṣaḥīḥ al-Bukhārī* [dual Arabic–English edn], Islamic Library Project (English), ed. and trans. Muhammad Muhsin, comp. Zayn al-Din al-Zubaydi (Riyadh: Maktaba Dār al-Salām, [1994]).

al-Bukhārī, *Ṣaḥīḥ: The Translation of the Meanings of Saḥîḥ al-Bukhārī* [dual Arabic–English edn], trans. Muhammad Muhsin Khan (Riyadh: Dār al-Salām, 1997), vols 1, 5.

Bunyan, John, *The Pilgrim's Progress*, ed. W. R. Owens, Oxford World's Classics (Oxford: Oxford University Press, 2003).

Chaucer, Geoffrey, *Geoffrey Chaucer, The Canterbury Tales*, trans. David Wright, Oxford World's Classics (Oxford: Oxford University Press, 1998).

Chaucer, Geoffrey, *The Merchant's Prologue and Tale: From the Canterbury Tales by Geoffrey Chaucer*, ed. Maurice Hussey (Cambridge: Cambridge University Press, 1966, repr. 2005).

Chaucer, Geoffrey, *The Riverside Chaucer*, ed. Larry D. Benson, 3rd edn (Oxford: Oxford University Press, 1988) [contains original text].

Clarke, Hugh and Bede Edwards, *The Rule of Saint Albert*, Vinea Carmeli 1 (Aylesford/Kensington: Carmelite Priory, 1973) [contains the Latin text of *The Rule of Saint Albert/Regula Sancti Alberti*, ed. with an English trans. by Bede Edwards].

Cloud of Unknowing and Related Treatises on Contemplative Prayer, The [original Middle English texts], ed. Phyllis Hodgson (Salzburg: Institut für Anglistik und Americanistik, Universität Salzburg/Exeter: Catholic Records Press, 1982).

Cloud of Unknowing and Other Treatises, The, ed. Justin McCann, commentary by Augustine Baker, 6th rev. edn (London: Burns & Oates, 1952).

Cloud of Unknowing and Other Works, The, trans. A. C. Spearing (London: Penguin Books, 2001).

Cloud of Unknowing and Other Works, The, trans. Clifton Wolters (Harmondsworth: Penguin Books, 1983)

[*Cloud of Unknowing*]: *A Book of Contemplation the Which is called The Cloud of Unknowing, in the Which a Soul is Oned with God*, ed. Evelyn Underhill, 6th edn (London: John M. Watkins, 1956).

al-Daylamī, Abū 'l-Ḥasan ʿAlī b. Muḥammad, *Kitāb ʿAṭf al-Alif al-Maʾlūf ʿalā 'l-Lām al-Maʿṭūf*, ed. J. C. Vadet, Textes et Traductions d'Auteurs Orientaux, vol. 20 (Cairo: Imprimerie de l'Institut Français d'Archéologie Orientale, 1962).

al-Daylamī, Abū 'l-Ḥasan ʿAlī b. Muḥammad, *A Treatise on Mystical Love*, trans. Joseph Norment Bell and Hassan Mahmood Abdul Latif Al Shafie, Journal of Arabic and Islamic Studies Monographs Series 1 (Edinburgh: Edinburgh University Press, 2005).

al-Daylamī, Abū 'l-Ḥasan ʿAlī b. Muḥammad, *Le Traité d'Amour Mystique d'Al-Daylamī*, Hautes Études Orientales, vol. 13 (Geneva: Librairie Droz/Paris: Librairie Champion, 1980).

de Lorris, Guillaume, *Le Roman de la Rose*, ed. Stephen G. Nichols (New York: Appleton-Century-Crofts, 1967).

de Lorris, Guillaume and Jean de Meun, *The Romance of the Rose*, trans. and ed. Frances Horgan, Oxford World's Classics (Oxford: Oxford University Press, 1999).

de Montfort, Louis Marie, *Treatise on the True Devotion to the Blessed Virgin*, 4th edn (England: Fathers of the Company of Mary, 1957).

de Sales, Francis (François), *Oeuvres*, ed. André Ravier and Roger Devos, Bibliothèque de la Pléiade (Paris: Éditions Gallimard, 1969).

de Sales, Francis (François), *Introduction à la vie dévote see* de Sales, *Oeuvres*.

de Sales, Francis (François), *Philothea or An Introduction to the Devout Life* (Rockford, IL: Tan Books & Publishers, 1994: paperback repr. of New York: Joseph Wagner, 1923/Philadelphia: Peter Reilly Co., 1942 edn).

de Troyes, Chrétien, *Romans de la Table Ronde*, ed. Jean-Pierre Foucher, Collection Folio (Paris: Éditions Gallimard, 1970, 1975).

de Troyes, Chrétien, *Lancelot, The Knight of the Cart*, trans. Burton Raffel (New Haven and London: Yale University Press, 1997).

Deonise Hid Divinite see Cloud of Unknowing …, ed. Hodgson.

Edwards, Bede (ed. and trans.), *The Rule of Saint Albert/Regula Sancti Albert see* Clarke and Edwards.

Epistle of Privy Counsel see *Cloud of Unknowing and Other Works* … trans. Wolters.,
al-Ghazālī, *Iḥyā' 'Ulūm al-Dīn*, 5 vols (Beirut: Dār al- Ma'rifa, n.d.).
al-Ghazālī, *Letter to a Disciple/Ayyuhā 'l-Walad* [English–Arabic edn], trans. Tobias Mayer (Cambridge: Islamic Texts Society, 2005).
Hava, J. G., *Al-Farā'id Arabic–English Dictionary* (Beirut: Dār al-Mashriq, 1970).
Hodgson, Phyllis (ed.), *see Cloud of Unknowing and Related Treatises on Contemplative Prayer, The*.
Holy Bible, King James Version (Oxford: Oxford University Press/London: Geoffrey Cumberlege, n.d.).
Holy Bible, ed. and trans. R. Knox (London: Burns & Oates/Macmillan, 1960).
Holy Bible, ed. and trans. Henry Wansbrough under the title *The New Jerusalem Bible* (London: Darton, Longman & Todd, 1985).
al-Hujwīrī, *Kashf al-Maḥjūb*, ed. V. A. Zhukovski (Dār al-'Ulūm Ittiḥād Jamāhīr Shūrawī Sūsiyālīstī, 1926).
al-Hujwīrī, *The Kashf al-Maḥjūb: The Oldest Persian Treatise on Sufism by 'Alī B 'Uthmān al-Jullābī al-Hujwīrī*, trans. from the text of the Lahore edn by Reynold A. Nicholson, E. J. W. Gibb Memorial Series, vol. 17 (London: Luzac, repr. 1970).
Ibn 'Abbād, *al-Rasā'il al-Sughrā/Lettres de Direction Spirituelle*, ed. Paul Nwyia, Recherches publiées sous la direction de l'Institut de Lettres Orientales de Beyrouth, Tome VII (Beirut: Imprimerie Catholique, 1958).
Ibn 'Abbād, *Ibn 'Abbād of Ronda: Letters on the Ṣūfī Path*, trans. John Renard, Classics of Western Spirituality (New York/Mahwah, NJ/Toronto: Paulist Press, 1986).
Ibn 'Abbād, *Sharḥ al-Shaykh Muḥammad b. Ibrāhīm al-Ma'ruf bi-Ibn 'Abbād al-Nafzī al-Rundī 'alā Kitāb al-Ḥikam li … Ibn 'Aṭā Allāh Sakandarī*, 2 vols in 1 (Cairo: al-Ḥalabī, 1939).
Ibn al-'Arabī, *Fuṣūṣ al-Ḥikam*, ed. Abū 'l-'Alā 'Afīfī (Beirut: Dār al-Kitāb al-'Arabī, 1946).
Ibn al-'Arabī, *Ibn al-'Arabi: The Bezels of Wisdom*, trans. R. W. J. Austin, Classics of Western Spirituality (Ramsey, NJ: Paulist Press, 1980).
Ibn al-'Arabī, *The Wisdom of the Prophets (Fusus al-Hikam)*, trans. Titus Burckhardt and Angela Culme-Seymour (Aldsworth: Beshara Publications, 1975).
Ibn al-'Arabī, *Shajarat al-Kawn*, ed. Riyāḍ al-'Abdallāh (Beirut: al-Markaz al-'Arabī li 'l-Kitāb, 1984).
Ibn al-'Arabī, *Ibn 'Arabi: The Tree of Being: Shajarat al-Kawn: An Ode to the Perfect Man*, interpret. Shaykh Tosun Bayrak al-Jerrahi al-Halveti (Cambridge: Archtype, 2005).
Ibn Baṭṭūṭa, *Riḥlat Ibn Baṭṭūṭa* (Beirut: Dār Ṣādir/Dār Bayrūt, 1964).
Ibn Baṭṭūṭa, *The Travels of Ibn Baṭṭūṭa* AD *1325–1354*, trans. H. A. R. Gibb (vols 1 and 2), trans. H. A. R. Gibb and C. F. Beckingham (vol. 4) (Cambridge: Cambridge University Press for the Hakluyt Society, 1958 (vol. 1), 1962 (vol. 2); London: The Hakluyt Society, 1994 (vol. 4)).
Ibn Ḥajar, *Kitāb al-Iṣāba* [*A Biographical Dictionary of Persons who Knew Mohammad*], 4 vols (Calcutta: Printed by T. J. M'Arthur, Bishop's College Press, 1856–88).
Ibn Hishām *see* Ibn Isḥāq/Ibn Hishām
Ibn Isḥāq, *Ibn Ishaq: The Life of Muhammad, Apostle of Allah*, ed. Michael Edwardes, trans. Edward Rehatsek (London: Folio Society, 1964, 2003).
Ibn Isḥāq, *The Life of Muhammad: A Translation of Isḥāq's Sīrat Rasūl Allāh*, trans. A. Guillaume, 20th imp (Karachi: Oxford University Press, 2006).
Ibn Isḥāq/Ibn Hishām, *al-Sīra al-Nabawiyya li-Ibn Hishām*, ed. Muṣṭafā Saqqā et al., vol. 1, 2nd edn, Turāth al-Islām (Cairo: Bāb al-Ḥalabī, 1955).
Ibn Kathīr, *Qiṣaṣ al-Anbiyā'*, ed. Muṣṭafā 'Abd al-Wāḥid, 2 pts (Cairo: Dār al-Kutub al-Ḥadītha, 1968).

Ibn Kathīr, *Stories of the Prophets*, trans. Rashad Ahmed Azami, 2nd rev. edn (Riyadh and Jeddah: Maktaba Dar-us-Salam, 2003).

Ibn Kathīr, *al-Sīra al-Nabawiyya*, ed. Muṣṭafā 'Abd al-Wāḥid (Beirut: Dār al-Ma'rifa, 1976), vol. 2.

Ibn Kathīr, *The Life of the Prophet Muhammad, Volume 2: Al-Sīra al-Nabawiyya*, trans. Trevor Le Gassick, Great Books of Islamic Civilization (Reading: Garnet, 1998, 2000).

Ikhwān al-Ṣafā', *Rasā'il Ikhwān al-Ṣafā'* (4 vols, Beirut: Dār Ṣādir/Dār Bayrūt, 1957), vol. 4.

al-Jīlī, 'Abd al-Karīm b. Ibrāhīm, *al-Insān al-Kāmil fī Ma'rifat al-Awā'il wa'l-Awākhir* (Cairo: Maktaba al-Thaqāfa al-Dīniyya, 2004), vol. 2.

Juan de la Cruz, *Obras Completas*, Maestros Espirituales Carmelitas, no. 3 (Burgos: Editorial Monte Carmelo, 1982).

Juan de la Cruz, *Noche Oscura see* Juan de la Cruz, *Obras Completas*.

Juan de la Cruz, *The Dark Night of the Soul*, ed., trans. and intro. John Newton and Benedict Zimmerman, Baronius Press Classics (London: Baronius Press, 2006; re-edn of London: Thomas Baker, 1916 edn).

Juan de la Cruz, *Subida del Monte Carmelo see* Juan de la Cruz, *Obras Completas*.

Juan de la Cruz, *Ascent of Mount Carmel*, trans. and ed. E. Allison Peers (London and New York: Burns & Oates, 1983).

Juan de la Cruz, *John of the Cross: Selections from the Dark Night and Other Writings*, Foreword by Ron Hansen, ed. Emilie Griffin, trans. Kieran Kavanaugh, HarperCollins Spiritual Classics (New York: HarperCollins, Harper San Francisco, 2004).

Juan de la Cruz, *The Poems of St John of the Cross*, trans. Roy Campbell (Glasgow: Collins Fount Paperbacks, 1983).

Juan de la Cruz, *The Poems of St John of the Cross* [dual Spanish–English text], trans. Kathleen Jones (London: Burns & Oates, 1993, 2001).

Julian of Norwich, *Julian of Norwich: Showings: Authoritative Text, Contexts, Criticism*, ed. Denise N. Baker, A Norton Critical Edition (New York and London: W. W. Norton & Co., 2005).

Julian of Norwich, *The Writings of Julian of Norwich: A Vision Showed to a Devout Woman and A Revelation of Love* [dual English–Middle English edn], ed. Nicholas Watson and Jacqueline Jenkins, Medieval Women: Texts and Contexts, vol. 5 (Turnhout: Brepols, 2006).

Julian of Norwich, *Revelations of Divine Love (Short Text and Long Text)*, trans. Elizabeth Spearing, introd. and notes by A. C. Spearing (London: Penguin Books, 1998).

Julian of Norwich, *Revelations of Divine Love*, trans. Clifton Wolters (Harmondsworth: Penguin, 1966, 1984).

Julian of Norwich, *A Revelation of Love*, ed. Marion Glasscoe, rev. edn (Exeter: University of Exeter Press, 2003).

Julian of Norwich, *Showing of Love*, trans. Julian Botton Holloway (Collegeville, MN: Liturgical Press, 2003).

al-Kalābādhī, *Kitāb al-Ta'arruf li-Madhhab Ahl al-Taṣawwuf*, ed. 'Abd al-Ḥalīm Maḥmūd and Ṭāhā 'Abd al-Bāqī Surūr (Cairo: al-Ḥalabī, 1960).

al-Kalābādhī, *Kitāb al-Ta'arruf li-Madhhab Ahl al-Taṣawwuf*, ed. Maḥmūd al-Nawāwī, 2nd edn (Cairo: Maktaba al-Kulliyāt al-Azhariyya, 1980).

al-Kalābādhī, *The Doctrine of the Sufis (Kitāb al-Ta'arruf li-Madhhab Ahl al-Taṣawwuf)*, trans. A. J. Arberry (Cambridge: Cambridge University Press, 1977, reprint of 1935 CUP edn).

al-Kisā'ī, *Qiṣaṣ al-Anbiyā' / Vita Prophetarum*, ed. Isaac Eisenberg (Leiden: E. J. Brill, 1922).

al-Kisā'ī, *The Tales of the Prophets of al-Kisā'ī*, trans. W. M. Thackston, Library of Classical Arabic Literature, vol. 2 (Boston: Twayne Publishers, G. K. Hall & Co., 1978).

Knox, R. (ed. and trans.) *see Holy Bible*

Liddell, H. G. (ed.), *An Intermediate Greek–English Lexicon*, Founded Upon the Seventh Edition of Liddell and Scott's *Greek–English Lexicon* (Oxford: Clarendon Press, 1968).
Lings, Martin, *Muhammad: His Life Based on the Earliest Sources* (London: George Allen & Unwin/The Islamic Texts Society, 1983).
Maḥfūẓ, Najīb, *Riḥlat Ibn Faṭṭūma* (Cairo: Dār Miṣr li 'l-Ṭibā'a, n.d.).
Maḥfūẓ, Najīb, *Naguib Mahfouz: The Journey of Ibn Fattouma*, trans. Denys Johnson-Davies (New York and London: Doubleday, 1992).
Malory, Sir Thomas, *Le Morte Darthur or The Hoole Book of Kyng Arthur and of His Noble Knyghtes of the Rounde Table*, Authoritative Text, Sources and Backgrounds, Criticism, ed. Stephen H. A. Shepherd, A Norton Critical Edition (New York and London: W. W. Norton & Co., 2004).
Malory, Sir Thomas, *Le Morte Darthur: The Winchester Manuscript*, ed. with intro. Helen Cooper, Oxford World's Classics (Oxford: Oxford University Press, 1998).
al-Mas'ūdī, *Murūj al-Dhahab* (Beirut: Dār al-Andalus, 1966, 1996), pt 3.
al-Mas'ūdī, *Murūj al-Dhahab/Macoudi: Les Prairies d'Or*, ed. C. Barbier de Meynard, Texte et Traduction (Paris: L'Imprimerie Nationale, 1914), vol. 4 [Arabic with French trans.].
al-Mas'ūdī, *The Meadows of Gold: The Abbasids*, trans. Paul Lunde and Caroline Stone (London and New York: Kegan Paul International, 1989).
McCann, Justin (ed.) *see Cloud of Unknowing and Other Treatises, The.*
Molière, *Oeuvres complètes* (Paris: Gallimard, 1971).
Molière, *The Misanthrope, Tartuffe and Other Plays*, trans. Maya Slater, Oxford World's Classics (Oxford: Oxford University Press, 2001).
Narshakhī, Muḥammad ibn Ja'far, *Tārīkh Bukhārā* (Tehran: Bunyād-ī Farhang-ī Īran, 1351/1972; ibid. (Cairo: Dār al-Ma'ārif, 1965).
Narshakhī, Muḥammad ibn Ja'far, *The History of Bukhārā*, ed. and trans. from the Persian abridgement of the Arabic original of Narshakhī, by Richard Nelson Frye (Princeton, NJ: Markus Wiener Publishers, 2007).
al-Nawawī, *Matn al-Arba'īn/An-Nawawi's Forty Hadith*, trans. Ezzedin Ibrahim and Denys Johnson-Davies, 3rd edn (Damascus: Holy Koran Publishing House, 1977).
Newton, Faye and Hazel Brooks, *Leaflet* [concert given during International Medieval Congress, University of Leeds, St Chad's Church, Leeds, 7 July 2008, entitled *Duo Trobairitz*].
Nurbakhsh, Javad, *In the Paradise of the Sufis*, 3rd edn (New York and London: Khaniqahi-Nimatullahi Publications, 1989).
Nurbakhsh, Javad, *The Psychology of Sufism (Del wa Nafs)* (London and New York: Khaniqahi-Nimatullahi Publications, 1992).
O'Donnell, Christopher, O.Carm. (rev. trans.), *The Rule of St Albert, as approved by Innocent IV (1247)*, leaflet circulated with the Carmelite Secular Order Newsletter, September 2003.
Padre Pio of Pietrelcina, *Letters, Volume 1: Correspondence with His Spiritual Directors (1910–1922)*, ed. Melchiorre of Pobladura and Alessandro of Ripabottoni, English version ed. Gerardo di Flumeri, 2nd edn (San Giovanni Rotondo: Edizioni/Editions Pio da Pietrelcina, 1984); *Letters, Volume 2: Correspondence with Raffaelina Cerase, Noblewoman (1914–1915)*, ed. as above, 3rd edn (2002); *Letters, Volume 3: Correspondence with His Spiritual Daughters (1915–1923)*, ed. as above, 2nd edn (2001).
Plato, *Phaedo* in H. N. Fowler (trans.), *Euthyphro, Apology, Crito, Phaedo, Phaedrus* [dual Greek–English text], Loeb Classical Library (London: W. Heinemann/Cambridge, MA: Harvard University Press, 1966).
Plato, *Symposium* [dual Greek–English text], ed. with intro., trans. and commentary by C. J. Rowe, Aris & Phillips Greek Philosophy Series (Warminster: Aris & Phillips, 1998); trans. Walter Hamilton (Harmondsworth: Penguin Books, 1972).

Plotinus, *Ennead III* [dual Greek–English text], ed. and trans. A. H. Armstrong, Loeb Classical Library (Cambridge, MA/London: Harvard University Press, 1993).

Qur'ān [Q.], trans. Abdullah Yusuf Ali: *The Holy Qur'ān: Text, Translation and Commentary* (Kuwait: Dhāt al-Salāsil, 1984).

al-Qushayrī, Abū 'l-Qāsim, *al-Risāla al-Qushayriyya fi 'Ilm al-Taṣawwuf* (Beirut: Dār al-Khayr, 1993).

al-Qushayrī, Abū 'l-Qāsim, *Sufi Book of Spiritual Ascent (Al-Risala al-Qushayriyya)*, abridged trans. by Rabia Harris, ed. Laleh Bakhtiar (Chicago: ABC Group International/Kazi Publications, 1997).

al-Qushayrī, Abū 'l-Qāsim, *Al-Qushayrī's Epistle on Sufism, Al-Risala al-qushayriyya fi 'ilm al-tasawwuf*, trans. Alexander D. Knysh, Great Books of Islamic Civilization (Reading: Garnet Publishing Ltd, 2007).

al-Qushayrī, Abū 'l-Qāsim, 'Qušayrī's Tartīb as-suluk' [Arabic–German text], ed. Fritz Meier, *Oriens*, vol. 16 (1963).

Rolle, Richard, *The Fire of Love*, trans. Clifton Wolters (London: Penguin Books, 1972).

Rule of Saint Linus, MS Lambeth 192.

Rūmī, Jalāl al-Dīn, *Mathnawī-i ma'nawi (Masnavi-ye ma'navi)*, ed. and trans. Reynold A. Nicholson, E. J. W. Gibb Memorial Series, n.s. 4 (London: Luzac & Co, 1925–33), vol. 3.

al-Sanūsī, Muḥammad b. 'Alī, *al-Manhal al-Rawī 'l-Rā'iq fī Asānīd al-'Ulūm wa Uṣūl al-Ṭarā'iq* in *al-Majmū'a al-Mukhtāra* (Beirut, 1968).

Shakespeare, William, *King Richard III*, ed. Anthony Hammond, The Arden Shakespeare (London: Thomson Learning, 2006).

Shakespeare, William, *The Merry Wives of Windsor*, ed. Giorgio Melchiori, The Arden Shakespeare (London: Thomson Learning, 2000).

Shakespeare, William, *William Shakespeare: The Complete Works*, ed. Peter Alexander, The Players' Edition (London and Glasgow: Collins, 1951, repr. 1961).

Simpson, D. P., *Cassell's New Latin–English/English–Latin Dictionary*, 3rd edn (London: Cassell, 1964).

Sir Gawain and the Green Knight, trans. Simon Armitage (London: Faber & Faber, 2007).

Sir Gawain and the Green Knight, trans. Brian Stone, 2nd edn (London: Penguin Books, 1974).

Sir Gawain and the Green Knight, Pearl, Cleanness, Patience, ed. J. J. Anderson [contains original Middle English text], The Everyman Library (London: J. M. Dent/North Clarendon, VT: Tuttle Publishing, 2005).

Spearing, A. C. (trans.) *see Cloud of Unknowing, The.*

al-Subkī, *Ṭabaqāt*, ed. al-Ḥūlw and al-Ṭanāhī (Cairo, 1386/1967), vol. 5.

al-Sulamī, *Kitāb al-Futuwwa*, ed. Aḥmad Farīd al-Mizyadī (Beirut: Dār al-Kutub al-'Ilmiyya, 2009).

al-Sulamī, *Kitāb al-Futuwwa*, ed. Sulaymān Ateş in Naṣr Allāh Pūrjāwādī (ed.), *Majmū'-yi āšār-i Abū'Abd al-Raḥmān Sulamī*, 2 vols (Tehran: Markaz-i Nashr-ī Dānishgāhī, 1980–3).

al-Sulamī, *The Book of Sufi Chivalry: Lessons to a Son of the Moment*, trans. Tosun Bayrak al-Jerrahi al-Halveti (New York: Inner Traditions International, 1983).

al-Sulamī, *see also* Taeschner

al-Ṭabarī, *Ta'rīkh al-Rusul wa'l-Mulūk/Annales*, ed. M. J. de Goeje (Leiden: E. J. Brill, 1882–5), Prime Series, vol. 3.

al-Ṭabarī, *The History of al-Ṭabarī (Ta'rīkh al-rusul wa 'l-mulūk), vol. VI: Muhammad at Mecca*, trans. W. Montgomery Watt and M. V. McDonald, Bibliotheca Persica, SUNY Series in Near Eastern Studies (Albany, NY: State University of New York Press, 1988).

Taeschner, Franz, 'As-Sulami's Kitāb al-Futuwwa' in *Studia Orientalia Ioanni Pedersen* (Hauniae: Einar Munksgaard, 1953).

Teresa of Ávila, *Camino de Perfección*, ed. Daniel de Pablo Manto, 7th edn, *Logos* vol. 58 (Madrid: Editorial de Espiritualidad, 2009).
Teresa of Ávila, *The Way of Perfection*, trans. 'A Discalced Carmelite' (London: Baronius Press, 2006, repr. of Glasgow: Sands & Co., 1942 edn).
Teresa of Ávila, *Castillo Interior o Las Moradas*, ed. José Vicente Rodríguez, 8th edn, *Logos* vol. 35 (Madrid: Editorial de Espiritualidad, 2006).
Teresa of Ávila, *The Interior Castle*, trans. 'Anon. Stanbrook Benedictine Nuns', rev. Benedict Zimmerman (London: HarperCollins, Fount Paperback, 1995).
Teresa of Ávila, *Epistolario*, ed. Luis Rodríguez Martínez and Teófanes Egido (Madrid: Espiritualidad, 1984).
Teresa of Ávila, *The Collected Letters of St Teresa of Ávila*, trans. Kieran Kavanaugh, 2 vols (Washington, DC: Institute of Carmelite Studies, 2001, 2007).
Teresa of Ávila, *Libro de la Vida*, ed. P. Enrique Llamas Martínez, 5th edn (Madrid: Editorial de Espiritualidad, 2000).
Teresa of Ávila, *The Life of Saint Teresa of Ávila By Herself*, trans. J. M. Cohen (London: Penguin Books, 1957).
Teresa of Ávila, *Libro de las Fundaciones* (Buenos Aires: Espasa-Calpe, 1951).
Teresa of Ávila, *see also* Mujica (in Secondary Sources, below).
Thérèse of Lisieux, *Histoire d'une âme*, nouvelle éd. critique par Conrad de Meester (Paris: Presses de la Renaissance, 2005; first publ. 1898).
Thérèse of Lisieux, *The Story of a Soul*, trans. and ed. Robert J. Edmonson (Brewster, MA: Paraclete Press, 2007).
Thomas à Kempis, *The Imitation of Christ* (London: Burns & Oates, n.d.).
Thomas à Kempis, *The Imitation of Christ*, trans. Anthony Hoskins with Preface by John Wesley (London: Folio Society, 2008, rev. edn of Oxford: Oxford University Press, 1903).
Thomas à Kempis, *The Imitation of Christ*, trans. Leo Sherley-Price (London: Penguin Books, 1952, repr. 1980).
Underhill, Evelyn (ed.) *see* [*Cloud of Unknowing*].
Wansbrough, Henry (ed. and trans.) *see Holy Bible*
Watt, W. Montgomery *see* al-Ṭabarī (and under Secondary Sources below).
Wehr, Hans, *A Dictionary of Modern Written Arabic*, 2nd printing (Wiesbaden: Otto Harrassowitz/London: George Allen & Unwin, 1966).
Wensinck, A. J., *Concordance et Indices de la Tradition Musulmane* (Leiden: E. J. Brill, 1962), vol. 4.
Wheeler, Brannon M. (trans.), *Prophets in the Qur'an: An Introduction to the Qur'an and Muslim Exegesis* (London and New York: Continuum, 2002).
Wolters, Clifton (trans.) *see Cloud of Unknowing and Other Works, The*; Julian of Norwich; Rolle, Richard.
Yāqūt, *Mu'jam al-Buldān* (Beirut: Dār Ṣādir, 1977), vol. 2.

Secondary Sources

Abbott, Christopher, *Julian of Norwich: Autobiography and Theology*, Studies in Medieval Mysticism, vol. 2 (Cambridge: D. S. Brewster, 1999).
Abdel Haleem, Muhammad, *Understanding the Qur'an: Themes and Style* (London and New York: I. B. Tauris, 1999).
Abun-Nasr, Jamil M., *Muslim Communities of Grace: The Sufi Brotherhoods in Islamic Religious Life* (London: Hurst & Co., 2007).
Ackerman, Jane, *Elijah: Prophet of Carmel* (Washington, DC: ICS Publications, 2003).
Addas, Claude, *Ibn 'Arabī: The Voyage of No Return*, trans. David Streight, Muslim Personalities

Series (Cambridge: Islamic Texts Society, 2000).
Anderson, William and Clive Hicks, *Green Man: The Archetype of Our Oneness with the Earth* (London and San Francisco: HarperCollins, 1990).
Antier, Jean-Jacques, *Teresa of Ávila: God Alone Suffices*, trans. Claire Quintal (Boston: Pauline Books & Media, 2007).
Arberry, A. J., *Sufism: An Account of the Mystics of Islam*, Ethical and Religious Classics of East and West, no. 2 (London: George Allen & Unwin, 1968).
Arnaldez, R. 'Al-Insān al-Kāmil', *EI²*, vol. 3.
Arthur, Rosemary A., *Pseudo-Dionysius as Polemicist: The Development and Purpose of the Angelic Hierarchy in 6th Century Syria*, Ashgate New Critical Thinking in Religion, Theology and Biblical Studies (Aldershot: Ashgate, 2008).
Aščeric-Todd, Ines, 'The Noble Traders: The Islamic Tradition of "Spiritual Chivalry" (*futuwwa*) in Bosnian Trade-guilds (16th–19th centuries)', *The Muslim World*, 97:2 (April 2007).
Asín Palacios, Miguel, *Saint John of the Cross and Islam*, trans. Howard W. Yoder and Elmer H. Douglas (New York: Vantage Press, 1981; first publ. as *Un Precursor Hispano-Musulman de San Juan de la Cruz*, Al-Andalus, 1, Madrid, 1933).
Atkinson, Morgan C. (ed.), with Jonathan Montaldo, *Soul Searching: The Journey of Thomas Merton* (Collegeville, MN: Liturgical Press, 2008).
Bagshaw, Dana, *Cell Talk: A Duologue Between Julian of Norwich and Margery of Kempe* (London: Radius, 2002).
Bailie, Eileen, 'Travelling with Elijah: A Journey into Darkness', *Mount Carmel [Special Issue: Elijah and the Rule]*, 56:2, Pillars of Carmel, 1 (April–June 2008).
Baker, Bruce and Gregory L. Klein (eds), *The Carmelite Rule* (New Jersey: Catholic Book Publishing Co., 2000).
Baker, Denise Nowakowski, *Julian of Norwich's Showings: From Vision to Book* (Princeton, NJ: Princeton University Press, 1997).
Baker, Rob and Henry Gray (eds), *Merton and Sufism: The Untold Story: A Complete Compendium* (Louisville, KY: Fons Vitae, 1999).
Baldick, Julian, *Mystical Islam: An Introduction to Sufism* (London: I. B. Tauris, 1989).
Barraclough, Geoffrey, *The Medieval Papacy* (London: Thames & Hudson, 1968, 1992).
Barthold, W. and R. N. Frye, 'Bukhārā', *EI²*, vol. 1.
Basford, Kathleen, *The Green Man* (Ipswich: Brewer, 1978).
Beckett, Lucy, 'The Mind's Journey' [Review of Harmless, *Mystics*, in] *Times Literary Supplement*, 8 August 2008.
Beer, Frances, *Julian of Norwich: Revelations of Divine Love [and] The Motherhood of God*, Library of Medieval Women (Cambridge: D. S. Brewer, 1998).
Begent, Peter J. and Hubert Chesshyre, *The Most Noble Order of the Garter: 650 Years* (London: Spink, 1999).
Begg, Ean, *The Cult of the Black Virgin* (London: Arkana, 1985).
Benedictine of Stanbrook Abbey, *Mediaeval Mystical Tradition and Saint John of the Cross* (London: Burns & Oates, 1954).
Bennett, Michael, 'Isabelle of France, Anglo-French Diplomacy and Cultural Exchange in the Late 1350s' in J. S. Bothwell (ed.), *The Age of Edward III*.
Berkeley, Gail Alva, *Julian of Norwich: The Rhetoric of Revelation*, PhD Diss., Princeton University, 1982.
Billy, Dennis J., *The Imitation of Christ [of] Thomas à Kempis: A Spiritual Commentary and Reader's Guide*, Christian Classics (Notre Dame, IN: Ave Maria Press, 2005).
Boase, Roger, *The Origin and Meaning of Courtly Love: A Critical Study of European Scholarship* (Manchester: Manchester University Press/ Totowa, NJ: Rowman & Littlefield, 1977).

Boitani, Piero and Jill Mann (eds), *The Cambridge Companion to Chaucer*, 2nd edn (Cambridge: Cambridge University Press, 2007).
Bosworth, C. E., *The New Islamic Dynasties* (Edinburgh: Edinburgh University Press, 1996).
Bosworth, C. E., 'al-Būṣīrī' *see* Meisami and Starkey (eds).
Bosworth, C. E., 'Sāmānids', *EI*², vol. 8.
Bosworth, C. E. et al. (eds), 'al-Būṣīrī'', *EI*², Supp. Fascs 3–4.
Bothwell, J. S. (ed.), *The Age of Edward III* (York: York Medieval Press/Woodbridge, Suffolk: Boydell Press, 2001).
Bourne, Peter, *St Teresa's Castle of the Soul: A Study of the Interior Castle* (Long Beach, CA: Wenzel Press, 1995).
Bowden, Henry Sebastian and Donald Attwater, *Miniature Lives of the Saints* (London: Burns & Oates, 1959).
Böwering, G., 'Al-Sulamī', *EI*², vol. 9.
Braudel, Fernand, *The Mediterranean and the Mediterranean World in the Age of Philip II*, trans. Siân Reynolds, abridged Richard Ollard (London: HarperCollins, 1992).
Brenan, Gerald, *St John of the Cross: His Life and Poetry* (Cambridge: Cambridge University Press, 1973).
Broadie, Alexander, 'Aquinas' *see* Honderich (ed.).
Bronner, Leah, *The Stories of Elijah and Elisha as Polemics against Baal Worship*, Pretoria Oriental Series, vol. 6 (Leiden: E. J. Brill, 1968).
Brown, Raymond E., Joseph A. Fitzmyer and Roland E. Murphy (eds), *The New Jerome Biblical Commentary*, 2nd edn (London: Geoffrey Chapman, 1989, repr. 1990).
Buckley, Ronald Paul, 'Al-Nasir, Ahmad B. al-Mustadi, Abu 'l-ʿAbbas (AD 1180–1225)' *see* Netton, *Encyclopedia.*
Bullen, Roger et al. (eds), *Complete Flags of the World*, 5th edn (London and New York: Dorling Kindersley, 2008).
Burrow, J. A., 'The *Canterbury Tales* 1: Romance' in Boitani and Mann (eds).
Burrows, Ruth, *Interior Castle Explored: St Teresa's Teaching on the Life of Deep Union with God*, 3rd edn (London: Burns & Oates, Continuum Imprint, 2007).
Cahen, Cl. and Fr. Taeschner, 'Futuwwa', *EI*², vol. 2.
Carra de Vaux, B., art. 'Djirdjis', *EI*², vol. 2.
Carrithers, Michael, *Buddha: A Very Short Introduction* (Oxford: Oxford University Press, 2001).
Carson, Thomas and Joann Cerrito (project eds), *New Catholic Encyclopedia*, 2nd edn (Detroit and New York: Thomson-Gale, in assoc. with Catholic University of America, Washington, DC, 2003), vol. 14.
Carver, Stephen James, *The Life and Works of the Lancashire Novelist William Harrison Ainsworth, 1805–1882*, Studies in British Literature, vol. 75 (Lewiston, Queenston, Lampeter: The Edwin Mellen Press, 2003).
Catholic Encyclopedia, The (New York: Robert Appleton Co., 1912), vol. 14.
Catholic Truth Society, *The Little Way of St Thérèse of Lisieux from the Saint's Own Writings* (London: CTS, 2005).
Celaya, Gabriel, *Exploración de la poesía* (Barcelona: Seix Barra, 1964).
Chalmers, Joseph, 'Prayer and Contemplation: In the Spirit of the Carmelite Rule (1)', *Mount Carmel [Special Issue: Elijah and the Rule]*, 56:2, Pillars of Carmel, 1 (April–June 2008).
Cheetham, Tom, *Green Man, Earth Angel: The Prophetic Tradition and the Battle for the Soul of the World*, SUNY Series in Western Esoteric Traditions (Albany, NY: State University of New York Press, 2005).
Cheetham, Tom, *The World Turned Inside Out: Henry Corbin and Islamic Mysticism* (Woodstock, CT: Spring Journal Books, 2003).

Chodkiewicz, Michel, *An Ocean without Shore: Ibn 'Arabî: The Book and the Law* (Albany, NY: State University of New York Press, 1993).
Clark, J. P. H., 'The "Cloud of Unknowing", Walter Hilton and Saint John of the Cross: A Comparison', *Downside Review* (1978), vol. 96.
Clinton, Kevin, 'Eleusis' *see* Hornblower and Spawforth (eds).
Cohn-Sherbok, Lavinia and Dan Cohn-Sherbok, *A Popular Dictionary of Judaism* (Richmond: Curzon Press, 1995).
Colin, G. S., 'Burda', *EI²*, vol. 1.
Collins, Hugh E. L., *The Order of the Garter 1348–1461: Chivalry and Politics in Late Medieval England*, Oxford Historical Monographs (Oxford: Clarendon Press, 2000).
Cooper, Helen, *The Canterbury Tales*, 2nd edn, Oxford Guides to Chaucer (Oxford: Oxford University Press, 1996).
Cornell, Vincent J., *Realm of the Saint: Power and Authority in Moroccan Sufism* (Austin: University of Texas Press, 1998).
Corner, Veronica, 'An icon of Elijah: A Gradual Revelation', *Mount Carmel [Special Issue: Elijah and the Rule]*, 56:2, Pillars of Carmel, 1 (April–June 2008).
Davies, Norman, *Europe: A History* (London: Pimlico, 1997).
Davis, Carmel Bendon, *Mysticism and Space: Space and Spatiality in the Works of Richard Rolle, The Cloud of Unknowing Author, and Julian of Norwich* (Washington, DC: The Catholic University of America Press, 2008).
del Gaudio, Antonio, 'The Transverberation', *The Voice of Padre Pio*, 38:4 (July–August 2008).
Denis, Gabriel, *The Reign of Jesus Through Mary*, 6th edn (England: Montfort Fathers, [1958]).
Dicken, E. W. Trueman, *The Crucible of Love: A Study of the Mysticism of St Teresa of Jesus and St John of the Cross* (London: Darton, Longman & Todd, 1963).
Dickens, Andrea Janelle, *The Female Mystic: Great Women Thinkers of the Middle Ages*, International Library of Historical Studies, vol. 60 (London and New York: I. B. Tauris, 2009).
Dieker, Bernadette, 'Merton's Sufi Lectures to Cistercian Novices, 1966–68' *see* Baker and Gray (eds).
Doel, Fran and Geoff Doel, *The Green Man in Britain* (Stroud: Tempus/Charleston, SC: Arcadia, 2001).
Dreyer, Edward L., *Zheng He: China and the Oceans in the Early Ming Dynasty, 1405–1433*, Library of World Biography Series (New York and London: Pearson Longman, 2007).
Dronke, Peter, *Medieval Latin and the Rise of European Love Lyric*, 2nd edn (Oxford: Clarendon Press, 1968), vol. 1.
Dukes, J. (rev.), *The Daily Missal and Liturgical Manual* (Leeds: Laverty & Sons, n.d. [1960]).
EI² see *Encyclopaedia of Islam*.
EIS see *Shorter Encyclopaedia of Islam*.
Eliade, Mircea (ed.-in-chief), *The Encyclopedia of Religion* (New York: Macmillan/London: Collier Macmillan, 1987), vol. 14.
Elliott, R. W. V., *The Gawain Country*, Leeds Texts and Monographs, new series, no. 8 (Leeds: University of Leeds School of English, 1984).
Emery, Ed. (ed.), *Muwashshah! Proceedings of the International Conference on Arabic and Hebrew Strophic Poetry and Its Romance Parallels, School of Oriental and African Studies*, London, 8–10 October 2004, Research Papers on Arabic and Jewish Strophic Poetry (London: SOAS/RN Books, 2006).
Encyclopaedia of Islam [*EI²*], ed. H. A. R. Gibb et al., 2nd edn, 12 vols incl. Supp (Leiden: E. J. Brill/ London: Luzac [for some vols], 1960–2004).
Encyclopaedia of Islam [*EI²*], Supp. Fascs. 3–4 (Leiden: E. J. Brill, 1981); vol. 12 = Supp. (Leiden: E. J. Brill, 2004).

Encyclopaedia of the Qur'ān [EQ], vols Two, Three, Four, Five, ed. Jane Dammen McAuliffe (Leiden and Boston: E. J. Brill, 2002, 2003, 2004, 2006).
EQ see *Encyclopaedia of the Qur'ān.*
Eravşar, Osman, 'Miniature Paintings of Prophet Elijah (Ilyas) and Al Khodor (Hidir) in the Ottoman Period', *ARAM*, 20 (2008).
Ernst, Carl W., *Words of Ecstasy in Sufism*, SUNY Series in Islam (Albany, NY: State University of New York Press, 1985).
Esler, Philip F. and Ronald A. Piper, *Lazarus, Mary and Martha: A Social-Scientific and Theological Reading of John* (London: SCM Press, 2006).
Filoramo, Giovanni, *A History of Gnosticism*, trans. Anthony Alcock (Cambridge, MA/Oxford: Blackwell, 1990, 1992).
Finlay, Victoria, *Colour: Travels Through the Paintbox* (London: The Folio Society, 2009).
Fitch, Eric L., *In Search of Herne the Hunter* (Chieveley: Capall Bann Publishing, 1994).
Fox, D. (ed.), *Twentieth Century Interpretations of Sir Gawain and the Green Knight* (Englewood Cliffs, NJ: Prentice-Hall, 1968).
Freely, John, *Istanbul: The Imperial City* (London: Viking, Penguin Books, 1996).
Frings, Theodor, *Minnesinger und Troubadours* (Berlin, 1949).
Frye, Richard Nelson, *Bukhara: The Medieval Achievement* (Costa Mesa, CA: Mazda Publishers, 1996).
Furlong, Monica, *Thérèse of Lisieux* (London: Darton, Longman & Todd, 2001).
Gaudreau, Marie M., *Mysticism and Image in St John of the Cross*, European University Papers, Series 23, Theology: vol. 66 (Bern: Herbert Lang/Frankfurt am Main: Peter Lang, 1976).
Geoffroy, E. et al., 'Ṭarīḳa', *EI*², vol. 10.
Gibb, H. A. R. *see Encyclopaedia of Islam*; *Shorter Encyclopaedia of Islam*
Gleave, Robert (ed.), *Books and Bibliophiles: Studies in the Bio-Bibliography of the Muslim World in Honour of Paul Auchterlonie*, Gibb Memorial Series (Oxford: Oxbow Books, forthcoming).
Good, Jonathan, *The Cult of St George in Medieval England* (Woodbridge: Boydell Press, 2009).
Goodrick-Clarke, Nicholas, *The Western Esoteric Tradition: A Historical Introduction* (Oxford: Oxford University Press, 2008).
Gordon, Richard L., 'Mysteries' *see* Hornblower and Spawforth (eds).
Görres, Ida Friederike, *The Hidden Face: A Study of Thérèse of Lisieux*, trans. Richard Winston and Clara Winston (San Francisco: Ignatius Press, 2003).
Graham, Terry, 'Christian Mysticism and Sufism', *Sufi*, 74 (Winter 2007).
Graham, Terry, 'Sufism: the "Strange Subject": Thomas Merton's Views on Sufism', *Sufi*, 75 (Summer 2008).
Green, Deirdre, *Gold in the Crucible: Teresa of Ávila and the Western Mystical Tradition* (Shaftesbury: Element Books, 1989).
Gregory, Russell, 'Irony and the Unmasking of Elijah' in Hauser and Gregory, *From Carmel to Horeb.*
Grossmark, Tziona, 'The Desert in Talmudic Travelers' Tales – Reality and Imagination': unpublished paper presented on 8 July 2008 at the International Medieval Congress, University of Leeds (7–10 July 2008).
Hageman, Howard G. 'Thomas à Kempis' in Eliade (ed.-in-chief), *Encyclopedia of Religion*, vol. 14.
Hall, M. A., 'An Ivory Knife Handle from the High Street, Perth, Scotland: Consuming Ritual in a Medieval Burgh', *Medieval Archaeology: Journal of the Society for Medieval Archaeology*, vol. 45 (2001).
Halm, H., art. 'Al-Ḳushayrī', *EI*², vol. 5.

Hamilton, Sue, *Indian Philosophy: A Very Short Introduction* (Oxford: Oxford University Press, 2001).

Hammond, Marlé, 'He Desires Her? Situating Nazhun's *Muwashshah* in an Androgynous Aesthetic of Courtly Love' in Emery (ed.), *Muwashshah!*

Harmless, William, *Mystics* (Oxford: Oxford University Press, 2008).

Hatton, David, *The Church of SS Peter and Paul, Clare*: www.clare-uk.com/Hatton_Book/Summary_church.pdf

Hatton, David, *Clare, Suffolk: An Account of the Historical Features of the Town, Its Priory and Its Parish Church* (Clare: SOS Free Stock, 1994).

Hatton, David, *Clare, Suffolk: Book IV: Clare Parish Church*: www.clare-uk.com/Hatton_Book/Clare_Book_IV.pdf

Hauser, Alan J., 'Yahweh Versus Death – The Real Struggle in 1 Kings 17–19' in Hauser and Gregory, *From Carmel to Horeb*.

Hauser, Alan J. and Russell Gregory, *From Carmel to Horeb: Elijah in Crisis*, Journal for the Study of the Old Testament Supplement Series, 85, Bible and Literature Series, 19 (Sheffield: Almond Press/Sheffield Academic Press, 1990).

Heng, Geraldine, 'Enchanted Ground: The Feminine Subtext in Malory' in Malory, *Le Morte Darthur*, ed. Shepherd (*see under* Primary Sources).

Hicks, Clive, *The Green Man: A Field Guide* (Fakenham: Compassbooks, 2000).

Higham, N. J., *King Arthur: Myth-Making and History* (London and New York: Routledge, 2002, 2009).

Hillenbrand, Carole, *Turkish Myth and Muslim Symbol: The Battle of Manzikert* (Edinburgh: Edinburgh University Press, 2007).

Honderich, Ted (ed.), *The Oxford Companion to Philosophy* (Oxford and New York: Oxford University Press, 1995).

Hornblower, Simon and Antony Spawforth (eds), *The Oxford Classical Dictionary*, 3rd edn (Oxford: Oxford University Press, 1999).

Horne, R. H., *A New Spirit of the Age* (London: Smith, Elder & Co., 1944), vol. 2.

Horovitz, J., 'Miʿrādj', *EIS*.

Howe, Elizabeth Teresa, *Mystical Imagery: Santa Teresa de Jesús and San Juan de la Cruz*, American University Studies, series 2, Romance Languages and Literature, vol. 76 (New York, Bern, Frankfurt am Main, Paris: Peter Lang, 1988).

Howells, Edward, '[Review of] Harmless, *Mystics*', *Eckhart Review*, 18 (2009).

Humphreys, Christmas, *A Popular Dictionary of Buddhism* (London: Curzon Press, 1984).

Ingledew, Francis, *Sir Gawain and the Green Knight and the Order of the Garter* (Notre Dame, IN: University of Notre Dame Press, 2006).

Irwin, R., 'Ibn Kathīr c. 700–74/c. 1300–73' *see* Meisami and Starkey (eds).

James, William, *The Varieties of Religious Experience: A Study in Human Nature* [Being the Gifford Lectures on Natural Religion Delivered at Edinburgh in 1901–1902] (London: Folio Society, 2008).

Janda, James, *Julian: A Play Based on the Life of Julian of Norwich* (New York: Seabury Press, 1984).

Johnson, Vernon, 'The Little Way' *see* Mary (ed.).

Johnston, William, *The Mysticism of the Cloud of Unknowing: A Modern Interpretation* (New York, Rome, Tournai, Paris: Desclée Co., 1967).

Jotischky, Andrew, *The Carmelites and Antiquity: Mendicants and Their Pasts in the Middle Ages* (Oxford: Oxford University Press, 2002).

Kanaan, Marlène, 'Legends, Places and Traditions Related to the Cult of St George in Lebanon', *ARAM*, 20 (2008).

Karamustafa, Ahmet T., *Sufism: The Formative Period*, The New Edinburgh Islamic Surveys (Edinburgh: Edinburgh University Press, 2007).
Katz, Steven (ed.), *Mysticism and Language* (New York: Oxford University Press, 1992).
Katz, Steven (ed.), *Mysticism and Philosophical Analysis* (New York: Oxford University Press, 1979).,
Katz, Steven (ed.), *Mysticism and Religious Traditions* (New York: Oxford University Press, 1983).
Katz, Steven (ed.), *Mysticism and Sacred Scriptures* (New York: Oxford University Press, 2000).
Keeler, Annabel, 'Ṣūfī *tafsīr* as a Mirror: al-Qushayrī the *murshid* in his *Laṭā'if al-ishārāt*', *Journal of Qur'anic Studies*, 8:1 (2006).
Keen, M. H., *England in the Later Middle Ages: A Political History* (London: The Folio Society, 1997).
Kelly, J. N. D., *Early Christian Doctrines*, 5th rev. edn (London: Adam & Charles Black, 1980).
Kennedy, Beverly, *Knighthood in the Morte Darthur*, 2nd edn (Cambridge: D. S. Brewer, 1992).
Keown, Damien, *Buddhism: A Very Short Introduction* (Oxford: Oxford University Press, 2000).
Kettlewell, Samuel, *Thomas à Kempis and the Brothers of Common Life* (London: Kegan Paul, Trench & Co., 1885; repr. Whitefish, MT: Kessinger Publishing, Rare Reprints, n.d.).
Khan, Hasan Ali, *Shi'a–Ismaili Motifs in the Sufi Architecture of the Indus Valley, 1200–1500 AD*, unpublished PhD Diss., London University (SOAS), 2009.
Kinross, Lord, *The Ottoman Empire* (London: The Folio Society, 2003; repr. of London: Jonathan Cape 1977 edn).
Knysh, Alexander, *Islamic Mysticism: A Short History*, Themes in Islamic Studies, vol. 1 (Leiden: E. J. Brill, 2000).
Knysh, Alexander, 'Ṣūfism and the Qur'ān', *EQ*.
Kselman, John S. and Ronald D. Witherup, 'Modern New Testament Criticism' in Brown et al. (eds), *New Jerome Biblical Commentary*.
Kurian, Alex, *Ascent to Nothingness: The Ascent to God According to John of the Cross*, ed. Andrew Tulloch (London and Maynooth: St Pauls Publishing, 2000).
Lambek, Michael (ed.), *A Reader in the Anthropology of Religions*, Blackwell Anthologies in Social and Cultural Anthropology, no. 2 (Malden, MA/Oxford: Blackwell Publishing, 2002).
Larrington, Carolyne, 'Knight Wear' [review of Ingledew, *Sir Gawain*], *Times Literary Supplement*, 21 July 2006.
Lee, Christopher, *This Sceptred Isle* (London: Penguin Books, 1998; first publ. London: BBC Books, 1997).
Leithart, Peter J., *1 and 2 Kings*, SCM Theological Commentary on the Bible (London: SCM Press, 2006).
Lewis, C. S., *The Allegory of Love: A Study in Medieval Tradition* (Oxford and New York: Oxford University Press, repr. 1985).
Lewis, Franklin D., *Rumi: Past and Present, East and West: The Life, Teaching and Poetry of Jalâl al-Din Rūmī* (Oxford: Oneworld, 2000).
Little, John T., '*Al-Insān al-Kāmil*: The Perfect Man According to Ibn al-'Arabī', *The Muslim World*, 77:1 (January 1987).
López-Baralt, Luce, *Islam in Spanish Literature from the Middle Ages to the Present*, trans. Andrew Hurley (Leiden, New York, Köln: E. J. Brill/San Juan: Editorial de la Universidad de Puerto Rico, 1992).
López-Baralt, Luce, *San Juan de la Cruz y el Islam. Estudio sobre la filiación semítica de su poesía mistica* (Colegio de México/Universidad de Puerto Rico, 1985; repr. Madrid: Hiperión, 1990).

Lory, P., 'Al-Shādhilī', *EI*², vol. 9
MacDermott, Mercia and Ruth Wylie, *Explore Green Men* (Loughborough: Explore Books, Heart of Albion Press, 2003).
Mackintosh-Smith, Tim, *Travels with a Tangerine: A Journey in the Footnotes of Ibn Battoutah* (London: Pan Macmillan, Picador, 2002).
Macphee, Wendy, *Programme Notes for Theatre Set-Up in William Shakespeare's* The Merry Wives of Windsor (London: Theatre Set-Up, 2004).
Madelung, W., ''Iṣma', *EI*², vol. 4
Madigan, Daniel A., 'Revelation and Inspiration', *EQ*.
Main, John, *The Way of Unknowing* (London: Darton, Longman & Todd, 1989).
Ma'oz, Zvi Uri, 'En-Nebī Khader (Khouder) at Bāniyās (Dan-Caesarea-Philippi-Paneas)', *ARAM*, 20 (2008).
Mary, Bro. Francis (ed.), *St Thérèse: Doctor of the Little Way* (New Bedford, MA: Franciscan Friars of the Immaculate, 1997).
Matthew, Iain, 'John and Daily Life' in McGowan (ed.), *A Fresh Approach*.
Matthews, John and Caitlín Matthews, *King Arthur: History and Legend* (London: Folio, 2008).
McAuliffe, Jane Dammen *see Encyclopaedia of the Qur'ān*.
McCaffrey, James, 'Focus', *Mount Carmel [Special Issue: Elijah and the Rule]*, 56:2, Pillars of Carmel, 1 (April–June 2008).
McCaffrey, James, 'Focus', *Mount Carmel [St Thérèse Issue Welcoming Her Relics]*, 57:3 (July–September 2009).
McCaffrey, James, 'The Prophet Elijah: Man of Prayer and Action', *Mount Carmel [Special Issue: Elijah and the Rule]*, 56:2, Pillars of Carmel, 1 (April–June 2008).
McGowan, John (ed.), *A Fresh Approach to St John of the Cross* (Slough: St Pauls, 1993).
McGowan, John (ed.), 'The Man, the Myth and the Truth' in McGowan (ed.), *Fresh Approach*.
McLean, Julienne, *Towards Mystical Union: A Modern Commentary on the Mystical Text* The Interior Castle *by Teresa of Ávila* (London: St Pauls, 2003).
Meier, Fritz, 'A Book of Etiquette for Sufis' in Meier, *Essays*.
Meier, Fritz, *Essays on Islamic Piety and Mysticism*, trans. John O'Kane, ed. Bernd Radtke (Leiden, Boston, Köln: E. J. Brill, 1999).
Meier, Fritz, 'A Resurrection of Muḥammad in Suyūṭī' in Meier, *Essays*.
Meisami, Julie Scott and Paul Starkey (eds), *Encyclopedia of Arabic Literature*, 2 vols (London and New York: Routledge, 1998).
Melchiori, Giorgio, *Shakespeare's Garter Plays: Edward III to Merry Wives of Windsor* (Newark: University of Delaware Press/London and Toronto: Associated University Presses, 1994).
Meri, J., *The Cult of the Saints: Muslims and Jews in Mediaeval Syria* (Oxford: Oxford University Press, 2002).
Merton, Thomas, *New Seeds of Contemplation* (New York: New Directions, 1962).
Merton, Thomas, *The Seven Storey Mountain*, 50th Anniversary edn (New York: Harcourt Brace, 1998; first publ. 1948).
Milton, Ralph, *Julian's Cell: The Earthly Story of Julian of Norwich* (Kelowna, BC: Northstone, 2002).
Miquel, A., 'Ibn Baṭṭūṭa', *EI*², vol. 3
Mirsky, Jonathan, 'Tribute, Trade and some Eunuchs' [review of Dreyer, *Zheng He*], *Times Literary Supplement*, 26 January 2007.
Morgan, Gerald, *Sir Gawain and the Green Knight and the Idea of Righteousness*, Dublin Studies in Medieval and Renaissance Literature (Dublin: Irish Academic Press, 1991).
Morrison, Craig, 'The Carmelite Rule: A Lectio Divina by Albert of Jerusalem (1)', *Mount Carmel [Special Issue: Elijah and the Rule]*, 56:2, Pillars of Carmel, 1 (April–June 2008).

Mujica, Bárbara, *Teresa de Ávila: Lettered Woman* (Nashville, TN: Vanderbilt University Press, 2009).
Mujica, Bárbara, *see also* Teresa of Ávila, *Epistolario*; idem, *Collected Letters* (under Primary Sources).
Mulhern, P., 'Thomas à Kempis' *see* Carson and Cerrito (eds).
Murdoch, Iris, *The Bell* (London: Chatto & Windus, 1958).
Murdoch, Iris, *The Black Prince* (London: Chatto & Windus, 1973).
Murdoch, Iris, *The Green Knight* (London: Chatto & Windus, 1993).
Murdoch, Iris, *Nuns and Soldiers* (London: Chatto & Windus, 1980).
Nasr, Seyyed Hossein, *Sufi Essays* (London: Allen & Unwin, 1972).
Netton, Ian Richard, ''Abd al-'Uzza b. 'Abd al-Muṭṭalib' *see* idem, *Popular Dictionary*.
Netton, Ian Richard, *Allāh Transcendent: Studies in the Structure and Semiotics of Islamic Philosophy, Theology and Cosmology* (London and New York: Routledge, 1989; repr. Richmond: Curzon Press, 1994).
Netton, Ian Richard, 'Badr, Battle of' *see* idem, *Popular Dictionary*.
Netton, Ian Richard, 'Baqā'' *see* idem, *Popular Dictionary*.
Netton, Ian Richard (ed.), *Encyclopedia of Islamic Civilisation and Religion* (London and New York: Routledge, 2008).
Netton, Ian Richard, 'Ibn Baṭṭūṭa' *see* idem, *Popular Dictionary*.
Netton, Ian Richard, 'Majlis Readings in the Golden Age of Islam: Text and Intertext' in Gleave (ed.), *Books and Bibliophiles*.
Netton, Ian Richard, 'al-Masad' *see* idem, *Popular Dictionary*.
Netton, Ian Richard, 'The Mysteries of Islam' in Rousseau and Porter (eds), *Exoticism in the Enlightenment*.
Netton, Ian Richard, *A Popular Dictionary of Islam* (Richmond: Curzon/Atlantic Highlands, NJ: Humanities Press, 1992, 1997).
Netton, Ian Richard, *Seek Knowledge: Thought and Travel in the House of Islam* (Richmond: Curzon Press, 1996).
Netton, Ian Richard, *Ṣūfī Ritual: The Parallel Universe* (London: Curzon Press, 2000).
Netton, Ian Richard, 'Ṭarīḳ', *EI²*, vol. 12 (= Supp.).
Netton, Ian Richard, 'Towards a Modern *Tafsīr* of *Sūrat al-Kahf*: Structure and Semiotics', *Journal of Qur'anic Studies*, 2:1 (2000).
Nevin, Thomas R., *Thérèse of Lisieux: God's Gentle Warrior* (Oxford: Oxford University Press, 2006).
Nicholson, Reynold Alleyne, *The Mystics of Islam* (London and Boston: Routledge & Kegan Paul, 1975; repr. of London: George Bell & Sons Ltd, 1914 edn).
Nicholson, Reynold Alleyne, *Studies in Islamic Mysticism* (Richmond: Curzon Press, 1994, repr. of Cambridge: CUP 1921 edn).
Nieva, Constantino S., '*The Cloud of Unknowing* and St John of the Cross', *Mount Carmel*, 27:4 (Winter 1979).
Noegel, Scott B. and Brannon M. Wheeler, *Historical Dictionary of Prophets in Islam and Judaism*, Historical Dictionaries of Religions, Philosophies and Movements, no. 43 (London/Lanham, MD: Scarecrow Press, 2002).
Nolan, Brian J., 'Theatre of a Saint: The Plays of Thérèse of Lisieux', *Mount Carmel*, 58:3 (2010).
Nwyia, Paul, 'Ibn 'Abbād', *EI²*, vol. 3
Nwyia, Paul, *Ibn 'Abbād de Ronda (1332–1390): un mystique prédicateur à la Qarawīyīn de Fes*, Recherches publiées sous la direction de l'Institut de Lettres Orientales de Beyrouth, Tome 17 (Beirut: Imprimerie Catholique, 1961).
Nwyia, Paul, 'Al-Kalābādhī', *EI²*, vol. 4

Obbard, Elizabeth Ruth (ed.), *Medieval Women Mystics*, rev. edn (Hyde Park, NY: New City Press, 2007).

O'Connor, D. J. (ed.), *A Critical History of Western Philosophy*, Free Press Textbooks in Philosophy (New York: The Free Press/London: Collier Macmillan, 1964).

O'Donaghue, Bernard, *The Courtly Love Tradition*, Literature in Context 5 (Manchester: Manchester University Press/Totowa, NJ: Barnes & Noble, 1982).

O'Neal, Miceál, 'A Prophet for the Church and the World: The Mission of Elijah for Today', *Mount Carmel [Special Issue: Elijah and the Rule]*, 56:2, Pillars of Carmel, 1 (April–June 2008).

Ormrod, W. M., *The Reign of Edward III: Crown and Political Society in England 1327–1377* (New Haven and London: Yale University Press, 1990).

Pantaleo, Jack, *Mother Julian and the Gentle Vampire* (Roseville: Dry Bones Press, 1999).

Paret, R., 'Al-Burāq', *EI²*, vol. 1

Parrinder, Geoffrey, 'Foreword' in Margaret Smith, *Way of the Mystics*.

Peers, E. Allison, *St John of the Cross and Other Lectures and Addresses, 1920–1945* (London: Faber & Faber, 1946).

Peers, E. Allison, *Spirit of Flame: A Study of St John of the Cross* (London: SCM Press, 1943, 1979).

Porter, J. R., *The Illustrated Guide to the Bible* (New York: Oxford University Press, 1995).

Porter, Pamela, *Courtly Love in Mediaeval Manuscripts* (London: British Library, 2003).

Queralt, Maria Pilar and Jaume Balanyā, *Montserrat* ([Montserrat/Barcelona:] Triangle Postals, n.d.).

Rahman, F., 'Baḳā' wa Fanā'', *EI²*, vol. 1.

Rego, Aloysius, 'Understanding the "Little Way": Thérèse's Gift to the Church', *Mount Carmel*, 57:3 (July–September 2009).

Reichert, Michelle, *Between Courtly Literature and al-Andalus: Matière d'Orient and the Importance of Spain in the Romances of the Twelfth-century Writer Chrétien de Troyes*, Studies in Medieval History and Culture (New York and London: Routledge, 2006).

Renard, John, 'Khaḍir/Khiḍr', *EQ*.

Ridgeon, Lloyd, 'Aḥwāl' *see* Netton (ed.) *Encyclopedia*.

Ridgeon, Lloyd, *Morals and Mysticism in Persian Sufism*, Routledge Sufi Series (London and New York: Routledge, forthcoming 2011).

Ridgeon, Lloyd, 'Al-Shadhili (1187–1258)' *see* Netton (ed.), *Encyclopedia*.

Ritter, H., art. ''Abd al-Karīm, Ḳuṭb B. Ibrāhīm al-Djīlī', *EI²*, vol.1.

Roberts, Alison, *Hathor Rising: The Serpent Power of Ancient Egypt* (Totnes: Northgate Publishers, 1995).

Rolheiser, Ronald, 'John and Human Development: The Dark Night of the Soul ... A Contemporary Interpretation' in McGowan (ed.), *Fresh Approach*.

Roman Catholic Daily Missal 1962 (Kansas City, MO: Angelus Press, 2004).

Rousseau, G. S. and Roy Porter (eds), *Exoticism in the Enlightenment* (Manchester and New York: Manchester University Press, 1990).

Ruffin, C. Bernard, *Padre Pio: The True Story*, rev. and expanded edn (Huntington, IN: Our Sunday Visitor Publishing Division, 1991).

Sacramentado, Crisógono de Jesús, *San Juan de la Cruz, su obra científica y su obra literaria* (Ávila, 1929).

Salih, Sarah, 'Julian's Afterlives': paper presented on 7 July 2008 at the International Medieval Congress, University of Leeds (7–10 July 2008).

Satchell, John, 'Green Man in Cumbria', *Folklore*, 110 (1999).

Satterthwaite, Philip and Gordon McConville, *Exploring the Old Testament, vol. 2: The Histories* (London: SPCK, 2007).

Schama, Simon, *A History of Britain: At the Edge of the World? 3000 BC–AD 1603* (London: BBC, 2000, 2002).
Scheindlin, R. P., 'Ibn 'Abbād al-Rundī (753–92/1333–90)', *see* Meisami and Starkey (eds).
Schimmel, Annemarie, *Mystical Dimensions of Islam* (Chapel Hill: University of North Carolina Press, 1975).
Schimmel, Annemarie, *Nightingales Under the Snow: Poems by Annemarie Schimmel* (London and New York: Khaniqahi Nimatullahi Publications, 1994).
Schnitker, Harry, 'England's Patron Saint and the Crusaders: St George', *Catholic Life* (April 2009).
Schricke, B., 'Isrā'', *EIS*.
Scott, Robert A., *Miracle Cures: Saints, Pilgrimage and the Healing Powers of Belief* (Berkeley, Los Angeles, London: University of California Press, 2010).
Scully, Vincent, 'Thomas à Kempis' *see The Catholic Encyclopedia*, vol. 14.
Seaford, R. A. S., 'The Mysteries of Dionysos at Pompeii' in Stubbs (ed.), *Pegasus*.
Seaford, R. A. S., '1 Corinthians XIII:12', *Journal of Theological Studies* (Notes and Studies), new series, 35:1 (April 1984).
Shaban, M. A., *Islamic History: A New Interpretation 2: AD 750–1055 (AH 132–448)* (Cambridge: Cambridge University Press, 1976).
Shorter Encyclopaedia of Islam [EIS], ed. H. A. R Gibb and J. H. Kramers (Leiden: E. J. Brill/London: Luzac, 1961).
Smart, Ninian, *Dimensions of the Sacred: An Anatomy of the World's Beliefs* (London: HarperCollins, 1996).
Smith, Bruce R., *The Key of Green: Passion and Perception in Renaissance Culture* (Chicago, IL and London: University of Chicago Press, 2009).
Smith, Margaret, *The Way of the Mystics: The Early Christian Mystics and the Rise of the Sufis* (London: Sheldon Press, 1976; repr. of 1931 edn).
Sorkhabi, Rasoul, 'Thomas Merton's Encounter with Sufism', *Interreligious Insight*, 6:4 (October 2008).
Spät, Eszter, *The Yezidis* (London: Saqi Books, 2005; first pub. 1985).
Speirs, J., 'Sir Gawain and the Green Knight', *Scrutiny*, 16 (1949); *see also* Fox (ed.), *Twentieth Century Interpretations*.
Starkey, David, *Six Wives: The Queens of Henry VIII* (London: Chatto & Windus, 2003).
Stephanie-Thérèse, 'Living by Love: Thérèse of Lisieux at Prayer', *Mount Carmel [St Thérèse Issue Welcoming Her Relics]*, 57:3 (July–September 2009).
Stoneman, Richard, *Alexander the Great*, 2nd edn (London and New York: Routledge, 2004).
Stoneman, Richard, *Alexander the Great: A Life in Legend* (New Haven and London: Yale University Press, 2008).
Stoneman, Richard, *The Greek Alexander Romance* (London: Penguin Books, 1991).
Storm, Rachel, *Myths and Legends of the Ancient Near East* (London: The Folio Society, 2003).
Stubbs, H. W. (ed.), *Pegasus: Classical Essays from the University of Exeter* (Exeter: University of Exeter, 1981).
Studia Orientalia Ioanni Pedersen (Hauniae: Einar Munksgaard, 1953).
Suárez, Aniano Alvarez, *Castillo Interior: Camino hacia el encuentro con Dios con Santa Teresa de Jesús*, Colección 'Karmel' (Burgos: Editorial Monte Carmelo, 2002).
Sykes, J. B. (ed.), *The Concise Oxford Dictionary of Current English*, 6th edn (Oxford: Clarendon Press, 1976, 1979).
Tausig, Michael, *What Color is Sacred?* (Chicago, IL and London: University of Chicago Press, 2009).
Thompson, Colin P., *The Poet and the Mystic: Study of the Cántico Espiritual of San Juan de la*

Cruz (Oxford: Oxford University Press, 1977).
Tottoli, Roberto, 'Elijah', *EQ*.
Tovmayan, Hasmik, 'St Sargis and al-Khadir: A Common Saint for Christians and Muslims', *ARAM*, 20 (2008).
Tranøy, Knut, 'Thomas Aquinas' in O'Connor (ed.), *Critical History of Western Philosophy*.
Trimingham, J. Spencer, *The Sufi Orders in Islam* (Oxford: Clarendon Press, 1971).
Turner, Victor, 'Liminality and Communitas' in Lambek (ed.), *Reader in the Anthropology of Religions*.
Turner, Victor, *The Ritual Process: Structure and Anti-Structure* (Chicago, IL: Aldine Publishing, 1969).
Underhill, Evelyn, *Mysticism: A Study in the Nature and Development of Man's Spiritual Consciousness*, University Paperbacks (London: Methuen, 1960, repr. from London: Methuen, 1911).
Vajda, G., 'Dhū 'l-Kifl', *EI*², vol. 2.
Vajda, G., 'Idrīs', *EI*², vol. 3.
Vajda, G., 'Irmiyā', *EI*², vol. 4.
Van Gennep, Arnold, *The Rites of Passage*, trans. Monika B. Vizedom and Gabrielle L. Caffee (London: Routledge & Kegan Paul, 1960; first publ. 1908).
Viviano, Benedict T., 'The Gospel According to Matthew' in Brown et al.(eds), *New Jerome Biblical Commentary*.
Viviano, Frank and Michael Yamashita, 'China's Great Armada', *National Geographic*, 208:1 (July 2005).
Von Balthasar, Hans Urs, *First Glance at Adrienne Von Speyr*, trans. Antje Lawry and Sergia Englund (San Francisco: Ignatius Press, 1986).
Von Speyr, Adrienne, *Mary in the Redemption*, trans. Helena M. Tomko (San Francisco: Ignatius Press, 2003).
Von Speyr, Adrienne, *The Mystery of Death*, trans. Graham Harrison (San Francisco: Ignatius Press, 1988).
Von Speyr, Adrienne, *The World of Prayer*, trans. Graham Harrison (San Francisco: Ignatius Press, 1985).
Waines, David, 'Trees', *EQ*.
Walker, Paul E., 'Impeccability', *EQ*.
Walsh, Jerome T. and Christopher Begg, '1–2 Kings' in Brown et al. (eds), *New Jerome Biblical Commentary*.
Waters, Colin, *A Dictionary of Pub, Inn and Tavern Signs* (Newbury: Countryside Books, 2005).
Watt, W. Montgomery, *Companion to the Qur'an* (London: Allen & Unwin, 1967).
Watt, W. Montgomery, 'Ḥalīma Bint Abī Dhu'ayb', *EI*², vol. 3.
Watt, W. Montgomery, 'Hidjra', *EI*², vol. 3.
Watt, W. Montgomery, *Muhammad at Mecca* (Oxford: Clarendon Press, 1953, 1972).
Watt, W. Montgomery, *Muhammad Prophet and Statesman* (London: Oxford University Press, 1967).
Watt, W. Montgomery, *Muslim Intellectual: A Study of al-Ghazali* (Edinburgh: Edinburgh University Press, 1971).
Waugh, Scott L., *England in the Reign of Edward III* (Cambridge: Cambridge University Press, 1991).
Welch, John, *The Carmelite Way: An Ancient Path for Today's Pilgrim* (Leominster: Gracewing, 1996).
Wensinck, A. J., 'Al-Khaḍir (al-Khiḍr)', *EI*², vol. 4.
Wensinck, A. J. and G. Vajda, 'Ilyās', *EI*², vol. 3.

Wesley, John, 'Preface' to Thomas à Kempis (see under Primary Sources above).
Wheeler, Brannon M., *Moses in the Quran and Islamic Exegesis*, RoutledgeCurzon Studies in the Qur'an (London: RoutledgeCurzon, 2002).
Wiener, Aharon, *The Prophet Elijah in the Development of Judaism: A Depth-Psychological Study*, The Littman Library of Jewish Civilization (London, Henley and Boston: Routledge & Kegan Paul, 1978).
Wilkins, Agnes, 'Louis Massignon, Thomas Merton and Mary Kahil', *ARAM*, 20 (2008).
Wilkins, Robert, *Death: A History of Man's Obsessions and Fears* (New York: Barnes & Noble Books, 1996).
Williams, A. R., 'Nile Style', *National Geographic*, 214:1 (July 2008).
Williams, Hugo, 'Freelance', *Times Literary Supplement*, 17 March 2006.
Wilson, Margaret, *San Juan de la Cruz: Poems*, Critical Guides to Spanish Texts, no. 13 (London: Grant & Cutler in assoc. with Tamesis Books, 1975).
Wolper, E. S., 'Khidr, Elwan Celebi and the Conversion of Sacred Sanctuaries in Anatolia', *Muslim World*, 90:3–4 (2000).
Ziegler, Philip, *The Black Death* (London: The Folio Society, 1997).

INDEX